Praise for *The Woman Who Ran for President*

"A convincing portrait, based on an impressive amount of original research. [Underhill's] attitude toward her subject is sympathetic without being sycophantic, intelligently critical but never condescending. . . . A lively biography."   —*The Wall Street Journal*

"A fast-paced account that reads like a detective story. In addition to her vibrant portrayal of Woodhull, Underhill has also convincingly re-created the nineteenth-century world of business and politics. . . . An absorbing biography of one of nineteenth-century America's most fascinating women."
                                                —*Rocky Mountain News*

"I would love to have known Victoria Woodhull. Forty-eight years before women got the vote, she ran for President. She became a stockbroker and possessed considerable wealth. She published a weekly newspaper. She founded a political party, the Equal Rights Party. She believed in free love. . . . Everyone interested in the history of women's rights will be fascinated by the story of this little-known pioneer."   —Katharine Graham

"An engaging biography"   —*Ms.*

"A must-read"   —*Feminist Bookstore News*

"Underhill writes with a flair that perfectly suits the savory, savvy nineteenth-century feminist whose life speaks to our own sensational and self-styling ear. . . . Underhill's agile and incisive prose makes this sprawling, unconventional life fluid and convincing."   —*Kirkus Reviews*

"A remarkably fair-minded and perceptive biography. . . . [An] endlessly fascinating story."   —*The Cleveland Plain Dealer*

PENGUIN BOOKS

THE WOMAN WHO RAN FOR PRESIDENT

Lois Beachy Underhill is a former advertising executive who has written and spoken extensively on family, health, and women's issues. She is a member of the Biography Seminar at New York University, and of Women Writing Women's Lives at the City University of New York

THE
WOMAN WHO RAN
FOR PRESIDENT

The Many Lives of
VICTORIA WOODHULL

LOIS BEACHY UNDERHILL

PENGUIN BOOKS

PENGUIN BOOKS

Published by the Penguin Group

Penguin Books USA Inc., 375 Hudson Street, New York, New York 10014, U.S.A.

Penguin Books Ltd, 27 Wrights Lane, London W8 5TZ, England

Penguin Books Australia Ltd, Ringwood, Victoria, Australia

Penguin Books Canada Ltd, 10 Alcorn Avenue, Toronto, Ontario, Canada M4V 3B2

Penguin Books (N.Z.) Ltd, 182–190 Wairau Road, Auckland 10, New Zealand

Penguin Books Ltd, Registered Offices: Harmondsworth, Middlesex, England

First published in the United States of America by Bridge Works Publishing Co. 1995
Published in Penguin Books 1996

1   3   5   7   9   10   8   6   4   2

THE LIBRARY OF CONGRESS HAS CATALOGUED THE HARDCOVER AS FOLLOWS:
Underhill, Lois Beachy
The woman who ran for president: the many lives of
Victoria Woodhull/Lois Beachy Underhill.—1st ed.
p.   cm.
Includes bibliographical references, notes, and index.
ISBN 1-882593-10-3 (hc.)
ISBN 0 14 02.5638 5 (pbk.)
1. Woodhull, Victoria C. (Victoria Claflin), 1838–1927.   2. Woman—United
States—Biography.   3. Feminists—United States—Biography.
4. Women in politics—United States—Biography.   5. Free Love—
United States—History.   I. Title.
HQ1413.W66U53   1995
973.8′092—dc20   94–49519
[B]

Printed in the United States of America
Set in Goudy Old Style
Designed by Eva Auchincloss

Dedication

For Richard Vincent, Lucille Beachy, and Tom Mathews

Contents

III
ENGLAND: 1877—1927

EPILOGUE
"Women Must Own Themselves"

Illustrations

Title page:

Victoria Woodhull c. 1870
Holland-Martin Family Archives

Following page 162:

Annie Hummel Claflin
Holland-Martin Family Archives

Reuben Buckman Claflin
John Miles Thompson, Jr., Papers

Family Portrait c. 1864–1865: Victoria Woodhull, Dr. Canning Woodhull, Byron Woodhull, and Zula Maud Woodhull
Holland-Martin Family Archives

Tennessee Celeste Claflin c. 1870
Holland-Martin Family Archives

Colonel James Harvey Blood
Holland-Martin Family Archives

Cornelius Vanderbilt
New-York Historical Society

Tennessee Claflin (*left*) and Victoria Woodhull (*right*) in the offices of Woodhull, Claflin & Company from *The Day's Doings*, February 26, 1870
Holland-Martin Family Archives

Acknowledgments

Robin Holland-Martin made the Holland-Martin Family Archives available to me, and my thanks to him know no bounds. He and Dominique made my stays in London a pleasure. His knowledge, diligence, discernment, and encouragement advanced my search for Victoria Woodhull immeasurably. I will always be grateful for the independence he granted me in carrying out my work.

I would like to thank John Miles Thompson, Jr., for making his family papers available to me, and for the hospitality he and Wanda extended to me. Their perceptive insights into the psyches of his remarkable forebears contributed significantly to my understanding.

Richard Davies shared the hospitality and history of Norton Park with me, and I appreciate his generosity. He has admirably preserved the house Victoria Woodhull occupied for so many years.

Madeleine Stern pointed me in the right direction at the start of my research, and I would like to express a special thank you for her guidance.

Alden Cohen's continuing advice and encouragement was a great source of strength, and I am forever in her debt.

I am profoundly grateful to the many archivists, scholars, experts, and friends who gave me their time, wisdom, and hospitality, among them Sal Alberti, Bertha Beachy, Pat Bertrand, Joseph and Beatrice Berg, Cameron Bloch, Penelope Bossom, Barney Bloom, Louisa Bowen, Jane Brabyn, Lisa Browar, Frankie Cadwell, Ruth Conkey, Gretchen and Paul Cornwell, Herman Davis, Karen Dricakmer, Ruth Dwyer, Doris Dysinger, Alex Eames, Bayard Forster, Janet Fox, Elizabeth Grenfell, Thomas Harkins, Dorothy Helly, Ronee Herman, M.D., Dagny Holland-Martin, Giles Holland-Martin, C.A., Tim Holland-Martin, Louise Kaplan, Julie Kitner, Kathy Kraft, Chris Leonard, C.P.A., Pam Livingston, Stanford Lotwin, James Lowe, Cynthia MacKay, M.D., Malcolm MacKay, Genifer Malden, Marion Meade, Stephen Michaud, Richard McBride, Melinda McIntosh,

Laura Monti, Phyllis N. Mott, Dona Munker, Katharine North, Jack Opperman, Judith Papachristou, Delcie Pound, Dan Rhodebeck, Marilyn Rossener, Ruth Sagar, Ruth Scott, Bayley Silleck, Sue Shapiro, David Shay, Eileen Simpson, Harriet Smythe, Marcelle Thiebaux, and Jon Underhill.

I deeply appreciate the encouragement, stimulation, and criticism offered by Aileen Ward and the members of the Biography Seminar at the New York Institute for the Humanities, New York University; by Carolyn Heilbrun and Deirdre Bair whose vision created the Women Writing Women's Lives Seminar; and by Marijane Meaker and the writers of the Ashawagh Hall Workshop.

Many libraries helped make this work possible. I would like to thank, particularly, Mark Piel of the New York Society Library, Mariam Touba of the New-York Historical Society, and the persistent detectives of the John Jermain Memorial Library: James Ashe, Pat Brandt, Jerilyn Rothman, and Dorothy Zaykowski.

My thanks go also to Barbara and Warren Phillips, the founders of Bridge Works Publishing Company, for their commitment to this book.

Introduction
Victoria Woodhull through Modern Eyes

By Gloria Steinem

> A pedestal is as much a prison as any other small space.
> —Anonymous

*A*bove the desk where I write, there is a framed letter from Victoria Woodhull, the most controversial suffragist of them all. People who see her big scrawled signature assume I must be looking for inspiration in her life as the first woman to address Congress, the first to run for president, the first to originate and run her own weekly newspaper, and one of the few women to live out in public the principles of female emancipation and sexual freedom that were not only unusual in her day but illegal. All of that is true, but hiding within her spidery script is a lesson I think I and many other women need even more: how not to be ladylike about money.

"My Dear Mr. Wilson," she begins her letter to a man who must have refused her lecture fee and offered her a percentage of the house instead. "I have propositions from several places in the far east, which makes it possible for me to amend my proposition to you. I will speak for you at some agreed night for ($100) one hundred dollars. I do not like to arrange for any part of net proceeds. Hoping this may meet your views, I remain—Yours truly, Victoria C. Woodhull."

I don't know about you, but I would have added apologies and explanations to such a request, and probably gone off in a corner to give myself a pep talk first. Women have had centuries of training to consider money impure, undeserved, mysterious, not our worry, or, as this mind set is sometimes reflected even inside current feminism, a male-imitative and politically incorrect concern. Yet Victoria Woodhull seemed free of all that. Though she was writing in 1873, when husbands and fathers could claim any wages their wives and

Reprinted with permission from an essay titled "A Matter of Class" in *Moving Beyond Words*, by Gloria Steinem (New York: Simon & Schuster, 1994).

daughters earned, she was negotiating for herself. She wasn't trusting this Mr. Wilson by relying on proceeds, knowing from experience that promoters didn't always count them honestly. Furthermore, she was demanding a large fee for public speaking, an act that was still illegal for women in some states. True, she was obviously coming back with a lower offer, but even that she couched in terms of being in demand in the New England area.

This was just the tip of the iceberg. A few years earlier, she had opened a Wall Street brokerage house with her younger sister, Tennessee Claflin, which made them the first women stockbrokers. It was backed by Cornelius Vanderbilt, whose proposal of marriage Tennessee had refused (she seemed to understand the power difference between wife/chattel and mistress/stockbroker, and probably remained his mistress), but the sisters did surprisingly well on their own. When the press ridiculed them as "The Bewitching Brokers" and worse, they attracted crowds by arriving each morning in an open carriage pulled by white horses, and displayed a large book of their clippings, good and bad, to customers. Instead of denying their checkered past as spiritualists they suggested that stock tips came to them in a trance—Vanderbilt himself touted this as his reason for following them—but they also made headlines with such unexpected street smarts as detecting a forged payment for gold.

At the same time that Victoria Woodhull was becoming an exception within the economic and social system, however, she was preaching its overthrow. Her popular weekly published the first American edition of Marx's *Communist Manifesto,* and her speeches advocated the one thing more shocking than Marx or suffrage: Free love, a serious movement against marriage law and the double standard. (Even Frederick Douglass, a former slave and great suffragist as well as abolitionist, declined to note in his autobiography that he had been nominated as vice president to run on the ticket with this scandalous woman.) "I have an inalienable, constitutional, and natural right," she declared in "The Principles of Social Freedom," "to love whom I may, to love as long or as short a period as I can, to change that love every day I please." She regretted that speeches on sexual matters got more publicity than those attacking the rich and hypocritical, but she gave both. In "The Impending Revolution," she said: "An Astor may sit in his sumptuous apartments and watch the property bequeathed to him rise in value from one to fifty millions . . . But if a tenant of his, whose employer had discharged him because he did not vote for the Republican ticket, fails to pay his month's rent to Mr. Astor, the law sets him and his family into the street."

Where did this outrageous strength come from? One source was her combination of a quick mind, charisma, and physical beauty, but there were other women who possessed those qualities in greater degree and still remained too fearful to speak up for themselves, much less to stand up to the powerful. I think it was something else: a question of class—in reverse. Victoria Woodhull was a rare woman who had escaped all training to be a lady—whether in school, family, or church. Because she and Tennessee were the main attractions of a traveling spiritualist and medicine show that supported their big, brawling family, they had the power of breadwinners. Though Victoria married at 14, her doctor husband turned out to be an alcoholic and a philanderer, whom she was also to support for most of her life. By the time she became a national figure in New York, her household included many siblings and their spouses and children, her parents, her own two children, the doctor she had divorced plus a freethinking second husband, various friends, lovers, and traveling radicals who often stayed for months—all supported by her newspaper, stock-brokerage, and charismatic speeches. With only three years of formal education, she became an intellectual influence of her age. Her name is found in the history of suffrage, socialism, and Wall Street, and in the pantheon of spellbinding orators.

But that framed letter is also a reminder of something else. Even Victoria Woodhull fell victim to the lady trap once she entered into its most powerful stronghold—the world of inherited wealth. This began with a growing vulnerability. She was arrested, imprisoned, and her newspaper was shunned for exposing the hypocrisy of one powerful and respected man too many; in this case, the famous preacher Henry Ward Beecher, whose well-known habit of taking mistresses from his congregation, while condemning sexual freedom for others, she had put into print. Forced to choose between a scandalous female accuser and a respectable male accused, society made a choice that would be familiar today. In the aftermath of this scandal that was described as the biggest story since the assassination of Lincoln, she took her sister, parents, and grown children, and escaped first to Paris and then to London. Tired of fighting, with a household that included a brain-damaged son requiring constant care, she must have looked upon the life of the British upper classes as safe and enviable. She and Tennessee began to trim their sails to attract rich and respectable husbands. Tennessee married a lord with a castle in Spain, Victoria found a wealthy banker, whom she had to wait years to marry (his mother disapproved), and the sisters settled into a life of expurgating and simply lying about their colorful past. Victoria even concocted and published a royal lineage for their parents—in reality the illiterate daughter of a German immigrant and a handyman often on the wrong side of the law—but society never really accepted them.

From a chaotic childhood and a painful early marriage, to public censure and a financial burden far beyond that imagined by most men, no force had been able to tame Victoria Woodhull—until she decided to become a lady. The woman who had become a public legend when a lady's name was supposed to appear in the papers only twice—when she was married, and when she died—now insisted she had never espoused free love, never believed in radical causes; it was all a misunderstanding due to articles written by others under her name. Her days devolved into lawsuits against authors who published accounts of her past, no matter how well documented, blaming her still-devoted second husband for everything, and a few disastrous trips to New York to "clear my name." Only after her English husband's death did some of the old Victoria come back—driving full speed around her estate in a sports car, opening a progressive kindergarten for children of the town, and becoming a benefactor to the poor in the surrounding countryside. Nonetheless, she denied her past to the end.

I think of this outrageous woman when I talk with the wives and daughters in families of inherited wealth who are beginning so bravely to rebel. To me, she symbolizes the strength they've often been denied and the seductive power of the ladylike training against which they must struggle. More dramatically than any other example I know of, Victoria Woodhull went from the bottom to the top of the class system. She found her strength at the bottom, used it to pioneer and triumph—but when the fruits of her own work were taken away, she lost her freedom by seeking refuge in an envied place.

This essay is my own journey of learning about class. I don't know if anyone's experience can counter the power of myth and make us rethink our assumptions that women are the same class as husbands or fathers, and that proximity to money is the same as its control. After an earlier version was published, I got skeptical, give-me-a-break letters from readers whose need for child care, housing, health care, and other basics was so painful that looking past them to different kinds of deprivation was impossible. Which is as it should be: survival takes priority. But there are important ways in which class works in reverse for women. Inherited wealth and power enforce patriarchy pure, and envy of this ladylike trap makes the rest of us behave against our own best interests. That will continue until women have a feminist class analysis of our own. We need to honor the strength and knowledge of women at the bottom, as well as the experience and access to resources of women at the top—and combine them to achieve power for females as a caste.

So as you read the next pages, ask yourself this question: What would happen if the women through whose wombs pass the concentrated power of this and other nations were to catch the spirit of the real Victoria Woodhull—not the other way around?

PROLOGUE
MAY 10, 1872

"Let Us Have Justice!"

On a warm May day in 1872, 668 delegates from the Equal Rights Party crowded into Apollo Hall, off Madison Square in New York City. Their mission was to pick a candidate to run against President Ulysses S. Grant. Hot-tempered city socialists traded opinions with prairie philosophers; moderate reformers mingled with utopian visionaries. Spiritualists and suffragists, labor organizers and temperance zealots, old abolitionists and new sexual radicals rubbed elbows, all determined to save the republic from what they saw as a great sump of corruption and injustice.

At twilight, a slim woman not yet 34 years old mounted the platform. Her eyes were blue and intense, her features delicately chiseled, yet determined. She wore a black dress. At her throat she had pinned a single fresh rose. If the effect was simple and modest, it was also studied and deliberate. She stood before the delegates holding her head at a slight angle, as though listening to a distant voice far above the hall. Finally, she raised her arms and stretched impulsively toward the delegates, almost as if she were pulling them to her breast. Through the open windows of the hall, the last rays of light were glowing, and the muffled clip-clop of horses' hooves could be heard outside on the cobbled streets of Madison Square. The delegates leaned forward as the speaker began, her voice soft but confident, her cadence biblical. "Go where we may in the land," Victoria Woodhull told them, "we see despotism, inequality, and injustice."

The woman in black was the most notorious free spirit in the country. Elizabeth Cady Stanton and Susan B. Anthony might organize women to press for the vote, but they were not fearless or reckless enough to run for president. Margaret Fuller might create an independent career in a world of men, but she didn't say to the newspapers, "Yes, I am a free lover." Victoria Woodhull's image provoked such strong emotions that Thomas Nast, America's most popular caricaturist, had drawn her for *Harper's Weekly* as a harpie with black wings. Nast called her Mrs. Satan.

For the next hour Woodhull called the delegates to a revolution—political and social, educational and industrial, economic and sexual. Congress had failed to act on suffrage for women. True reform, she declared, would come only through a new constitution, a great upheaval that would purge the country of political trickery, despotic assumption, and all industrial injustice. "Shall we be slaves to escape revolution?" she asked the delegates. "I say never. I say away with such weak stupidity." A great roar swelled up from the hall. She held up a hand for quiet. Then, face flushed, she said, "Let us have justice though the heavens fall!"

As she had anticipated, the delegates jumped to their feet, shouting her name until she stepped to the front of the stage and bowed again and again. The frenzy of the ovation was so loud it startled passersby outside on Broadway. Finally she withdrew to an anteroom, the cheers of the delegates still echoing in her ears.

From offstage Woodhull could hear the voice of Judge A. G. W. Carter, a stout and hearty man who worked for women's suffrage in Cincinnati. "The time for words has passed," he said. "We want action . . . Without any more words, I propose the name of Victoria C. Woodhull to be nominated president of the United States."

"All who are in favor of the nomination, say 'Aye,'" shot back J. D. Reymart, the president of the convention, a well-known New York lawyer and reformer.

Shouts of "Aye, aye, aye," rang out. Men jumped up onto their seats and threw their hats in the air, women waved their handkerchiefs above their heads. Voices chanted, "Victoria . . . Victoria . . . Victoria . . ."

It was a tumultuous moment in American history. Never before had an American woman dared to seek the White House as anything but a wife. Women couldn't vote in 1872; the franchise was still 48 years in the future. But the workings of power, money, and sex that silenced most women in the nineteenth century had only emboldened Victoria Woodhull. There was no one like her in the United States, no one so adored by her followers or so loathed by those she challenged. She had made herself the country's first woman stockbroker and an independently wealthy woman. She and her beautiful sister, Tennessee Claflin, published *Woodhull and Claflin's Weekly,* one of New York's most provocative newspapers. She was a nationally famous lecturer. She had a devastating effect on men. Her admirers were figures like Commodore Cornelius Vanderbilt, the robber baron who built the New York Central Railroad. Her enemies included Henry James, the novelist, who couldn't bear the threat she presented to his fastidious sense of woman's conventional role.

In one respect, James was right. Woodhull had rejected the nineteenth century's definition of women. In her life and views, she was more than a century before her time. She had appeared before the public, practicing what she called her spiritual art as a medium and medical clairvoyant, early in her life. Within a world of profound spiritualists and transparent quacks, she developed enormous charismatic power. Then she went into business, accumulating a fortune. Now she was ready for something far more ambitious, challenging the manly status quo through national politics, threatening the very balance of power among men and women.

Woodhull had conceived the Equal Rights Party and organized the convention, using her speeches, her fortune, and the *Weekly* to bring it to New York. Still, there was no guarantee that the delegates would choose her. Other candidates were circulating with their own ambitions. The spiritualists—splintered, naive, never before politically active—expected to provide the single largest interest group at the convention. They debated the qualifications of Andrew Jackson Davis and Robert Dale Owen, two of their established leaders. Suffragists thought Elizabeth Cady Stanton, a moderate, would be more acceptable than Woodhull, a firebrand, to their large, middle-class constituency. The Labor Party was supporting Judge David Davis of Illinois, highly regarded among labor reformers. Radicals trying to establish Karl Marx's International Workingmen's Association in the United States were promoting Wendell Phillips, an abolitionist who had run for governor of Massachusetts. And the forces for temperance were putting forth their strongest voice, George Francis Train.

As it happened, Woodhull's real nemesis was not in Apollo Hall. A few weeks earlier the *New York Herald* had printed a letter proposing a different candidate for the consideration of the reformers: the Reverend Henry Ward Beecher. Beecher had won fame in the abolition movement. He had become a leading figure in the American establishment, an editor, author, and the most popular preacher of the day. Every Sunday, eager crowds turned out to hear the orotund sermons he delivered from his pulpit at Plymouth Church in Brooklyn Heights. The *Herald* letter praised Beecher's character, pointing out the "exoticism" of a political platform built on agitation for women's rights, spiritualism, and free love. A candidate who ran for the White House solely on those issues was sure to be abused, ridiculed, and defeated. Beecher, the letter argued, would have a fair chance for election in November.

Woodhull had not financed the convention to nominate Beecher. Their relationship was complex. They had been lovers briefly, they were rivals, and the intersection of their lives would ultimately be disastrous for both of them. She responded to the *Herald* letter in the pages of the *Weekly*. "We want no expediency here," she wrote. "The convention should not seek to make itself respectable by hanging on to the tail of any kite." She succeeded in turning the reformers' attention away from Beecher.

He preferred to distance himself from reformers in any case. Privately he had told Woodhull that if he preached radical ideas to his congregation, he would soon be talking to empty seats. His well-known face, with its hooded, gray eyes, was not among the delegates.

With Beecher out of the running, Woodhull had calculated that her best hope for success lay in a modest demeanor and careful timing. She would await the delegates' call to the hall, neutralizing her image as Mrs. Satan by presenting herself to them as less outspoken and more properly conventional than she really was, adopting a propriety the convention members would consider womanly. In response to their summons, she would deliver a speech intended to inspire prompt action. Without her direction, the reform factions—temperamentally suited as they were to argument—would simply talk the convention to death. If she could preempt the debates that would introduce the names of other candidates, she might win a unanimous nomination. The strategy required restraint, but she had believed it could produce an immediate victory.

Now she waited decorously in the anteroom, listening to the delegates shout her name again and again, until Reymart came to escort her back to the platform.

Then, in a low calm voice, she said, "Friends, from my inmost heart I thank you . . . for the great honor you have shown me in making me your standard bearer." Her manner was a model of modesty as she acknowledged the accolades of the crowd.

When she finally left the platform, the throng moved with her to the anteroom where she received well-wishers. Flowers banked the walls of the room, rustic baskets brimming with tulips and lilacs. Friends crowded around Woodhull, kissing her and kissing each other, laughing and crying. "For the first time in history," Woodhull later wrote in the *Weekly,* "the comrades of reform had united and a new political party had been born."

Colonel James Harvey Blood, Woodhull's husband, stood nearby, stolidly retaining his composure despite the confusion in the anteroom. Dark hair in perfect order, side whiskers elegantly clipped, he carried himself with authority, the bearing he had gained as a young Civil War officer. He had his own ambitions, but knew they would find their best outlet as Woodhull's adviser and alter ego. Now he stood watching Woodhull receive the embraces of the crowd.

The reporter from the *Cincinnati Commerical* counted Woodhull's kisses for his readers. He had never before seen so much kissing and hugging in public, nor in private. "Men were not afraid to pass hands round women who were not their wives, and women also indulged in political osculation," he reported. "Mrs. Woodhull was in ecstasy, and so was her sister Miss Claflin."

Tennie Claflin was across the room, her face beaming, her curls held in place under a smart black hat. She had followed Woodhull onto the lecture circuit. Her own promotional posters touted her as "beautiful, bright-eyed, blond, young, sprightly and smart." It was an open secret that Commodore Vanderbilt, who was about to celebrate his seventy-eighth birthday, had proposed marriage to her. Gossip said Claflin had been the Commodore's mistress, and that perhaps she still was. Throughout the convention day she had remained subdued, adopting for herself Woodhull's strategy of womanly rectitude. Now she broke her silence, accepting congratulations on her sister's behalf, kissing women and men without discrimination.

The New York press had depicted the Equal Rights Party as a collection of "wild men and women." After the meeting, the *Weekly* reported that not a single tobacco stain could be found in the hall; none of the established political parties could make the same claim, the paper commented primly.

But Woodhull's attempts at modesty did not impress the *New York Times.* With a patronizing sneer, the *Times* said, "The career of Victoria Woodhull cannot but be entertaining as she gains public attention by hook or by crook . . . Mrs. Woodhull, with an ambition worthy of a female Napoleon, goes for the presidency and strikes immediately at the White House."

Ignoring the mockery, Woodhull republished the article in the *Weekly*. The attack meant less than the broad public exposure the press had given to her plans.

I

MIDWESTERN
UNITED STATES

1838–1867

1
"A Favoring Omen"

What possessed Victoria Woodhull, this woman-who-would-be-president? To say that she was ambitious explains nothing. Unconventional ambitions alone meant very little in an age that so often and effectively suffocated women's aspirations. One accidental clue to Woodhull's nature can be found in the "Mrs. Satan" caricature drawn by Thomas Nast. In the foreground, shrouded in black and equipped with hooked wings, stands the Victoria of 1872, a female gargoyle poised to destroy the country's fondest notion of the Good Woman. Off in the background, far harder to make out, a dutiful wife carries her drunken lout of a husband and squalling children up one of those trackless hills of adversity so admired by nineteenth-century moralists. The drawing is smug: the wife prefers the nettled path to the free-spirited temptations of Mrs. Satan. What Nast didn't know was that for many years Woodhull had lived the life of that dutiful wife. Without Woodhull the Good Woman, there would have been no Mrs. Satan.

Victoria Claflin Woodhull was born in 1838, an inauspicious year squeezed materially between the economic panic of 1837 and the depression of 1839, and tossed on the spiritual turbulence of the Great Awakening. Her father, Reuben Buckman Claflin—known to his friends as Buck—combined the best traits of frontier self-reliance with a streak of the rascal and confidence man. Her mother, Roxanna Hummel Claflin, called Annie, seemed frail, even angelic, compared with her robust and athletic husband, but she was no ephemeral flower. She was intelligent, ambitious, and absolutely persuaded that the child she carried—the seventh of her ten children—was no ordinary being. Annie's folk wisdom told her a seventh child brought luck. She embellished the circumstances of Victoria's birth and childhood with fanciful tales that evolved into family legends. In the last months of her pregnancy, Annie was "sanctified" at a religious revival. Dreams and visions had come to her, convincing her she would bear a remarkable child. She and Buck named their daughter Victoria, after the 18-year-old queen of England. As an adult, Victoria believed that being her mother's seventh child brought her good fortune, and that her name was a "providential and prophetic" choice on the part of her parents, a "favoring omen" for the course of her life.

Victoria's early empire was a small white cottage in Homer, Ohio, with a high peaked roof and a porch running around three sides. A garden stretched in a jumble of colors between the Claflin house and Main Street, and the fragrance of flowers drifted inside through tall open windows. As a child, Victoria played beside the great central fireplace. She watched the black iron kettle, hanging from its crane, and learned the rich smells of the daily meals simmering on the fire. Outside the back door and a few steps across the lawn, a mill race flowed in a deep ravine. There ducks paddled silently, and every now and then a turtle lifted its head. Birds swooped overhead and then sank down, disappearing from view among the cattails and marsh grasses.

From her front door Victoria could look west along Main Street toward the new Methodist church, where Annie unsettled the more staid members of the congregation with her ecstasies during services. Annie's religious impulses were eclectic. They traced back to influences she had absorbed among her German-speaking relatives in Pennsylvania. Her grandfather, John Jacob Hummel, had arrived in Berks County, Pennsylvania, in 1743. Her father, John, had migrated farther west with his wife, Margaret Moyer Hummel. In 1793 they had settled at a crossroads called Dry Valley in the Susquehanna Valley, where John opened Hummel's Tavern. Annie, born in 1804, was the last of her parents' seven children. Her father died at 41, the year she was born, and her mother spent Annie's first year in mourning for her husband.

The Hummel family lived on the banks of the Susquehanna River in a Pennsylvania German world that abounded in mysteries, superstition, and folklore. Annie knew the secret but sure signs of impending death: a dog howling near a window, a fruit tree that blossomed in the fall. She heard hidden rituals whispered in darkened rooms behind closed doors, chants to ward off illnesses, and lines of the hex to cast a spell. Annie believed that words had magical properties beyond their literal meaning. She accepted an omnipotent inner world in which thoughts could bring an event to pass, a world beyond rationality, a zone whose surest emanations appeared in dreams. All her life Annie clung to the innocent magical beliefs of a child who hasn't learned the operation of cause and effect, and she passed her eccentricities along to her daughter.

A gift for the spiritual was not one of Buck Claflin's qualities. A materialist and adventurer, he was always in ardent pursuit of the main chance. His family traced themselves back to Robert Mackclothlan, a Scottish soldier who had settled and prospered in Wenham, Massachusetts, sometime before 1661. As the generations of Claflins multiplied and land grew scarce, the younger Claflins pushed westward. Buck's mother, Anna Underwood, claimed a sea captain as a grandfather. She had come down a bit in the world when she married young Robert Claflin, Buck's father. Buck and his twin brother, Samuel Carrington Claflin, were born in 1796 in Sandisfield, Massachusetts, a dark little valley hemmed in by the Berkshire Mountains. It had become a stagecoach stop between Albany and Hartford. After the twins' birth, Anna and Robert obtained some land in Troy, Pennsylvania, and added 11 more children to their family.

Samuel became a well-known hunter and farmer in the area, but Buck despised the physical drudgery of the farm and rebelled against backwoods life. For a while he read some law and worked in a store. Then he turned to logging, a major industry along the Susquehanna River. He became a river man, a rafter who knew rocks and currents, the sort of man needed to navigate timber downriver to the sawmills. After the hazardous trips, he would sit in the riverside taverns, his feet propped up on a wooden whiskey keg. It was a setting he found convivial. He flourished in the company of hard-drinking, hard-gambling men who drew their living from the Susquehanna. But Buck was not universally admired. German-speaking raftsmen in their fur caps, heavy red-checked woolen shirts, and trousers coated with pitch called him "the Englishman." Behind his back they spoke of him as a gambler and a sharp trader, not one of them.

One of Buck's sidelines was buying and selling horses. Through this interest, he met John Snyder, the son of Simon Snyder, the first governor of Pennsylvania. Handsome John, as John Snyder was known, hired Buck to train his horses. What appealed to Buck most was the way his new employer liked to live. Handsome John had set himself up as a country gentleman on an estate he called Freedom. He owned a paper mill, a sawmill, and many acres of land. He raised fine horses and raced them on his own track. (Gambling for high stakes had become such a vice among the river men that upright citizens like the Hummels had formed an association to abolish public tracks.)

No account of Buck and Annie's introduction survives, but the circumstances of Susquehanna Valley life suggest they met at a tavern called the Rising Sun, owned by Annie's uncle, John Jacob. Whether Buck saw advantages beyond love in the niece of a prosperous tavern owner, there is no way to know. The Hummel family would have known of Buck's reputation. They would not have approved. But Buck's style and ambitions appealed to Annie.

She married Buck in 1825. They left the Susquehanna Valley and the disapproving Hummels and, after a brief visit to Buck's family in Troy, began a nomadic river life. Buck lived by his wits. Constantly on the move, he left Annie for a month or more each spring and fall to transport 180 to 200 rafts of lumber and 8 "arcs," covered rafts that carried produce. He put his profits into taverns and stores, which he ran in the winter months when the rivers were frozen.

Buck plunged into the canal age, on the Susquehanna around Harrisburg, then on the Monongahela near Pittsburgh. The construction of the Ohio and Erie Canal took Buck to Ohio, first to Cleveland, and eventually to Homer. During the frenzied real estate boom after the 308-mile waterway opened in 1832, Buck boasted that he had made half a million dollars. According to family legend, he then built a resort hotel in Streetsboro, outside Cleveland, but what he called a resort hotel was actually a country tavern. Eventually he sold the Streetsboro business and retired to Aurora, where he raised "fine horses" and raced his favorite, named Paul Jones. Buck's description of life in Aurora sounded more like Handsome John's Freedom than anything Buck could have afforded.

Whatever the case, falling real estate values brought on by the 1837 recession probably drove Buck and Annie from Aurora. Homer caught his fancy because he hoped the North Fork of the Licking River, which ran through Homer, would become a feeder canal into the Ohio and Erie. When he got to Homer, Buck presented himself as a man of means, destined to put the town on the map. He arrived with just enough cash to establish credit. He purchased the local grist mill, but he had no intention of becoming a miller. He meant to enlarge the grist mill, add a sawmill, build a race with a watercourse a mile and a half long, and assemble 500 acres of land as an investment. He contracted to pay $4,000 for the tract, an impressive sum for the time.

Annie was once again pregnant. Since 1825 she and Buck had produced a new Claflin every other year of their married life. This time it was Victoria. When she was born, her two older sisters, Margaret and Mary, were 11 and 7 years old, and her two brothers, Maldon and Hebern, were 5 and 3. Two other sisters, Delia and Odessa Maldiva, had died before Victoria's birth. Later two younger sisters joined the family, Utica in 1841 and Tennessee Celeste in 1843. Annie's last child, Hester Ann, was born in 1849 and died in early childhood.

Three years separated Victoria and Utica. During those years Annie inducted Victoria into her own unusual world of superstition, spiritualism, and religion. The family remembered her laughing with pleasure and calling her baby "my little queen." Victoria was extravagantly loved, the Claflins' petted baby. She gained an unshakable sense of her own worth.

The aura of sanctification emanating from Annie was probably first instilled at one of the popular camp meetings organized in the summer by the proselytizing Methodists. Worshippers would erect white tents on wooded hills and light great bonfires. At twilight, the sound of a trumpet would start the meetings, and hymns would follow. Preachers spoke in rotation, day and night, urging every "sister, dear sister" to come forward and make a confession. Sobs would mingle with prayers and shouts of "Glory, Glory, Jesus, Jesus." The redeemed would wring their hands, tear at their hair, and call for mercy. Reaching a state of frenzy, they would speak in tongues, believing that the incomprehensible words came as a gift from God, the most direct and intimate form of communication with Him.

As a child, in white summer dresses or dark winter mufflers, Victoria walked with her mother to morning services every Sunday and nighttime prayer meetings every Wednesday. Annie carried a Bible under her arm, a heavy volume with dark brown covers and gilt-edged pages. It recorded the births of all the Claflins. Annie sometimes allowed Victoria to hold her Bible as they sat together listening to the direct, forceful sermons of the circuit-rider ministers, most of them self-taught. Victoria absorbed the preachers' measured biblical cadences, moral zeal, pursuit of higher truth through mystical insight, and eagerness for social reform. At her mother's side Victoria anticipated the Methodist millennium, foretold in the Book of Revelation, that glorious moment when holiness would triumph and bring joy and freedom from wickedness to all those who believed.

At prayer meetings Victoria watched her mother rise with a strange, contorted look on her face to pour out passionate halleluyahs. When the spasm passed, Annie returned to her seat, her face aglow with the euphoria of her glossolalia. But over the years, Annie's ability to achieve this trance state dissipated. Victoria's encounters with her mother's ecstasies became less frequent, and eventually they stopped.

Annie's behavior squared poorly with Homer's standards for womanly virtue. The town matrons, perhaps envying the handsome mother and her pretty daughters, scrutinized Annie. Not only was her religious style peculiar, but her housekeeping did not match up. One day a delegation arrived—footsteps clattering along the porch, a knock sounding sharply at the door—to offer the outsider some good advice. Faced with Annie's unwavering gaze, the women soon came to the point: there were no curtains on her windows. One hundred and fifty years later, people still tell the story. "Windows are for light and air," Annie told the blue noses and sent them on their way.

The spurned neighbors discovered that Annie was illiterate and snubbed her. Apart from her childhood religious training in German, Annie had received no education. She spoke English fluently without an accent, but she could not read or write. She quoted long passages from the Bible, but she couldn't read it. She had learned the words, chapter and verse, by memorizing them as they were read aloud. It is possible that she had some form of reading disability, for her daughter Utica later suffered from dyslexia. Whatever the case, Annie's illiteracy confirmed for the better-educated matrons of Homer that Annie was not quite one of them. Undaunted, she ignored their judgment and, her children in hand, followed her own lights.

When Victoria was three a calamity befell Buck. In 1839, another financial panic, fueled by excessive real estate speculation, initiated a great depression. Shipbuilding stopped, construction stopped, businesses and banks failed, and thousands were out of work. Buck was forced to take out a loan on the mill, and he failed to make the first payment on his land. He had borrowed money against real estate that had become worthless, and he had no way of recovering. In 1841, at age 45, he was left with only the mortgaged grist mill and his house.

Trying to put a good face on his situation, Buck later told an 1850 census taker that he was a lawyer. His Pennsylvania horse-training job was reinvented as a legal career devoted to the service of his oldest friend, the governor of Pennsylvania. This statement was simply untrue. Governor Simon Snyder had died in 1819, when Buck was 23 years old, and it's unlikely the two ever met. Buck's claim to be a lawyer did have some foundation in his work as a clerk in a Pennsylvania law office; in early nineteenth-century Ohio almost anyone could title himself a lawyer. But in 1853 a long-awaited legal reform, the Ohio Code of Civil Procedure, replaced the old Ohio common law system and made self-proclaimed lawyers like Buck obsolete.

For Victoria the legacy of these years was a life-long obsession with regaining her father's lost fortune. As an adult she gave a brief account of the catastrophe: "He suddenly lost all that he had gained, and sat down like a beggar in the dust of despair . . . Father, in the opinion of many, became partially crazed; he would take long and rapid walks, sometimes of twenty miles, and come home with bleeding feet and haggard face . . . Mother, never wholly sane, would huddle her children together as a hen her chickens, and wringing her hands above them, would pray by the hour that God would protect her little brood. Intense melancholy—a misanthropic gloom thick as a sea fog—seized jointly upon both their minds."

Buck's reaction was predictable and unpleasant. He spent his days in taverns, returning late at night to expend his drunken rage on his children. He kept braided willow switches in a barrel of rain water, ready to use for whippings. Victoria's older brother Hebern ran away from home at age 13 to escape his father's abuse. When Victoria appealed to her mother for protection, Annie sided with her husband, laughing hysterically at the beatings, looking crazily delighted and clapping her hands. At other moments she would be angelic, fondling her children, caressing them, lifting up her arms to thank God for them. But then, for no apparent reason, she, too, would strike them angrily. Victoria later described her mother as "one of the most erratic of mortals." The trauma instilled in her a sense of distrust that shaped her closest relationships for the rest of her life.

Faced with these accumulating pressures, Victoria had to develop extraordinary powers of self-defense. Just as her father's economic fortunes began to disintegrate, she lost an important source of emotional support. Rachel Scribner, the woman who helped Annie care for her brood, suddenly died. At the moment of Rachel's death, Annie claimed, Victoria entered a trance that lasted three hours. When the little girl opened her eyes again, she spoke with great excitement of seeing Rachel alive. Listening, Annie transformed Victoria's dreams into a vision: Victoria had floated through space with Rachel, "seeing scenes of wondrous beauty."

After Rachel's death Victoria invented two imaginary playmates. Annie observed that they were constantly present, and that Victoria talked to them as a girl would to her dolls. Annie identified these imaginary friends as the two sisters, Delia and Odessa Maldiva, who had died before Victoria's birth. Annie had been mourning Odessa when she became pregnant with Victoria, and Victoria had become an emotional replacement, doubly shaped by her mother's needs and dreams.

During the years that followed, with Rachel Scribner gone and Buck Claflin often off chasing new pipe dreams, Victoria grew into another role as family caretaker. Another family story illustrates this development. Walking to prayer meeting one evening, Victoria stretched out her arms dramatically and said, "Mamma, stop to hear voices!" She clasped her mother tightly, indicating she must not make a noise. The "voices of the air," as Victoria later identified them, had told her that two men were planning to rob their house. Forewarned, she devised a simple protective ruse: when she returned home she lit every lamp in the house. According to Victoria, the robbers did come at two that morning, but finding the lamps ablaze, they didn't dare break in. It was a triumph of imagination, one that surely pleased Annie. The form young Victoria's imagination took is intriguing: she would protect her family—and in a grandiose way.

On another occasion Victoria was sitting sleepily by a cradle, rocking a sick baby sister. Feeling her eyes closing, she fought to stay awake. In that tense and fearful household, she couldn't permit herself the smallest dereliction. Even so, she fell asleep. When Annie unexpectedly entered the room, Victoria woke up, immediately inventing a new vision: two angels had come to help her, gently pushing her away from the cradle so they could fan the feverish baby with their own white hands. Meanwhile, she said, they had put Victoria into a trance. That was why her face had been turned upward toward the ceiling. In a disordered household with no rational rules, Victoria was learning how to manipulate her parents, imitating Annie's own coping devices. Annie believed Victoria's explanation and even accepted it with pleasure.

Eventually Buck's situation began to improve—a year as postmaster in 1843 helped—but he seemed to have lost his old spirit. He spent his time beside the fire telling long, rambling stories designed to impress anyone who would listen that he had known better days.

In 1846, at the age of eight, Victoria started school. The town soon discovered that she possessed a remarkable mind. Annie announced that the tough little mysteries stumping the brains of other students were as clear as sunshine to Victoria, that she was the quickest pupil in her school. She apparently had a photographic memory. She could glance at a page and repeat it by heart. Annie's pride exaggerated Victoria's accomplishments, but she was correct in believing her daughter possessed unusual intelligence. Victoria's schooling totaled less than three years at broken intervals between her eighth and eleventh birthdays. She attended classes in the Methodist church whenever a teacher was available to conduct them, but her formal education was haphazard. The Akron Law of 1848 reorganized the Ohio state school system, and Victoria's younger sisters, Utica and Tennessee, benefited from the new program. But the changes came too late to educate Victoria. Of necessity she came to accept her mother's assessment that her intellectual skills were a miracle granted by heavenly spirits to prepare her for a special destiny.

Isolated from Homer society, Victoria and her mother jointly exercised their gifts of fantasy. Watching her mother's silent prayers, her moving lips, Victoria said later that she believed the prayers were offered to a supernatural audience "whose watchful eyes are always on us." Victoria became convinced that some subtle power of transmutation was at work between her mother and herself. These marvelous expectations were more thrilling than anything else in Victoria's life. They left an enduring legacy: her conviction that unknowable powers, bestowed by her mother, ordered her life.

Her father's legacy was far more ambiguous. In 1853 Buck lost his mill. In the dead of winter, a lamp overturned in the dry grain, and a blaze instantly lit up the cold night. As Homer filled with shouts, children's cries, and the stamping of horses' feet, the townspeople organized a bucket brigade and worked desperately to save the building, but the water arrived too late to put out the flames. In less than an hour, nothing remained of the mill but charred beams and a gaping black hole.

On the night of the fire, Buck was away in nearby Mount Vernon, and Annie was left to face the disaster alone. Victoria watched while her stricken mother gathered her children on a bridge overlooking the smoldering ruins. Acrid fumes drifted up as Annie stretched her arms over their shivering heads and poured forth a prayer: "O merciful Father, send relief or we perish."

Around Homer, no one considered Buck Claflin's loss a tragedy. No one rallied around the family. Gossips immediately accused Buck of setting the fire himself to collect insurance money, for fire insurance had just become available in Homer, and everyone knew that Buck had been hard-pressed to repay the mortgage on the mill. With real estate prices down, an insurance settlement would bring in more cash than selling the property. Buck was more than capable of working out the equation. These rumors were spread out of spite. Buck had arrived in Homer talking big, only to become the scapegoat for hard times that no one understood. His pretensions had never gone down well, and now Homer had a chance to put him in his place. Years later, townspeople would still describe the Claflins as arrogant people who put on airs.

Buck was never charged with wrongdoing after the fire. He said himself that he had failed to insure the mill at its full value, and no evidence exists to indicate how much money, if any, he collected. The trajectory of his subsequent life indicates he was dead broke. He was now 57 years old. The expectations of wealth he and his wife had shared at the time of Victoria's birth were gone. He had nothing left but his bravado. True to his character, he maintained a pretentious facade and spoke airily of losing a great deal of money speculating.

At the time, Victoria wanted to believe her father's tales. Whatever the facts, he managed to convince his daughter that the family had lost its rightful place in the world. Over the years, her view of her father changed, but she still clung to the vestiges of her early idealization of Buck Claflin as a man of wealth fallen on hard times. As a grown woman, she and her sister Tennie both talked obsessively about the fortune their father had lost and their desire to "regain what should have been our own."

When Buck was at his best, Victoria experienced him as a powerful force to be adored and placated, but one of limited helpfulness to her. At his worst, he was mean-spirited and vicious. She could not remember a single fatherly kiss. Conditioned by Buck to expect little of men, she would soon marry someone very much like him, a man with pretensions to gentility who was also undependable and abusive.

Buck knew when to put Homer behind him, but it was Annie, as always, who packed up the children and followed him to Mount Gilead, Ohio. Victoria felt the weight of Homer's rejection as she left behind the only home she had ever known.

2

"Send for the Spirits"

*F*or the next 14 years, the record offers only occasional glimpses of Victoria, flashes of family history and emotions that she measures out to us and for which she is the only source. Beginning in adolescence, she composed and recomposed her autobiography, reinventing her life as she moved through time, altering the story to serve her changing needs. She learned early how to hold an audience, how to win sympathy and approval. With remarkable resourcefulness, she turned that talent into one of her strongest coping skills. Her account of those 14 years—subjective, melodramatic, highly colored and self-serving—was recorded in 1871 by a sympathetic memoirist, Theodore Tilton, who would play an important role in her life. His work, based on a generally accurate chronological framework, offers a sympathetic introduction to her life and work.

Victoria told Tilton about a signal summer in 1853, when she was 14 years old and living in Mount Gilead, Ohio. The Claflins had taken refuge with Victoria's oldest sister, Maggie, and her husband, Enos Miles, a successful businessman and partner in the Hewitt and Miles Drugstore. Shortly before Independence Day Victoria fell ill with a fever, and the family summoned Dr. Canning Woodhull to treat her.

The Claflins, including Victoria, were impressed by the young man's appearance. He was handsome, with black hair and dark eyes, 28 years old and unmarried. As Victoria spun the story years later, Dr. Woodhull exhibited "the respectability of his family connections—his father being an eminent judge, and his uncle the mayor of New York." Adopting the mode of a fairy tale, she cast the doctor as a "prince." She told Theodore Tilton that he had come to find her "as Cinderella," ill and worn from helping with the care of her younger sisters, "a child of the ashes."

"Being a trained physician," she reported, the doctor arrested her decline. One day, before she had entirely recovered, and still looked

haggard and sad, he had stopped her in the street and said, "My little chick, I want you to go with me to the picnic." No glass slipper
appears in this story, but a pair of shoes does play a part. Annie gave
Victoria permission to attend the Independence Day picnic, but Buck
set a condition that first she should earn enough money to buy new
shoes. "So the little 14-year-old drudge became for the nonce an apple merchant," Victoria remembered. "With characteristic . . . energy [she] sold her apples and bought her shoes."

On the Fourth of July, Victoria put on her white summer dress and
her new shoes, pinched her cheeks to give them color, and decorated
her hair with hollyhocks, as was the custom. Canning appeared in
the white suit men commonly wore in hot weather, and off they went
to the picnic, the handsome doctor and glowing child.

Independence Day, Mount Gilead's favorite holiday of the year,
celebrated high summer as well as the birth of the nation. Across the
state, patriotic citizens decked their cities and towns with bunting of
red, white, and blue. Newspaper editorials offered their annual cau-
tion: intoxication was not necessary to celebrate the Fourth, advice
that would be cheerfully ignored as the day progressed. In Mount
Gilead the band played, the volunteer militia marched, and the
mayor solemnly read the Declaration of Independence. Then the pic-
nickers gathered around trestle tables that creaked under the weight
of hams and turkeys, pies and cakes. Beer and cider washed everything down. Flasks of home-brewed whiskey appeared. Men dipped
into their tobacco pouches, and the green grass around the picnic tables turned brown. Chunks were chipped from blocks of ice cream,
and everybody licked the sticky treats in their hands.

Independence Day was the ninth wedding anniversary of Enos and
Maggie Miles. Their son John was two; Maggie's first three children
had died as infants, but she would bear three more children, two of
them daughters who would become Victoria's much loved nieces.
Mary, Victoria's next older sister, had also married a Mount Gilead
man named Ross Byrnes. They, with their two toddlers, were part of
the celebration. But Victoria's brothers were missing. Maldon had
married and moved to Pennsylvania, and Hebern refused to spend a
night under the same roof as his father.

At the end of the picnic, Victoria recalled, on coming home, Dr.
Woodhull was inspired with a sudden and romantic interest in this
"artless maid," as she described herself. "My little puss," he told her,
"tell your father and mother that I want you for a wife."

At 14, Victoria was becoming aware of how attractive she was to men. Still, she was genuinely surprised and upset by the proposal. According to Tilton's account, she "quivered with anger," and with "timorous speed fled to her mother . . . feeling as if some injury was threatened her, and some danger impended." But her parents were delighted with the unexpected offer. "A grand match," they said. A marriage contract was made.

Victoria later portrayed herself as being forced into marriage against her will, but that seems unlikely. She rarely did anything against her will, and however frightened she may have been, she had every reason to look on Dr. Woodhull's proposal as an attractive idea. Life with her family was a never-ending round of making fires, washing, ironing, baking, cutting wood, spading the vegetable garden, running errands, and tending infants. She had been out of school for three years; common practice had required her to stay at home when her youngest sister, Hester Ann, was born.

Four months later, not long after her fifteenth birthday, Victoria married Dr. Woodhull. Of her wedding day, the moment young girls of the time dreamed about, Victoria said only that "she accepted the change." A marriage certificate, filed with the Probate Court Records of Cleveland, showed that Victoria Claflin married Canning Woodhull on November 23, 1853. Both their names were misspelled on the document. The wedding took place in Cleveland, where Canning lived, not in Homer or Mount Gilead. The ceremony was performed by a Presbyterian minister who was a stranger to the bride and groom. After the ceremony, as winter winds began to blow across Lake Erie and dry leaves scuttled across the brown grasslands, Canning took his bride to his lodgings.

Canning had painted a fine but deceptive picture of himself. His father the judge was actually a justice of the peace. It was true that a Caleb Woodhull had once been mayor of New York, but Canning had never met him; he had no idea if they were related. The young doctor had yet to establish himself in the medical profession, and for good reason. In Ohio during the 1850s, thousands of men were competing for patients after completing medical degrees based on eight months of study and a short apprenticeship. New doctors often moved to frontier areas. Canning had associated himself with the Hewitt and Miles Drugstore, another method young doctors used to find new patients, but for all real purposes Victoria's new husband was a doctor without a practice.

Victoria discovered almost immediately that she had escaped from one hard life only to begin another even harder. Tilton unfolded the story she told him in the florid, self-dramatizing prose favored at the time. "Her captor, once possessed of his treasure, ceased to value it. On the third night, after taking his child-wife to his lodgings, he broke her heart by remaining away all night at a house of ill repute. She soon learned, to her dismay, that he was habitually unchaste, and given to fits of intoxication. She was stung to the quick. The shock awoke all her womanhood. She grew ten years older in a single day. A tumult of thoughts swept like a whirlwind through her mind, ending at last in one predominate purpose, namely, to reclaim her husband. She set herself religiously to this pious task—calling on God and the spirits to help her in it. Squandering his money like a prodigal, he suddenly put his wife into the humblest quarters, where, left mostly to herself, she dwelt in bitterness of spirit. Sometimes, with uncommon courage, through rain and sleet, half clad and shivering, she would track him to his dens, and by the energy of her spirit compel him to return. At other times all night long she would watch at the window, waiting for his footsteps, until she heard them languidly shuffling along the pavement with the staggering reel of a drunken man, in the shameless hours of the morning. During all this time she passionately prayed Heaven to give her the heart of her husband, but Heaven decreeing otherwise, withheld it from her."

Victoria would learn that Canning's "disease," as she came to call his chronic alcoholism, was something she could do nothing about. Whenever she looked back on these events she would accuse herself of being "ignorant," "innocent," and "simple."

Victoria next offers us a picture of herself pregnant, in a small frame house in Chicago during a winter so cold she visualized icicles clinging to her bedposts. On December 31, 1854, attended by her husband, who was drunk during the delivery, she gave birth to a son. The boy had the Woodhull family's dark hair and black eyes. They named the baby Byron after his grandfather. But according to Tilton's account, "To add to her misery, she discovered that her child, begotten in drunkenness and born in squalor, was a half idiot, predestined to be a hopeless imbecile for life, endowed with just enough intelligence to exhibit the light of reason in dim eclipse: a sad and pitiful spectacle [roaming] from room to room, muttering noises more sepulchral than human; a daily agony to the woman who bore him . . . the uncommon sweetness of his temper [wins] everyone's love, [and] doubles everyone's pity . . ." The "dismal fact" of her son's "half-idiocy" so preyed upon her mind that "in a heat of morbid feeling she fell to accusing her innocent self for his misfortunes. The sight of his face rebuked her."

Victoria spent the rest of her life trying to understand her son's mental incapacity. She went through the medical curriculum, at least as far as Canning understood it, to come to terms with Byron's condition. Barely out of childhood herself, she was now faced with a crushing reality. She changed from a light-hearted young girl to an intense, humorless woman bent on survival.

After a visit with her mother, Victoria returned to Chicago with her handicapped son. She still hoped to reform her husband, a dream as forlorn as Tilton's prose: "Once, after a month's desertion by him, until she had no money and little to eat, she learned that he was keeping a mistress at a fashionable boarding house under the title of wife. The true wife, still wrestling with God for the renegade, sallied forth into the wintry street, clad only in a calico dress . . . and shod only with india-rubber shoes, entered the house, confronted the household as they sat at table, told her story to the confusion of the paramour and his mistress, and drew tears from all the company till, by a common movement, the listeners compelled the harlot to pack her trunk and flee the city, and shamed the husband into creeping like a spaniel back into the kennel which his wife still cherished as her home."

Although the account reeks of melodrama, there is every reason to believe that it represents an actual event. Whatever enjoyment Victoria experienced during this performance—along with the slim victory of bringing her husband home—it did not eliminate her misery. But at the very least the story suggests that she had found a way of gaining the first small measure of mastery over her chaotic life.

In the tradition of martyred wives, Victoria tried to inspire her husband to begin a new life. The Woodhulls moved to San Francisco. The gold rush days were past, but, like Chicago, San Francisco was one of the fastest growing cities in the country. Change of sky was not change of mind, Victoria observed later. Along with their luggage her husband took his habits, and she took her misery from East to West.

In San Francisco an actress named Anna Cogswell met Victoria and, sizing up her talents, nudged her toward the stage. The poor transient with a drunken husband and an incapacitated son suddenly landed a significant job. Tilton says her role was the part of a country cousin in *New York by Gaslight*. The text was given to her in the morning, she learned and rehearsed it during the day, and was a "fair hit" in it that night. For six weeks thereafter she earned $52 a week. "Never leave the stage," said some of her fellow performers. "But I do not care for the stage," she replied, "and I shall leave it at the first opportunity. I am meant for some other fate. But what it is, I know not."

Victoria's sense of the theatrical, coupled with her childhood gift for visions, brought forth a flamboyant new character and role. "One night," Tilton recounts, "while on the boards clad in a pink silk dress and slippers, acting in the ballroom scene in the *Corsican Brothers,* suddenly a spirit voice [said], 'Victoria, come home.'"

At that moment, Victoria said, she saw a vision of Tennie distinctly enough to notice that she was wearing a striped French calico frock and standing beside their mother. "Victoria come home," the messenger said again, beckoning with her tiny forefinger.

Victoria "burst away at a bound behind the scenes" and, without waiting to change her dress, ran through a foggy rain to her hotel. She packed up her few things that night and took herself with her husband and child to the morning steamer bound for New York, eventually reaching her mother's home in Ohio. She came upon Tennie dressed in the same dress as in the vision, and on asking the meaning of the message, she was told that at the time it was uttered her mother had said to Tennie, "My dear, send the spirits after Victoria to bring her home."

An artful performer emerges in these episodes. When San Francisco did not offer Victoria a broad enough stage, she drew from her mother, her original wellspring, to improve her possibilities. But it is too easy to be cynical about these developments. Victoria's spiritual messenger was very much in keeping with the times. Nationwide interest in spiritualism had been aroused by Margaret and Kate Fox of Hydesville, New York. In 1848 the sisters had discovered, through powers that their followers considered supernatural, that they could deduce a message from mysterious rappings in their family cottage. They spent the summer of 1850 at Barnum's Hotel in New York City, and after Horace Greeley's *New York Tribune* gave favorable notice to their seances, they emerged as the leading figures in a new and lucrative field. Though there is no indication that Victoria ever met the Fox sisters, she was familiar with their careers, and later wrote about the knocks that had begun their movement.

The obsession with spirit communication was not new in America. Believers could point to incidents in the Bible, to the poltergeist that had disturbed the home of John Wesley, the founder of Methodism, to reports from mediums within American Shaker communities. America had also been introduced to mesmerism by itinerant magnetizers and lecturers. Franz Anton Mesmer had excited Paris in the 1780s with his demonstrations of hypnotism. Mesmer believed he had identified the source of spirit communication, an invisible fluid he called animal magnetism which connected soul and body as well as the spiritual and material worlds. Mesmerizers, adept at or-ganizing these connections, practiced in the same manner as mediums.

While spirits knocked, another invisible force, electricity, was animating the country. By the 1850s telegraph keys tapped throughout the United States. Believers in spirit communication used the new technology to argue that certain people were charged with an aura that made them "batteries" for spiritual telegraphy.

Victoria was searching for a new career, but she required something more substantial than spirit knockings. She found it one day in Indianapolis. Canning had disappeared on an alcoholic binge, and Annie was caring for Byron. When Victoria returned to their hotel, she learned from her mother that Byron had become suddenly ill with a high fever. Distraught, Annie wailed hysterically, "Your boy died two hours ago." He had apparently contracted scarlet fever, the disease that had taken Hester Ann Claflin, Victoria's youngest sister, five years earlier. Victoria cried, "No, I will not permit his death."

Later she dramatized the events that followed: "Without knowing what I did, I ripped my clothes open from my breast and clasped Byron to it with all my strength. As I did so the ceiling of the room disappeared from my view, and the form of the Savior descended. I stood fixed in the middle of the room with [Byron] thus clasped in my arms for seven hours. When I returned to consciousness and released him from my arms he was not only restored to life, but the disease was gone . . . just as if nothing had occurred to him. The child that had been thought dead was brought back again to life."

Victoria told the world that the spirit of Jesus Christ had brought Byron back from death, that He had "rewrought the miracle of

Lazarus" for her sake. She translated the curing of her son into a "calling," which she described as a "penetrating spiritual insight applied to the cure of disease." She said that she had been "directed" to announce herself as a medium to "treat patients." Suddenly she "discovered" that she was able to obtain "miraculous cures." And Victoria made other claims, as well. According to one of them, a woman who was expected to die was brought to her by a priest. For ten days and nights Victoria stayed with the ill woman without even leaving her for meals. After the tenth day the patient was able to walk downstairs and travel to Marquette, Michigan. Victoria believed that her own skin had become transparent and that her face had a light about it after her ten-day vigil, proof—to her—that her gift had a supernatural source.

In her new vocation, Victoria used no medicines, nothing but her presence, her touch, and her sympathetic ear, a technique that might today be called a form of intuitive psychotherapy. Whatever her impulses or motives may have been, she seems to have had a rare gift granted to a few individuals: a capacity for helping others to heal themselves.

The stories Victoria told of her step-by-step entry into her calling have a core of sincerity. But she used her considerable gifts of showmanship to embellish them. And as she traveled from city to city, she polished the practice she described as her "spiritual art."

Victoria had, she tells us, "prayed to God for another child, a daughter to be born with a fair body and a sound mind." On April 23, 1861, at 53 Bond Street in New York City, her prayer was granted. "The babe entered the world at four o'clock in the morning, handled by the feverish and unsteady hands of its intoxicated father, who . . . cut the umbilical cord too near the flesh and tied it so loose that the string came off. [He] laid the babe in its mother's arms—and then staggered out of the house. Nor did he remember to return. Meanwhile the mother on waking was startled to find that her head on the side next to her babe's body was in a pool of blood—that her hair was soaked and clotted in a little red stream oozing drop by drop from the bowels of the child."

Victoria was helped by a kind neighbor. Three days later, when she saw her husband staggering up the steps of a house across the way, mistaking it for his own, she asked herself, "Why should I any longer live with this man?" Victoria's older sister, Mary, had divorced her husband after ten years of marriage when he abandoned her and their two children. The laws of the state of Illinois granted divorce on any reasonable grounds. Victoria would soon return to Chicago to end her own marriage.

She gave her daughter an unusual name, spelled variously as Zula, or Zulu, Maud. The provenance of the name remains a mystery, but it was sufficiently meaningful to the Claflins that Victoria's sister Maggie gave the same name to her own daughter born six months later, Carrie Zula. Zulu, the name of the African people, was also a nineteenth-century name for a dark tulip with blackish lights, described as murrey velvet. These Zulu tulips could have been out at the time Zula Maud was born in May. Or perhaps Victoria had simply heard the word and liked the sound of it.

Victoria imbued her daughter's normalcy with special significance. She said later that they were more than mother and daughter, that a unique tie bound them together. Bearing a healthy baby freed Victoria's psyche from the emotional pall that Canning and Byron had cast over it. She later incorporated this positive experience into her social theories, using it to confirm her belief that only sexually-knowledgeable parents who wanted children should have them.

During these years Victoria's sister Tennie became her closest partner. One year the entire family gathered in Cincinnati to celebrate another Fourth of July. At that time Buck and Annie had Tennie going around the country telling fortunes, a role Victoria romanticized as the "damsel mentioned in the Acts of the Apostles, who brought her masters much gain by soothsaying." But Tennie, with Buck's sponsorship, had been doing considerably more than fortune-telling. It's unclear how much Victoria actually knew about their activities, but she knew enough to accuse her father of "adding to much that was genuine in her mediumship more that was charlatory . . . I believe Tennie ought to use the gift God has given her, but not in the mercenary way she was forced to use it," she declared. "She had no right to prostitute her powers."

Victoria's version of events was that she had "clutched Tennie as by main force and flung her out of this semi-humbug." But Tennie was supporting the family with her fortune-telling, and Victoria's rescue "excited the wrath of all these parasites." As the Claflins gathered in Cincinnati, hot words in loud, angry voices filled the house. When Tennie told her family she wanted to be rid of the "dead weight," they shouted back, "We will show you up, we will put you in the newspapers, we will ruin you." The scene would be enacted again and again over the years as the Claflin family repeatedly squeezed the sisters for every cent they could.

What we know about Buck and Tennie's activities starts with an ad he placed in a Columbus, Ohio, newspaper in 1859:

A WONDERFUL CHILD
MISS TENNESSEE CLAFLIN
WHO IS ONLY FOURTEEN YEARS OF AGE

This young lady has been traveling since she was eleven years old, and . . . has been endowed from her birth with a supernatural gift to such an astonishing degree that she convinces the most skeptical of her wonderful powers . . . She may be consulted in her room, United States Hotel, High Street, Columbus, from the hours of eight o'clock A.M. to nine o'clock P.M. Price of consultation $1.00.

The Fox sisters had created a public appetite for child mediums. To feed it, Buck had subtracted two years from Tennie's age. She fit the part. With round cheeks and wide blue eyes topped by a halo of red-gold ringlets, she still looked like a child. She wore a simple calico dress to enhance the illusion. Tennie thrived on the excitement. She said, "I told such wonderful things . . . that my father made from $50 to $100 a day at hotels simply by letting people see the strange clairvoyant child."

For their dollar, Tennie's clients received messages from absent friends, living and dead, and tales of events from the past, the present, and the future. The young woman was facile and quick-witted; her mix of artfulness and naive sincerity was extremely appealing. When circumstances required it, Tennie could go into an unconscious state. She claimed to find lost money and identify thieves.

Buck next decided they should go into healing. Medical testimonials soon appeared in his ads. A Mr. E. Bacus, Sr., said he had obtained immediate relief after Tennie prescribed medicine and operated on him with her hands. His friend Mr. Bambrough, of 41 Long Street, Columbus, had begun to recover from a paralytic stroke after receiving Tennie's treatments.

Tennie also sold a medicine called Miss Tennessee's Magnetio Life Elixir for Beautifying the Complexion and Cleansing the Blood.

Price, $2.00 per bottle. The elixir was warranted to be perfectly harmless and purely vegetable, to be taken three times a day, one-half hour before each meal. Buck had ordered up bottles and printed quantities of labels displaying Tennie's face. From Columbus the elixir was introduced to Chicago at the Wonderful Child Miss Tennessee's Magnetio Infirmary, 265 Wabash Avenue. Pittsburgh followed Chicago, and then all the new midwestern cities were introduced to the wonderful child and her elixir.

Buck expanded their confidence game. He began touting himself as the "American King of Cancers, Dr. R. B. Claflin." In 1863 the Ottawa, Illinois, *Free Trader,* reported the doctor had arrived in town. The Claflins rented the Fox River House Hotel and converted it into an infirmary. Following their established routine, they distributed circulars quoting satisfied patients. Mrs. Rebecca Howe told the town that she had been cured of breast cancer. It wasn't long until all 15 of the infirmary beds were filled.

But a year later, Mrs. Howe's health had deteriorated, and she had second thoughts. On June 4, 1864, she published her change of heart in the *Ottawa Republican.* "To whom it may concern," her statement read, "Miss Tennessee Claflin, having published a card addressed to the public, touching her treatment of myself for cancer, which statement was prepared by Miss Claflin herself, and which is in many respects false and untrue and calculated as I believe to mislead the public . . . I make this statement realizing the fact that I have but a short time to live, and that it is my wish to prevent . . . sufferers . . . apply[ing] to Miss Claflin, whom I believe to be an imposter . . . wholly unfit for the confidence of the community."

When Rebecca Howe died, a grand jury was convened to look into the cause of her death. It found she had died from drugs administered by Tennessee Claflin. Tennie's elixir was only a placebo, but no one in town believed that, and she was indicted for manslaughter. By the time the indictment was issued, Tennie had fled the state. The Claflins left their patients behind in the infirmary. Four were dying of cancer, too ill to be moved. Utterly callous toward the dying, Buck placed an ad in the *Free Trader* urging Tennie's patients in Illinois to continue purchasing their medicines by mail.

Tennie was not the only talented youngster who supported her family by fraud and deception. The Fox sisters, who had started the trend, ultimately confessed that they had produced their knocks by the simple expedient of cracking their toe joints. They had entertained each other with the trick as children, calling the sound Mr. Splitfoot.

Given the hyperspirituality of the nineteenth century, it is just possible that some young women started out believing in the unique quality of their gifts as mediums. They soon realized, however, that embellishments made them more persuasive. It was easy to cheat the many unsophisticated country and frontier people who were attracted to their marvels. Conscious deception became part of their practices, as it had with Tennie.

Competition was fierce and showmanship essential for a medium's survival. Cora Hatch, a young practitioner, captivated her audiences with her bare shoulders and arms, which she raised in the attitude of a clergyman. Her masses of golden curls and the white rose she always tucked into her belt became famous. Achsa Sprague enveloped herself in flowing dresses of bold stripes and wrapped bright ribbons around her wrists.

Successful mediums were the first women many Americans saw speaking in public. They became stage performers, speaking in trance on any subject the audience selected. Alone and vulnerable looking on the platform, they made a powerful impression on their followers. An admirer declared that Cora Hatch's entrancing eloquence made his heart throb with sacred emotion. Achsa Sprague, who never married, received three letters proposing marriage in the course of a single week. Cora Hatch did marry—three times. For a young medium, the public acclaim and adoration were a heady experience, far more exciting than traditional marriage and babies.

Neither Victoria nor Tennie went on the stage as a trance medium, but both were prepared by their experiences as clairvoyants to become public figures. Most mediums associated their first awareness of spirits with childhood reveries. Like Victoria, they turned to spirits again during a desperate period in their lives. Again like Victoria, they were often poorly educated, and their prospects were limited. Mediumship offered riches and a better life. Those mediums who succeeded developed impressive talents for extemporaneous speaking.

Tennie had not undergone the illness and suffering that were considered precursors to mediumship. She loved playing center stage and ran the risk of becoming psychologically dependent on the role. She knew the importance of establishing an honest image and worried about being exposed as a fraud.

Victoria presented herself as sensitive, somewhat nervous and sincerely convinced of her calling. She said she considered it a religious vocation. Victoria could be comfortable as a clairvoyant only by asserting her sincerity. She maintained that she, more than most human beings, scorned a lie, that she would rather burn at the stake than practice a deceit. Her exaggerated words suggest the fierceness of her own inner struggle. She had stitched a talisman against any temptation toward untruthfulness—the words from Psalm 120, "Deliver my soul O Lord from lying lips and from a deceitful tongue"—into a sleeve in each of her dresses. For two years she protected herself with this charm, she said, and she felt that in the process she had acquired an intuitive power to detect a lie at the moment it was uttered.

At about this time, Woodhull and her sisters made a sharp impression on a minor celebrity of the day. Jesse Grant, father of General Ulysses S. Grant, lived in Covington, Kentucky, across the Ohio River from Cincinnati. In his later years he grew increasingly hard of hearing. The medical doctors he consulted offered no effective treatment, attributing the disorder solely to advancing age. In his search for a remedy, Grant found himself on a cool and shaded veranda with Victoria Woodhull, the most famous local practitioner of medical clairvoyance.

Grant was a tanner, unhappily married to a reclusive and unsettled woman. In his job he heard animals scream as they died, then he tore off their hides and soaked them in lye and tannic acid—a filthy livelihood. Although his parents had abandoned him as a boy of 11, he had managed to educate himself. Like many untutored but intelligent men, he had harbored a lifelong ambition to become a man of letters. He had even written a novel. In his seventies he still composed verses under his pen name, the Bard of Covington.

Woodhull had been well schooled by her father in the ways of pleasing old men. She held Grant's hands in her own, looked directly into his eyes, seemingly oblivious to the sexual invitation implied, and listened intently. Jesse Grant could feel all at once that he was the center of the universe, that anything was possible. With the acute sensitivity to subtle cues that had made her such a successful clairvoyant, she gave him sympathy and gentle advice, all part of the practice of her "spiritual art."

Woodhull's two younger sisters, Tennessee and Utica, were also present, both endowed with the same exceptional beauty and sensuality as Victoria. Jesse Grant memorialized the occasion with an ode that began:

> *Three sisters fair, of worth and weight;*
> *A queen, a city and a state*

Well after nightfall, still hard of hearing but with a beatific smile on his face, he bid the sisters farewell and departed with an unsteady gait. He ultimately found a couplet to finish his poem:

> *Each bewitching little gypsy*
> *got that day a little tipsy.*

In the next glimpse Victoria offered of her life, she was in St. Louis, in April of 1864. A Union officer, Colonel James Harvey Blood, called to consult her as a "spiritualistic physician." He was tall, broad shouldered, dark eyed, and wore the romantic mantle of a war hero. Woodhull liked what she saw.

Blood had just returned to St. Louis after the Civil War battles of Lookout Mountain and Missionary Ridge. Three years earlier he had helped organize the Sixth Missouri Volunteers, raising funds and re-cruiting men for the regiment after President Abraham Lincoln's call for volunteers.

Blood had been born in Dudley, Massachusetts, on December 29, 1833. His forebears had lived in Massachusetts since 1617, but after the panic of 1857 he had come West with his parents to make a fresh start. Blood got a job in the city comptroller's office, his brother George worked as a bookkeeper, and his brother John became a clerk. Seth, the youngest, was still in school.

When war broke out, St. Louis was a bitterly divided city, but the Bloods maintained their strong New England antislavery loyalties. Blood and his younger brother John enlisted. During almost three years of continuous fighting, they had seen action in virtually every major battle in the war's western theater. Promoted to commanding officer of his regiment, Blood fought the military bureaucracy to gain adequate pay and promotions for his men. He was leading the regiment south when news arrived of Lincoln's Emancipation Proclamation of January 1, 1863. He and John were both wounded while under General Grant's command at Vicksburg, but they recovered to return to more heavy fighting. By the time Blood's enlistment was up, in the spring of 1864, the war in the west was over. He chose to identify himself by his military title for the rest of his life.

The Colonel and John returned to St. Louis, and the hero's welcome which awaited them in their home at 453 Pine Street. Waiting there also was Blood's wife, Mary, who had left her family behind in Massachusetts to move west with her husband. They had a daughter, Carrie, now five years old. His wife and daughter lived, and had been living all through the war, with his parents on Pine Street.

There was another side to the Colonel, quite different from the military man or the methodical careerist. He had helped organize the St. Louis Society of Spiritualists, serving as secretary of the new organization. Among spiritualists he was considered a man of a "philosophical and reflective cast of mind," a figure who more than most was "a student of the higher lore of spiritualism." On his return his fellow spiritualists selected him their president.

For reasons given variously as his own health (he was said to carry seven bullet holes in his body), or his wife's health, Blood called on Woodhull, the "spiritualistic physician." In Woodhull's account of their meeting, she said Blood was "startled" to see her pass into a trance. The Colonel was forced to lean close to her lips to hear her words. She spoke slowly, seemingly "unconsciously to herself," as she put it, whispering to the Colonel that his "future destiny was to be linked with hers in marriage."

These were the overtures of a sexually experienced woman. Woodhull was later quoted, second- or thirdhand, as saying she had lived the life of an "abandoned woman" until she made "a connection" with Colonel Blood. She denied the quote and bristled at the phrase "abandoned woman," but the expression does sound like her. It represents the style she was to develop to exquisite perfection. Her choice of words left the listener to decide if she had been abandoned, as of course she had been, many times, by her alcoholic husband, or if she had lived a life of sexual abandonment. This ambiguity came from the lips of an immensely attractive and sensuous woman, one who showed herself to be quite capable of acting in response to the needs of her own libido. The listener was faced with a deliciously titillating dilemma: whether to feel sympathy for her plight or sexual interest. Most men felt both.

Woodhull concluded her account of her first encounter with Blood in a spritely euphemism: "To their mutual amazement, but to their subsequent happiness, they were betrothed on the spot by the 'powers of the air.'" We can safely assume that "betrothed on the spot" implied a sexual encounter, and that the lovers thereafter pleasantly filled many springtime hours. The treatment for whatever ailed Blood pleased both of them.

The Colonel saw his new love through experienced eyes. He had scheduled trance speakers into St. Louis before the war. The best-known had come: brilliant Emma Hardinge, who became Mrs. Britten; her equally famous rival, Cora Hatch, now Mrs. Richmond; the philosophical Andrew Jackson Davis and his partner Mary Love, who lived with him in a free-love "marriage." Woodhull was younger, lovelier, more compelling than all the others. Blood knew he had discovered a great talent.

In the St. Louis elections of 1865, on the first Monday in April, Blood won a three-year term as auditor, a position that paid $2,500 per year, one of the city's highest salaries. With the job came his own office in the courthouse. He also became president of the St. Louis Railroad, a line of horse-drawn cars. But immediately after election day, Blood left his wife and moved into a boarding house on Washington Avenue, and not long afterward he left the state altogether. He never returned to his office in the courthouse, his family on Pine Street, or his wife and daughter.

Woodhull also left St. Louis to attend to some unfinished business. She tracked down Canning and divorced him in Illinois. At the same time she indulged herself in an odd whim. She arranged to have a family portrait painted. The picture shows an ideal Victorian family. Canning stands at the center of the scene, dominating the image, his family clustered around him. He is fashionably dressed in a frock coat. Byron, showing no hint of his impairment, is dressed to match his father in every detail, including his own little necktie. Woodhull stands to one side watching over her little flock with a serious look on her face. It may be Christmas, for she has decorated her hair with a sprig of holly, and Zula, carried on her father's arm, holds another cluster in her hands. Zula, outfitted in white and lace with blue ribbon trim and a blue sash around her waist, is the one bright spot in the otherwise dark composition.

The portrait is false. Canning was not what he seemed; his eyes reveal a sadness that verges on depression. Byron was not what he seemed. Woodhull, far from the ideal Victorian wife and mother, was in fact newly divorced. Only the little girl in white was true. Her shy smile is the only smile in the picture.

It is possible that the portrait was meant for Zula. Victoria also had a minature made, which she carried in her watch all of her life. Whatever the facts of her chaotic life, she needed a permanent image of an ideal family to pass on to her daughter.

Woodhull moved with Blood to Ohio—not to Cincinnati, where the Claflins still lived, but to Dayton, a town known for its liberal-mindedness. Dayton accepted the remarriage of divorced men and women more readily than Catholic Cincinnati. Blood engaged a fashionable Presbyterian minister, the Reverend Thomas E. Thomas, to perform the marriage ceremony (a note in the minister's book indicates the Colonel paid $5). Dayton had fought to free the slaves, and Dr. Thomas, one of the city's most outspoken abolitionists, was willing to oblige a Union officer and war hero who wanted to remarry. On Saturday, July 12, 1866, at the Phillips House Hotel, he joined Blood and Woodhull in marriage.

After the ceremony there was some confusion about the formalities. The minister neglected to file a confirmation. Years later his daughter said that her father had simply forgotten and had left the papers in his pocket. The state of Missouri has no record of Blood's divorce before his July 12 marriage to Woodhull. Blood did fill out an application for a marriage license. The partially completed form can still be found among the Dayton courthouse records. Perhaps Blood had paused at the words, "He has no lawful wife living . . . he knows no legal objection to the marriage contemplated betweem him and the said Victoria Claflin," the name he had entered on the license. The application remained forever incomplete, and the minister's record of the marriage forever unfiled.

Blood and Woodhull made many contradictory statements about their marriage—that they were later divorced, that their marriage had been annulled, that they had remarried in Chicago (where the great fire of October 1871 destroyed all the city's civil records so no marriage of this period can be substantiated). But they did go through the motions of a wedding ceremony in Dayton, and thereafter they lived as husband and wife.

After a short stay in Cincinnati, the couple moved to Pittsburgh, where their lives took a new direction. New post-war medical standards imposed by state authorities began to put spiritualist healers out of business. Legislatures had started banning the activities of

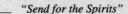

mediums, and courts were levying fines against violators. Charles Colchester, who had made his name by claiming to have conducted seances for President Lincoln, was arrested in Buffalo and fined $40 plus $743 in court costs. This changing climate of opinion jeopardized Woodhull's calling and she reassessed her talents.

II
NEW YORK CITY
1867–1877

3
Commodore Vanderbilt

*I*n the spring of 1868, Victoria Woodhull met Cornelius Vanderbilt, the richest man in America. Evidence suggests that she and Tennie went to New York with their sights deliberately set on the Commodore. Vanderbilt had a well-known soft spot for clairvoyants and a sharp eye for female beauty. The sisters, aware of their assets on both counts, had apparently decided to display themselves and their talents with the object of becoming his personal clairvoyants. Meeting Vanderbilt was not difficult: he had an open-door policy. The trick was to get more than his usual look of amused contempt, his brusque, "Come, speak quick and be off."

The Commodore, at 74, was a familiar sight on the streets of New York in his frock coat, high collar, flowing white cravat, and top hat. He had named a New York Central locomotive the Commodore Vanderbilt and decorated its headlights with his portraits. His private railroad car, yellow with red trim, was also named the Vanderbilt. A 50-ton bronze frieze of his railroads and steamships was under construction at the St. John's freight terminal on Hudson Street, and a colossal Commodore in bronze would stand at its center. He had had his face engraved on the New York Central's stock certificates. He was fond of saying that "many young ladies bought the stock that they might possess [my] picture."

The great railroad man spent the working part of his day, which he kept brief, in his sparsely furnished quarters on Bowling Green or in a new but equally bare one-room office on West 4th Street, directly behind his mansion at 10 Washington Place. He was accessible but impatient. To a young man seeking wisdom on how to make his way in the world he barked, "Say, sonny, lookahere. Let me give you a word of advice. Pay ready money for everything you buy and never sell anything you don't own. Good morning, sonny." He turned down all requests for charity. "Let others do what I have done and they need not be around here begging," he would snap. He was always interested, however, in more intriguing proposals.

On a promising day in the spring of 1868, the sisters made their way to Vanderbilt's door. They presented him with two business cards, expensively and delicately engraved. These tokens of respectable propriety identified the handsome brunette as Mrs. Victoria Woodhull and her younger, lighter-haired, and more voluptuous companion as Miss Tennie C. Claflin, clairvoyants. (Significantly, in bowing to the new realities of the time, Woodhull identified herself as a clairvoyant, not a medical clairvoyant.)

What Woodhull and Tennie remembered of this meeting, at least as far as they later shared it with the public, was that they had been "directed by some kind spirit hand" to Vanderbilt's "fatherly care and kindness." Their language employed the cloying phrases that were the currency of spiritualistic mediums, a style that the Commodore recognized and understood.

Woodhull later told and retold the story of the impulse that had led her to New York. It reveals a performance carefully prepared for Vanderbilt's sensibilities. A guiding spirit had directed them to a mysterious destination, a "place unknown to them," where they would find a house "that had been prepared for their comfort and use . . . in a city surrounded by tall ships." Vanderbilt could hardly fail to understand that "tall ships" referred to the tall-masted piraguas that transported his freight and the coasting schooners that ferried his passengers.

Woodhull's story was artfully transparent. "For many years, although an almost daily visitant, my principal spirit guide refused to reveal his name, promising to do so in due time . . . One night . . . he suddenly appeared and began to write upon the table. The letters were of fire and lighted up the room distinctly. When done he turned and commanded me to read. I did so, and it was, 'Depart thence' . . . I was to go to New York . . . There, in New York, I would find the house I was to occupy at number 17 Great Jones Street, which had been prepared for me."

The Commodore would have recognized the destination, for 17 Great Jones Street was on the stretch of East 3rd Street that ran between Broadway and the Bowery, a few doors from where they were sitting in his office behind Washington Place. Woodhull had suggested just enough to let Vanderbilt make his own deductions about the spirit guide that had led her to his own door. It was a bold advance transmuted by ladylike behavior into the accepted convention of spirit guidance.

A game was being played, the rules understood by all the participants. Nobody was fooled, least of all Vanderbilt. The sharp-eyed Commodore knew a good performance when he saw one. He recognized Woodhull and Claflin immediately as "ladies of resource."

The destination, which Woodhull had so ingenuously said was unknown to her, was actually the neighborhood of the city where she had lived briefly in the spring of 1861 when Zula Maud was born. At that time she'd had plenty of opportunity to absorb the lore about the Commodore. It was popular currency: all New York traded in it. He had truly loved his mother, Phebe Hand, the one person he could never outfox. Her death had torn a great hole in the fabric of his life. He had also loved his last child, George Washington Vanderbilt, born in 1839, the son most like his father. George had attended West Point and fought in the Civil War. At Shiloh he had contracted tuberculosis and died soon afterward.

Gossips had talked with spurious sagacity of the great man's deep mourning. In his efforts to communicate with the spirits of his mother and son, he fell back on half-forgotten practices he had known as a boy on Staten Island. He had once believed that clairvoyants could see the inside of the human body, that diseases could be discovered from miniatures or locks of hair and cured by mesmerism. A Mrs. Tufts from Staten Island had become his private medium, and there had been others as well. Despite his inclination to doubt, he was a reluctant skeptic who wanted to believe. So it was no coincidence that Woodhull leased a house on Great Jones Street, and when she and her sister walked through Vanderbilt's door, they were putting into action a carefully thought out plan.

The Commodore, apparently, was utterly charmed. An almost immediate rapport developed between the city's great financier and the two Midwestern clairvoyants. Throughout that spring, as twilight slowly descended into long evenings, the sisters often dined at his table. He also went to the house on Great Jones Street, so near his own back door, where Woodhull conducted private seances in the darkened drawing room. Gilded armchairs glittered faintly as heavy curtains were drawn over each tall window.

"Do as I do, consult the spirits," the Commodore told New York businesswoman Susan A. King, advising her to put her money in his own New York Central common stock. "It would go up 22 percent in three months," he said. Mrs. Woodhull said so "while in a clairvoyant state." One gets the sense that Vanderbilt was entertaining himself at the expense of the newspapermen who reported these stories, while not entirely disbelieving, either. Woodhull said later that the most wonderful prophesies of her life occurred at the house on Great Jones Street.

Tennie applied a more direct technique to the Commodore. She told him that she was a magnetic healer, a gift she had first become aware of when she was a girl of 11. By touching and massaging a patient's body, she said, she could transmit vital and healing forces. One hand provided positive energy, the other hand responded with a complementary negative force. Magnetic healing was a popular nineteenth-century form of the spiritual "laying on of hands." It obviously had the potential for provocative sexual experience as well. After Tennie demonstrated her unique body massage on the Commodore, he felt for himself certain vital forces reawakening.

There is little doubt that Tennie and Vanderbilt became lovers, though no evidence exists to prove it. Vanderbilt was a well-known womanizer. Tennie's life had offered her many opportunities for sexual adventures, and there is every reason to believe she had taken advantage of them. Her unusual combination of physical—even animal—allure was enhanced by her facade as a proper lady. Her only comment on the subject was, "Commodore Vanderbilt knows my power."

Tennie often went to Vanderbilt's office to read to him from the newspapers. When he dozed off, associates remembered, Tennie would perch on his knee, pull at his whiskers, box his ears, and say, "Wake up, old boy." Lazily opening his eyes, Vanderbilt would put his arm around his "little sparrow." Silvery peals of laughter echoed through the room. "Oh that Ten, Ten, Tennessee!" the Commodore was heard to exclaim. It seems clear that he enjoyed Tennie's favors to the full extent permitted by his aging but responsive body.

There was nothing easy or gentle about the Commodore. But Tennie, an expert at manipulating her own parents, knew instinctively how to handle Vanderbilt. He was a man of her parents' generation, a monument to the frontier mentality. Born in 1794, two years before her father, he had been adept at everything he put his hand to except school. He could swim, row, sail, wrestle. Even though his father whipped him repeatedly over his failures in his school work, he refused to read anything longer than a few lines. Like Annie Claflin, he may have had a reading disability. In any case, he found it convenient for Tennie to read to him. Sensitized by life with her mother to the testiness that frustrated dyslexics often display, she became known as the only person, other than Vanderbilt's mother, who could manage his arrogance.

Tennie's air of higher purpose, entirely a reflection of her more formidable sister, pleased the Commodore—in direct contradiction to the condescension that marked his usual attitude toward women. Vanderbilt cared little or nothing for social amenities. He was a trader. He took what he wanted and was willing to pay for it. There can be no question, considering his generosity during the following years, that he was truly fond of Tennie. They developed an amiable quid pro quo: a deal was a deal, and they both gave good value for what they received.

Woodhull and Claflin's extraordinary attractiveness to Vanderbilt, and to other powerful men of the nineteenth century, was no accident. The sisters projected good breeding and sexual availability, gentility and sensuality: "ladies" in the drawing room, lovers in the bedroom. Always totally feminine, they understood the masculine psyche of their day and put their understanding to their own use. Both women had extraordinary physical presence, a "wonderful magnetism," in the phrase of one contemporary. Tennie developed the style of a natural, easygoing courtesan, impetuous, uninhibited, seemingly shallow. Woodhull was loftier, more idealistic. She needed a high-minded rationalization to justify her unconventional sexual behavior.

The sisters were looking for power, ideas, riches of their own. They started with what they knew best, clairvoyance. If medical clairvoyance could no longer be practiced safely, they would explore other possibilities. The New York of the "flash age" was a wide-open city. Merchants, financiers and contractors ran the place, along with William Marcy Tweed, "Boss" of Tammany Hall, the Democratic political machine, and corruption ruled city politics. Since the Civil War, moral, religious, and social standards had relaxed. New millionaires, war profiteers, entered New York society to find husbands for their daughters.

Greed was a virtue if it made one rich; winning was the measure of success. Strong nerves, unlimited energy, fast reflexes, sharp trading—Vanderbilt embodied the spirit of the day. He played by his own rules and took satisfaction in trampling his opponents. It was a spirit akin to that which Woodhull and Claflin knew from primitive, frontier America. They could model themselves on the ultimate robber baron as they searched for money and power.

The Commodore could not endure office work. His business day consisted of the hour or so each morning he spent dictating his few, brief letters to a secretary. Incoming mail that ran to more than 15 lines he threw to his clerk saying, "Here, see what this damned fool is driving at and tell me the gist of it." He kept his records in his well-trained memory and reckoning in a little book he carried in his vest pocket. His desk drawer contained a box of cigars and not much else.

Vanderbilt usually stopped at his stables before lunch. His coach house stood at the rear of his residence on West 4th Street, near his office. He inspected his trotters, peering into their eyes, lifting up their dainty white feet, admiring their small, fleet builds. He knew every horse's temperament and called each by name—Post Boy, Plow Boy, Mountaineer, Doctor, Flying Dutchman, Princess, Mountain Maid, Mountain Boy. He occasionally issued invitations, highly prized, for others to accompany him on this ritual.

In the afternoons the Commodore liked to drive up Bloomingdale Road (Upper Broadway) where, from four until sunset, New York gentlemen with fast horses went trotting. Vanderbilt usually sat alone at the reins gulping a wine glass of gin and sugar. He would cross the tracks of the Harlem and Hudson Railroad as the Express approached, his carriage wheels just clearing the tracks before the train passed behind him. "There is not another man in New York who could do that," he shouted. Then he would return home to Washington Square, or dine out with Tennie, thoroughly invigorated and ready for supper. "I don't stuff," he would say unconvincingly as he indulged his tastes for Spanish mackerel, woodcock, and venison.

Each summer Vanderbilt left Washington Place to take his trotters to Saratoga. The summer of 1868 was no exception. The hours and intimacies the sisters had been sharing with him all spring were interrupted in July when he left the city.

Sophia, his wife, remained behind. The Commodore disliked his family. Though he had fathered 13 children, he'd had scant affection for any since George's death. Cornelius, his oldest son, had accumulated $80,000 in debt and was in the process of declaring bankruptcy. "I'd give a hundred dollars not to have named him Cornelius," was the Commodore's comment. William he called a "blatherskite." His daughters fared no better. "Women are not fit to have money anyhow," he said.

Vanderbilt had married his cousin, Sophia Johnson, in 1813 when he was 19. She had tried all her life to please her husband. At first he had been ardent and affectionate, but then he became imperious and selfish. In 1846 he shipped her off to Canada so he could bed a governess. When Sophia returned and refused to move from Staten Island to Manhattan, he committed her to a lunatic asylum until she agreed. By 1868 she was frail, in poor health, and spending most of her time on Staten Island with her daughter Marie Louise and son-in-law Horace F. Clark. On August 17, 1868, Vanderbilt received word in Saratoga that the long-suffering Sophia had died. Horace Greeley, one of the pallbearers at the funeral, wrote in the *Tribune* that Sophia had lived nearly 74 years without incurring reproach or provoking enmity.

At 17 Great Jones Street, Woodhull and Tennie welcomed Vanderbilt back, expressing the appropriate condolences. Then the Commodore took an unexpected step. He proposed marriage to Tennie, promising to "make her a queen." This proposal does not appear to be anything that Tennie had engineered. It startled her.

Tennie had a secret that even her sister may not have known about at this time. She had been married briefly to a man named John Bortel. When the story of the marriage came out many years later, Tennie would claim that she had been divorced from Bortel almost immediately, and that the Chicago fire of 1871 had destroyed all the records. But Chicago had not yet burned when Vanderbilt asked Tennie to marry him. Tennie may not have been legally free to marry. She knew that a living husband might inconveniently reappear if she married a public figure like Vanderbilt. Tennie enigmatically put off Vanderbilt's offer and her refusal seemed to make her even more desirable to the Commodore.

While Tennie equivocated, both sisters said they would always bless the Commodore's kindness, and wear him "in their hearts in deepest gratitude and reverence." In May of 1869 they celebrated with Vanderbilt his seventy-fifth birthday. Tennie had dug down into her own pockets to find an appropriate gift. She spent $2,000 for an oil painting titled *Aurora* depicting a life-size Venus trailing wisps of gauze and playing with Cupid. Tennie's choice suited Vanderbilt's taste, and he hung *Aurora* at Washington Place.

In July of 1869 Vanderbilt left for his usual summer stay in Saratoga. What Tennie didn't know was that a new force was at work against a possible marriage. That force was the Commodore's son William.

Billy, as the Commodore usually called him, appeared bland and innocuous. But his appearance was deceiving. Years earlier when Vanderbilt had banished him to a barren farm on Staten Island, William had made the farm profitable. Eventually the Commodore arranged to have him appointed receiver of the small Staten Island Railroad. William had cut expenses and connected the line by ferry to the city. Its stock had risen, and the railroad began paying a 10 percent dividend. The Commodore rewarded him with a large stone house at 459 5th Avenue and the vice presidency of the Harlem and Hudson Railroad. William mastered every nuance of the railroad business and his father made him a vice president of the New York Central.

Thinking to make a fool of his ever-more-competent Billy, the Commodore passed him a tip that the Harlem and Hudson stock was falling. But William knew his father too well to believe his words without doing some checking of his own. He learned Vanderbilt was buying Hudson, not selling. When the stock had peaked, finally, reaching 130, the Commodore asked William how much he had lost.

"I went in at 110 on 10,000 shares," William responded. "That ought to make me $200,000."

After that the Commodore was overheard telling a friend, "Billy will make a good railroad man."

William was far too wise to oppose his father's feeling for Tennie in her presence. But in Saratoga, Vanderbilt was away from Tennie's influence. That August, Tennie and Woodhull were shocked to learn that Vanderbilt had remarried. The bride, Miss Frank Crawford of Mobile, Alabama, was a tall, handsome woman, just a few years older than Tennie, one of William's distant cousins. After losing everything during the war, Miss Crawford and her mother had come to New York. The Commodore had been putting them up in his own house as a favor to poor relations, or so he had led others to believe. The 75-year-old groom and his young bride eloped to Canada and were married August 21. Back in the steamy city, the hottest summer in memory, New Yorkers who had clucked over the Commodore's peccadillos guessed that William had procured a young cousin for his father because she would satisfy the old man's appetites and be content with a more modest financial settlement than the spirited Tennie.

Though the marriage took Woodhull and Tennie off guard, they kept their counsel, telling friends only that the Commodore was the man to whom they owed "all that they had done," and that they would always bless his "fatherly care." He had introduced them to New York's free-for-all rules, and they were learning to play the game. If Vanderbilt now felt he owed them a favor, they held a powerful hand.

4

"The Coming Woman"

Despite the Commodore's little surprise, 1869 turned out to be an annus mirabilis that completely reshaped Victoria Woodhull's ideas and prospects. Earlier that year she had attended the first national convention of the women's suffrage movement. It gave her a grander sense of purpose. "Visions of the offices I might one day hold danced before my imagination," she said later.

Woodhull traveled from New York, a city smoldering under its January miasma of coal fires, to the marginally milder climate of Washington with its lofty, though drafty, chambers of power. She described later the start of the suffrage meeting in Caroll Hall, on the 19th of January. She saw the leading advocates of women's rights in action: Elizabeth Cady Stanton, elegant, logical, forceful; Susan B. Anthony, aggressive, earnest, uncompromising; and the gentle, saintly Quaker, Lucretia Mott. "The three chief figures [sat] in joint council like the . . . Fates of a new dispensation," one suffragist named Grace Greenway wrote, capturing the excited mood of the day. Woodhull got caught up in the charged atmosphere, convinced that a new day for women was "soon to materialize . . . Really, at the time, I thought the millenium was at hand," she wrote years later in a short memoir.

"Senator [Samuel C.] Pomeroy from Kansas was present and made an able speech," she recounted. Pomeroy was a vocal proponent of universal suffrage. He believed that the United States Constitution gave all citizens, women included, the right to vote. Pomeroy's speech introduced Woodhull to a concept that she would mull over and one day make her own.

As the day continued "everything was in fine working order except the furnace," Woodhull noted. "When Pomeroy announced that he must go to the Capitol, Susan [Anthony] charged him with trying to avoid the smoke."

"Elizabeth Cady Stanton made a great speech the evening of the

19th," wrote Woodhull. For her, this speech was the emotional high point of the convention. "The need of this hour is . . . a new evangel of womanhood to exalt purity, virtue, morality, true religion, to lift man up into the high realms of thought and action," Stanton said. Her words stimulated the euphoria that Woodhull and the other women present were already feeling.

But Stanton intended this Washington convention to accomplish something more solid than emotional uplift, and something more specific than Pomeroy's vaguely worded claim for universal suffrage. She expected to awaken Congress, to redirect its attention from the plight of emancipated Negroes to the rights of women. In drawing up the Fifteenth Amendment, which guaranteed voting rights to black men, the lawmakers had not been persuaded to include the vote for women. Stanton urged immediate action by Congress "for a Sixteenth," to enfranchise women, Woodhull remembered.

Overall, the tone of Stanton's argument was thoughtfully reasoned and positive. But she had been negative in the past. In 1867, an amendment to the Kansas state constitution had proposed full voting rights for women and blacks. Republicans had refused to campaign for women in Kansas because they feared women's claims might hold back blacks. National leaders spoke out—Horace Greeley in the *New York Tribune,* Theodore Tilton in the *Independent,* and Wendell Phillips in the *National Anti-Slavery Standard*—but only for black male suffrage. Stanton and Anthony were outraged and had gone to Kansas to campaign for women. In the heat of the conflict, they implied that the black men were lesser intellects than the white women, words that imparted an ugly, racist tone to the campaign. Abolitionists fought back, and a quarrel began that would have unfortunate and long-lasting consequences. The immediate result in Kansas was that neither women nor black men won the vote.

After Kansas, the abolitionists had looked to the federal government, rather than individual states, to protect the rights of black citizens. The Fourteenth Amendment, guaranteeing rights of citizenship, had been ratified in July of 1868. Congress was now debating the Fifteenth Amendment and black voting rights.

"Shall American statesmen . . . make their wives and mothers the political inferiors of unlettered and unwashed ditch-diggers [and] boot-blacks . . . fresh from the slave plantations of the South . . ." Stanton asked the suffrage convention. "Think of Patrick and Sambo . . . who do not know the difference between a monarchy and a republic, who can not read the Declaration of Independence or Webster's spelling-book, making laws for Lucretia Mott, Ernestine L. Rose and Anna E. Dickinson," Stanton elaborated in her speech, naming several women prominent in the suffrage movement.

Frederick Douglass stood to challenge Stanton. He had been a slave himself; he had escaped to become the great orator of abolition. In the resonant voice that always thrilled his audiences, Douglass made a powerful plea for putting black suffrage ahead of women's. The full text of his speech has not survived, but he recorded his sentiments in a letter written after the convention.

> The right of women to vote is as sacred in my judgement as that of man, and I am quite willing to hold up both hands in favor of this right . . . I am now devoting myself to a cause [if] not more sacred, certainly more urgent, because it is one of life and death to the long enslaved people of this country, and this is: Negro suffrage. While the Negro is mobbed, beaten, shot, stabbed, hanged, burnt and is the target of all that is malignant in the North and all that is murderous in the South, his claims may be preferred by me without exposing in any wise myself to the imputations of narrowness or meanness towards the cause of women. As you very well know, woman has a thousand ways to attach herself to the governing power of the land and already exerts an honorable influence on the course of legislation. She is the victim of abuses, to be sure, but it cannot be pretended, I think, that her cause is as urgent as . . . ours."

Douglass went on to say that the conduct of white women suffragists who held to the principle that no Negro shall be enfranchised while women are not, "does not seem generous."

Stanton and Douglass debated for the first time in a series of heated exchanges. Word by word, the women in the audience felt forced to choose sides, and many of them, including Woodhull, sympathized with Douglass. Suffrage leaders all knew that a protracted conflict would hurt the women's rights movement, but they couldn't mend the differences.

Stanton's racism expressed her own elitism and that of many suffragists. Most women drawn to the suffrage movement were from upper middle-class, privileged, and propertied backgrounds. Their leaders were articulate women who spoke with authority and were ready to enter the public life of the country as the equals of men. Stanton came from a wealthy upstate New York family that had made its fortune before the American Revolution. She encouraged other suffragists to feel that their social and economic status made them the "most refined and elevated women of the North" and entitled them to power even if their sex did not. Her words during this period express an unmistakable arrogance toward those she perceived to belong to the lower orders among women as well as blacks. Operating with a marked double standard, she argued that the special mission of the suffrage movement was "to awaken women everywhere to a proper self-respect." Then, immediately, she translated that same "proper self-respect" into entitlements for women of privilege. The convention introduced Woodhull to the social snobberies of blueblood reformers.

With her critical eye, Woodhull studied the genteel ladies around her as they congratulated themselves on being nothing like "the rude, uncultured women generally represented by the opposition, but in point of intelligence, refinement, appearance and all the feminine virtues, far above the ordinary standard." She watched the members of the pearl-brooched set arrogate to themselves the authority to keep out "ignorant" women and to "silence persons unfit to appear before an intelligent and refined audience." An unlettered, unknown woman had a long way to go to become prominent in their suffrage movement. In this setting, the concept of clairvoyance, the "calling" that Woodhull had practiced and treasured, was at best provincial and at worst highly suspect. Her work had earned Woodhull considerable income and provided an approbation which she described as "golden opinions." But her past successes counted for nothing here. Among the better educated and socially connected women of the convention, she was a nobody. The history of the movement that Stanton and Anthony wrote a few years later doesn't even mention her attendance.

Rather than taking offense at this elitism, Woodhull considered it a challenge. She registered the conflicts between the suffragists and the abolitionists without openly taking sides. Instead, she looked for ideas she might turn to her own use. Virginia Minor of St. Louis, Missouri, spoke that evening, arguing that the Constitution, and the recently passed Fourteenth Amendment granting Negroes citizenship, also gave women the vote, if inadvertently, as a right of citizenship. It was a novel concept, erected on the building blocks of Pomeroy's views. Virginia Minor's argument got lost in the drama of more exciting conflicts, but Woodhull remembered it.

She had one small triumph during the convention. Several newspapermen assigned to cover the convention noticed her. Among them, Woodhull captivated the widely-read reporter from the *New York World* who signed his columns "Alpha." "Mrs. Woodhull takes the most lively interest in all the genuine reforms of the day and entertains her own distinctive views," he told his readers. "Upon the woman question I deem her particularly sound . . . She has just been attending the National Female Suffrage Convention but only partially agrees with the doings of that body." Woodhull told "Alpha" that while she "believed in woman most completely," she "also believed in man just as thoroughly." Her words reflected the sympathy she felt for Douglass's argument at the convention.

"Alpha" chose to see another interpretation of Woodhull's belief in man, an interpretation not entirely absent from her intentions. He composed paragraphs of honeyed puffery, infatuated litanies to her fine and commanding figure, her spiritual eyes, her intellectual genius, her "womanly tenderness, [as] she listens to the sad story of some sick, unfortunate sufferer whose life is nearly quenched in night, and gently as a careful and skillful nurse . . . administers the healing antidote." The *Washington Star* had been the first significant newspaper to interview Woodhull, and "Alpha" wrote, "I can fully agree with the writer in the Washington paper that this woman is to rise to a very conspicuous position . . . destined to act a part in the coming conflicts and reforms in the country." He called Woodhull "The Coming Woman."

5

"Gold, Gold, Gold Was the Cry"

Woodhull returned to Great Jones Street from Washington with a new conception of women's possibilities. She adopted a lower profile for several months. From time to time, she was seen with Tennie in Vanderbilt's company, but she seemed thoughtful, almost subdued. She gave up medical clairvoyance. She spent quiet evenings with Colonel Blood. It was a period of germination, gestation.

Then, in September 1869, she reappeared as a highly visible player in the "great bear gold panic" on Wall Street. On September 24, Black Friday, she sat in her carriage outside the Gold Exchange from "morning til evening, watching . . . and operating heavily." On that notorious September day, the Commodore's old rivals Jay Gould and James Fisk, Jr., almost succeeded in cornering the gold market. They failed, but by the time the day was out, Woodhull had made a fortune.

Never before had an American woman made quite such a public splash on Wall Street. To understand this particular episode in her life one must understand the financial markets of the time. Gould and Fisk—two deviously resourceful speculators in their early thirties—had cut their teeth on the Commodore during an earlier contest for control of the Erie Railroad. Gould looked deceptively fragile. Sallow skinned and black bearded, he was self-effacing and secretive. Fisk, not as bright, but far bolder than Gould, was a reddish-blond extrovert, vain but likable, a "prince of peddlers" who gambled and womanized flamboyantly. The public loved his style and forgave his indiscretions. Vanderbilt said his railroad war against the two had "taught me that it never pays to kick a skunk."

A lively market in gold trading had developed as a result of Lincoln's fiscal policies during the war. The trading was institutionalized in the Gold Room, as it came to be known, on Broad Street. Greenbacks issued to finance the war, non-interest-bearing, green-colored

Treasury notes that served as legal tender, were not backed dollar for dollar by gold. Instead, they were backed by the pledge of the government. Government policy was to buy back greenbacks at a discount, for currency that was redeemable in gold. The policy increased the demand for the precious metal. When Grant became president in 1869, gold was selling at $130 an ounce. To defeat speculators, the government kept gold bullion valued at $100 million in its vaults.

Gold attracted Gould. During the spring of 1869 he bought $7 million worth, the first act in his scheme to corner the market. For Gould to succeed, he had to prevent the government from selling its gold. He arrogantly sought to enlist the president for his campaign. He made his approach through Abel Corbin, a zealous churchgoer like himself, a lawyer and a lobbyist who had just married Jenny Grant, the president's middle-aged sister. Gould convinced Corbin the economy would benefit from high-priced gold. He also set up a $1.5 million gold trading account for Corbin's wife. Through the Corbins, he was able to entertain President Grant himself with champagne, fine food, and cigars. That summer Gould bought virtually all the gold that remained in circulation, and had contracts for twice as much again.

Gould spread the word that the government would not sell its gold. Through Fisk, he also planted the story that Mrs. Grant, the first lady, had allowed gold to be purchased on her behalf. When Grant finally learned the full extent of his brother-in-law's plans, he dictated a letter from his wife to his sister: "Tell Mr. Corbin that the President is very much distressed by your speculations and you must close them as quickly as you can." Corbin showed the letter to Gould, who knew his only hope now was to sell his gold as quickly as possible. But through Fisk he told the Gold Room, "I'll bet any part of $50,000 that gold will go over $145."

On September 24, as Woodhull sat in her carriage on the street outside the Gold Room, thousands of businessmen paced the pavement, hatless, collarless, shouting and screaming. Traders, unaware of Grant's signal to Corbin, had packed the area, and the action had started early. The indicator in the Gold Room opened at 150, then rose to 160. "Gold, Gold, Gold was the cry," the *New York Herald* reported the next day. Fisk later told a congressional committee that in his years on Wall Street he had never seen anything to match Black Friday.

The commotion reached such a frenzy that a Brooklyn regiment was ordered to its armory. In the event that troops were needed to restore order, they could be quickly ferried across the river to Manhattan. Then word came that Grant had ordered the government to sell $4 million of the country's gold reserves. "Suddenly selling began," Fisk recalled. "There is no fright as great as the fright in Wall Street when the [speculators] become panicky. Burnt brandy won't save 'em." Speculators had been purchasing gold on credit. When payment was called for, the collateral, whether gold or other assets, had to be sold in a rapidly falling market. Within 30 minutes gold dropped 30 points, back down to the 130 level it had traded at before Gould's speculations began.

Throughout the United States, brokers and bankers gathered around the telegraph wires for the latest readings. The crisis threatened to engulf the stock market. To prevent the panic from spreading, Vanderbilt put $1 million into stocks. He intended the move to stabilize the market and protect his own interests. His actions were successful and the panic remained limited to gold.

But more than a dozen Wall Street firms, and hundreds more across the country, faced ruin. The Gold Exchange itself never recovered. Gould had gained $11 million, some said, while others claimed that his finances were in disarray, that there was "nothing left of him but a heap of clothes and a pair of eyes."

Woodhull, uncharacteristically reticent, said, "I came out a winner." She had arrived in New York a wealthy woman. She later claimed that she had earned "nearly $100,000" as a medical clairvoyant (almost $1 million in today's dollars). Her father's daughter where money was concerned, she had risked the lot speculating in the gold market. She now knew the gambler's rush of adrenaline, the neuron explosion of success, the invulnerable feeling of being, for an instant, a "master of the universe."

By the end of 1869, Woodhull put her worth at $700,000 (more than $6 million in today's dollars). Given her talents for inventing a good story, we can assume that the $100,000 she claimed to have brought with her to New York, as well as its overnight transmutation into $700,000, were exaggerated. The figure $700,000 had too nice a ring to it to be believable—seven being her lucky number. But whatever the actual amount, Woodhull was now immensely wealthy.

After Black Friday, the Commodore had called her a "bold operator," a compliment she carefully recorded in her notes for an autobiography many years later. Undoubtedly Vanderbilt's tutelage had emboldened her. Though the market stabilized after the panic, stocks were down all fall, and the Commodore bought some bargains. Among other prizes, he gained control of the Lakeshore and Michigan Railroad. Woodhull may have followed his lead. Evidence suggests that after the Black Friday scramble, she also held some new stock purchases.

The Commodore's standing had never been higher. He left the house on Washington Place several times to steady the market. His presence alone was calming. Moving along, scattering nods here and there, he never stopped to talk.

"Central's coming up," someone would yell.

"Top o' the heap still, my boy," Vanderbilt would shoot back.

As his protégés, Woodhull and Claflin prospered with him. They made regular calls at the Commodore's office. With characteristic tactlessness he blurted to Tennie one day that she might have been Mrs. Vanderbilt, but the family arranged it otherwise. Then he put an arm around her waist and drew her close to him. Marriage had not ended Vanderbilt's fondness for the two sisters.

Tennie was too shrewd to believe Vanderbilt. She knew that family wishes had little impact on his behavior. Even so, the sisters' relationship with the Commodore was about to change. The new Mrs. Vanderbilt was forging a powerful family alliance with her stepson, William. One of the objectives of that alliance was to eject Woodhull and Claflin from the Commodore's life.

6
Woodhull, Claflin & Company

William Vanderbilt tried first to remove the sisters from his father's life by enticing them with a long trip to Europe. They were far too quick for him. Claflin and Woodhull's next visit to West 4th Street was made to share a bit of information about themselves that they believed had been withheld from the Commodore. They had recently, they said, "received the most urgent and flattering inducements to make a European trip, which was to consume the entire year."

When Woodhull told this story later she did not mention any names. However, events themselves identify William Vanderbilt as the unnamed underwriter of the trip abroad. The prospect of a European trip was "so seductive," Woodhull said. "We had gone so far . . . as to pack our trunks and decide upon the ship in which to sail . . . During the night before we were going to select our staterooms sister and I were both raised up simultaneously in bed, and each said to the other while yet unconscious of what we were doing, 'We must not go to Europe now.'"

It was not in the nature of the two unconventional sisters to let William Vanderbilt eject them unchallenged. They recognized that they had a unique opportunity, and they found a startling way to put Vanderbilt's influence to work to further their own ambitions.

Woodhull elaborated, coloring her words for the Commodore's spiritualistic sensibilities: Her spirit guide had explained, she said, that "instead of on the morrow going to secure staterooms for Europe, we were to go down to Wall Street."

Pause.

". . . and secure a banking office."

The pitch was incredibly audacious. The sisters were fully aware of New York's conventional wisdom regarding Vanderbilt: one, that he did not believe in charity, and, two, that he could always be interested in a sound business proposition.

This one fascinated the Commodore. He understood at once the adroit proposal, as well as his son William's role in the diversionary trip to Europe. Victoria and Tennie had so much "spirit," as the Commodore liked to say, enjoying his little pun. The sisters soon had a check for $7,000, written in Vanderbilt's own hand, and they could now exhibit his signature as evidence that he was their backer.

One of the Commodore's favorite maxims was, "All you have to do is to attend to your business and go ahead. Never tell nobody what you're doing 'til you do it." Clearly Woodhull and Tennie had learned the lesson. They later wrote to him, thanking him for giving them their start, and their words give some clues as to what followed.

> It was you, Commodore, who first extended your hand to aid two struggling women to battle with the world; it was you who encouraged them to break away from the fetters that held them captive to public opinion, and to go out into the world to claim a recognition as individuals upon the talent that they possessed; it was you who gave them wise counsel, and showed them the shoals and rocks upon which so many men are wrecked; it was you who stood by them when they ventured into the financial heart of the country, which had so long been monopolized by men; it was your check with your name written by your own hand that was the open sesame to its charmed precincts, which otherwise had been closed against them, heralded all over the world with theirs, making them your financial protégés, that gave prominence and importance to their venture. It was the goodness of your heart, directed by some kind spirit hand, or else your prescient knowledge of what was to come, that led you to do all this for them.

Tennie deposited Vanderbilt's check with Henry Clews, a prominent New York banker, and word of Vanderbilt's new "investment" immediately spread through the city's financial circles.

A few days later Tennie drove up to Clews's office. As he later recalled, "She wore a look of enthusiasm and pleasant surprise, appearing to have a heavy thought to divulge."

"I have a point," she said, "that came from the highest source."

Clews had no doubt who Tennie's highest source was, and his interest rose sharply.

Tennie said she planned "to buy 1,000 shares of New York Central."

Clews tapped his little bell, his office messenger appeared, and Clews instructed him to tell the cashier to adjust Miss Claflin's account. Tennie accepted the check, which included interest for the few days of her deposit, and left Clews's office. She then drove to the Fourth National Bank, where Vanderbilt kept an account, and presented the check for the stock purchase. She returned to Clews's office a short time later, saying, "Mr. Clews, the bank wishes to have me identified."

Clews called an office boy and told him to accompany Miss Claflin to the bank and identify her as being entitled to the amount of the check. This little maneuver enabled Tennie to use Clews's endorsement to establish her credit at the bank. Both Clews and the Fourth National Bank would become known as sponsors of the sisters' new endeavor.

On Thursday, January 20, 1870 the *New York Herald* published a sighting:

> The general routine of business in Wall Street was somewhat varied today by the mingling in its scenes of two fashionably dressed ladies as speculators. Who they were few seemed to know . . . Where they obtained their knowledge of stocks was a matter of puzzling conjecture with those whom they met. After investing to the extent of several thousand shares in some of our principal stocks and selling others, and announcing their intention to become regular habitués of Wall Street, they departed, the observed of all observers.

Woodhull made her Wall Street debut on the same day another suffrage convention was starting in Washington, intending her financial prominence to lay groundwork for her nascent political ambitions. As she explained her design later, a "female invasion of the masculine precincts of finance" would "secure the most . . . prominent notice to the world." The delegates to the suffrage convention could not miss this kind of notice.

It was the first of many occasions on which Woodhull offered herself as a "representative woman," a woman moving into situations where no woman had gone before. Ego and ambition motivated her. But she sincerely believed that all women benefited from seeing one woman publicly take her place on male terrain. This kind of eminence for a woman had, she thought, a value for all of womankind.

On January 20, the same day Woodhull appeared on Wall Street, the *Herald* received a note written in an elegant hand on fine-quality paper: "We were not a little surprised at seeing our appearance in Wall Street noticed in your columns of today," she wrote. "As we intend operating as mentioned, we should be glad to make your acquaintance. Woodhull, Claflin & Company."

Enclosed were two new business cards, delicately engraved. Woodhull was discovering in herself an astute instinct for publicity. The word clairvoyant did not appear on either card. Woodhull was moving on to a new career.

The *Herald* responded with alacrity and promptly sent a reporter named Thomas A. Masterson to obtain an "on scene" interview, a technique the paper had used to build its circulation to the highest in New York.

"You are a member of the firm of Woodhull, Claflin & Company?" Masterson asked, taking out a little notebook in which he meticulously recorded his interviews, "and you are doing business as stockbrokers and bankers?"

Tennie shook his hand assertively, like a man. "Yes," she replied. "Myself and my sister, Mrs. Woodhull, are the active members of the firm."

In the modulated tone she had adopted for the occasion, she explained that Woodhull would join them shortly. In the meantime she would be glad to answer any questions he might have. She had put on a plain dress to appear businesslike. "We have been interested in stocks in this city some two or three years," she said in a nonchalant way, giving the impression of experience in financial matters. "We have lately used these apartments as our offices." The two small, comfortable rooms fronting on the avenue, their windows heavily draped against the January cold, were parlors 25 and 26 in the Hoffman House Hotel on Madison Square. A religious motto—"Simply to Thy cross I cling"—hung conspicuously on the wall, conveying an air of religious sincerity and respectability. "Within a few weeks we shall have suitable offices for the transaction of our business in Wall Street, or in that vicinity."

"It is a novel sight to see a woman go on the Street as a stock operator, and I presume you find it rather awkward," Masterson said.

"Were I to notice what is said by what they call 'society,' I could never leave my apartments, except in fantastic walking-dress or in ball-room costume," Tennie replied, looking Masterson directly in the eye. "I think a woman is just as capable of making a living as a man . . . I don't care what society thinks; I have not time to care. I don't go to balls or theaters. My mind is in my business, and I attend to that solely."

"But stock speculations are dangerous, and many persons of great experience, and with large capital at their backs, have been swamped, as you are aware, and I presume your experience is rather limited."

"I studied law in my father's office six years," Tennie said, improvising quickly. "I know as much of the world as men who are older. Besides we have a strong back." Tennie gestured toward a large photograph of the Commodore hanging on the wall. Apparently concerned that she may have been too frank, she added "We have the counsel of those who have more experience than we have, and we are endorsed by the best backers in the city." With these words, Henry Clews and the Fourth National Bank were implicitly accorded the sponsorship roles Tennie had allocated to them.

It was the "strong back" that Masterson's editor, Ashley Cole, had sent him to investigate. "I have been told that Commodore Vanderbilt has been working in the interest of your firm. It is stated that you frequently call at his office in 4th Street about business. Is this true?"

"I know the Commodore, and frequently call to see him on business," Claflin replied, angling for the public attention that Vanderbilt's name would bring to Woodhull, Claflin & Company, but choosing her words carefully because she couldn't be certain how much publicity the Commodore would tolerate. "I am not prepared to state anything as to whether he is working with us. I will say that we have the advice and assistance of the shrewdest and most respectable financiers in the city."

Woodhull had put off the moment she was to join Tennie, and she now entered the room somewhat nervously. Masterson looked her over carefully and jotted down that she wore a single rose "tastefully inserted in her hair." He noted her "sanguine, nervous temperament" in his little book. She "seemed to feel uneasy." But whatever her initial uneasiness, he observed, she immediately entered into the spirit of the conversation.

Once started, Woodhull talked with great animation about the Arcade Railway. The sisters had helped Melville C. Smith, the line's promoter, interest the Commodore in the project, a ground-level railroad with a pedestrian mall overhead, designed to relieve New York City traffic congestion. She then turned the subject to a silver company in Nevada that she believed would return large profits.

The conversation continued, with Masterson filling his notebook. "We have made about $700,000 and expect that when we establish an office in Wall Street and go in earnest into gold and stocks, we will do much better," Woodhull said, as she escorted him to the door with a smile. The figure $700,000 had become the official estimate of her personal fortune.

On Saturday January 22, 1870, the day after his interview, Masterson's story appeared. The sisters had found a new and valuable sponsor in the *New York Herald*. "The firm looked contented and happy and seemed to be doing well," he reported in his long account. "It would seem as though the mantle of the genial old Commodore had descended on their shoulders, his photograph on the wall seems to indicate that his spirit was there—and they are not prepared to deny that they know a thing or two about the Commodore's notions of the rise and fall of stocks."

The article was accompanied by a long editorial. "We congratulate the brokers that their labors are to be shared by the fair sex. How refreshing the time when the halls of the Stock Exchange shall exhibit a variety of costume as diverse as the floors of a ballroom," it concluded jovially.

The weeks of publicity that followed established Woodhull and Claflin clearly in the public eye. Headlines named them "Queens of Finance," and "Bewitching Brokers." Their move to new quarters at 44 Broad Street in February provided a fresh lead for the story of the "Female Sovereigns of Wall Street." Their magnificent office furnishings and their up-to-the-minute telegraph lines were all documented in print. The Wall Street luminaries who stopped by to meet them were catalogued, and among them were the famous speculators, Daniel Drew and Jay Cook.

Interestingly enough, the visitor whose name Woodhull most cherished, one that she recorded in her autobiographical notes years later, was Walt Whitman, America's *Leaves of Grass* poet. He grasped immediately Woodhull's view of herself as a representative woman. As she recounted it, he said, "I came here to see . . . two great children of nature in this swarming vortex of life . . . You have given an object lesson to the whole world . . . You are a prophecy of the future."

The press found the "Wall Street ladies" to be full of pluck and determination, ready to see a good thing and grasp it, able to talk of financial matters intelligently, businesslike in manner, thoroughly posted on all points, making altogether a favorable impression. Columns of print went on at length about their lithe figures, transparent complexions, and wide-awake blue eyes. The press anointed them "straightforward, well-bred American women who were perfectly capable of taking care of themselves in the dangerous byways of Wall Street."

This male press chorus brought Woodhull the notice she sought from the suffragists. Susan B. Anthony, who with Elizabeth Cady Stanton had started a suffrage newspaper called *The Revolution,* came down to 44 Broad Street in early March to conduct her own interview. She began by complaining in her tart way about the bad habits of Wall Street men who stared at every woman on the pavement except the apple sellers. "The advent of this woman firm in Wall Street marks a new era," she said, "and we concluded to see for ourselves how it looked for women to be at the head of a banking institution, surrounded by . . . those evidences of masculine superiority that men have plumed themselves upon so long."

It was with Tennie, not Woodhull, that Anthony talked, perhaps by chance, but perhaps because the occasion was so important to Woodhull that it brought on an attack of the nervousness Masterson had noticed during his interview. In any case, by the time Woodhull entered the room Anthony had already left. But Tennie, on her own, had acquitted the new firm well.

Anthony, a dour and severe Quaker, found Tennie as attractive as had her male interviewers. She described Tennie as a handsome blond attired in a plain suit of blue cloth trimmed with black astrakhan, astrakhan muff, and black velvet hat with black feathers.

After greeting the visitor, Tennie removed her hat, an age-old female gesture that said she was letting down her hair for a good chat. She led Anthony to her private office at the back of the building and seated her on a comfortable green lounge.

Anthony began rather stiffly. "What first suggested to you the idea of coming into the rush and tumble of Wall Street?"

"The necessity for earning a livelihood . . . and unfitness for the slow, dreary methods by which women usually earn a living," Tennie replied. Her disarmingly candid reply softened Anthony's reserve, and she warmed to her subject.

"How did you obtain the sort of education necessary to fit you for this kind of life?" Anthony's question was appropriate, but ticklish for Claflin.

"Natural aptitude, principally, together with early familiarity with the details of business management. I am related to the great Claflin," she said, shaving the truth to make a better story. The Claflin she referred to was a well-known retailer, and he was related to Tennie only by the most tenuous connection—descent from the old Scottish soldier Robert Mackclothlan. Tennie ran quickly through her family, improving on the facts once again: "My father was once a very successful merchant, and the possessor of a large fortune. He lost it mainly in speculations." That part of the statement, at least, contained some truth, and Tennie went on to express that article of material faith she shared with Woodhull: "If my sister and I get any part of it back, we shall only regain what should have been our own."

In a strange lapse, Anthony identified her subject as Jennie C. Claflin, though Tennie's name had been widely published before this interview. Anthony showed herself to be familiar with the newspaper stories, stating that the firm's name had been paraded in the daily and weekly papers, and paid Tennie a rather left-handed compliment: "I think you have got off very easy so far as the newspapers are concerned. They have had nothing very dreadful to say against you."

"Look at this office. Is it not better than sewing drawers at ten cents a pair?"—Tennie couldn't resist spicing her story with a racy word—"or teaching music at ten dollars a quarter? Within the last ten days we have made five hundred dollars in commissions on sales alone. This is called very good for a beginning."

Agreeing, Anthony wrote in conclusion, "These two ladies (for they are ladies) are determined to use their brains, energy, and their knowledge of business to earn them a livelihood . . . The advent of this woman's firm in Wall Street marks a new era."

Toward the end of the month, *The Revolution* followed up the story and joined the male chorus. "The new firm, Mesdames Woodhull, Claflin & Co., who have made such a sensation in Wall Street, [will] stimulate the whole future of women by their efforts and example. They are full of pluck, energy and enterprise, and are withal most prepossessing in personal appearance, in manners, and ladylike deportment; moreover, they 'know what they are about,' and are calculated to inspire confidence by the sound sense, judgement and clear-sightedness they show in financial matters." Anthony, *The Revolution* and the suffrage movement gave their blessing to Woodhull, Claflin & Company. That it had taken the approbation of the male press to gain the attention of the suffragists was a lesson not lost on Woodhull.

The Commodore, ever close-mouthed, made no public comment about the new firm or his protégés. Randall Foote, who executed brokerage orders for Woodhull and Claflin and who was close enough to Vanderbilt to have witnessed one of his wills, remembered Vanderbilt "making his salutation at their welcoming salon" and arranging to offer a call on several thousand shares of Erie stock to Gould through the firm. A "psychology gamble" was under way, Foote remembered; Vanderbilt was testing Gould's intentions regarding the railroad.

Gould, too, began using Woodhull, Claflin & Company as a psychological gamble. With uncharacteristic frankness he later explained that through them he could piggyback off the Commodore. "I picked the ladies' firm myself—without them realizing it—because, you see, the Street when Woodhull and Claflin sold would just naturally jump to the conclusion that the principal was Cornelius Vanderbilt . . . Rather neat finesse I thought that was . . . When the Stock Exchange was surest we were squeezing Vanderbilt . . . I was supplying them with all the stock their unkind suspicions would bid for . . . [and] paid Victoria and Sister Tennie $1,000 a day commission through quite a . . . spell."

The sisters quickly created remarkable public roles on Wall Street. This, in fact, was their primary objective. They did not spend their days reading prospectuses or sitting on high stools adding up long columns in ledger books. They probably never conceived of the serious professional study of the investment business that a later generation would assume on the part of the organizers of a new firm. They no more intended to be day-to-day brokers than Buck Claflin had intended to be a miller. Their goals were more imaginative. Their most forthright statement on the subject was that they wanted "to know the secrets of money that had heretofore been a male preserve."

7

The Art of the Soirée

*H*enry Clews, the banker Tennie had so adroitly made into a Woodhull, Claflin & Company backer, reflected in his memoirs that office hours at 44 Broad Street extended beyond the traditional ten to three into evening soirées and Sunday salons. Mathew Hale Smith, another Wall Street personality, remembered the hospitality of the "lady brokers" in a book he published in 1870. He recalled their "very popular after-business levees," noting that they took costly rooms at the Astor House Hotel, hired a private table, invited friends, extended general invitations, and held open house.

Though only fragmentary accounts of the popular occasions survive, a guest list, published later by the New York papers, was impressive. It included, in addition to Clews and Hale, William Orton, president of Western Union; William S. Hillyer, President Grant's wartime chief of staff; Albert Brisbane, a Fourierist reformer from a well-to-do New York family; the Reverend Octavius Brooks Frothingham; A. F. Wilmarth, president of the Home Fire Insurance Company; T. J. S. Flint, president of the Continental Bank; Thomas C. Durant, vice president of the Union Pacific Railroad; Jesse Wheelock, president of the Stock Exchange Board; and Josiah Warren, the founder of American philosophical anarchism.

Reporters from all the newspapers were regulars at the open houses. After the roast beef and the pudding, Tennie could be counted on to be pleasingly spontaneous. "No women had ever been stock or gold brokers," she said. "Wall Street was tabooed to petticoats . . ." But "we did not intend to let our petticoats interfere with anybody, or take up any more room in the street than the other brokers' trousers . . . Why shouldn't [women] just as well be stockbrokers as keep stores and measure men for shirts? We couldn't see why. So, you see, here we are—brokers—and we mean to be so."

It was good copy, and Tennie luxuriated in it. "We like newspapers and newspapermen," she said. "They are the salt of the earth [and]

keep everything from spoiling . . . We do not want flattery, we do not
want detraction, we want fair play—nothing more . . . We ask to be
taken for exactly what we are good for, as men are."

Woodhull's style was more restrained. She would say simply, "We
like all the newspapers. They have been very kind to us."

On January 22, the date of the sisters' long interview with the *Herald,* the *New York Tribune* commented sympathetically on the
"Women in Wall Street." Woodhull promptly wrote to the new managing editor, Whitelaw Reid. Her words were a surprisingly forthright, if properly worded, invitation for one of her Saturday evenings.
"Will Mr. Reid do me the favor of calling at my parlors this evening,
for just a few moments, and by so doing very much oblige." She
signed it, "Yours very respectfully, V. C. Woodhull."

Among the many newspapermen in post-Civil War New York,
Reid was a special case. He moved with ease among the affluent and
privileged of New York society. He was confident and handsome,
with black hair and deep-set eyes. He affected an oversize moustache,
apparently feeling that he needed to minimize the one poor feature a
contemporary photograph reveals, a rather insignificant chin. An
Ohio boy, he had made his name as the Washington correspondent
for the *Cincinnati Gazette.* Two years earlier Horace Greeley had
brought Reid to the *Tribune.* Despite Greeley's anti-sensationalist editorial policies—unique among the New York papers of the period—
the *Tribune* and Reid's reputation had continued to grow.

Woodhull was interested in Reid for another reason. He had found
a young orator named Anna Dickinson and made her nationally famous. Reid had interviewed Dickinson after one of her abolition
speeches in 1863 when she was only 21 years old. His newspaper
coverage helped her establish a reputation as the Joan of Arc of the
Union cause. Now her penetrating gray eyes, prominent nose and
ample mouth, her curly black hair cut short like a man's, were known
everywhere. Reid reported on her activities regularly in the pages of
the *Tribune.* The precedent was not lost on Woodhull.

When Reid received the invitation to attend one of Victoria's Saturday evenings, he accepted and enjoyed the sisters' hospitality. Afterward, Woodhull wrote him: "Accept the thanks of sister and
myself for the generous appreciation in which you held our feelings . . . The editorial was all we could have wished, and much more
than we could have thought of asking, and was entirely satisfactory
to our best friend the Commodore, who first called our attention to

it, as we were dining with him, the day of its issue." The Commodore's name having been dropped, and her intimacy with him underlined, Woodhull made a further overture: "We should be glad to see you soon on something of importance. Will you please signify through bearer when we may expect you so as not to be previously engaged. Yours respectfully. . ."

Woodhull and Reid seem not to have hit it off, at least initially, but the correspondence is intriguing, primarily because it illustrates the straightforward approach she made to those she thought could help her ambitions.

Tennie, her female antennae as usual at full scan, found the up-and-coming editor romantic. She took him up. In a Sunday morning note, she wrote, "I trust you rested well last night and that you find yourself refreshed therefrom: for myself . . ." At this point she broke into the meter of what sounds like a popular song of the day, "I'm lonely today / Love without you / I sigh for one . . ." She stopped and, playing the coquette, replaced what was no doubt the word "kiss" with "smile," continuing, "which I hope to see tomorrow A.M." The sexual overture was unambiguous. Tennie, too, understood the role Reid could play in advancing the enterprises of Woodhull, Claflin & Company.

The sisters used men rather than being used by them. Their relationship with Blood followed this pattern. He helped them overcome the limits of their early lives. An astonishing fact about the notes to Reid was the penmanship; a close analysis shows that Blood wrote them. His distinctive, elegant script is unmistakable. His correspondence had a style and polish neither sister had yet mastered, so they used him as their secretary.

Woodhull and Claflin recognized the limits of their early lives; they were not country bumpkins. They had schooled themselves in manners and spoke grammatially correct English. Their vocabularies went well beyond the words they learned in their few years of schooling. They were shrewd in assessing their strengths and weaknesses, and they knew how to get help when they needed it. We can assume that when they borrowed Blood's penmanship, it was not the first time they found a sponsor to give them polish.

The patterns of the sisters' relationships with men can be seen in a brokerage firm contract they made with Blood. They shared magnanimously, but they retained control. They never gave "ownership" of themselves—Woodhull's term for it—either financially or emotionally to anyone else. The contract gave no indication that Wood-hull and Blood were husband and wife. It was strictly business, but it was a sweet deal for Blood. He put no capital of his own into the venture, but he received an equal share of the profits (and losses), as well as a salary of $75 a month, in exchange for his management. Blood's experience as a military officer, his training as an accountant, and his brief effort as City Auditor of St. Louis gave him management experience. But Blood could not withdraw substantial funds or make financial decisions that might incur losses without the prior approval of Woodhull or Tennie. The agreement was signed on a wintry day in March 1870. Tennie's handwriting was an immature scrawl. Woodhull signed after her sister; though she would often in the future allow Blood to sign her name, this was a private, not a public, signature and she wrote it herself in an angular, hastily scrawled, not particularly beautiful but entirely legible script.

During this period, Blood's secretarial services extended to most of Woodhull's correspondence. Sometimes she dictated to him, sometimes Blood composed entire letters and signed her name to them. The letters she wrote in later life show the same impatient scrawl as the brokerage contract signature. Her writing is unencumbered by punctuation and often oversize, though the spelling and grammar are correct. In those days before typewriters and word processors, Woodhull must have felt that Blood's work would make a better impression than hers.

The Colonel exhibited no jealousy or resentment toward the other men in the sisters' lives. In fact, he aided them in seducing men of power and influence to their causes, by staying out of the way. For instance, he never joined the sisters at Commodore Vanderbilt's table. His composition of Tennie's romantic note to Reid at the *Tribune,* so obviously an invitation to seduction, leaves an unpleasant sense of the Colonel as a secret partner in Tennie's liaisons. It is possible he became Tennie's scribe in order to stay abreast of her intimate involvements.

Blood's motives in his relationship with Woodhull are equally unclear. From the start, Woodhull was the luminous star, Blood the man in the background, the "expectant believer in [her] stupendous destiny." Hers was the more outgoing personality, his the more subdued. She never used the Colonel's name, explaining that she was following "the example of many actresses, singers and other professional women whose names have become a business property to their owners." Blood took his place behind the scenes, and Woodhull came first, as she always would.

Blood's devotion to Woodhull seems to have masked his own private ambitions for wealth and fame. He had a powerful need to see himself in altruistic terms, and seemed unable to acknowledge his underlying self-interest, even to himself. He once said, "When anyone can't understand me well enough to know that I am working for the human race, not for Colonel Blood, I don't care to have very much to do with them."

Blood's partnership in the firm remained something of a secret. The name remained Woodhull, Claflin & Company, and Blood never appeared in the sisters' extensive press coverage. Blood's intimates defended his secretive ways, maintaining that the Colonel's "natural modesty" caused him to "sequester his name in the shade." On the other hand, the enigmatic Blood's modesty may have had more to do with the mother of his young daugher, whom he had left back in St. Louis, and with whatever legitimate financial claims she may have had on him, than with Woodhull's ambitions or his own.

In the public mind, Tennie more than Woodhull was synonymous with Woodhull, Claflin & Company. Her relationship with the Commodore had launched and promoted it, her deposit with Clews had given it credit. Tennie's foresight now gave the company another boost. Soon after the contract was signed, an attempt was made to defraud the firm with a doctored check. Tennie, not Blood, prevented the fraud. A businesslike man representing himself as an agent for Park and Tilford's, a well-known grocery firm, presented Tennie with a check for $6,600, requesting a gold purchase for $5,500 and a check for the balance. The grocery firm had purchased gold through Woodhull, Claflin & Company previously, but this agent was a stranger. Tennie took the precaution of having his check certified by the New York County Bank, on which it had been drawn. The teller there started to sign it routinely, then had second thoughts and sent the check to Park and Tilford's for verification. The grocers puzzled over the check and soon realized that the so-called "agent" had cleverly altered their check for $66 to read $6,600. The "agent" had meantime disappeared. Tennie's care in having the check certified saved the firm $6,600.

Of greater value than the money was the publicity the incident received. "The ladies of the firm have come out of the affair with flying colors," said the *World*. "Their shrewd management and business tact were equal to the emergency, and the precautions they took in regard to certification guarded them from all loss." Had they written the story themselves, Woodhull and Tennie could have found no better way to reassure the public that they could hold their own in the treacherous world of Wall Street.

At the end of the day the Street gossiped and fed at Charlie Delmonico's genial tables. Woodhull and Tennie chose to follow the crowd, knowing full well that women were expected to have male escorts at the restaurant. When Charlie Delmonico, full of apologies and expressing his high regard for his two guests, claimed he could not "create a precedent," Tennie marched into the street, pulled the first coachman she found into the restaurant, and ordered "tomato soup for three." Wall Street gave the new firm added points for ingenuity.

Tennie's sights stayed on Wall Street, but Woodhull's ranged further. Power and ideas interested her. The political ambitions she had conceived in Washington germinated. She made her parties a democratic mix of capitalists and anarchists, business leaders and politicians, preachers and social theorists.

One of them, Stephen Pearl Andrews, became her intellectual guru. A radical reformer, he was also a pioneer sociologist, a lawyer who held a medical degree, a linguist who developed Alwato, intended like the later Esperanto to be a universal language, and a phonographer, skilled in Isaac Pitman's system of phonetic transcription, which he developed into an effective technique for teaching illiterate people to read. Andrews's best known work, *The Science of Society,* was a lucid expression of American anarchism. His utopian community on Long Island, called Modern Times, had disbanded and he had formed Unitary Home, a row of houses on 14th Street with communal parlors and kitchens. It had been an incubator for new ideas, intermingling sophisticated learning and naive idealism. The Unitary Home had disbanded and Andrews had fallen on hard times, but he was still a utopian romantic. Cultivating the image of a seer, he wore the flowing beard of an Old Testament prophet. A photograph of him at the time shows a man with stern and judgmental eyes over a hawk's beak of a nose. The *New York World* called him one of the era's "Queer Philosophers."

For all his philosophical pretensions, Andrews was no more immune to Woodhull's beauty and sensuality—or her money—than other men. And he, more than most of the guests who drank her champagne, made an instant and magnificent impression on *her*. He could casually mention Herbert Spencer's sociology and Charles Fourier's communal phalanxes in the same sentence; he argued the ideas of all the European social theorists, Bakunin, Proudhon, Saint-Simon, Hegel, and Comte, and then promoted the American Josiah Warren's "sovereignty of the individual" and "equitable commerce" or John Humphrey Noyes's stirpiculture and free love.

Woodhull instantly saw Andrews as another man who could help her overome her limitations, an intellectual resource for her political ambitions, and perhaps even more, a means of establishing herself as the representative woman of the time. In many ways their mutual attraction seemed a misalliance, he an anarchist reformer and she the first woman stockbroker. But Woodhull listened to Andrews and was dazzled.

Andrews became a regular at Woodhull's soirées. He was 61, she was 31; mentor and protégé pooled their resources and contacts. Andrews gave her a sophisticated education in social theory and reform. His philosophy of individualism enabled her to interpret her own life through a new theoretical frame. He may also have helped her with the basics of reading and writing which she had covered so sketchily as a child. Under Andrews's tutelage, Woodhull found intellectual self-confidence.

He set himself the task of radicalizing Woodhull, seeing in her a means to get his ideas before the public. Known around New York since the 1850s, less for *The Science of Society* than for a celebrated three-way debate on the subject of free love in the pages of the *New York Tribune* with Henry James, Sr., and *Tribune* editor Horace Greeley, Andrews had denounced the "interference of the state in his morals . . . Freedom in love was . . . the culminating point toward which all other reforms tend," he said. Andrews and Woodhull discussed free love in all its nuances.

Andrews later said that Woodhull's evenings resembled "the Salon of Mme. Roland during the first French Revolution—a rendezvous for men of genius, and women of genius, and the men interested in radical progress, and the women of similar interest . . ." With Andrews at her elbow, Woodhull was now poised to take a plunge more daring than her operations on Black Friday. This time she would gamble everything on politics.

8

"I Announce Myself as a Candidate for the Presidency"

On Tuesday April 5, 1870, Woodhull moved into an imposing brownstone in the opulent Murray Hill area of New York City. Everything sparkled, from her elaborate entryway of polished marble to her immense mirrors in gilt frames. The sofas and chairs in her drawing room were ribbed in a blue rep silk, and plush carpets covered the floors. She had created a setting for her "at homes."

All of her extended family joined her—Blood, her children, Tennie, her sister Maggie and her family, who had followed her to New York, as well as a staff of servants. Even Stephen Pearl Andrews would soon take up residence.

Woodhull could ascend to her rooftop and look out on a panoramic view of the expanding city, to the south where tall ships still waited in the harbors, and to the north, where freshly laid-out city streets checkered the countryside. The view fit her mood and expectations.

A week earlier she had offered herself to the country as a candidate for president. She did so by the simple expedient of sending a letter to the *New York Herald*. Her declaration got right to the point.

> As I happen to be the most prominent representative of the only unrepresented class in the republic, and perhaps the most practical exponent of the principles of equality, I request the favor of being permitted to address the public through the *Herald*. While others of my sex devoted themselves to a crusade against the laws that shackle the women of the country, I asserted my individual independence; while others prayed for the good time coming, I worked for it; while others

argued the equality of woman with man, I proved it by successfully engaging in business; while others sought to show that there was no valid reason why women should be treated, socially and politically, as being inferior to man, I boldly entered the arena of politics and business and exercised the rights I already possessed. I therefore claim the right to speak for the unenfranchised women of the country, and believing as I do that the prejudices which still exist in the popular mind against women in public life will soon disappear, I now announce myself as a candidate for the Presidency.

The letter was bold and well timed. Woodhull had picked a moment when the suffrage movement was badly divided over strategy and tactics to make her own play for attention. Her larger purpose was to force the country to face up to the "women question" in the election of 1872. She felt certain that grassroots support for women's suffrage ran far deeper than anything the established political parties had been able to absorb. She also argued shrewdly that neither the Republicans nor the Democrats had any major issue to put before the public. The Republicans, who had for so long stood for the high principles of abolition, had accomplished their objective. They had nothing of equal magnitude to capture the attention of the voters. Suffrage for women had the potential to become such an election issue. "The present position of political parties is anomalous," she wrote.

> They are not inspired by any great principles of policy or economy; there is no live issue up for discussion. A great national question is wanted . . . That question exists in the issue, whether woman shall . . . be elevated to all the political rights enjoyed by man. The simple issue whether woman should not have this complete political equality . . . is the only one to be tried, and none more important is likely to arise before the Presidential election.

In making her case, Woodhull drew on two highly unusual precedents. The first was the progress of blacks in securing the franchise, the second was the determination of women to run for office even without the vote. "The blacks were cattle in 1860," she wrote. "A Negro now sits in Jeff Davis's seat in the United States Senate." Should the country do any less for women?

The second precedent, unmentioned by Woodhull in her letter, had been established by Elizabeth Cady Stanton. Three years before the 1869 suffrage convention, Stanton had nominated herself as an independent candidate for Congress from New York City's Eighth District. She argued that the Constitution did not prevent women from holding office, whether they could or could not vote. She had addressed a letter to her district, advocating "free speech, free press, free men and free trade," as well as women's rights. The press had been kind, if condescending. The *Herald* had called Stanton a "lady of fine presence and accomplishments" who would wield "a wholesome influence over the rough and disorderly" elements of Congress.

The divisions between the abolitionists and suffragists had grown worse since the 1869 convention in Washington. In May of 1869 a loose affiliation of reformers created to bring unity, the Equal Rights Association, had split apart. The Stanton-Anthony bloc formed its own organization, the National Woman Suffrage Association, headquartered in New York. In November of 1869 the abolitionists organized the American Woman Suffrage Association headquartered in Boston. Lucy Stone, Henry Blackwell, Julia Ward Howe, Thomas Wentworth Higginson, and Mary Livermore were its leaders, and they asked Henry Ward Beecher to be their president.

Theodore Tilton, the reform-minded editor of the *Independent*, was a close friend of Stanton's. He took the initiative to resolve the differences and restore unity. On March 14, 1870, Tilton had sent an open letter to Stanton as head of the New York wing and Beecher as titular head of the Boston wing, on behalf of the Equal Rights Association. He proposed a meeting on April 6 to discuss reunion. He wanted to name a neutral party, the lecturer, Anna Dickinson, to head a new united society.

Woodhull stepped into this crisis with her letter to the *Herald*. Like Dickinson, she was a neutral. She was neither famous enough nor respected enough to win the sort of position Tilton was dangling before Dickinson, but she could gain public recognition by introducing her name before a wide audience at the moment suffrage politics threatened to boil over. Hence, the comments in her letter about others who crusaded for suffrage while she asserted her independence, others who prayed for it while she worked for it, others who argued the equality of women while she proved it by engaging in business.

Woodhull timed her letter so that it would appear on Saturday April 2, four days before the suffrage union meeting. It was also Wall Street's half day. She would be able to receive visitors and congratulations in her office at 44 Broad Street all afternoon.

On skimming through the *Herald* that Saturday, passing the classified ads, telegraphic world news, and Washington news, she read on page eight, at the top of the page on the right-hand side, a bold typeface headline:

> THE COMING WOMAN. VICTORIA C. WOODHULL . . . TO RACE FOR THE WHITE HOUSE—WHAT SHE WILL AND WHAT SHE WON'T DO—HER VIEWS ON HOME AND FOREIGN POLICY—NEW IDEAS ON GOVERNMENT.

The *Herald* not only published the letter but also printed its own highly favorable editorial. Woodhull's financial credentials, as "the lady broker," were appreciated and featured.

> Mrs. Woodhull, the lady broker of Broad Street, independent of all suffrage tea-parties and Grundy associations, proclaims herself as a candidate for the occupancy-in-chief of the White House, and asks it on the score solely that she has the means, courage, energy and ability necessary to contest the issue to its close. Now there can certainly be no objection to such a competition as this: it possesses the merits of novelty, enterprise, courage and determination. Women always take the part of each other, and if the women can be allowed to vote, Mrs. Woodhull may rely on rolling up the heaviest majority ever polled in this or any other nation. Her platform, which will be found in another column, is short, sharp, decisive and has the true ring in it. Now for victory for Victoria in 1872.

The *Herald* took Woodhull's announcement as an opportunity to give its support to the Sixteenth Amendment, which Stanton had proposed. The paper, along with a great many voters, expected the amendment would soon extend the franchise to women:

The passage of the Fifteenth Amendment to the Constitution of the United States has had at least one beneficial effect, so far as our political status is concerned in this country—to wit, the clearing of the track for the Sixteenth and as many other amendments as may be deemed necessary and becoming toward the attainment of a liberal and benignly comprehensive system of representation, and participation both in the making and the administration of laws.

Despite its position supporting a Sixteenth Amendment, the *Herald* took a high-handed attitude toward the suffrage movement, reflecting a widespread attitude that the suffragists spent too much time fighting among themselves. It urged women to vote for Woodhull, to show their might, "independent of any of these petty organizations."

Woodhull's large front office on Broad Street overflowed with visitors offering their congratulations that Saturday afternoon. Vile rainy weather did not dilute the infectious enthusiasm. Woodhull presided, simply attired, her usual fresh rose her only decoration. She came forward to greet visitors with her arms outstretched, her face flushed and wreathed in smiles. She clasped their hands and shook them warmly, accepting their encouragement graciously. Gone was the nervous sister who had followed Tennie's lead with the press. A sensitive reporter from Philadelphia noticed that the sisters were, as usual, inseparable, but he found Mrs. Woodhull "to have more sagacity and depth" as she "received guests, both business and private, with perfect ease, and without either confusion or hurry."

Woodhull had already begun to prepare the next steps in her campaign for president, a series of position papers. They started as a thoughtful article, "The Basis of Government," which dealt primarily with women's claims to equality with men. But they developed into considerably more. A series with an imposing title, "The Origins, Tendencies and Principles of Government," was emerging, the brainchild of Stephen Pearl Andrews. With these papers, Woodhull could project herself as a learned and thoughtful woman qualified to be president.

She seemed more concerned about where the papers would appear than what was in them. Woodhull approached Reid about publishing them in the *Tribune*. The paper had more stature among serious-minded people than the popular *Herald.* Their discussions progressed; the paper set the first of the articles in type. Then Woodhull followed up by asking Reid to consider placing them in the weekly edition of the *Tribune,* which had a circulation of 200,000, as well as the daily. She felt sufficiently confident that his response would be favorable to ask him to "be kind enough to give me a splendid editorial such as you so well know how to write."

But this time she overplayed her hand. Reid began avoiding her. His editor, the famous Horace Greeley, was having second thoughts. Greeley had founded the paper in 1841 and had become the outstanding newspaper editor of his time. An abolitionist and reformer, he had become a master of astringent prose despite his lack of formal education. He declared his eccentricity by wearing a countrified white duster and low-crowned, wide-brimmed hat all over the city. The great reform editor had another eccentricity; he claimed to be in favor of women's rights, but he was opposed to suffrage for women. He had no interest in publishing Woodhull's ideas.

Not yet aware of Greeley's veto, Woodhull wrote to Reid on Friday, April 8: "I retired last night at 11:30 having given up your coming. I trust you will . . . not forget to call again when it will not interfere with your duties." She added a postscript: "If you do not come over this evening, please send me word when the Basis etc. will appear."

Later that day she received the bad news from Reid, and she replied, "I comply with your request . . . as you seem unwilling to give it space I trust you will do me the favor to furnish me proofs and accept my thanks for courtesies conferred."

Woodhull immediately turned to Ashley Cole, city editor of the *Herald,* to publish the position papers. Cole had already done a Sunday follow-up to the Saturday editorial, calling Woodhull's announcement of the previous day "a powerful document on behalf of women's rights." "Mrs. Woodhull," he wrote, "may be considered in the field, and, being of the female firm in Wall Street of Woodhull, Claflin & Co., who can tell the extent of her financial resources among the brokers, bulls and bears? A woman, and a smart and handsome woman, she is the proper person to stand forth against the field as the woman's rights candidate for the White House."

On Saturday, April 16, the day before Easter Sunday, "The Tendencies of Government" appeared on page five of the *Herald.* It was introduced enthusiastically by Cole as Woodhull's "bull" on "social laws." The timing was perfect from Woodhull's point of view; just two weeks had passed since her announcement. She had been able to persuade Cole to run the series on the basis of the first article alone, without, as he put it, knowing "whether her conclusion will agree with her premises." Such was his response to her spell.

Ever mindful of his readers' interest in Woodhull's Vanderbilt connection, Cole reminded them again that she was the Commodore's protégé. She had "undertaken the difficult task of correcting popular errors on the science of government," he said. "The document will be found exceedingly interesting as showing the quality of the female mind against which the money changers of Wall Street will have to contend."

What followed, as it turned out, was not a position paper at all. Instead the readers of the *Herald* received a pyrotechnic display of Andrews's learning. "As far back into the past as our historic lights enable us to see, and still much further even behind the appearance of man upon the face of the planet, the existence of government can be plainly traced." A sociological discourse followed, citing the social theorists Spencer and Comte, and Maine's *Ancient Law,* to establish a "chain of progression" of government. A second article followed, comparing the evolution of government to the evolution of the simplest organic forms. A third discussed the subject of reconciling sacred and profane history. The series went on to trace the rise and fall of nations throughout history. The object was to find a course for the United States to follow to become the first "universal government." Andrews was airing utopian theories that had little connection with the real world of the 1870s. The *Herald* expressed itself dazzled by the profundity of the series, but the average newspaper reader's eyes, accustomed to daily reports of mayhem and scandal, must have glazed over.

Still the loyal Cole and the *Herald* continued this farrago. On April 25 the paper declared, "Mrs. Victoria C. Woodhull, head of the firm of female brokers . . . has undertaken the difficult task of enlightening the public mind on the best means of running the governmental machine of America." On May 9 the *Herald* mixed its metaphors in describing the woman who had "delved deep into the mines of governmental lore, and is vigorously training for the Presidential sweepstakes of 1872." On May 16 the paper published what it described as Woodhull's "Last Lesson in Political History," saying that she had "devoted herself to enlightenment of our statesmen . . . [as well as] consenting to fill the office of President of the United States," and that her last letter "will be found quite as interesting reading as any of her previous letters on the same subject."

Then on May 27, Cole gave Woodhull what she had been angling for, an editorial on her fitness for office. He congratulated her for the way she had sought "not only to study and perfect herself in the nature of the functions which she seeks to exercise . . . but, to give her opinions to the people, that they may judge of her ability and the correctness of her views."

Woodhull's apparent fitness for office was based on a large measure of deception. Cole apparently didn't realize that Andrews was the actual author of all this heavy prose he had published. Occasional traces of Woodhull's lighter touch were apparent, but even those faded away after the first three articles. The work was so obviously not Woodhull's that a reader today is left with an uncomfortable sense of misrepresentation. The modern convention of ghostwritten works for public figures was not accepted nineteenth-century practice. But Woodhull was riding high, and she swept over these inconvenient details. Cole had no interest in undermining his story, either. If he ever discovered the truth, he maintained the fiction. Even 40 years later, long after Woodhull had forgotten him, he wrote to her recalling how much "delight" he had taken "in receiving and printing your special articles." He signed the letter, "Yours with undiminished felicity and esteem," expressing nothing but sincere admiration. Eventually some readers who knew Andrews's work recognized his style and ideas. In response to their questions, Woodhull said airily that it made no "difference to us from whence the truth comes, only so that it comes."

The *Herald* was so pleased with the series, the paper encouraged Woodhull to continue beyond her "Last Lesson." A total of ten articles appeared; the series ran into July. In 1871, Woodhull published them as a book, and she did not acknowledge Andrews's contribution.

One revealing paragraph appeared in the third article, a story about the ancient Assyrian queen Semiramis. She was Woodhull's first discovery in a restless search through history and legend for female rulers. The article described the queen as a "beautiful and extraordinary woman who possessed the most marvelous control over all she came in contact with. Her simple presence was sufficient to quell any tumult . . ."

Woodhull liked to think of herself as a profound thinker who combined a "singular masculine grasp" with "womanly intuition." In her experience, women were "quicker witted" than men, able to "arrive at conclusions easier and sooner." "While man is toiling up the rugged steep by slow and painful steps, woman instantly flies to the summit and wonders that man should be so obtuse and slow." But Woodhull's appeal would lie not so much in learned ideas as in her courage and daring, her willingness to take chances, her innovation. She had raised a "flag" for women with her announcement for president, and now she intended to make herself a suffrage leader.

Reigning over her elegant drawing room, entertaining her friends from the press, Woodhull let it be known that she would "spend a fortune" in advocating her views on "equality and governmental policy," and hinted that she had a new surprise in store for the republic—something that would both "interest and astound the political world."

9
Woodhull and Claflin's Weekly

Woodhull's secret was *Woodhull and Claflin's Weekly,* a newspaper that appeared on New York City newsstands in early May 1870. "This journal will . . . support Victoria C. Woodhull for president . . . and will advocate suffrage without distinction of sex," the editorial page proclaimed. UPWARD AND ONWARD urged the paper's motto. The timing of the first issue was carefully planned to coincide with a May meeting of the warring Boston and New York suffragists. The April union effort had failed but a new attempt was underway. Once again Woodhull was putting her name before a wide audience at a time of suffrage turmoil.

But the *Weekly* was no one-shot venture. It was a sustained effort on Woodhull's part to place herself as a "representative woman" of the time, a means of portraying herself as destined for leadership.

Woodhull called the *Weekly* her "pet." Throughout the spring of 1870, she sat surrounded by her circle, sometimes at her business office on Broad Street, sometimes at the printer on Park Row, but most frequently on the blue silk sofas at 38th Street, where fresh flowers scented the room, and a decanter of cognac waited on the sideboard. Woodhull worked among mountains of clips from daily newspapers, stacks of articles offered for publication, long proof sheets from upcoming issues. She issued her orders. All around her, pens scratched down her words. Many members of her inner circle drafted copy, edited, and ghosted articles.

Woodhull's idiosyncratic imprint imbued the paper with its enduring character. From the start, the *Weekly*'s identity became synonymous with hers; no reform slogans, nothing like Stanton's *Revolution,* obscured her presence; instead, the names Woodhull and Claflin arched across the entire top of the page. Woodhull's name appeared first, as always.

Everything that touched women's lives interested Woodhull. Educate daughters and give them practical training, just like sons, she told her readers. Women need education to be self-sufficient. A woman can be a man's equal in all the rights and privileges of life. The average price for women's labor is $7 per week, while men get $12 to $40. Women need help or they may slip down to prostitution. Women can work as well as men in scores of callings, and be paid as well. The *Medical Gazette* is finally recognizing women in the medical profession. Rutgers female college is expanding its departments. Women printers attended the Printers Convention in Cincinnati. Women are being poisoned by hair dye. Even women who are willing to remain as mere appendages to men with no individuality outside of wifely submission must keep up with the progress of the world in order to be good companions.

Woodhull followed the activities of women lecturers—Anna Dickinson, "the only pecuniary success of the women's movement"; the young Bostonian Kate Field; the gentle Southerner Laura C. Holloway—and the efforts of "high born English women" who were supporting women's rights. Her experience with Canning Woodhull, her first husband, prompted a story on a nursing home in Brooklyn where alcoholism was being treated as a disease rather than a moral failing, though soon after the article a poem on the sad lot of the drunkard's wife appeared. And her personal interest can be detected in a piece signed "Omega." It pointed out that "ambition, love of power, and love of fame are not necessarily evidences of insincerity."

A "Paris Letter" appeared, along with "From Washington," written by a columnist who signed his name "Crescent," and "News Foreign and Domestic." The paper covered the arts in its "Poetry and Fiction" section. Every issue included poetry, often printed on the front page, verses that sound sentimental today but that appealed to Woodhull's taste—and she herself provided the subject for many of them. Under "New Publications," the works of George Eliot and Anthony Trollope were registered and applauded. Charles Dickens's death was mourned, but a novel by Sarah A. Wright was curtly dismissed for its character's emotional weakness and involuntary self-sacrifice "for want of knowing how to take care of herself."

The *Weekly* covered financial news and made pronouncements, ("the grand bull movement in Wall Street began about April 23 . . .") that were taken to reflect the Commodore's views. A regular feature was "Wall Street Yesterday," offering stock listings. Even sports news was reported, another nod toward the Commodore. "Yachting Notes" reported a race off the English Channel in which an American yacht, *Sappho,* defeated an English competitor, *Cambria,* on its own British waters.

For the front page of the *Weekly's* first issue, Woodhull printed the first installment of a novel by George Sand, *In Spite of All (Malgré Tout),* which was just appearing in *Revue des Deux Mondes* in Paris. Translated expressly for the *Weekly,* probably by Andrews, Sand's novel told the story of a beautiful and ambitious woman's rise to power. The model, reported the *Weekly,* was the French Empress Eugenie.

Sand had sparked a hot controversy among the suffragists. In a review of her earlier novel *Consuelo,* Harriet Beecher Stowe, the bluenose author of *Uncle Tom's Cabin,* had excoriated Sand for her irregular sex life. Stowe was allied with the Boston wing of the suffrage movement, the conservative group headed by her brother, Henry Ward Beecher.

Elizabeth Cady Stanton of the New York wing, objecting to Stowe's point of view, would later write a defense; saying, "George Sand has done a grander work for women, in her pure life and bold utterances of truth, than any woman of her day and generation." Stanton attacked Stowe for vacillation and timidity on women's issues. By placing Sand on the cover of the first *Weekly,* Woodhull allied herself with Stanton and the New York liberals. But as the episodes of *In Spite of All* progressed in the *Weekly,* it became obvious that Sand was painting a scathing picture of an unscrupulous upstart. No longer eager to identify with the heroine, Woodhull buried the last episodes at the back of the paper.

From the first issue, the *Weekly* had a look of quality. Its 16 pages were laid out cleanly on heavyweight paper of larger-than-average page size, and set in easy-to-read type. The copy was well written, professionally edited, and virtually free of errors, grammatical or typographical. The editorial page of the first issue apologized in advance for any unintentional slips, putting the readers on notice that the *Weekly* had set itself high standards. No advertising appeared on the front page, a departure from the custom of the time. The paper did not prepare scurrilous personal stories in order to blackmail the well known or powerful. Everything about the *Weekly* reflected good taste.

From May 14, 1870, until June 10, 1876, the paper arrived each week on the newsstands and at the homes of subscribers, a total of 288 issues. During those six years, Woodhull faced the unremitting pressure of deadlines, payrolls, and printing costs. For only six months during that time was she unable to get the paper out. But she brought her "pet" back stronger than ever, saying, "We nursed it into life, age and strength and why should we not love it next to life itself?"

The first issue offered, in a politic gesture, the *Weekly*'s compliments to its "elder brethren" of the press, mentioning specifically James Gordon Bennett, the editor of the *Herald,* whose staff had treated the sisters so well so many times in its pages, Horace Greeley of the *Tribune,* and half a dozen others.

Woodhull also made overtures to suffrage leaders, complimenting stout and middle-aged Elizabeth Cady Stanton on her personal appearance, cooing about her "not unwieldly figure," her "active movements." It also praised her ideas, her opposition to the political and social subordination of single women and restrictions on the property rights of married women. In the same pages, Woodhull offered small bouquets to Lucy Stone and Lucretia Mott.

A column on suffrage titled the "Sixteenth Amendment" ran regularly, expressing Woodhull's support of Stanton and the New York wing. But having paid her dues to the suffrage leaders, Woodhull used the editorial page to spin out her own position on suffrage, first only in faint outline. Her stand would soon propel her to the suffrage leadership position she desired. Women were entitled to the vote because they were citizens, she argued. Women were taxed for their property the same as men, a burden she herself bore as a successful broker. Therefore, the state owed women complete rights of citizenship.

Cordial as Woodhull was to the suffragists, her most extravagant compliments were lavished on her patron, Commodore Vanderbilt. The *Weekly* described the ruses Vanderbilt had used to gain control of the New York Central Railroad, parlaying 2 percent of its stock into control of the entire line. The paper enthused, "Thus can one man with great brains . . . carry out a scheme which is the grandest in the history of railroads . . . [it] almost staggers belief." Vanderbilt's name appeared in the paper frequently, an effort on Woodhull's part to please the attention-loving Commodore. And every time the sisters associated themselves with his name, they augmented their own stature. Tennie delivered copies of the paper to Vanderbilt's office and stayed to read them to him.

The Commodore provided his experience and funds to make the

paper commercially sound. Stories in the *Weekly* itself over the years indicate a starting budget of about $35,000, underwritten in part—probably about half—by the Commodore, with the remainder financed by Woodhull and Claflin. "The Commodore is like heaven—he helps those who help themselves—and we intend to help ourselves—you may rest assured of that," the sisters said. They predicted that the *Weekly* would be making a profit by the end of its second year. A printing of 20,000 was planned, increasing to 50,000. The American News Company handled distribution. There is no way to verify the circulation levels that the paper awarded itself. The *Weekly,* like every new publication, saw itself flying from the presses into eager hands. But later events do confirm that the initial business plan was sound, and that the paper got off to a good start.

The sisters mailed their unsold papers to daily newspapers and influential people as complimentary copies. The editorial page asked for responses to these copies, and printed positive replies as part of the paper's promotional campaign.

Initially, Tennie—chosen for the "abundance of her assurance"—sold ads. Competitors and even a few prospects said she dragooned men into subscribing and buying space. She would find a man in his office and fluster him seductively. Sometimes the outcome of her visit was "a footrace around the rolltop desk," according to gossip. Whatever the game, Tennie made her sale; new names were added daily to the paper's list of advertisers. But Tennie did not intend to go it alone indefinitely. The first issues printed a "help wanted" notice for two men to handle advertising.

By the end of June, H. L. Ostrander, the new advertising agent, was in place to handle subscriptions and ad sales. He established a businesslike rate card that started at 60 cents a line with discounts for larger ads and continuing campaigns. The *Weekly* started with three pages of advertising and eventually grew to four. Some still-famous names found their way into the paper: Tiffany watches, Brooks Boots and Shoes, Steinway Pianos. Forty-one advertisers appeared in the first issue, along with listings for six theaters. And the numbers grew. Clothing, hats, hotels, carriages, stationery, medicines, soaps, cosmetics, office furniture, insurance companies, railroads (led, of course, by Vanderbilt's New York Central and Harlem and Hudson). The list would lengthen to include Wall Street firms, books, magazines, and the Louisiana State Lottery.

Undoubtedly some of these ads were run at little or no charge in exchange for the prestige they gave to the paper's advertiser list. And some ads must have been "trades" in exchange for products or services. But whatever special deals were made, the collection of advertising sponsors was impressive, a remarkable performance for two beginners.

As the *Weekly's* package of business and editorial clicked, and as issue followed issue, the paper drew attention and compliments from beyond the sisters' immediate circle. "Handsome and readable," said the *New York Standard*. The *Day* in Philadelphia called the *Weekly* "undoubtedly the ablest journal of its class, [it] can hardly fail of success." The *Inquirer* concurred, saying the newcomer possessed "more than ordinary merits."

After two years on the newsstands, the *Weekly* was recognized as a solid success. Frederick Hudson's volume, *Journalism in the U.S.,* published by Harper and Brothers in 1873, summed it up: "a 16-page paper [that] dealt in finance and fashion, stock jobbing and strong-minded women, sporting[s] . . . , politics and president-making, supporting a woman even for the executive mansion . . . [published by] two sisters who seem capable of accomplishing what they undertake." Women took off their aprons and took up their pens to write to the *Weekly* in such numbers that Woodhull finally had to tell them, reluctantly, that her "Women's Drawer" was full.

In a gesture of greater significance, the *Herald* used the birth of the *Weekly* to criticize the divisions between the Boston and New York wings of the suffrage movement. "While the two hostile divisions of women righters are passing their time in refusing to coalesce with each other and in flooding the country with resolutions and chatter," the *Herald* wrote, "there are at least two advocates of the woman movement that endeavor to show by example and precept that their sex, with ordinary fair play and industry, can take care of itself . . . The example of Woodhull and Claflin is a highly commendable one, as they do more and talk less than any two divisions of female agitators put together."

Two suffrage papers were already being published. *The Revolution,* Stanton and Anthony's paper that represented the New York interests, was approaching the end of a short, debt-ridden life. Woodhull and Claflin had run an ad for their brokerage firm in its pages. The Boston wing had just started publishing the *Woman's*

Journal, edited by Julia Ward Howe and Mary Livermore. The February 19 issue had recognized Woodhull, Claflin & Company. But both of the earlier papers devoted more attention to ideology than the bottom line and depended on underwriters for financial support.

Theodore Tilton's *Brooklyn Independent* provided a better model for the *Weekly* than the suffrage papers. As editor, Tilton had made himself influential, a power even in Washington. He had transformed the *Independent* from a small religious journal into a widely read and influential newspaper, outspoken in its support of abolition and other radical causes. The *Independent* still carried religious news, but it also covered general news, Washington correspondence, financial and commercial news, books, poetry, and advertising, the kind of broad-based editorial coverage that the *Weekly* had adopted for itself. The *Independent* prided itself on publishing a wide range of opinions on every subject, opening its columns to opposing viewpoints, "free and uninfluenced utterances that [have] genuine value." Tilton's paper claimed 500,000 readers, and the publisher, Henry Bowen, made $50,000 to $60,000 each year from the *Independent.* Woodhull admired Tilton's success, and his name appeared in the *Weekly* with some frequency during the summer of 1870.

In each issue of the *Weekly,* Woodhull promoted her presidential campaign. She started making Washington contacts; she recorded General Benjamin Butler's activities. The radical congressman from Massachusetts, famous as a Union general, was a supporter of women's rights and a power in the capital. The paper reported Butler's legislative proposals, his recommendations for regulating working hours and conditions, the activities of his family, even his whereabouts on the Fourth of July.

In June, Woodhull sent her own ambassador, Tennie, to Washington to scout the terrain. She was introduced around the city by "Crescent," the *Weekly*'s Washington columnist. Tennie, Crescent reported, had been welcomed by everyone with "all honors," and had even been received by President Ulysses S. Grant himself. The president and his family immediately became the subjects of a *Weekly* campaign of flattery. The two editors purred over the several poems and articles by the first lady. She "appears to have bequeathed her talent to her daughter," they wrote about Nellie Grant, who was described as a "fair-haired young beauty of fifteen." Then they printed "The Tear," her sweet doggerel:

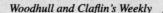

> *There stood a glistening tear*
> *In her blue and sorrowing eye;*
> *Reserved till the time drew near*
> *To say a last good-bye . . .*

Woodhull and the *Weekly* had located the president's weakest line of defense in their first sortie on Washington.

10
Whispering in the President's Ear

*L*ate in the fall of 1870, Woodhull moved into the Willard Hotel in Washington and set herself up as a lobbyist on behalf of suffrage for women. It was another simple expedient that got right to the point. Suffrage for women would be won in the nation's capital, not at conventions.

The Willard was an attractive place. Its handsome arched doorway led into bright rooms gleaming with white paint and lined with Windsor chairs. The halls and sitting rooms were jammed with senators, representatives, members of the president's cabinet, clerks, contractors, railroad men, entrepreneurs. After one visit to the Willard, Nathaniel Hawthorne said, "You adopt the universal habit of the place, and call for a mint-julep, a whiskey-skin, a gin-cocktail . . ." Women held court in the rooms upstairs, wives and daughters of the men downstairs. Female lobbyists, who were generally considered to be women of dubious reputations, also reigned upstairs. It was all part of the well-established and accepted Washington scene when Congress was in session—the parties, the entertaining, the young, unattached women on the guest lists. The Willard was talk, smoke, and power.

"Everybody knows what the 'third house' in Washington is," Woodhull said later. "It consists of the lobbyists who are there to obtain legislation—to push this little scheme or that small appropriation. Large sums of money are expended by this lobby. When a particular scheme is to come up, its friends distribute ten, fifteen and even twenty thousand dollars among the mistresses of these houses. Why? To secure their influence with representatives and senators. You needn't take my word for this; anybody who will inquire can learn the truth."

Woodhull found no shortage of people willing to introduce her to Washington's facts of life. Her initial goal was to secure a Sixteenth

Amendment enfranchising women. She remembered later that the Democratic members of Congress first opened her eyes to the difficulties that lay in the way. Playing all the angles against the center, they told Woodhull that the suffrage leaders would simply "quarrel with each other" when they came to Washington. The Democrats meant to throw kerosene on the fire. They advised Woodhull that while the suffragists argued, she could quietly push her own program and "get the victory and the credit." She listened carefully. If these politicians wanted to use her, she would use them.

The Fifteenth Amendment, which had caused so much controversy at the suffrage convention in 1869, had passed Congress, been ratified by the states and become the law of the land on March 30, 1870, well before Woodhull arrived at the Willard. Stanton, speaking for the New York wing, had called it "an open, deliberate insult to American womanhood." Abby Kelly Foster had countered on behalf of the Bostonians that she believed that it was the "Negro's hour," and she would consider herself a "monster of selfishness" to put her daughter's political equality ahead of black men's. Positions had become so polarized that suffragists would not reunite for 20 years. Only in 1890 would they finally become the National American Woman Suffrage Association.

The Republican Party, which stood for abolition and reform, didn't want to get drawn into the suffrage conflict. The Democrats in Congress had fomented further dissension by supporting Stanton's and Anthony's suffrage petitions and bills. Their tactics worked. The two suffrage leaders were accused of allying themselves with racist Southern Democrats. They defended themselves with the lame explanation that the hypocrisy of Democrats served them better than the treachery of Republicans.

A bill for a Sixteenth Amendment granting suffrage to women had been introduced into the House of Representatives by George W. Julian of Indiana in 1869. It was referred to the House Committee on the Judiciary and had been languishing there for over a year. Frederick Douglass had joined those supporting the amendment, making a statesmanlike effort to heal the wounds between himself and the New York suffrage wing. But the bill stayed in committee. President Grant was considered to be sympathetic toward suffrage for women, but he had not acted. When Stanton and Anthony went to the Hill that fall to urge the passage of the Sixteenth, Isabella Beecher

Hooker, who had accompanied them, said they were told that Congress "had no time to attend to such a question even if they thought it worthy of consideration."

Woodhull's first maneuver was to build her own contacts with the members of the House Judiciary Committee who were holding the Sixteenth Amendment hostage. She sought out General Benjamin Butler, the influential member from Massachusetts, whose interest she had already been cultivating. Butler's unprepossessing appearance belied the powerful role he played in Washington. He stood five feet, four inches tall and waddled as he walked. His enormous head, bent slightly forward, was recognized throughout the city. "The truth," one Washington insider said at the time, "is that Butler's big head contains a good share of the brains of the House, and he possesses qualities that would make him a leader in any cause he might espouse."

Before the war, Butler had been a Democrat, associated with the Southern wing of the party; but after the war broke out he had became a strong Unionist. He obtained a political appointment as an officer. Later John Hay, secretary to President Abraham Lincoln, passed the word that Butler was "the smartest damn rascal that ever lived." During the war, Butler and Grant had had a stormy relationship, but by the time of Grant's inauguration, Butler had more influence with the president than anyone else in the House of Representatives, where he was now Grant's champion. The grateful president had, in turn, made Butler his spoilsman and officebroker, giving Butler a base of power that extended well beyond the boundaries of Massachusetts.

The entire city recognized Butler's genius for bending the rules to his own advantage. Woodhull's real help would come from Butler personally, not the Democrats. He was in a position to let her know that Congressman Julian's Sixteenth Amendment bill had come to its final resting place in the Judiciary Committee, that there was no hope of its ever reaching the floor.

It was characteristic of Butler's contrary personality to engage the suffrage issue just when his fellow Republicans refused to touch it. He had become famous for an ingenious wartime evasion of the Fugitive Slave Act. Asked to return a slaveowner's Negroes in accordance with the law, he had declared them to be "contraband of war" and refused to release them. His action won the applause of the abolitionists and overcame their aversion to his prewar affiliations with the South. The government later upheld Butler's interpretation of the law, and his use of the term "contraband" was widely adopted.

Woodhull cultivated the plump little general, and the two of them soon drew the eye of the city's gossips. In one story that made the rounds, Butler offered to help Woodhull's cause in exchange for "an opportunity to feast his eyes upon her naked person." The rumor expressed, no doubt, the fantasy of more than one member of Congress who felt her charm. "Half-truths kill," was Butler's evasive response to the rumors.

The full truth was complicated. Butler was devoted to his wife, Sarah, an actress who had given up a successful career 30 years earlier to marry him. She had taken her place in Washington society and was considered a woman of intelligence and cultivation, with the manners of an empress. She and her daughter Blanche, married to Senator Adelbert Ames of Mississippi, supported suffrage for women.

Sarah, however, was not in Washington in the fall of 1870. Woodhull had chanced on Butler during the loneliest autumn of his life. Suffering from thyroid cancer, Sarah was spending five months in Heidelberg, Germany, where her sons had been sent for a European education. "I am very lonely although very busy; but the time when business is over is the lonely hour," Butler wrote to her in a letter that fall. Two weeks later he wrote again, "You have been away 51 days now and it seems months. Call it what you will, use, habit, wont, association, friendship, love, 27 years of intimacy cannot be broken off without wrenching the heart . . . I am writing this past midnight, I do not feel like going to bed . . . But why annoy you with all this! You have enough disquiets and troubles without mine which cannot be remedied at present."

In many ways, Woodhull was a young, fresh version of Sarah. When she and Butler began their collaboration, their working relationship was highly charged sexually and emotionally. Butler's little habits and mannerisms became familiar to Woodhull—his late-night snacks of whiskey and doughnuts, the unnerving sight of his unlit cigar going round and round in his mouth, a habit he had developed to relieve his nervous tension when he had tried to stop smoking.

There is little doubt Woodhull and Butler had an affair. Years later, Woodhull told her daughter about it as she dictated recollections for a biography. It was one of her typically ambiguous sexual statements. While she was in Washington, she said, she "went at night and asked him to open the committee for me." The phrase "went at night" certainly suggests a sexual encounter. In Butler, Woodhull had found Washington's strongest power behind the scenes, and she entered into a brief, intense connection that brought her something more than sex.

Butler had the matter of his own reelection to the House occupying his attention that fall. But soon after election day, his collaboration with Woodhull on suffrage began to show results. Neither Woodhull nor Butler left a record of their exchanges, but we can see the partnership unfold in the pages of the *Weekly*.

On November 19 the paper ran a dramatic headline: "STARTLING ANNUNCIATION . . . SIXTEENTH AMENDMENT A DEAD LETTER." The accompanying editorial was one of the few ever to carry Woodhull's byline. It expressed, in her own language, the preliminary outlines of what would come to be known as her Memorial on suffrage. A Sixteenth Amendment was not necessary, she wrote, because if the Constitution were interpreted properly, women as citizens had already been granted the vote. The women of Wyoming had just acted on their right to vote. Wyoming had become a territory in 1868, and its first territorial legislature had granted voting rights to women in 1869. The territory became known as the equality state, even though Wyoming was not formally admitted as the forty-fourth state in the Union until 1890. Woodhull was undeterred by the technicalities of statehood or territorial status. She quoted Article 4, Section 2 of the Constitution to make her case that the rights exercised in Wyoming belonged to the citizens of all states—the passage that said, "The citizens of each state shall be entitled to the privileges and immunities of citizens in the several states."

With Butler away in Massachusetts, Woodhull consulted J. D. Reymart, the New York lawyer and reformer who was active in Democratic politics and president of the Hercules Insurance Company. He was a friend in whose judgment she had confidence. He considered Woodhull's idea legally sound and encouraged her to pursue it. "I do now proclaim to the women of the United States of America that they are enfranchised," Woodhull declared in the *Weekly*.

The Constitution, she pointed out quite rightly, nowhere uses the word "man" in contradistinction to "woman." The founding fathers had avoided both terms. Instead they used the word "persons." Not until 1868, with the passage of the Fourteenth Amendment, was the word "male" used for the first time, and then only in conjunction with some supplementary enforcement language. "Divine guidance" had led the framers of the Constitution to "form a perfect equality for male and female," Woodhull wrote. Woodhull believed that the language the founding fathers used had been inspired by a special wisdom that the authors themselves may not have been aware of. Woodhull herself often felt "inspired" by wisdom she did not fully comprehend. She printed the entire Constitution in the *Weekly,* so that readers could judge the merits of her argument. Her editorial was innovative, strong, and provocative. The *New York Commercial Advertiser* declared itself impressed by the "brass" of her assertion.

Since the first issue of the *Weekly,* Woodhull had been saying that suffrage was a civil right of all citizens; that women were citizens as surely as men, since they were required as citizens to pay the same taxes. She added to this the argument that Virginia Minor of Missouri initially had made at the 1869 convention, that the Fourteenth Amendment had established women's right to vote when it stated, "All persons born or naturalized in the United States, and subject to the jurisdiction thereof, are citizens of the United States . . . No state shall make or enforce any law which shall abridge the privileges or immunities of citizens."

Even John A. Bingham of Ohio, chairman of the House Judiciary Committee, who was the author of the Fourteenth Amendment, became convinced that his wording bore within it "a richer burden of meaning than he had meant to freight it with." When Woodhull took her claim to him, he first said, "Madam you are not a citizen." Then she pointed out to him his own phraseology, "All persons born or naturalized . . . are citizens." He put on his spectacles to read the words from his own hand a second time. Finally he reluctantly acknowledged the merit of what she said.

In the December 31 issue of the *Weekly,* distributed on December 17, Woodhull added the argument that states ratifying the Fourteenth or Fifteenth Amendment had, by that action, nullified any prior state legislation forbidding women to vote. Bit by bit, she put her unconventional case together.

Woodhull made her next move under Butler's guidance. On Monday December 19, she petitioned Congress to pass "enabling legislation" to confirm her interpretation. On Wednesday December 21, "The Memorial of Victoria C. Woodhull" was presented to the Senate by Senator John S. Harris of Louisiana and to the House by Congressman Julian of Indiana, author of the now-dead Sixteenth Amendment bill. Harris and Julian requested that the Memorial be referred to the Senate and House judiciary committees. Butler's timing was clever, for most members of Congress were preoccupied with the Christmas holidays. He may have written the Memorial, for it included none of Woodhull's rhetorical flourishes.

As submitted to Congress, the Memorial concentrated its argument on the Fifteenth Amendment, saying that since its adoption, no state or territory had "passed any law to abridge the right of any citizen to vote . . . on account of sex or otherwise," and that laws adopted prior to the amendment were "void and of no effect." Most significantly, the Memorial requested that Congress pass the additional legislation necessary to enforce this interpretation of the Fifteenth Amendment, "such laws as in the wisdom of Congress shall be necessary and proper for carrying into execution the right vested by the Constitution in the citizens of the United States to vote, without regard to sex." Such an act of Congress would make the amendment binding in all states, whether they had ratified the Fifteenth Amendment or not. Butler, as a member of the House Judiciary Committee, had participated in the enactment of the Enforcement Bill of May 31, 1870, which had been designed to end intimidation of black voters after the passage of the Fifteenth Amendment. He was following the same precedent here, this time to guarantee voting rights to women through the same Fifteenth Amendment.

The Woodhull-Butler collaboration produced a remarkable new direction for the suffrage movement. Woodhull couldn't have succeeded without Butler's adroit political tactics, and he wouldn't have persevered without her persuasive influence. She spent that Christmas Day in Washington, so Butler's Christmas was not a lonely one, despite the absence of his wife and sons. Woodhull returned to New York for New Year's Day, to receive callers in the accepted New York tradition, but she was soon back in Washington.

The suffragists were also arriving in force. Another convention was to meet in Washington on Thursday, January 11. Isabella Beecher Hooker was considered to be its "leading spirit," and she later wrote a wonderfully gossipy account of the events surrounding this convention and Woodhull's impact on them.

Hooker was unaware of Woodhull and Butler's activities before Christmas. "When I got to Washington at the end of the month [Woodhull] had been there quietly but persistently at work," she wrote. "I found her respected and listened to, by such men and women as Mr. Julian and his wife, Laura Giddings, Senator Pomeroy, Mrs. Griffing, Judge Woodward of Pennsylvania . . . and twenty more members I can't stop to name—and there was not one word of scandal about her among them but on the contrary profound admiration and respect."

From Butler and this Washington inner circle, Woodhull had secured a commitment to let her present her Memorial in person before the House Judiciary Committee while the suffrage convention was in session. The idea was pure genius. She would become the first woman to address a congressional committee at that level, and she would do it when virtually everybody interested in suffrage would be in Washington. As the Democrats whispered, she would surely steal "the victory and the credit."

Accounts of reactions among the suffragists vary. Most of them hadn't heard of Woodhull's coup until they read about her imminent appearance at the Capitol in the Washington papers on January 11. Stanton did not attend the convention, apparently convinced that further efforts in Washington were useless at that time. Anthony arrived at the last minute, interrupting her schedule of speaking engagements to be present.

Hooker met Woodhull, and they talked for two hours. Hooker marveled later that Woodhull had "actually feared us." She commented on the power of what might be called Woodhull's star quality. She impressed Hooker "profoundly, and in a manner I could never describe, with the conviction that she was heaven sent for the rescue of woman from her pit of subjection. She has ever since appealed to me as then—as a womanly woman, yet less a woman than an embodiment of pure thought, soul and reason—a prophetess, full of visions and messages to the people which it would be woe unto her to refrain from proclaiming, even though martyrdom were sure to follow. She is an idealist—a visionary perhaps—but she is without consciousness of self and absolutely without selfishness. Her standard of benevolence is unapproachable to most of us—and she has lived up to it."

The suffragists cancelled their session the next morning so delegates could hear what Woodhull would tell Congress. Hooker was staying with Senator Pomeroy. Various attempts to discredit Woodhull as "a shyster from Wall Street who had nominated herself for president," caused the senator to offer some practical advice: "Men could never work in a political party if they stopped to investigate each member's antecedents and associates. If you are going into a fight, you must accept every help that offers." His advice carried the day.

The committee room was crowded Thursday morning. Bingham, the chairman, was nominally in charge, but Butler ran the show. Other committee members present were Burton C. Cook of Illinois, John A. Peters of Maine, Ulysses Mercur of Pennsylvania, William Loughridge of Iowa, Michael C. Kerr of Indiana, Giles W. Hotchkiss of New York, and Stephen W. Kellogg of Connecticut. For the suffragists, Hooker had rounded up, in addition to Susan B. Anthony, Lillie Devereux Blake of New York, Reverend Olympia Brown of Connecticut, Paulina Wright Davis of Rhode Island, Josephine Griffing, and Belva Lockwood of Washington, D.C. Butler also "allowed" a number of newspaper correspondents to attend.

And of course Tennie was there, having come from New York to share this victory with her sister. She sat quietly, almost demurely, her face impressing Hooker with the look of "a sweet innocent child."

Bingham opened the meeting promptly at ten, and Woodhull stood before a significant public audience for the first time in her 32 years. "Her voice trembled with emotion and she started hesitantly almost gasping for breath," one suffragist remembered. She also recalled Tennie's "look of prayerful sympathy" for her sister's discomfort, describing it as "one of the most beautiful expressions" she had ever seen on a human face. Woodhull's voice gained strength, and her hesitant beginning seemed to make her subsequent reading more effective.

First she offered her claims that the Constitution made no distinction of sex, that women were citizens and so had the rights of citizens to vote, that "the citizen who is taxed should also have a voice in the subject matter of taxation." Then she made an impassioned plea for fair play for women, a ringing call for recognition of the moral rightness of her position. Woodhull's "inspiration" had found a voice:

> Women constitute a majority of this country—they
> hold vast portions of the nation's wealth and pay a
> proportionate share of the taxes. They are entrusted
> with the most vital responsibilities of society; they
> bear, rear and educate men; they train and mold their
> characters; they inspire the noblest impulses in men;

they often hold the accumulated fortunes of a man's life for the safety of the family and as guardians of the infants, and yet they are debarred from uttering any opinion by public vote . . . when they propose to carry a slip of paper with a name upon it to the polls, [men] fear them . . .

The American nation in its march onward and upward, cannot publicly choke the intellectual and political activity of half of its citizens by narrow statutes. The will of the entire people is the true basis of republican government, and a free expression of that will by the public vote of all citizens, without distinctions of race, color, occupation or sex, is the only means by which that will can be ascertained. As the world has advanced into civilization and culture; as mind has risen in its dominion over matter; as the principle of justice and moral right has gained sway . . . as the might of right has supplanted the right of might, so have the rights of women become more fully recognized . . .

It was reserved for our great country to recognize by constitutional enactment that political equality of all citizens which religion, affection, and common sense should have long since accorded; it was reserved for America to sweep away the mist of prejudice and ignorance, and that chivalric condescension of a darker age, for in the language of Holy Writ, "The night is far spent, the day is at hand, let us therefore cast off the work of darkness and let us put on the armor of light. Let us walk honestly as in the day.

Further legal arguments followed; appropriate precedents were cited. The option of allowing the courts to decide the issue was powerfully expressed. Butler's guidance of the argument was clear, although the rhetoric now was mostly Woodhull's.

Woodhull closed by offering the grace notes a sage petitioner was expected to bring to a congressional request: "Believing firmly in the right of citizens to freely approach those in whose hands their destiny is placed under the Providence of God, your memorialist has frankly, but humbly, appealed to you, and prays that the wisdom of Congress may be moved to action in this matter."

Then she smiled, bowed gracefully, and resumed her seat.

In the pause that followed, Anthony said, with force and humor, "Now I wish, General Butler, that you would say 'contraband' for us." And everyone had a good laugh.

Other speeches were made that day, but to the *New York Herald,* at least, Woodhull had captured the committee. She had presented the case, one of the committee members acknowledged, "in as good a style as any congressman could have done." No longer chiding the suffragists for their divisions, the *Herald* announced, "There is no disguising the fact that the women suffrage advocates are making headway in Washington."

Amid hurrahs, Woodhull was carried off to Lincoln Hall to present her address to the entire suffrage convention.

Even Horace Greeley's antisuffrage *Tribune* covered the event. Scanning the horizon for a new star, the paper said, "All the past efforts of Miss Anthony and Mrs. Stanton sink to insignificance beside the ingenious lobbying of the new leader and her daring declaration . . . Mrs. Victoria C. Woodhull and her sister were the chief ornaments of the Convention."

Isabella Beecher Hooker agreed. Woodhull "alone of all the women in the United States succeeded in getting a hearing . . . out of a dead Congress," she said. "This woman is a born queen, and I owe her the allegiance of my heart." In the days that followed, word spread, attributed to no less a source than Anthony, that Woodhull was being seen now, even in the White House, "whispering in the president's ear."

The president was considered a populist. Born in Woodhull's home state of Ohio, he came from the American heartland. The electorate had endowed him with an authenticity to which Woodhull could respond. She had paved her way to the White House with more than the poetry of Nellie Grant. An editorial in the *Weekly* earlier that month had flattered the president, saying: "He stands as uncorruptible in his simple honesty, his directness of purpose, his pure integrity . . . [and anyone who believes the contrary] should receive the scorn and contempt of every honest mind throughout the country."

Whether it was the flattery, curiosity, or simply a pragmatic eye on the wives of the voters, Grant succumbed. Woodhull received an invitation to the White House. Doorkeepers, in the blue military uniforms the Union general had brought with him to the capital, promptly ushered her into a crowded anteroom warmed by a coal fire. The smell of fresh paint confirmed that Mrs. Grant's reported renovations had begun. But eastern elegance had to coexist with western habits. The floor and carpet were already spotted with the unmistakable brown of fresh tobacco stains.

When Woodhull entered the president's office, the poisonous aroma of the president's famous black cigar assaulted her well before she caught sight of him slouched, as was his habit, over the heavy oak arms of his chair. Light streamed into the room from long windows. Grant leaned forward to put out his cigar, and the gray smoke crossed and silvered as it drifted up toward the ceiling.

A reticent man, the president politely stood to greet Woodhull, motioning her to his own chair. He said, in his brusque way, perhaps intending to flirt, "Some day you will occupy that chair." Woodhull told friends later that she believed him, that she *would* occupy his chair as the first woman president of the country. Grant, in her view, had been directed by some higher power to deliver a special message to her.

In his inaugural address the president had supported the Fifteenth Amendment guaranteeing voting rights to blacks. To date, he had sidestepped the issue of suffrage for women. Reputed to distrust reformers, he had revealed his own suffrage plan to Mrs. Grant, "I would give each married woman two votes. Then both husband and wife would be represented at the polls without there being any divided families on the subject of politics," he said.

During their meeting, the president acknowledged to Woodhull that the suffrage movement was right and just and deserved to succeed. Then, the audience was over.

On leaving the White House, Woodhull was vague about the details of her brief exchange with the president. And she continued to be reticent about their meeting. But she believed the president would take a position favorable to her cause, and that he could be counted on to hold it. "The president is with us," she said later.

Grant's support seemed reconfirmed when Woodhull learned that Mrs. Grant had joined her cause. Again it was Anthony who spread the news. She wrote Woodhull a letter saying, "And so Mrs. Grant has filed in. Let them [all] come."

Elizabeth Cady Stanton was more cautious. She wrote to Woodhull to offer her support, but said she suspected a "Republican dodge."

The real test of Grant's support lay with the reluctant chairman of the House Judiciary Committee, John A. Bingham. It was he who had said to Woodhull, in all sincerity, "Madam you are not a citizen." He eventually agreed to her appearance before his committee, but all indications were that he would report unfavorably on her Memorial. Woodhull still hoped that the influence of Grant's office would bring Bingham around.

Her optimism was misplaced. Bingham's report for the majority of the committee denied Woodhull's petition and recommended that a resolution discharging the committee from further consideration of the subject be passed. If the right of female citizens to suffrage was vested by the Constitution, he said, that right could be established by the courts. No Woodhull bill would come out of the House Judiciary Committee.

General Benjamin Butler, loyal to Woodhull, issued an able minority report in her support. The president said nothing. He appeared to have found in her Memorial no more than an opportunity to pay lip service to women's suffrage. He apparently hoped that the issue would just go away. Unless new measures were found to bring it back to life, the Memorial was headed for the same certain death in the Judiciary Committee as the proposed Sixteenth Amendment.

The president dropped instantly in Woodhull's esteem. She agreed to discuss her feelings in an interview published by Charles Gibson Dana's *New York Sun*. Dana didn't like Grant, and the *Sun* may have twisted her statements into a more negative indictment of the president than she intended, for the words attributed to her run contrary to her usually tactful manner toward powerful men. But then Grant was no longer a man who could be trusted or put to good use.

> [President Grant] has got so many . . . weak men in his Cabinet who control him that he is afraid to do what he knows to be right . . . Politically the administration is throughout weak and corrupt . . . We would be glad to have the president's assistance because he is president; but he knows very well that we don't care for him and mean to depose him. If he had done what he knew to be right at the outset we would

have sustained him, and he would have been strong today; but his weakness and cowardice have been his ruin.

Though Grant had failed her on suffrage, he had acknowledged her White House ambitions. For that, she would always be fond of him. But on suffrage, she would have to go her own way.

11
The Woodhull

*F*rustration only stimulated Woodhull's imagination. If Republicans and Democrats thought they could thwart her, she would form her own third force. Her idea quickly spilled out on the front page of the *Weekly*.

COSMO-POLITICAL PARTY.
NOMINATION FOR PRESIDENT OF THE U.S. IN 1872.
VICTORIA C. WOODHULL
SUBJECT TO RATIFICATION OF
THE NATIONAL CONVENTION

read one set of headlines above a story reporting that "a new party and a new platform is proposed for the consideration of women and men."

Woodhull based the new independent party on her Memorial. In moving away from a Sixteenth Amendment and toward a "declaratory act," Woodhull had taken the position that voting was no longer a privilege granted to women. It was a constitutional right they possessed as citizens, a right they had been denied. If Congress, through Bingham's committee, wouldn't recognize that right, she would go to the full House of Representatives. If turned down there, she would go directly to the people.

Woodhull repeated her arguments on suffrage in the *Weekly*, meticulously delineating the steps she had attempted within the existing political party machinery. Though unsuccessful, they justified her new initiative. As an added measure, the *Weekly* printed a Memorial from Claflin to the New York State Legislature. It mirrored Woodhull's, and confronted the established system at the state level in New York.

The memorialist who had "humbly appealed" to the "wisdom of

Congress" spoke now with a new tone tinged with exasperation. "The male citizen has no more right to deprive the female citizen of the free, public, political expression of opinion than the female citizen has to deprive the male citizen," she said. Her rhetoric was taking on a sharper edge.

As details of Bingham's negative majority report came out, Woodhull took him to task. She recognized his strategy of deferring to the courts for what it was: evasion. "The point is shirked," she said. "An attempt will be made in the House to shut off all debate upon the question."

When the full report became available and she had had a chance to examine it thoroughly, she confessed to "not a little surprise at [its] character."

> I am satisfied that no unprejudiced person can read it and not become convinced that all citizens, whether they are male or female, should be protected in the exercise of equal rights. It cannot be said of Mr. Bingham's report that it evinces either remarkable clearness or remarkable correctness. In fact it put one in mind of nothing so much as a bull which has determined by sheer force to butt an object out of the way . . . This is perhaps as cool a dodging of an issue as ever was made in the halls of Congress.

She awaited the minority report by Butler, expected at the end of January, and when it came out she said his "manliness" stood out in sharp contrast to Bingham's pusillanimity

Woodhull then took another extraordinary step. She requested an opportunity to make her argument, in person, to the entire House of Representatives in the House Chamber. She believed she had 79 votes committed to her Memorial by members of the House, and she hoped to add to that total with a personal plea. But Bingham could block Woodhull's access to the House. Butler, perhaps abashed by the aggressiveness of his protégé, was unwilling or unable to intervene, and Woodhull's request was denied.

Butler's minority report had limited itself to supporting a declaratory act admitting women as voters in contests for election to the House of Representatives. After Woodhull's request to address the House was denied, she took issue with Butler, now chiding him for his timidity. In the *Weekly* she proposed to the House the wording for her own declaratory act, a more forthright, less ambiguous statement: "Resolved, by the House of Representatives, that the right of suffrage is one of the inalienable rights of citizens of the United States, subject to regulation by the states, through equal and just laws. That this right is included in 'privileges of citizens of the United States' which are guaranteed by the 14th Amendment to the Constitution of the United States; and that women citizens, who are otherwise qualified by the laws of the state where they reside, are competent voters for Representatives in Congress."

Woodhull hired Lincoln Hall, the largest auditorium in Washington, for February 16,1871, and prepared to take her case directly to the people. She enlisted the help of most of the suffragist leaders. Isabella Beecher Hooker appeared as a cosponsor of the event, though Woodhull paid the bills. In an elegant typeface, tickets to the event announced the topic as "Constitutional Equality, a Legal and Moral View." Woodhull and Hooker gave themselves equal billing, though Woodhull's name appeared first on the ticket.

Suffrage leaders joined Woodhull and Hooker on the platform. They had accepted Woodhull pragmatically, for her money and her success in reawakening interest in suffrage. Now they were ready to associate their names with her. Woodhull's sharp words to the powerful Washington politicians excited suffrage admiration. The new assertive attitude she had brought to suffrage, "the consciousness of a right unjustly withheld [that] must be pronounced and admittted," as Josephine Griffing, the group's Washington secretary, wrote, appealed to these women emotionally as well as intellectually.

Newspapers reported the audience to be the largest ever at Lincoln Hall. Long before the lecture started, all the seats were taken. Ushers searched futilely for extra chairs. Latecomers stood elbow to elbow on both sides as well as at the back of the auditorium. The sound of many voices built a sense of anticipation.

Butler was to introduce Woodhull, but by eight o'clock he still had not appeared. Suffragist leader Paulina Wright Davis, seated beside Woodhull on the platform, stepped in to replace him. Advancing to the footlights, she said, "The objective of this lecture is to present to you concisely the legal and moral arguments in favor of enfranchising one half the citizens of the United States . . . If neither of the parties existing now are ready to take this issue, which is the only live one of the day, a new one will spring up that will grind these to powder." Davis spoke in the new aggressive suffrage language. "The one demand is for equal justice," she said, "not reformed laws, not crumbs and favors, but equal justice." She then introduced Woodhull as "the first woman to see clearly and present persistently the demand for suffrage as a right plainly guaranteed by the Constitution and its amendments."

Woodhull sat through Davis's remarks with "perfect composure," the *Washington Chronicle* reported. "Those who knew her face saw at a glance that nothing but a tremendous effort of will enabled her to maintain that demeanor." When she started to speak her face was "perfectly colorless, and she was obliged to stop an instant between each sentence to gain strength to go on to the next." Hooker stepped to Woodhull's side and put an arm around her, "involuntarily" called to her aid, Hooker said later.

In a voice that could barely be heard, Woodhull began, "I have no doubt it seems strange to many of you that a woman should appear before the people in this public manner for political purposes." Her voice grew stronger. "And it is due both to you and myself that I should give my reasons for so doing . . . I am of that portion of the people who are denied the rights of citizens." She reviewed her Memorial: "When I was before Congress I said to Mr. Bingham, 'I want to vote because I am a citizen.' He replied, 'you are not a citizen.' 'What am I?' I asked. 'You are a woman,' he said. I told him I knew that before I came to Washington." She was talking not about a privilege, but about a right, Woodhull said.

> I hold then that, in denying me this right without my having forfeited it, departure is made from the principles of [the] Constitution . . . If the free man pays no taxes without representation, how is it that the free woman is compelled to do so? Not long since I was notified by a United States tax officer that if I did not pay a certain tax the government had imposed upon me, my property would be levied upon and sold for that purpose. Is this tyranny . . . ? I am subject to tyranny. I am taxed in every conceivable way. For publishing a paper I must pay—for engaging in the banking and brokerage business I must pay—of what

it is my fortune to acquire each year, I must turn over a certain per cent . . .

I do now claim that I am, equally with men, possessed of the right to vote, and if no others of my sex claim it, I will stand alone . . .

Therefore, I would have Congress, in the pursuit of its duty, to enforce the Constitution by appropriate legislation, pass a declaratory act plainly setting forth the right of all citizens to vote . . .

If Congress refuses to legislate appropriately in the matter, every woman who desires to vote should take all the steps required . . . to become qualified . . . If they do not wish to vote, I alone, however, will stand and reiterate my claim. My paper, *Woodhull and Claflin's Weekly,* is devoted to this and every glorious and ennobling cause. But I do not believe I stand alone, and could we but get forwarded to Congress the names of those women who wish to vote the question would be speedily settled.

Woodhull held the attention of the huge crowd for an hour and a quarter, and the response was vocal and positive. "Mrs. Woodhull has opened her presidential campaign with a very effective speech," the *New York Herald* announced the next day. "The parts of the speech hitting hard at Bingham, and the members of Congress who refused to allow Mrs. Woodhull to have the Hall of the House for her speech, were loudly applauded. Altogether it was a great success." We "listened with rapt attention to the masterly argument," said the *Chronicle.* Her speech was "applauded throughout," said the *Washington Sunday Gazette.* A "brave, eloquent and unanswerable argument," said the *Washington Daily Republican.*

After Woodhull had bowed in thanks to her audience, Hooker prepared to speak on the moral view of the question. Fairly new to the lecture platform, she appeared "graceful and ladylike" to the *New York Tribune,* and had "developed a wonderful aplomb since her first appearance last winter."

But the audience called for Butler. He had finally arrived while Woodhull was speaking, and, with his son-in-law, Senator Ames of Mississippi, had taken his seat on the platform. Watching the progress of Woodhull's lecture, he had looked extremely happy, and the *Herald* speculated that he seemed to be thinking of the excellent chance he would have of being elected president when women could vote, provided Woodhull was not a candidate. Hooker "graciously" yielded her time to Butler, and he gave, in his "peculiarly terse and vivid manner," according to the *Chronicle,* "a summary of his minority report of the Judiciary Committee on the Woodhull Memorial."

Whatever reservations had delayed Butler's arrival evaporated as he had listened to his protégé speak. Afterward he told Woodhull, as she remembered it years later, "You are going to become a great orator." He passed along his advice on public speaking. She remembered his saying, "Put that glass of water down. Never touch it while you are speaking." And when he learned she had no printed copy of her speech available for the press, he advised her for the future to have her speeches set in type and distributed in advance of her appearances. (Butler was known for printing his speeches with parenthetical pronouncements of "prolonged cheers" and "extended audience applause," well before the day of delivery.) Woodhull seems to have followed his advice, for although no copy of her first speech has survived exactly as delivered, her subsequent speeches were regularly printed in advance and made available to the press. Eventually they were sold directly to the public at lecture halls and through the *Weekly.*

Congratulations surrounded Woodhull. Elizabeth Cady Stanton wrote, "We have waited 6,000 years, and the time has fully come to seize the bull by the horns, as you are doing in Washington and Wall Street, and show the John Binghams that we who pay millions in taxes every year propose to be something more than members of the state." Susan B. Anthony set off on a lecture tour supporting Woodhull's Memorial with a speech she titled "The New Situation."

Once again, Woodhull took her case directly to the people, this time in the pages of the *Weekly.* As she had in her Washington speech, she appealed to readers to petition Congress for a declaratory law:

> Everyone should feel that he or she is a leader and should set about the good work; should draw a petition and sign it themselves and get everybody else whom it is possible to do the same, and then forward it either direct to their representative in Congress or

to Mrs. Josephine Griffing, Secretary of the National
Suffrage Association, Washington, D.C., who will see
everything of this kind properly attended to . . . A
million names should show Congress . . .

Not only must these petitions flow from the people
upon Congress so as to overwhelm it, but the same
power should be brought to bear upon the legislature
of every state . . . friends of the cause should act in
concert. Their real power has never been felt.

A sample petition was printed in the *Weekly,* appearing on the editorial page each week.

Hooker composed her own declaration and pledge. The paper
printed and endorsed it along with Woodhull's. Hooker asked
women to send their signatures to Washington to be entered in a volume of petitions kept by Griffing for that purpose, and thanked
Woodhull for the gift of "three grand books for record keeping."

By mid-March Woodhull had sent out 5,000 copies of her Memorial to interested readers and, on Mrs. Griffing's behalf, she promised
to print and send any number of the Judiciary Committee's majority
and minority reports. It was a substantial media campaign. In a rash
moment, Woodhull had volunteered to donate $10,000 to the suffrage cause, or so it was reported. She was quite capable of making
such an impulsive gesture, and she later claimed to have met the
obligation by printing and distributing thousands of the reports on
her Memorial.

Woodhull disappeared from Washington but left, said Hooker, "a
most enviable position behind." In March 1871, Woodhull spoke at
Cooper Institute in New York, at the Brooklyn Academy of Music, at
the Academy of Music in Philadelphia, and at the Boston Music Hall.
Newpapers and audiences were lavish with their praise. Even the
conservative *New York Times,* which shunned "all fantastic schemes
of reform" and disapproved of Woodhull's presentation to the Judiciary Committee, now reported that she had been loudly cheered at
Cooper Institute and that the hall could have been filled twice over.

Everyone acknowledged Woodhull's power as a speaker. When she
stood before an audience, her beauty aroused energy; her voice—
strong but feminine—drew everyone in. Her physicality, which included a strong measure of sexuality, connected with her listeners.

The nineteenth century word for it was "magnetism." Woodhull magnetized the crowds.

It was as if her entire life had prepared her for this moment. Whatever the limits of her education, they were irrelevant when she spoke. In her early experience, true wisdom had come from personal insight or inspiration, as she called it, and the spoken word. Her mother, who couldn't read, had not sat beside her at bedtime with a book in her hands. She had told the little girl tales. The Methodist preachers Victoria had listened to also practiced oral traditions. They didn't concern themselves with doctrine or intellectual analysis; they transmitted the fire of the Scriptures through the spoken word. Over time, Woodhull would pay lip service to the values of a more lettered society but, consciously or unconsciously, she would hold to her own approach. Speaking represented the excitement of life.

Woodhull was often the first woman public speaker that many women in her audience had seen. She had scoffed at suffrage tea parties. But the talk, talk, talk of suffrage meetings offered its own kind of consciousness raising, and now her lectures added their challenge to women's political consciousness. Woodhull believed her visibility as a "representative woman" empowered all women, and believing helped make it so.

Already, she had outstripped in celebrity and political influence the suffragists whose attention she had struggled to win. Paulina Wright Davis began introducing her as the Joan of Arc of the suffrage movement. As her earliest supporter, the *Herald,* put it, "She seems to be the head and front of the movement now, having pushed the others aside, who never could manage to stir up public enthusiasm and enlist prominent politicians in the cause as Mrs. Woodhull has done."

Preparations were under way for another suffrage meeting in May. People were already calling it "The Woodhull" convention.

12
The Great Secession Speech

On May 8, 1871, as the suffragists were gathering in New York for their convention, Woodhull spoke before the Reform Labor League at Cooper Institute. Her ostensible purpose was to obtain support for suffrage, but she used the occasion to present the issue in the context of a broader, "humanitarian" reform program. She was starting to think of her presidential ambitions as more than a "flag" for women; she was laying the groundwork for bringing two groups with humanitarian goals in common—the suffragists and the labor reformers—into the new political party she would lead.

Woodhull dazzled the labor reformers. She ranged far beyond the suffrage issues of her previous public speeches. She spoke in detail about the evils of the existing political parties and their allied special interests, particularly land-grabbing schemes, railroad monopolies, excessive profits of national banks, the corrupt civil service, and the resulting "unequal distribution of material possessions."

"I tell you the first principles of life have been utterly lost sight of," she said, "and we are floundering about in the great ocean of material infidelity . . . A party which would become successful and remain in power must be . . . firm in the advocacy of all growth and reform . . . All sectionalism, all favoritism, all specialism must be swallowed in the greater interests of the whole."

The next day the *Times* reported that Woodhull's speech had abounded with extracts from government reports, library quotations, and statistical tables, and had dealt with moral, social, and political questions of vital importance to the human family. The paper conveyed the image of a speaker well versed in a wide range of issues and reforms, a leader whose practical and philosophical ideas were worthy of attention. This favorable picture of Woodhull greeted the suffragists as they picked up their morning papers.

All through that spring Woodhull had been preparing a move to broader ground. Though her speeches continued to discuss suffrage, the *Weekly* had shifted its emphasis to other reform issues, and to Woodhull herself, calling her an "embodiment of the movement." Woodhull's declaration for president continued to run on the front page of the paper, where it had appeared every week since January, a "continual warning that some woman will be the next president."

The suffragists, nevertheless, remained essential to Woodhull's success, and she worked hard to forge alliances. During her spring speaking tour, she sought out suffrage leaders in each city she visited, wishing to become personally acquainted with them. She made sure they received complimentary tickets to her lectures. And in her conversations with them she introduced the subject of broader reform.

Woodhull felt confident of Lucretia Mott's support. The "Quaker gentlewoman" who was "first and foremost in everyone's opinion," had invited Woodhull to dinner in Philadelphia. Though senior among the suffragists, Mott was still open to new ideas and was interested in Woodhull's proposal to form a new political party. Woodhull was grateful for Mott's broadmindedness. She later wrote Mott, "You won my heart under peculiarly impressive circumstances, which have ever caused a sort of reverence to fill my soul for you. I felt that of all women who seemed to understand me somewhat, you understood me best . . . Your affectionate would-be daughter."

Woodhull also met Mott's influential family, her sister Martha Coffin Wright, and Mott's daughter and son-in-law, Maria and Edward Davis. "We were all charmed with her beauty and grace and knowledge and enthusiasm and were not half ready to have her go," Wright wrote afterward to her daughter Ellen Wright Garrison in Boston, who was married to William Lloyd Garrison II, son of the great abolitionist. "She [Woodhull] said both parties were utterly corrupt and a new one, Labor and Woman Suffrage, would be formed. She was full of enthusiasm and faith in the coalition."

Paulina Wright Davis of Providence, Rhode Island, had become Woodhull's strongest ally. After her quick thinking, when Butler had failed to arrive on time, had rescued Woodhull's first speaking engagement, she and Woodhull had become personal friends. Woodhull had written in April, "A thousand thanks for your evidences of love and solicitude. I did not know there could be such unselfish devotion, and I have more immediate faith in humanity for knowing you."

A more subtle element also contributed to this friendship. The two women shared a common interest in spiritualism. Woodhull's strongest bonds evolved with those who, like herself, lived by intuitive convictions. Many women of the day who dared to be different fortified themselves, as Woodhull did, with a subjective and religious spiritualism. The use of code words such as "intuition" created what might be called a secret sisterhood among them. The word "humanitarian" carried another special meaning, conveying the nonmaterial values of spiritualism. The secret sisterhood crossed socioeconomic boundaries and included bluebloods such as Davis as well as those, like Woodhull, from more humble backgrounds. These women drew confidence from the conviction that they were destined to achieve important goals, despite the discouraging realities of the man's world in which they lived. But knowing that their beliefs in spiritualism could subject them to ridicule, they were careful about sharing them. The sisterhood remained behind the scenes, holding informal power within the suffrage movement. It provided a ready-made alliance and strong lasting friendships for Woodhull. Where suffrage leaders stood in relation to the spiritualistic sisterhood would, over time, largely determine where they stood in relation to Woodhull.

Davis, nearing 60, was tall, elegant, and still beautiful, though her golden hair and blue eyes had paled. One admirer described her gentle earnest manner as "graceful audacity." She had studied anatomy and physiology, and lectured on health reform, illustrating her talks with a mannequin imported from Paris. Some of her listeners went on to become the country's first women doctors. Having accompanied her husband, Thomas Davis, to Washington when he was elected to Congress in 1852 for a single term, she had also acquainted herself with the realities of politics.

For several years Davis had published *Una,* one of the first publications devoted to women's rights, and she was now putting out *New World,* which Woodhull supported with generous notices in the *Weekly.* The two women saw each other when they could, relaxed and gossiped together, always looking forward to their infrequent visits. They traded opinions on fashion ("the watch is too old-fashioned to make it desirable," Woodhull worried), health news ("I had a serious attack but am again revived. Colonel has been very sick for the last ten days, seriously so some of the time"), and suffrage bulletins ("I spoke by special invitation in Syracuse to a good audience. I made Mrs. Gage's acquaintance. She has some influence there and should be brought right, if possible. She is bitter on some of the old leaders"). Woodhull's letters to Davis were signed, "Your affectionate daughter," expressing both women's interpretation of the relationship.

More than any other established suffragist, Davis would support Woodhull's candidacy for president and her agenda for broad social reform for women. She wrote that suffrage alone "will not give women social equality—any more than it gives it to the Negro now; it is but a stepping stone." But the warm bond between Woodhull and Davis would soon be strained by a long separation. Crippled by rheumatic gout, Davis was leaving public life for a long trip abroad. Before her departure she promised Woodhull that "though I may be on the other side of the globe I shall come home to vote for you in 1872."

Elizabeth Cady Stanton, the acknowledged leader and most powerful personality in the suffrage movement, a woman in her prime at 56, supported Woodhull for pragmatic reasons. The two women had not yet met, though Woodhull had received several cordial letters from her. On February 20 Stanton had written, "I have watched the grand work inaugurated by you in Washington this winter with the deepest interest and fully agree with the position you so eloquently and logically maintained in your demand for 'a declaratory act.'" Stanton was not part of the spiritualistic sisterhood. She appears to have looked on spiritualism with a bemused and benevolent tolerance, accepting spiritualistic leanings as a harmless folly to which a number of her friends were subject.

Having lived through the struggles of *The Revolution* (the paper was now being edited by Laura C. Bullard and would be discontinued in February 1872), Stanton had concluded in her February 20 letter to Woodhull, "I read your journal with great pleasure. It is the ablest women's journal we have yet had, discussing, as it does, the great questions of national life." Woodhull looked forward to meeting Stanton at the May convention, and expected to be able to win her further support.

Though absent from the recent convention in Washington, Stanton had immediately recognized that Woodhull could be useful to the suffrage cause. She overlooked any elitist reservations she held about Woodhull in favor of Woodhull's talents and money. Stanton spread this attitude throughout the suffrage movement in private letters that were passed from hand to hand among the suffragists.

> I have thought much . . . of our dear Woodhull, and
> all the gossip about her, and come to the conclusion
> that it is a great impertinence in any of us to pry into
> her affairs . . . This is one of man's most effective en-

gines for our division and subjugation. He creates the public sentiment, builds the gallows, and then makes us hangman for our own sex. Women have crucified the Mary Wollstonecrafts, the Fanny Wrights, the George Sands, the Fanny Kembles of all ages, and now men mock us with the fact, and say we are ever cruel to each other. Let us end this ignoble record and henceforth stand by womanhood. If Victoria Woodhull must be crucified, let men drive the spikes and plait the crown of thorns.

Stanton's attitude created a groundswell of pro-Woodhull feeling for the convention.

Susan B. Anthony's support for Woodhull was more reserved. At 51, she was often portrayed as a vinegary old maid. In fact she was a vital woman with a merciless wit, unending energy, and rocklike strength of character. She had grown up on a farm near Rochester, New York, reared by Quaker parents who supported the abolition and temperance movements. At 30 she had left teaching to devote herself to the women's movement. Anthony was a first-rate organizer. While Stanton was the star, possessing a personal charm and popularity that Anthony lacked, she collected money, circulated petitions and tracts, and testified before legislatures. Anthony accepted second place willingly, loyally subsumed by the cause.

While on a lecture tour in support of what she was calling the "new and living gospel," Anthony wrote Woodhull from Kansas City. "Go ahead bright, glorious, young and strong spirit, and believe in the best hope and love and faith of S. B. Anthony . . . I have never in the whole 20 years good fight felt so full of life and hope . . . I am sure you and I, and all women who shall wish to, will vote for somebody—" but here Anthony stopped short of endorsing Woodhull and completed her sentence with the words "if not for Victoria C. Woodhull." Enthusiasm, quickly checked, prefigured the pattern of their relationship.

Anthony disdained spiritualism. She also adamantly opposed broad reform efforts, insisting over and over that the suffragists must give single-minded support to the issue of gaining the vote. Personality differences divided the two women as well. Anthony was willing to take second place to Stanton, but she would never willingly take second place to Woodhull.

Isabella Beecher Hooker, the suffragist who wrote so glowingly of Woodhull from Washington and had helped sponsor Woodhull's first speech, would become her most enduring friend among the suffragist leaders. Hooker found Woodhull sympathetic, because of the "spiritual" qualities she perceived in her. Hooker summed them up to her own satisfaction: Woodhull's "whole nature is spiritual in an uncommon degree," she said, and she had "visions inspired by spiritual influences" very much like Hooker's own. The flavor of her spiritualism can be found in a letter to Woodhull: "You were drawn to me . . . my dear friend, believe me, because it has been my blessed fortune to live near the heart of my dear Heavenly Father that something of his great tenderness has passed into my soul, and I too love all mankind with a great yearning love. This shines through word and look, I suppose, and souls are warmed and fed and sometimes they are led to feel, perhaps, that I could give them great peace and perpetual refreshment." If the secret sisterhood of spiritualism could be said to have a leader, it was Hooker.

A handsome woman of 49, with an imposing manner and striking eyes, Hooker was a new convert to suffrage. The Washington convention with Woodhull had strengthened her suffrage convictions. Hooker's straitened financial circumstances caused her frustration and anxiety and she constantly lamented the lack of funds for the suffrage cause as well. She had found Woodhull even more appealing when she discovered the stockbroker was a woman of wealth. She urged her friends to support "such a powerful woman" as Woodhull "both because of her own brain and heart and because of her command of money (a thing we have never had in our ranks before)."

As the convention neared, Woodhull hoped Hooker's support would help her silence her most outspoken enemies, Hooker's famous Beecher sisters. Catharine Beecher and Harriet Beecher Stowe opposed suffrage in general and Victoria Woodhull in particular. They did not attend suffrage conventions, but their opinions influenced women who did. The Beechers were blessed with a gift for words, whether from the pulpit, between the pages of a book, in newsprint, as letter writers, or simply in dinner party conversation. In 1871 alone there were two novels by Harriet Beecher Stowe, collections of sermons and lectures from Henry Ward Beecher, and a volume of advice from Catharine Beecher. Henry Ward Beecher, at 58, was the most famous of the six Beecher brothers, an immensely popular and effective preacher. His brothers, William, Edward,

Charles, Thomas, and James, like their father Lyman, were all preachers and authors. (One sister, Mary Perkins, had no public career.) Whatever the Beechers thought received extensive media exposure. A long-time family friend, Dr. Leonard Bacon of Yale, summed up their influence when he said, "This country is inhabited by saints, sinners, and Beechers."

Catharine, the eldest of the Beecher siblings, was a famous teacher and author. Almost 71, tall, angular, and imperious, she attacked the suffrage movement for destroying the family with free love, free divorce, and the avoidance of motherhood. She warned that suffrage would allow society to fall into the hands of the ignorant. Although there was no question in her mind that she was qualified to vote, she was not so sure about other women. Her sister, Isabella Hooker, had not been able to change her mind.

Woodhull had aggressively attacked Catharine Beecher in the *Weekly* for her anti-suffrage position, asking, "Is it not possible to drive Miss Beecher for very shame out of her unholy position? . . . She seeks . . . to deprive woman of her legal right to vote, . . . let these wagers of war against women's rights . . . these Miss Beecher women especially . . . remain under the bondage [of men], let them remain under it by all means, and lick the dirt from the naked feet of their oppressors; but do not let them interfere with that grand and sublime majority of noble women who prefer freedom and the full rights of American citizenship . . ." This attack set in motion a series of destructive encounters with the Beecher family.

Harriet Beecher Stowe was better known than Catharine. When President Abraham Lincoln said, on meeting Stowe, "So this is the little lady who made the big war," he expressed the widespread belief that Stowe's book, *Uncle Tom's Cabin,* had readied the country for the abolition of slavery.

Stowe stayed away from suffrage to avoid controversy because she had recently burned her fingers on scandal. When an unflattering biography of the poet Byron's wife appeared, almost ten years after Lady Byron's death, Stowe wrote in the *Atlantic Monthly* and in *Macmillan's Magazine* in London, "The True Story of Lady Byron's Life." She revealed that Byron had treated his bride cruelly and had eventually told her of his love affair with his half sister Augusta Leigh. Some Byron biographers believe Stowe's account was accurate and that Byron, in fact, married to conceal the affair, but no definitive evidence has ever been found. Outraged disbelief greeted Stowe's disclosures, and she was accused of being vile. Stowe's response was to amplify her charges in an 1870 book, *Lady Byron Vindicated*, but the publicity gave her a brush with disrepute that she found unbearable.

Elizabeth Cady Stanton had hoped that Stowe would do for suffrage what she had done for abolition, but when Stowe's new novel, *My Wife and I,* appeared as a serial in the *Christian Union,* it was immediately clear that Stowe was writing satire. Stowe's leading character, Mrs. Cerulean, presided over "New Dispensation Salons," and proposed "a simple remedy for the reconstruction of society." Give the "affairs of the world into the hands of women . . . the superior . . . the divine sex." Stowe, mocking Woodhull and her "at homes," acknowledged in her preface that she had not met the original for Mrs. Cerulean, but she had heard her described. The author drew a far harsher caricature of a young woman, deliciously named Audacia Dangyereyes, who goes into men's business offices and virtually forces them to subscribe to her paper, as she tells them,

> "Call me Dacia for short. I don't stand on ceremony. Just look on me as another fellow. And now confess that you've been tied and fettered by those vapid conventionalities which bind down women till there is no strength in 'em. You visit in those false, artificial circles, where women are slaves, kept like canary birds in gilded cages . . . Now I'm a woman that not only dares say, but I dare do. Why hasn't a woman as much a right to go round and make herself agreeable to men, as to sit at home and wait for men to come and make themselves agreeable to her? I know you don't like this, I can see you don't . . . but I'm going to make you like me in spite of yourself. Come, now, be consistent with your principles; allow me my equality as a woman, a human being."

Making her opinions explicit, Stowe called Audacia a tramp. Tennie may have fumed at this epithet, but ironically Stowe's fictional suffragists are colorful, clever, and full of life, whereas her protagonists are dull and insipid. The *Christian Union* doubled its circulation while *My Wife and I* ran. Woodhull's *Weekly* commented simply that Stowe's book was "amusing readers" as it "arrays the Bible against the modern view of women's rights."

As Woodhull had hoped, Hooker attempted to play the peace-maker between her sisters and Woodhull, believing that they would be convinced of Woodhull's "purity and goodness" if they knew her. Shortly before the May convention, she persuaded Catharine to pay a call on Woodhull. The two women took a carriage ride in Central Park. Perhaps it was the soft breeze, or the fresh green of the trees, or Woodhull's charm and sympathy, but the two women appeared to have had a cordial conversation. Hooker reported to a friend: "My sister Catharine says she is convinced now that I am right and that Mrs. Woodhull is a pure woman . . . and ought to be treated with kindness . . ." Woodhull remembered that they talked about Henry Ward Beecher and his wife, Eunice, considered a "griffin," and Catharine Beecher had confided in Woodhull "how unhappy Henry Ward Beecher's home life was." Woodhull could take some satisfaction in Catharine's silence though she had to endure Stowe's satire.

Anna Dickinson was another detractor Woodhull hoped to silence as the convention approached. The young orator Woodhull had once hoped to emulate had become an outspoken critic. A suffrage supporter wrote Stanton that Dickinson "does not hesitate to give it as her opinion that Mrs. W. is an unprincipled woman . . . Anna Dickinson expressed surprise and much regret that Mrs. Stanton and Susan B. Anthony should cooperate with her in any way."

Stanton provided the defense Woodhull needed, pragmatic as always:

> All the women most interested in our cause feel that [Woodhull] is a valuable addition . . . Anna Dickinson [has never] thought enough of our movement to make a speech on our platform, and it ill becomes [her] to question the wisdom of Susan B. Anthony or myself in welcoming anyone to our ranks who is ready to share our labors.

Still hoping she might become the mediator of the two suffrage wings, Woodhull made what she called a "personal and private appeal" for unity. On the eve of the convention, she approached the Boston wing through the editor of the *Woman's Journal*. Her hopes proved unrealistic and she was rebuffed.

The New York wing, however, gave her support through the Washington Suffrage Committee, an organization formed to compile the signatures of women petitioning for a "declaratory act." Sarah

Stearns of Minneapolis offered a resolution so strong that it amazed even Hooker, who had not been present when the subject was discussed.

Stearns's words were printed by the *Tribune* May 10, 1871, the day before the convention started. "We honor Victoria C. Woodhull for her fine intellectual ability, her courage and independence of character, her liberality and high moral worth, and since every word, look and act impressed us with the conviction that she is profoundly in earnest, we feel that for this earnestness and fearlessness we, as women, owe her a debt of gratitude which we can only repay by working with and for her with our whole hearts."

On May 11, the convention was called to order in Apollo Hall. Woodhull sat on the platform in a place of honor between Stanton and Mott. The speakers of the day included Hooker, Davis, Mott, Anthony, Stanton and Woodhull, among others, but Woodhull's speech dominated the meeting. To the message she had been delivering since February, she now added some dramatic changes.

> I have had ample occasion to learn the true worth of present political parties . . . What do the Republican leaders care for the interests of the people? . . . They have prostituted . . . the whole power of the government to their own selfish purposes . . . Shall we turn to the Democratic party? . . . Can we expect anything better from them? . . . where they have the power their leaders do not hesitate to make the most use of it to their own aggrandizement.
>
> It is my conviction, arrived at after the most serious and careful consideration, that it will be equally suicidal for the Women Suffragists to attach themselves to either of these parties . . . If Congress refuse to listen to and grant what women ask, there is but one course left them to pursue . . .
>
> We will have our rights. We say no longer by your leave. We have besought, argued and convinced, but we have failed; and we will not fail.
>
> We will try you just once more. If the very next Congress refuse women all the legitimate results of citizenship; if they [refuse to pass] a proper declaratory act . . . then we give here and now, deliberate no-

tification of what we will do next . . . one year . . . from this day . . . we shall proceed to call another convention and to erect a new government . . .

We mean treason; we mean secession . . . we will overslaugh this bogus republic and plant a government [that] derive[s] its power from the consent of the governed.

The fired-up convention delegates called it Woodhull's "Great Secession Speech." With her emotionally assertive attitude, her demand for rights denied, her quality of impassioned determination, Woodhull became the fulcrum of the meeting. Her concept for broadening the reform efforts of the suffragists received an extended hearing. Davis read a series of "Woodhull resolutions" on broader reform goals, generalized statements that had the unmistakable flavor of Stephen Pearl Andrews's authorship ("The woman's movement means no less than the complete social as well as the political enfranchisement of mankind"). Lucretia Mott asked Woodhull to read her party platform, a document that had been published in the *Weekly*. The platform was another Andrews composition, but Woodhull added her own opening and closing remarks. The platform went well beyond suffrage, supporting Woodhull's new political party and calling for labor reform; regulation of special interests; nationalizing of railroads; and tax, prison, and civil-service reform.

Lucretia Mott proved to be a staunch Woodhull supporter throughout the convention, believing, as she said, that among the Quakers the larger issue all along had been "human rights." Woodhull wrote her later, "I scarcely know how to tell you how much I bless your dear self for the nobleness, kindness and love you have shown me . . . I never will prove unworthy of your esteem." In Quaker style she signed the letter, "Your affectionate daughter in truth." Mott replied, "Victoria, my heart and home are ever open to thee."

Paulina Wright Davis, too, gave Woodhull her full backing. She had just completed a pamphlet called "A History of the National Woman's Rights Movement." When she published the booklet later that year, she included Woodhull's "Great Secession Speech" as part of her history.

Elizabeth Cady Stanton and Woodhull finally became acquainted. During the convention, Stanton was among Woodhull's guests at 38th Street. Though Stanton declined to go so far as Davis and endorse Woodhull for president, she did say that she was willing to work outside the established political parties and willing to support the formation of a new reform party. She suggested the organization be called the People's Party. Always interested in a wide range of social reforms for women, Stanton said later, "I have worked 30 years for woman suffrage, and now I feel that suffrage is but the vestibule of woman's emancipation."

Wright wrote to her daughter in Boston that Woodhull had been "affectionately welcomed and listened to with the greatest interest." Her daughter replied, expressing the expected Boston reaction and the response of others who were not present to feel the mood, that Woodhull's "rebellion threat" seemed "absurd."

Although the Bostonians remained stony about Woodhull, the attitude of the New York press was almost universally positive. On May 12 the *Tribune* applauded "the lady whose intellectual ability and high moral worth we lately endorsed. For ourselves we toss our hats in the air for Woodhull. She has the courage of her own opinion."

Woodhull selected a costume she would wear as president of the United States, showing it briefly to an astonished reporter from the *New York Sun*. Pants of dark blue cloth reached to her knees and buckled over light blue stockings. They were topped by a dark blue tunic with a man's collar and a cravat. Her hair had been cut as short as a boy's. The reporter quipped, "Mrs. Woodhull, if you appear on the streets in that dress the police will arrest you."

"No they won't," she replied severely. "When I am ready to make my appearance in this dress, no police will touch me." The reporter interpreted her comment to mean that the president of the United States was above common arrest.

She also began polishing her handwriting, striving for presidential quality by imitating Blood's beautiful script. An autograph of hers from this time, generally accepted as her work, not Blood's, and sold as such by collectors over the years, is a perfect match for Blood's well-turned style.

The convention had given Woodhull a perfect forum. She had every reason to feel confident that she had broadened her public image from suffragist to humanitarian, and that many suffragists supported her new direction. She could count on them as she moved ahead with her presidential campaign.

13
Muckraking Days

Woodhull's political campaign was succeeding beyond even her best hopes. But while she was reaching her highest peaks of rhetoric, the ground was crumbling beneath her brokerage business.

Since Black Friday the sisters had been buying and selling gold. As Tennie put it, "For myself, I have at least one financial opinion, and that is that gold is cash; and as a consequence to have plenty of it is to be pretty nearly independent of everything and everybody." Her words made good copy for the *Herald,* but bad management policy. Woodhull, Claflin & Company had been speculating in gold on margin, a high-risk investment activity. The firm accepted accounts on margins of 10 percent, charged interest at "street rates," and charged commissions of one-eighth percent. These margin transactions were a common business practice of the time, but they were also more of a gamble than an investment. For more than a year, gold had been unstable, swinging widely at each new rumor of war in Europe. Woodhull, Claflin & Co. had been guessing wrong more often than right.

Colonel Blood, as the firm's manager, had the job of breaking the bad news to clients. Most of Blood's correspondence, at least the letters that have survived, served to inform clients of losses and to close out accounts. To one business client, Hudson and Hickey, he wrote, "We are sorry you are compelled to withdraw just now as we are always unwilling to close our customers out at a loss." The message to others was much the same. Could their account have been "held a few days longer it would have been a profit rather than a loss."

Blood handled the speculative transactions properly, issuing the appropriate paper work in a careful and timely fashion. But the records indicate that he placed inexperienced investors in the firm's high risk activities, a practice that raises questions about his judgment if not his ethics. For example, two women with no previous investing experience, a Mrs. Tucker and a Mrs. J. D'Taime, had entered into a gold-trading pool. The women seemed to have believed that the female ownership of the firm would protect them from losses. It did not.

The interests of Woodhull, Claflin & Company were intermingled with the interests of the *Weekly*. Blood wrote a financial column in the paper, factual reports of Wall Street activities written in his straightforward style that were intended, in part, to attract brokerage customers. He also opened the editorial pages to Woodhull, Claflin & Company clients. Mrs. Annie L. Swindell, a teacher with writing aspirations, did an article for the *Weekly* that appeared in September. It was no coincidence that she had opened a brokerage account at the same time.

Similarly, the business side of the paper mixed with the editorial side. Though no partnership contract survives, Blood's role at the paper seems to have mirrored his role at the brokerage firm, with one exception; he did not share the profits or losses. He managed day-to-day business operations, subject to Woodhull's or Claflin's approval of major decisions. He was conscientious and businesslike in a fast and loose era, but he considered the editorial and business interests of the paper to be one and the same. If, in the process, he made judgments that would appear ethically questionable today, his style of operation was common practice at the time.

On July 16 Blood wrote an editorial stating that women should be more involved in purchasing life insurance—a remarkably far-sighted concept. He announced plans to "praise the meritorious" insurers and "expose schemes." The articles that followed were intended, in part, to augment the paper's roster of insurance advertisers, and they did. To its original two advertisers, Hercules Mutual and Widows and Orphans, the *Weekly* added four more, North America Mutual, Government Security, the Ben Franklin Company, and Craftsmen's. By September 10, 1870, the *Weekly* was carrying almost half a page of insurance advertising each week. The threat to "expose schemes" undoubtedly helped the *Weekly* gain the new advertisers. Neither Woodhull nor Claflin seems to have challenged what they called "Blood's department".

The editorial pages of the *Weekly* would have benefited from more of Blood's innovations. With both Woodhull and Blood preoccupied, Stephen Pearl Andrews found himself with a free hand. Long-winded essays on social theories, free masonry, spiritualism, the "social issue"—meaning free love, and the licensing of prostitution—appeared under his byline. He rode his favorite hobby horses back and forth over the *Weekly*.

Blood took command of the paper and, just one step ahead of bankruptcy at Woodhull, Claflin & Company, the principals turned into crusaders against corruption.

On September 10, 1870, the *Weekly's* lead editorial was startling: "Frauds in Existing and in Projected Railroads—Their Forthcoming Complete Exposure." Woodhull seems to have found time for this project despite her other commitments; the language of this announcement is in her style:

> We entered upon the walks of money "change" to do a legitimate business in American securities. That business has been of vast extent and profitable to our clients. It opened to us unusual facilities and sources for correct information. The natural, the hereditary keen intelligence of our race and sex was brought with all its force upon the subject, and soon revealed the startling fact that frauds existed in many of the securities deemed first class and current upon the market. We were enabled to save many of our customers from serious losses. In doing this we discovered that larger, bolder and deeper frauds were contemplated by petroleum and shoddy bankers, who, like scum, had risen to the surface in boilings of the dishonest caldrons of war.
>
> We have employed the ablest detective talent of the country; this talent has closely and carefully watched the bankers, brokers, directors and officers of the existing and projected companies, and we are prepared with the names of each party, the description and extent of the frauds perpetrated, the swindles intended, the quantity or amount of bonds and shares in many cases which gratuitously and dishonestly went to each director, banker, Congressman, Governor and State Legislator. Each in their turn will be brought to light.

Woodhull called the exposé "The Mysteries and Romance of Fraud," anticipating the "curious interest" to be found in peeling back, layer by layer, hidden transactions, until the secret fraud lay exposed. She had selected a revealing title, for she, personally, had flirted with the romance of fraud. "More anon," she promised.

The would-be robber baroness of Woodhull, Claflin & Company reinvented herself as the watchdog of Wall Street, ready to call all "pseudo bankers" to account. Together she and Blood, with Claflin's concurrence, made an astute judgment: in a darkening financial climate, more could be gained by exposing rascals than by banking their dollars. Certainly there would be more readers for the paper in exposures—and more votes for Victoria Woodhull as well. It was not a move away from capitalism—yet. It was a move in favor of honest, fair capitalism.

For the first time the *Weekly* named a publisher, Walter Gibbon, so that Blood could be free to produce editorials week after week. "Railroad frauds humbug, cheat or swindle the rich, middle and laboring classes out of more money than is necessary to build and equip the road, leaving a clear profit to the rascals or leaving a debt so arranged that it will fall almost costless into their hands." An informed public could invest more wisely, the *Weekly* said. "Railroad milkers" beware, the paper threatened. "We shall lead where the truth points." Browsing today through the now brown and brittle pages of the newspaper, a reader is overwhelmed by the relentless details arduously collected and printed, issue after issue.

Names familiar and unfamiliar—the New York and Westchester County Railroad Company, the New York and Boston Railroad Company, the Pennsylvania Railroad Company, the West Shore Hudson River Railroad Company, the New York and Fort Lee Railroad Company, the Indianapolis, Bloomington and Western Railway—were examined for "effervescence" versus substance and found wanting. The Air-Line Railroad (the New Haven, Middletown and Willimantic) was chided for estimating its start-up costs at $3.5 million and then piling up at least a million more in overruns. "Ginger pop banking," snorted the *Weekly*.

The *Weekly* intended to expose the frauds of Jim Fisk's Erie Railroad early on, to deflate his "coarse and vulgar puffing." But the paper found the "details of the rapacity, rascality, gross immorality, defiance of public opinion, and perpetration of outrages" too extensive to fit into the available space. The "fatal odor of the Erie 'dead cat' [will swing] in the face of every American" before the end of the year, the investigators promised.

Insurance companies were called to account for setting aside insufficient reserves for their policyholders, for assessing real estate at inflated prices that falsified their reserves, for paying their executives excessive salaries. Names were cited: Home Fire Insurance Company, Farmer's and Mechanics Insurance Company, Peabody Life Insurance Company. "Men who cannot earn their salary in any other way place no bounds to their self rated value when once made officers of modern insurance companies . . . The extravagance is unexampled!" cried the *Weekly*. Northwestern Mutual Life Insurance Company was singled out for publishing impossible dividends in its promotional pamphlets.

On October 22, the *Weekly* turned its attention to bogus Mexican bonds, and it put the story on the front page October 29.

In November, the paper gave top billing to frauds in Southern states' bonds, "carpet baggers' operations" in North Carolina, where state bonds enriched the state's seven railroads at the taxpayers' expense.

On December 17, the Pacific Mail Steamship Company, controlled by Jay Gould and Russell Sage, was the target. The company provided transportation to California through the profitable Isthmus of Panama route. The two men had bought and sold their own stock, sending it violently up and down, and in a short time they had been $5 million richer.

During the same month, the *Weekly* poured its ink onto the "vampire real estate speculators of New York," predicting that the real estate "bubble" was about to collapse. On December 10, the paper warned that "real estate speculation bought on margin will soon be in foreclosure."

A week later the paper followed up: "The real estate market is still falling. There were fifteen additional foreclosure suits filed in five days about one week ago. Real estate, we now say, will fall much lower. It will not, in this generation, reattain such inflated prices . . . and we advise speculators and persons who are holding merely for investment to sell out in time."

These exposures were a source of pride to Woodhull, and she remembered them with satisfaction many years later in her autobiographical notes, saying that the "financial schemes then flourishing . . . by which the unsuspecting public . . . were inveigled into the purchase of securities that . . . would soon be worthless . . . receive[ed] their death-blows through the columns of our paper."

To draw maximum attention to their investigations, Woodhull designed a cleaner, fresher front page for *Woodhull and Claflin's Weekly* with striking, bold type. A new logo followed: "Progress! Free Thought! Untrammeled Lives! Breaking the Way for Future Generations."

The *Weekly* proprietors had anticipated the wave of revulsion toward "King Money" that would soon roll through the country. Their crusading exposés placed them among the early and honorable voices of those who came to be called muckrakers.

14
Annie's Day in Court

W oodhull's house on New York City's 38th Street was spacious, but it was not large enough to contain the Claflin family peacefully. During her many absences the disputatious Claflins filled the house with sulks, pets, shouts and snits. The worst came from Woodhull's mother, Annie Claflin.

On May 15, 1871, apparently to Woodhull's complete surprise, Annie brought a complaint against her son-in-law, Colonel Blood, in Essex Market Police Court. She stated in an affidavit that Blood had alienated her from the affections of her daughters and threatened her with bodily harm, causing her much "unnecessary dread, anguish of mind and other discomfort." Annie was convinced that only a court of law could enable her to "resume the tranquility desirable to one of her advanced stage of life." The charges were groundless, and lawyers attempted to settle the matter, but Annie insisted on her day in court.

The "peculiar old lady of determined mien and expression indicative of unrepenting purpose," as a reporter from the *Herald* described her, "proceeded to relate the story of her wrongs and domestic tribulations."

"Judge," she said, "my daughters were good daughters and affectionate children until they got in with this man (she paused for emphasis) Blood. He has threatened my life several times, and one night last November he came into the house on 38th Street and said he would not go to bed until he had washed his hands in my blood."

Realizing that he was hearing about Colonel James Harvey Blood of the banking house of Woodhull, Claflin & Company in Broad Street, the *Herald*'s reporter began to record every word. The *Herald*'s account, one of many made of the legal proceeding, appears to be among the most accurate. It was also the most widely distributed.

Annie was not to be stopped: "I'll tell you what that man Blood is.

He is one of those who have no bottom in their pockets; you can keep stuffing in all the money in New York; they never get full up. If my daughters would just send this man away, as I always told them, they might be millionairesses and riding around in their own carriages. I came here because I want to get my daughters out of this man's clutches. He has taken away Vickey's affection and Tennie's affection from poor old mother."

As Annie spluttered out her rage, the aura of gentility that Woodhull had carefully built around herself ebbed away. "S'help me God, Judge, I say here and I call Heaven to witness that there was the worst gang of free lovers in that house in 38th Street that ever lived—Stephen Pearl Andrews and Dr. Woodhull and lots more of such trash."

At this point Annie's lawyer tried to silence her, but she outshouted him. "Yes, Yes; I'll keep quiet; but I want to tell the judge what these people are. I was afraid for my life all the time I was in the house. It was nothing but talking about lunatic aslyums. If God had not saved me, Blood would have taken my life long ago."

Lunatic asylums. These two words explain Annie's motivation in insisting on appearing before the judge. She had heard the story all New York knew, about Mrs. Vanderbilt being sent to an asylum. Would the same thing happen to her? Having gotten her anxiety out into the open, Annie finally left the stand. It's hard to see in this garrulous old woman the mother whose imagination had set Woodhull in motion, but Annie was apparently frightened and thought she was fighting for her life.

Mary Sparr, Woodhull's next-older sister, divorced from her first husband and married now to Millard F. Sparr, then took the stand. Greedy and jealous of her more successful younger sister, she nurtured and then took advantage of Annie's insecurities. She supported Annie's charges.

Colonel Blood was called next. He seems to have been caught unprepared, as though he didn't expect to testify. Perhaps he had assumed that the judge would refuse to hear the case. Blood denied everything the two women had said.

"Did you never make any threat to Mrs. Claflin?" he was asked.

"Nothing except one night last fall when she was very troublesome I said if she was not my mother-in-law I would turn her over my knee and spank her."

"Would you really do that?"

No answer. Then the questions took a decidedly different course. "When were you married to Mrs. Woodhull?"

"In 1866 in Chicago." If this response of Blood's is accurate, the Dayton ceremony of 1866 must have been followed by a more legally binding civil ceremony in Chicago.

"Were you married before that to anyone?"

"Yes, I was married in Framingham, Massachusetts."

It is difficult to understand why Blood's legal counsel did not object to these questions. His marriage to Woodhull had never been discussed publicly by either of them, and up to this point he had avoided any examination of his private life. The questions were not germane to the allegations, and the answers could only hurt Woodhull and himself.

But the counsel for the plaintiff pursued the subject, and Blood replied.

"Were you divorced from your first wife?"

"Yes."

"Was Mrs. Woodhull divorced when you married her?"

"I don't know."

A stunning admission. The statement did not support Woodhull's own version that she and Canning Woodhull were divorced in Chicago in 1863.

"Were you not afterwards divorced from Mrs. Woodhull?"

"Yes, in Chicago in 1868."

A second stunner.

"How long were you separated from her?"

"We were never separated; we continued to live together and were afterwards remarried."

The most likely explanation for the marriages and remarriages was that one or both of the partners had not been legally free to marry at the time of their "wedding" in Dayton—hence the unfinished marriage application. The truth may never be known. As already mentioned, the documents conveniently went up in flames later in the year, on October 8, 1871, when the great fire of Chicago destroyed all the city records.

Canning Woodhull's name was introduced, a new and potentially even more damaging subject.

"When have you seen Dr. Woodhull?"

"I see him every day. We are living in the same house."

A third blow.

"Do you and Mrs. Woodhull and Dr. Woodhull occupy the same room?"

No answer.

"Now, Mr. Blood, please tell the court why Dr. Woodhull lives in the same house, and who supports him."

"The firm of Woodhull, Claflin & Co. has supported the whole of them; Mrs. Woodhull's first child is idiotic and Dr. Woodhull takes care of him."

Blood's maladroit performance eventually came to a close. Woodhull and Claflin would be called to the witness stand the next day.

On Tuesday, the setting of the Essex Market Police Court degenerated into a mob scene. "Physicians, lawyers, social reformers, cooks, chambermaids, brokers, and gentlemen of elegant leisure arrayed in velvet and tuberoses" crowded the passageways and pushed against the railings, hoping to get a glimpse of the sisters. When they arrived, they were dressed in similar black silk suits, jockey hats, and unconventional short curls, all appreciated by the crowd.

Woodhull testified first. She had not found a way to avoid the demeaning moment. Instead she threw herself into it, apparently thinking she would gain public sympathy for the humiliation inflicted by her family. As reported by the *New York Herald,* she testified, "My name is Victoria C. Woodhull. Colonel Blood is my husband; Dr. Woodhull was my husband. I was near fourteen years of age when I married Dr. Woodhull. I have lived eleven years with Colonel Blood. [The *Herald* reporter must have misheard seven, the length of time Woodhull and Blood had been together, for eleven.] My mother has lived with me three years at 17 Great Jones Street and at East Thirty Eighth Street. My father lived there also. This man Sparr and his family, four children, Mrs. Miles and her four children, Dr. Woodhull, myself and my husband, Colonel Blood, and my sister Tennie. Colonel Blood never treated my mother otherwise than kind. Sometimes when she would become violent he would utterly ignore her presence. I thought at times that she was insane and not responsible for what she said. I never thought my mother in danger of any violence from Colonel Blood. The most I ever heard him say was when she would come up to the door and abuse him frightfully, as if she were possessed by some fiend, 'If you do not leave that door I will go out and push you from it.' I never knew him to put his hands on her.

She left my house on the first of April and went to the Washington Hotel to board. All bills for her maintenance there were paid by the firm of Woodhull, Claflin & Company . . .

"I have always pitied my mother. She always seemed to have a desire to have her own way, and seemed to know better what her children wanted than they did themselves. My father is still living with me. Dr. Woodhull and my children are also with me."

"What evidence of insanity have you noticed in your mother's conduct?" she was asked.

"Sometimes she would come down to the table and sit on Mr. Blood's lap and say he was the best son-in-law she had. Then again she would abuse him like a thief, calling him all the names she could lay her tongue to, and otherwise venting her spleen—all without any cause whatsoever.

"The whole trouble was that mother wanted to get Tennie back going around the country telling fortunes."

She was asked, "Did you ever hear your mother complain that Blood claimed the money that came in through your sister Tennie?" The implication was that the funds Vanderbilt provided as backing for the new firm had been appropriated by Blood for his own purposes. The brokerage firm contract, however, strictly limited Blood's control over the firm's funds.

Woodhull's lawyer objected to the question and it was ruled out of order, but Woodhull intervened: "I will answer him . . . she was determined to ruin Blood . . . she would have him in the penitentiary before she died . . . he would end his life there."

"What was the violent language or abuse that your mother used toward Colonel Blood?"

"It was the same that most mothers-in-law give their sons-in-law."

"Did you ever say that you would put your mother in a lunatic asylum?"

"Her other daughter, Mrs. Brooker, [Woodhull's younger sister Utica] told her that if she did not keep quiet it would be her duty to put mother in some such place."

"Did your mother have any means?"

"When she left us and went to the Washington Hotel we paid all her bills."

Woodhull clearly didn't realize that her prominence would subject this testimony to close public scrutiny.

Tennessee Claflin was called to the stand. She looked earnestly at the Judge, greeted her counsel with a friendly nod, and stared squarely at the opposing counsel. Then, the *Herald* reported, she looked "meltingly" toward the 25 reporters waiting for her to testify. The *Herald* reporter added that Claflin had "good eyes" and knew "her power."

On being sworn in, Claflin "kissed the book with an unctuous smack," clearly enjoying the attention. She began her testimony: "I am Tennie C. Claflin; I am one of the firm. Mr. Blood is my sister's . . . husband. I have lived with them since the firm was first started. Before that my mother and father lived with me. I am the martyred one." Tennie, too, expected public sympathy. She turned toward the opposing counsel with a smile and said, "Now go on. You may cross-examine me as much as you like. I never knew the Colonel to use any violence towards mother. He only treated her too kind. In fact I don't see how he stood all her abuse."

Tennie resumed, carried away with herself. "I have been accused of being a blackmailer. If I am a blackmailer, I want it ventilated. I can stand ventilating." Tennie was not naive, but she was careless and irresponsible. By bringing up the subject of blackmail she did not clear herself but instead raised a lot of questions. Both Woodhull and Claflin felt they were being blackmailed by Annie and her manipulators within the family, who threatened to disclose the secrets of the sisters' past lives if they were not supported in a more princely style.

"What was the reason your mother quarreled with Colonel Blood?"

"Hadn't I better begin and tell the whole trouble from the commencement? My mother is insane on spiritualism. But she is my mother and I love her. She has not slept away from me five minutes until lately."

"You and your mother have been on most intimate terms?"

"Yes, since I was 11 years old I used to tell fortunes with her . . . She wants me to go back with her to that business. But Vickey and Colonel Blood got me away from that life, and they are the best friends I ever had. Since I was 14 years old I have kept 30 or 35 deadheads . . . I am a clairvoyant. I am a spiritualist. I have power and I know my power. Many of the best men in [Wall] Street know my power. Commodore Vanderbilt knows my power."

Up to now Tennie had handled her relationship with the Commodore with consummate, and, in fact, uncharacteristic discretion. Caught up in the excitement of the moment she talked on, unwisely.

Vanderbilt's patience would be tested when he learned of Tennie's testimony, and the first signs of an estrangement would soon appear in the relationship.

"I have humbugged people I know," Tennie continued. "But if I did it was to make money to keep these deadheads. I believe in spiritualism myself. It has set my mother crazy because she commenced to believe when she was too old."

Tennie turned to the bench. "But Judge, I want my mother. I am willing to take my mother home with me now, or pay $200 a month for her in any safe place. I am afraid she will die under this excitement. I am single myself, and I don't want anybody with me but my mother."

A long argument between counsel and the judge followed. Suddenly Tennie left her seat, dashed unexpectedly to her mother's side, and put her arms around her. Annie returned her embrace, and they kissed and hugged each other.

Colonel Blood came forward, patted Tennie on the cheek, and put her disheveled hair back in place. "Retire, Tennie," he whispered, "do retire, my dear. You are only making yourself conspicuous." She nodded and left the court room.

The reporters concluded that silver-tongued Tennie had won the round. But it was Woodhull's public persona that had been badly damaged. As the newspapers arrived at 38th Street the next day, she discovered that sympathy had not materialized. She had become a figure of fun.

In the next installment of _My Wife and I,_ Harriet Beecher Stowe chortled, "There's a precious row . . . in Police Court. Our friend Dacia Dangyereyes is up for blackmailing and swindling; and there's a terrible wash of dirty linen going on."

The unorthodox marriage arrangements between Woodhull and Blood titillated the gossips. Stowe later found Blood's first wife in Framingham, Massachusetts, and wrote a friend,

> Did I tell you that here in Framingham lives one wife
> of that Colonel Blood whom this wretched woman
> has seduced and infatuated to be her tool and slave.
> Mrs. Blood is a lovely . . . accomplished woman with
> a daughter twelve years of age. Her husband, she tells
> me, was a young man of one of the best families in St.
> Louis, had served with honor in the army, was in high

position with every prospect of rising in the world, perfectly content in all his habits and devoted to her and her child. This Woodhull woman set up in St. Louis as a clairvoyant physician and Blood consulted her as to his wife's health. Immediately this witch set her eye on him and never left practicing every diabolical art til she finally got him to give up his family, his position, his prospect in life, his wife and his child, to follow her in a life of infamy as he has been doing ever since.

Woodhull tried to keep to the high road, writing to a friend about Stowe's assault, "Mrs. Stowe has been so outrageously bitter an[d] denunciatory of me and all I have attempted to do, that some of my warmest friends insist that a lesson be taught her. I personally prefer to leave her to her conscience and her God, and my defense and exculpation also to Him."

Meanwhile, Stowe wrote a letter to her sister Isabella:

A gentleman who is a member of brother Henry's church came to me last night and said that he wished me to write you as follows: that he travelled on the night cars with Mrs. W to Washington having never seen her before and not knowing who she was. She was with a Senator of his acquaintance and kept up such a talking after he wanted to sleep that he spoke out and requested her to stop. The next morning at Washington she introduced herself as Mrs. Woodhull and asked him to wait on her to her hotel. He did so and at her request secured her rooms and took breakfast with her, she stating that she wished to have a conversation with him. She began then and narrated the whole history of her life—of her husband's profligacy and of her having for some years lived the life of an abandoned woman. She said in the end that she now had frequent offers of that kind but that she had formed a connection with Colonel Blood and should remain constant to it. He said that the freedom of speech in that conversation was something perfectly astonishing to him, neither could he understand any object but one for making him the recipient of such details. After hearing her a while he rose to go and she invited him to return and come to her room in the evening—but he hurried and paid his bill and left the hotel feeling that it was no place for him.

When this story reached Isabella Beecher Hooker, she passed it along to Elizabeth Cady Stanton, saying that the best thing to do would be to confront Woodhull directly with it, for "my prevailing belief is in her innocence and purity. I have seldom been so drawn to any woman and I talked earnestly with her many times . . . I shall always love her—and in private shall work for her redemption if she is ensnared—for I never saw more possible nobilities in a human being than in her."

Hooker told friends that she had been trying to get specific evidence about Woodhull. She speculated that Woodhull had married Blood, then divorced him, then continued to live with him as his wife, "I suppose, simply [as] a protest . . . against human laws of marriage and divorce which seem to them unjust and demoralizing."

Woodhull wasted no time in recriminations and regrets. She started putting together what she considered her "perfect" defense.

15

"I Do Not Intend to Be the Scapegoat"

Three days later, on Saturday, May 20, Woodhull's defense was ready. She submitted it as a letter to the editor of the *New York Times:* "Because I am a woman, and because I conscientiously hold opinions somewhat different from the self-elected orthodoxy . . . [the press] endeavors to cover my life with ridicule and dishonor. This has been particularly the case in reference to certain law proceedings into which I was recently drawn by the weakness of one very near relative."

Woodhull's strategy for damage control was to shift public attention to harsh press criticism of her and away from Annie's "weakness" and Tennie's wilder disclosures. Altruism motivated her household arrangements, she said, praising Blood as the enlightened husband who approved of her support of Canning Woodhull: "One of the charges made against me is that I lived in the same house with my former husband, Dr. Woodhull, and my present husband, Colonel Blood. The fact is a fact. Dr. Woodhull, being sick, ailing, and incapable of self-support, I felt it my duty to myself and to human nature that he should be cared for, although his incapacity was in no wise attributable to me. My present husband, Colonel Blood, not only approves of this charity, but co-operates in it. I esteem it one of the most virtuous acts of my life."

Many today would agree with her that caring for an alcoholic former husband in her own home was a selfless and charitable act, not a symptom of depravity. She continued judiciously: "My opinions and principles are subjects of just criticism. I put myself before the public voluntarily. I know full well that the public will criticize me, and my motives and actions, in their own way and at their own time. I accept the position." Then Woodhull the street fighter emerged: "But let him who is without sin cast his stone. I do not intend to be made the scapegoat." She came out of the closet: "I advocate free love in the highest purest sense as the only cure for the immorality, the deep damnation by which men corrupt and disfigure God's most holy institution of sexual relations."

Advocating free love publicly was Woodhull's calculated stance to show that her private life was a matter of principle rather than convenience. She knew that if she didn't neutralize the revelations, her political ambitions were dead. Her unconventional marriage arrangements could withstand public scrutiny only if she could justify them, and free love provided her rationale. It was a desperate act that placed Woodhull in the center of the hottest social issue of the day, and put her public career on a new course.

Woodhull claimed her right to the same free-for-all rules by which men played, the same sexual freedom many of them practiced. The sexual double standard of her "judges," who "preach against free love openly and practice it secretly," she scorned as cowardly.

She entered further dangerous terrain by saying: "I know of one man, a public teacher of eminence who lives in concubinage with the wife of another public teacher of almost equal eminence. All three concur in denouncing offenses against morality. 'Hypocrisy is the tribute paid by vice to virtue.' So be it. But I decline to stand up as 'the frightful example.' I shall make it my business to analyze some of these lives, and will take my chances in the matter of libel suits. I have small faith in critics, but I believe in public justice."

The "public teachers" she threatened to expose would have been immediately identified by her readers; Henry Ward Beecher was widely understood to have had a sexual affair with his parishioner Elizabeth Tilton, the wife of his protégé, Theodore Tilton.

Woodhull was charging full tilt at the united front of the American establishment. Free love had been a part of the American scene for many years. The term had been invented by John Humphrey Noyes for his utopian Oneida community, where "perfectionists" practiced "Bible communism" and rejected monogamy in favor of complex marriages with multiple wives and husbands. Woodhull had adopted the Oneida creed as interpreted by Stephen Pearl Andrews—the view Andrews had been urging on her since they first met. Experimental communities such as Oneida were often ridiculed and condemned, but they were usually left alone. By proposing free love as a way of life for the larger society, by advocating it as preferable to hypocrisy and the sexual double standard, Woodhull opened an explosive social debate. She turned to free love in self-defense, but it grew to be the subject with which her public life would be most identified. She made it compelling, insisting that women had the right to say no to loveless marriage and no to unwanted sexual advances, that they had the right to own their own bodies.

Woodhull had selected the *New York Times* for her defense, both for its stature and because it had not treated her with jocularity. The *Times* ran the letter the following Monday on page five, under the headline "Mrs. Woodhull and Her Critics," and made no further comment.

Woodhull immediately composed a second letter to the *Times* reiterating her charge that she had become the scapegoat for those opposed to the women's movement. She claimed that "Woman's Suffrage and Woman's Rights being the issue, and there being no defense, I am taken as the representative woman, and my personal character being maligned and depreciated, the cause suffers." To those who said she was "unfit to present and advocate the woman's cause," she restated her right to play by men's rules:

> What man with sufficient ability and wealth to support a party is ever attacked on the score of his immorality or irreligion—in other words for his drunkenness, blasphemy or licentiousness? These are his private life. To go behind a man's hall-door is mean, cowardly, unfair opposition. This is the polemical code of honor between men. Why is a woman to be treated differently? I claim as a matter of justice, by no means as of "gentle courtesy," that the same rule be observable toward the woman journalist or politician as toward the man. . . . Is it fair to treat a woman worse than a man, and then revile her because she is a woman?

The *Times* ran this second letter and Woodhull published it in the *Weekly.*

Horace Greeley's *Tribune,* which had so recently applauded Woodhull's "high moral worth" and her "sagacious courage," now led the attack Woodhull had anticipated. Greeley, whose personal life was considered to be spotless, wrote that he opposed suffrage for women on the basis of "immorality and unchastity." Without naming Woodhull he said: "Let her be the one who has two husbands after a sort, and lives in the same house with them both, sharing the couch of one but bearing the name of the other . . . my conviction of the proper indissolubility of marriage is the mainspring of my hostility to woman suffrage and to the social philosophy from which many vainly seek to separate the woman movement . . . My conception of the nature and scope of the marriage relation renders my conversion to woman suffrage a moral impossibility."

Woodhull used Greeley's words to launch another counteroffensive in the *Weekly*. "The allusion by Mr. Greeley to me and my domestic affairs is too pointed and direct to be misunderstood." she shot back. "To no other woman than to me has this avalanche of maglignant venom any applicability. This is, therefore, my conflict . . . He has chosen to invade my family sanctum. He will not object to my invading his."

Invade she did. The *Weekly* stated, "Mr. Greeley's home has always been a sort of domestic hell. I do not mean that Mr. Greeley has proved an unfaithful husband." She lashed out at hm for quelching the interest in suffrage and the aspirations for self-development shown by his wife and two daughters. "Nothing can bemore aggravating to a woman and a mother than a senseless indifference on the part of a husband and father to all the aspirationsof mother and daughters for some wide career or some greater security of condition than that which marriage affords . . . there is a Mrs. Greeley also in the case, and one who had the bravery to head a movement for suffrage directly in the teeth of Mr. Greeley's insulting assumption of being himself the only party entitled to havean opinion on the subject. So much for Mr. Greeley's domestic family."

Carrying out her early threats in the *Times* to analyze some of these lives, Woodhull's *Weekly* attacked Greeley's employees and colleagues. "A word now in respect to his official family, his editorial staff and his political favorites and associates . . . Allow me to present to you Whitelaw Reid, John Hay and other youngsters of the establishment . . . we have been told that some of the most brilliant of the *Tribune's* edtorials against free-love are written by a gallant whose presentation of the beauty of virtue . . . shines with a light reflected from the gayety of the night's amours."

Woodhull chastized men who sexually harassed women in public life, saying, "Nobody has such an opportunity to know the world as a public woman whose opinions are known to favor social freedom . . . nearly every male biped of the genus [thinks] that every woman who believes in freedom is, therefore, free in his sense of the word and ready to throw herself into the arms of every man who approaches her."

Introducing in the *Weekly* what was to become a refrain in her sexual dogma—women must have the right to say "No"—Woodhull said, "It is one of the first and best uses of social freedom that in the rebuffs that such men receive they get a lesson in true purity and in the dignity of woman's nature which the legal crampiness of the marriage relation never allows to be given. . ."

Woodhull's prompt and outspoken defenses began to establish a public stance that convinced many. She was succeeding in shifting the focus of the controversy away from her chaotic personal life and onto the issue of free love.

The suffragists began to rally around her. Stanton's earlier defenses received new circulation. Anthony, despite her reservations, expressed new, pragmatic support for the brains and the cash Woodhull brought to suffrage. Stanton wrote Woodhull directly, her tone and attitude generous and broadminded as usual: "The grief I felt in the vile raking of your personal and family affairs was threefold—sympathy for you, shame for the men who persecuted you, and the dangers I saw in the abuse of one of our greatest blessings, a free press."

At Stanton's urging, other suffragists began to defend Woodhull. They grumbled about Stephen Pearl Andrews and attributed to his influence all Woodhull's actions they considered unwise. Isabella Beecher Hooker supported Woodhull over the objections of her sisters. She wrote that Paulina Wright Davis had been the leader of those "standing by Mrs. Woodhull, and I never admired anything more in my life."

But Sarah Stearns of Minneapolis—who had, in a burst of enthusiasm, introduced the eloquent resolution praising Woodhull at the time of the May convention—could not be won over. She regretted her earlier spontaneous act. She felt, she said, a "tender pity" for the tribulations of Woodhull's "poor old mother," and thought it "unnatural and evil" of Annie to parade her own daughter before the public. But, she told Woodhull, although Mott and Stanton and Hooker "resolved to stand nobly by you," she found that she could not join them. Woodhull's stand on free love was "contrary to all ex-

pectations" and compelled her to take back what she said in her resolution about Woodhull's "high moral worth."

Still, on balance, Woodhull felt reassured. By the end of June she
was writing privately to a friend that "already the reaction has set in
and [we have made many] new and valuable friends, besides
strengthening all the old ones."

16
"The Sweeter Impulses of Nature"

The same day Woodhull's letter appeared in the *Times*—May 22, 1871—a man burst into her office at 44 Broad Street and confronted her with a copy of the paper. He pointed to the words "a public teacher of eminence" and demanded, "Whom do you mean by that?"

Woodhull immediately recognized the man as Theodore Tilton. Their paths had crossed at the suffrage convention earlier in the month, and once seen, Tilton was easy to remember. He was a handsome man with dark, brooding eyes and heavy auburn hair, which he wore long in the "Grecian" style. His impeccable but unconventional soft collar and tie and the loose jacket he preferred to the usual frock coat all set him apart in a manner appropriate to the half dozen volumes of romantic poetry he had published.

Tilton's aggressive attitude did not intimidate Woodhull.

"I mean you and Mr. Beecher," she replied. She had, she said, "a mission" to bring Beecher's hypocrisies "to the knowledge of the world," and she had nearly determined to do so.

"Mrs. Woodhull," Tilton responded, "You are the first person I have ever met who has dared to . . . tell me the truth. But, do not take any steps now . . . I have carried my heart as a stone in my breast for months, for the sake of Elizabeth, my wife, who is brokenhearted as I am. I have had courage to endure rather than to add more to her weight of sorrow. For her sake, I have allowed this rascal to go unscathed. I have curbed my feelings when every impulse urged me to throttle and strangle him. Let me take you over to my wife, and you will find her in no condition to be dragged before the public; and I know you will have compassion on her."

Woodhull dined with the Tiltons. Elizabeth Tilton was small and pretty, a dark-haired, dark-eyed woman with a gentle manner. She and Tilton managed, for this evening, to return to their marital roles and best company manners, even though Elizabeth Tilton made no secret to Woodhull of her affair with Beecher. She gave Woodhull a book of poems, inscribing it, "To my friend Victoria C. Woodhull."

Tilton had told Woodhull that his wife was often absent from home for days at a time, and he believed she was bent on destroying her life. Woodhull agreed that she was "a wretched wreck of a woman whose troubles were greater than she could bear." Moved by her plight, Woodhull said nothing more about publishing an account of the Beecher-Tilton affair.

Theodore Tilton himself had a reputation for being irresistible to women. One friend ascribed it to his eyes, "very expressive, piercing yet with an almost dove-like softness and tenderness." He was widely understood to have had his own liaisons with various women in the suffrage movement, one so well known that rumors of an imminent elopement had circulated the previous year. The relationship had since ended.

Tilton admitted to Woodhull that he was "not exactly a vestal virgin." She told him she thought he was as much a hypocrite as Beecher. As Woodhull remembered their conversations later, she had said that his resentment of his wife's affair was the old "barbarous idea of ownership in human beings"; he was "playing the part of the fool and tyrant . . . true manliness would protect the absolute freedom of the woman who was loved."

Tilton responded to Woodhull's forthrightness. He took her rowing on the Harlem River. They shared long carriage rides along shaded lanes and enjoyed leisurely picnics on the beach at Coney Island.

They made a handsome couple, a golden pair that attracted attention whenever they were together. An intense sexual connection began, a tangle of libido and manipulation. Woodhull was later quoted as saying, "He slept every night for three months in my arms. Of course we were lovers, devoted, true, faithful lovers." Woodhull denied the quote, but at least one intimate of hers, whose account appears reliable, quoted Woodhull as having confided to him that she'd had sexual relations with Tilton. She gave herself away, saying on one occasion that, "a woman who could not love Theodore Tilton, especially in reciprocation of a generous, impulsive, overwhelming affection such as he was capable of bestowing, must indeed be dead to all the sweeter impulses of nature."

There were love letters, too. One note Tilton wrote was published by the papers several years later. "June 15, [1871], My dear Victoria:

Put this under your pillow, dream of the writer, gather the spirits about you, and so good night. Theodore Tilton."

Woodhull and Tilton's favorite escape was the rooftop at East 38th Street. On the warm June evenings when light lingered until after eight o'clock they could always find a cool breeze and watch the darkness fall. In the distance, the East River first gleamed, then faded, as the dim glow of a million gaslights rose up. The first stars would appear, filling the sky above the almost-empty city blocks that developers had laid out to extend the city uptown. Tilton said of this refuge later, in his sentimental style, "She never goes to any church— save to the solemn temple whose starry arch spans her housetop at night . . . where she sits a worshipper in the sky."

Tilton made the affair public by expressing "his willingness to answer questions" put to him by a reporter from *Pomeroy's Democrat* and published in the paper June 25, 1871. The reporter pointed out that Tilton and Blood arrived at 44 Broad Street together, apparently amiable friends.

"Mr. Tilton, have you known Mrs. Woodhull long?"

"Only since the Woman's Convention at Apollo Hall. Since then I have sought an intimacy with her and her family. She interests me very much."

"How?"

Tilton smiled. "If the woman's movement has a Joan of Arc, it is this gentle, yet fiery spirit, Victoria Woodhull. She is one of the most remarkable women of her time. Little understood by the public, she has been denounced by people who cannot appreciate her moral worth. She is called a free lover owing to her own mistaken use of the term. She is a 'purist' of the first water. Her sincerity, truthfulness, nobility and uprightness of character rank her, in my mind, as a pious Catholic would rank St. Teresa. She is a devotee, a religious enthusiast, a seer of visions."

The reporter recognized he had stumbled on a good story and said to Tilton, "You astonish me."

"Not more than I was myself astonished at the singular revelation of her character to me as one of the most upright, truthful, religious, unsullied souls I have ever met," Tilton replied.

During this interlude, Woodhull was able to put together the story of Tilton's life, and she published many of their conversations in the *Weekly* about a year later. She said then that she had kept some notes but also had worked from memory. Her account agrees sufficiently with the many other versions of these events later published that it appears to be reasonably reliable.

Of Tilton's early years, Woodhull later said little, but Tilton had been considered a young man of great promise from an early age. He was born in New York on October 2, 1835, and attended the Free Academy, later called the College of the City of New York. Tilton had learned phonography, a form of shorthand, before he was 15, and that skill, combined with a gift for flattering older men, had led him to a series of career opportunities. He worked for the editor of the *New York Observer* as a stenographer, and his pleased employer gave him a job on the paper. He did some work for the *Tribune* as well, and came to Horace Greeley's attention. He attended Plymouth Church and was hired by one of the members to report Beecher's sermons. He contrived a small desk in his pew, and every Sunday he "took" Beecher's words. On his twentieth birthday he married Elizabeth Richards, a sister of a childhood schoolmate. Six months later, in the spring of 1856, he was offered a job on the *Independent*, Henry A. Bowen's religious newspaper published in Brooklyn. Tilton turned it into the successful paper Woodhull had admired. In 1860 Tilton bought a house at 174 Livingston Street, near Plymouth Church in Brooklyn Heights. The Heights considered itself the last outpost of New England gentility, a refuge from the vulgarities of Manhattan. His home soon overflowed with four children. The previous year, 1870, Bowen had offered Tilton the editorship of the *Brooklyn Union,* a secular paper that Bowen owned, in addition to Tilton's job at the *Independent.* Tilton seemed to have everything an ambitious and talented man of 36 could want.

Tilton had the temperament to match his energy and imagination. He published the poems of Elizabeth Barrett Browning in the *Independent* and wrote poetry himself—light, romantic verse. He developed a dramatic speaking style and traveled frequently on successful lecture tours. He was popular, particularly with younger people, one of whom as an old man still remembered Tilton: "He was histrionic, vain, extravagant and loved to pose, but also attractive and inspiring. He did a lot of good. He did me good."

Throughout his meteoric rise, Tilton's guiding star was Henry Ward Beecher. Beecher wrote a popular column for the *Independent,* but it did not come easily to him. He was notorious for missing deadlines. Bowen discovered that Tilton had developed a knack for imitating Beecher's style—helped, no doubt, by the experience of recording Beecher's sermons. Bowen made Tilton Beecher's ghost-writer, and between 1856 and 1860 Tilton wrote at least 30 Beecher columns.

The two men were more than professional associates at the paper. They wandered through bookshops and picture galleries together. They worked together for Plymouth Church—Tilton, for a time, as superintendent of the Sunday school. Tilton commissioned a portrait of Beecher and hung it on the wall at 174 Livingston. He and Beecher and Henry Bowen were considered by some to be "the Trinity of Plymouth Church."

Tilton wrote Beecher, "What hours we had together . . . What mutual revelations and communings! What interchanges of mirth, of tears, of prayers! The more I think back upon this friendship, the more I am convinced that, not your . . . fame, not your genius, but just your affection has been the secret of the bond between us; for whether you had been high or low, great or common, I believe that my heart, knowing its mate, would have loved you the same."

But the "trinity" was not without dissension. In 1862 Henry Bowen had told Tilton, in strictest confidence, that on her deathbed his wife had confessed to a love affair she'd had with Beecher. Bowen hinted to Tilton of other secrets as well, secrets he kept to himself because, Bowen's biographers have theorized, Bowen feared that their revelation would harm Plymouth Church, which he had fathered and financed.

Starting in 1866, while Tilton was away from Brooklyn on lecture tours, Beecher became a regular caller at his home. Elizabeth Tilton wrote to her husband that she was thrilled by these visits from the "great man," whom she had secretly loved since before her marriage to Tilton. Tilton wavered between jealousy and pride that Beecher had chosen his home in which to spend his time.

Then, on July 3, 1870, Elizabeth Tilton confessed to her husband that, since October of 1868, Beecher had been more than her pastor. She had surrendered only after "long moral resistance," assured by Beecher that their sexual union was "pure." It had begun in a period of vulnerability after the death of her son Paul, when Beecher had comforted her during Tilton's absences.

Woodhull told Tilton that she had first heard about his secret in the winter of 1870 in Washington. While gathered with the suffragists in the committee room they used for their meetings in Washington, she had been told that Isabella Beecher Hooker might snub her because of her social opinions and her antecedents. A man Woodhull had never met had then stepped forward and said, "It would ill become these women and especially a Beecher to talk of antecedents or to cast any smirch upon Mrs. Woodhull, for I am reliably assured that Mr. Beecher preaches to at least 20 of his mistresses every Sunday."

The remark, Woodhull said, had subdued rather than angered the people in the room. "The women who were there could not have treated me any better than they did. Whether this strange remark had any influence in overcoming their objections to me I do not know, but it is certain they were not set against me by it; and all of them, Mrs. Hooker included, subsequently professed the warmest friendship for me."

Woodhull had put the matter out of her mind, occupied with other matters, until Paulina Wright Davis brought it up. Tilton's wife, Woodhull told him, had confided in Davis. "She spoke freely of a long series of intimate and so-called criminal relations on her part with a certain clergyman . . . of years standing . . . that she loved him before she married [you]." Woodhull had received a letter from Davis that referred to the subject, and urged her to expose the affair. It read, "Dear Victoria: I thought of you half of last night, dreamed of you and prayed for you. I believe you are raised up of God to do a wonderful work, and I believe you will unmask the hypocrisy of a class that none others dare touch. God help you and save you. The more I think of that mass of clerical corruption the more I desire its opening. Ever yours, lovingly, Paulina Wright Davis." And most recently Woodhull had heard the same story from Elizabeth Cady Stanton. Woodhull told Tilton that she and Stanton had talked at some length when Stanton visited her at home during the recent Apollo Hall convention.

Tilton acknowledged that everything Woodhull had heard was true. She had no idea of the extent of Beecher's "depravity," he said, and told his melancholy version of the story. He had first begun to have his own suspicions of Beecher on his return from a long lecture tour in the West, Tilton said. He questioned his daughter privately in his study regarding what had happened during his absence. "The tale of iniquitous horror that was revealed to me was enough to turn the heart of a stranger to stone, to say nothing of a husband and father." The intimacies had been carried out in his own house, with his children at home.

"These things drove me mad," he said, "and I went to my wife and confronted her with the child and the damning tale she had told me. My wife did not deny the charge nor attempt any palliation. She was then enceinte, and I felt sure that the child would not be my child. I stripped the wedding ring from her finger. I tore the picture of Mr. Beecher from my wall and stamped it to pieces. Indeed I do not know what I did not do. I only look back to it as a time too horrible to retain any exact remembrance of it. She miscarried the child and it was buried. For two weeks, night and day, I might have been found walking to and from that grave, in a state bordering on distraction. I could not realize that I was what I was. I stamped the ring with which we had plighted our troth deep into the soil that covered my wife's infidelity. I had friends, many and firm and good, but I could not go to them with this grief, and I suppose I should have remained silent through life had not an occasion arisen which demanded that I should seek counsel.

"Mr. Beecher learned that I had discovered the fact and what had transpired between my wife and myself, and when I was absent he called at my house and compelled or induced his victim to sign a statement he had prepared declaring that so far as he, Mr. Beecher, was concerned, there was no truth in my charges and that there had never been any criminal intimacy between them. Upon learning this, as I did, I felt, of course, again outraged and could endure secrecy no longer. I had one friend who was like a brother, Mr. Frank Moulton."

The two men had gone to college together. Moulton, an amiable man and a junior partner in the export firm of Woodruff & Robinson, was widely respected and his presence inspired confidence.

"I went to him," Tilton continued, "and stated the case fully. We were both members of Plymouth Church. My friend took a pistol, went to Mr. Beecher and demanded the [Elizabeth Tilton statement] . . . under penalty of instant death." Beecher begged Moulton not to expose him to the public, Tilton continued. Moulton had obtained the letter and reassured Tilton that he had put it in his safe. After that, Tilton said, he seldom ate or slept at home, but stayed often with the sympathetic Moulton.

During this period of trauma, the relationship between Tilton and Bowen cooled. They'd had some disagreements over editorial policies at the *Independent,* but these seemed to be a pretext for their personal differences. Bowen was displeased by rumors he had heard of Tilton's infidelities and objected as well to Tilton's support of women's rights.

On December 1, 1870, an editorial appeared in the *Independent* that became notorious as Tilton's free-love editorial. In it he supported freer divorce laws, saying, "A public opinion which compels the juxtaposition, or which forbids the disconnection, of an unmated pair—who are tied, not knit—chained, not wedded—violates the ethics of him who, preaching from the mountain-top of morals, taught so terrible a distinction between love and lust. Marriage without love is a sin against God."

After the editorial appeared, Bowen eased Tilton off the *Independent,* offering him a substantial salary to edit the *Brooklyn Union,* his secular paper. Then he abruptly fired him at the end of 1870. Frank Moulton, concerned about his friend Tilton and about Plymouth Church, and hoping to calm these explosions of mercurial temperaments, took on the role of mediator. He and his business partners put up $10,000 for Tilton to launch a new weekly, *The Golden Age.* He convinced Beecher to contribute an additional $5,000, though Beecher had to mortgage his house to do it.

Woodhull had been keeping an eye on Tilton, and had written in *Woodhull and Claflin's Weekly,* not long after the *Golden Age* appeared in March, that it was "as brilliant as its editor-in-chief, Theodore Tilton. Can anything stronger be said? To the few who do not know the force of our comparison we can only recommend the *Golden Age* as bright, witty and wise."

Moulton had talked Beecher and Tilton into resuming their friendship. Then Woodhull's threatening letter appeared in the *Times.* The three men reacted to it with alarm, hurriedly reconnoitering to work out a Woodhull containment strategy, hatching a plan to put her under "social obligation" to them. They charged Tilton with carrying it out. But, as the summer wore on, Tilton had become recklessly infatuated with Woodhull and appeared to have changed sides.

Woodhull had wanted to publish a biography of herself, thinking she could entrust her "justification" to such a work. She believed that if the story of her life were known, she would receive sympathy and understanding from the public rather than censure. The disclosures in court in May, and the subsequent press mauling she had received, further convinced her of the usefulness of such a publication. Blood had attempted to write a biography, but Woodhull had been dissatisfied with his efforts.

Tilton took Blood's notes and spent an entire night with them, pen in hand. A valuable account of Woodhull's early life emerged, wrapped, however, in the cloying style of Tilton's own infatuation: Woodhull's countenance was famed for its "striking spirituality," he said; she was "blushing, modest and sensitive," and "the Sermon on the Mount fills her eyes with tears."

The biography appeared in September, 1871, and sold for 10 cents a copy, published by Tilton's *Golden Age* under the title, "Mr. Tilton's Account of Mrs. Woodhull." It is a measure of Tilton's ego that, although this is the story of Woodhull's life, his name appeared before hers in the title. Woodhull acquiesced in his self-involvement, and achieved her own goal—close identification with Tilton's highly regarded name.

She found the biography entirely to her liking, and said it "sparkled in every line like rare old wine, which was to be accounted for only [because] he was newly and madly in love, for nothing else would have inspired him to write so grandly." Before the summer was over, Tilton had written another pamphlet for Woodhull, supporting her Washington Memorial.

Woodhull had accomplished much of what she had hoped to gain from her association with Tilton. She had achieved public identification with him. He had written extensively on her behalf. But she was having less success persuading him to take a public stand "wholly and unreservedly" in favor of free love. His position on the subject at the *Independent* had resulted in so much trauma, it now seemed that he might "vacillate or go backward." And Tilton had yet to support Victoria Woodhull for president. On that subject, he had said only that "should she be elected to the high seat to which she aspires (an event concerning which I make no prophecy) I am at least sure that she would excel any Queen now on any throne in her native faculty to govern others."

17

The Grand Endowments
of Henry Ward Beecher

"*I*t was at this time that Mr. Tilton introduced Mr. Beecher to me, and I met him frequently at Mr. Tilton's and Mr. Moulton's," Woodhull said later. Woodhull had wanted to meet Beecher for some time. When Tilton set out to "quiet" her with "social obligations," she had made the most of his talents on her behalf. Beecher could bring even more to her cause than Tilton.

A note from Tilton started things. "My dear Victoria: I have arranged with Frank [Moulton] that you shall see Mr. Beecher at my house on Friday night. He will attend a meeting of the church at ten o'clock and will give you the rest of the evening as late as you desire. You may consider this fixed. Meanwhile on this sunshiny day I salute you with a good morning. Peace be with you. Yours, T. T."

Woodhull found a 60-year-old man with graying hair who weighed more than 200 pounds. Photographs of the time show pensive eyes, stringy hair and flaccid jowls. If the camera wasn't kind to Beecher, however, his congregation was. He projected vitality. "Beecher, Beecher, Beecher! . . . Don't ask me what I think of him. I . . . only know that I am intensely interested," Susan Howard, the wife of a church trustee, wrote to her brother soon after Beecher came to Plymouth Church in Brooklyn. "There is a sort of fascination about the man . . . He carries one along with him by the power of his own flow."

Beecher's talent as a preacher lay in acting, not in theology. He went through the motions of his family's religious vocation without strong convictions, but he came alive before an audience. A listener who watched him early in his career saw a "stout and clumsy figure," the face "full, heavy and flushed," an altogether unimpressive appearance. But when he started to speak he was transformed, "inspired, radiant, glorified, transfigured, face aflame, eyes flashing, voice reverberating." He established an unusual intimacy with an audience. He said, "I want them to surround me, so that they will come up on every side, and behind me, [and] surge about me." When he preached about the joy of God in nature and about submission "to the heart's instincts," his parishioners loved the performance and loved him.

He followed his instincts, responding to the luxuries of life and enjoying sybaritic indulgences. He loved precious stones of every variety and took endless pleasure in carrying them in his pocket, taking them out, and rolling them in his hand. He called them his "opiates."

When Woodhull finally met Beecher at ten o'clock on a warm Friday evening in 1871, they discussed, she said, the "social problem" in all its "varied bearings." Ten o'clock at night was a late hour for two leaders to meet, and it suggests that both were allowing for more than a discussion of social problems. The evidence indicates that they found it—that the two leaders shared a brief but mutually exciting and satisfying sexual encounter. An intimate of Woodhull's said she told him she'd "had sexual relations . . . with Beecher." "I believe that she told the truth," he added.

Woodhull was highly disingenuous in the way she juggled her elaborate sexual adventures between Tilton and Beecher, enjoying fleeting trysts with both men during the summer of 1871 and at the same time expressing an apparent sympathy for Tilton's wife. Elizabeth Tilton had learned that Beecher had another sexual partner, and, Woodhull said, "her sorrow was greatly augmented by the knowledge that the clergyman was untrue." Woodhull elaborated further saying Beecher, despite his "repeated assurances of his faithfulness" to Elizabeth Tilton, had "recently had illicit intercourse, under the most extraordinary circumstances, with another person." Woodhull was talking about her own relations with Beecher.

She did not comment on the peculiar circumstance that Beecher and Tilton were, once again, sexually involved with the same woman, this time willing partners in a ménage à trois. The pattern of the two men's behavior suggests that their emotional involvement with each other outdistanced their feelings for the women in their lives, Elizabeth Tilton and Victoria Woodhull alike.

For her part, Woodhull simply accepted and enjoyed Beecher's sexuality. She wrote in the spirit that animated free love:

The immense physical potency of Mr. Beecher, and the indomitable urgency of his great nature for the intimacy and embraces of the noble and cultured women about him, instead of being a bad thing, as the world thinks, or thinks that it thinks, is one of the noblest and grandest of the endowments of this truly great and representative man. The amative impulse is the physiological basis of character. It is this which emanates zest and magnetic power to his whole audience through the organism of the great preacher. . . . Passional starvation, enforced on such a nature, so richly endowed, by the ignorance and prejudice of the past, is a horrid cruelty. The bigoted public . . . condemned him in their ignorance, to live without food. Every great man of Mr. Beecher's type has had, in the past, and will ever have the need for, and the right to, the loving manifestations of many women, and when the public graduates out of the ignorance and prejudices of its childhood, it will recognize this necessity and its own injustice. Mr. Beecher's grand and amative nature is not, then, the bad element in the whole matter, but intrinsically the good thing, and one of God's best gifts to the world.

This defense of Beecher says more about Woodhull than Beecher, about her own "amative" nature, which she believed was "intrinsically" a "good thing," a gift from God. In writing this account of Beecher for the *Weekly*, Woodhull was explaining herself to the world. The concept that physical sexuality was to be encouraged as healthy and normal for both men and women would become a theme of her future lectures. She would expand it further and say explicitly that a woman had the same rights to sexual satisfaction that a man had.

The role of Frank Moulton in these clandestine meetings changed over the summer. At the start he was simply helping Tilton put Woodhull under obligation to him. But as he got to know Woodhull better, he came to like her. Moulton had talked about Woodhull with his wife, Emma, asking her opinion. He said later, "My wife is a broadminded, self-preserving woman, able to take care of herself.

We accept life on the theory of human imperfection." The Moultons treated Woodhull with courtesy and respect.

Years later Emma Moulton became an important primary source for the first Beecher biography to offer anything other than hagiography. The author, Paxton Hibben, was convinced that Woodhull and Beecher had been lovers. Though he didn't use this material in his book, he did state his conclusion in his correspondence with Woodhull's heirs. In the biography, he ventured another conclusion: "Victoria Woodhull understood Henry Ward Beecher perfectly. She was perhaps the only human being who ever did."

Certainly, Woodhull understood Beecher's sexual nature, and she calculated she could use that knowledge to her advantage. She wanted more than a sexual adventure; she wanted his support for her free-love position. If Beecher, with his high position, would publicly stand by her side, the opprobrium attached to her would be deflected considerably. Hypocrisy and a double sexual standard were the evils she perceived, and she took the chance that Beecher would oppose these evils with her. She said she thought Beecher was "a man that would care a great deal for the truth, and that, having lived the life that he had, and entertaining the private convictions he did, I could perhaps persuade him that it was his true policy to come out and openly avow his principles, and be a thorough, consistent radical, and thus justify his life in some measure, if not wholly, to the public."

But Woodhull was indulging in wishful thinking. Beecher was not the man to take a stand on principle. Beecher's brother Thomas compared him to a watchman who sees the first turn of the tide and shouts discovery. He was known as an abolitionist, yet he had straddled the fence for 20 years before taking a stand on slavery.

Woodhull soon learned about Beecher's cautious nature. He told her that he "was 20 years ahead of his church," that he "preached the truth" only as fast as his people "could bear it." "I know that our whole social system is corrupt," he said, and added, no doubt thinking of his own unhappy marriage, "I know that marriage, as it exists today, is the curse of society." These were frank, private statements, but Beecher had no plans to repeat them in public as Woodhull urged. To raise the issue of sexuality at all was shocking enough, but to advocate sexual activity outside of marriage went far beyond anything the era would accept. Beecher understood this reality only too well.

Since Woodhull now knew from personal experience that Beecher practiced free love in private, as she phrased it, she had some pressure she could bring to bear on him to take the step she desired. She was prepared to do whatever was necessary to bring him around. The highly manipulative nature of her own sexuality did not strike Woodhull as weakening her case. She simply ignored it.

Though Beecher was reluctant to lend his stature to free love, Woodhull found another name, highly prestigious, to fortify her position. Goethe had brought Europe's attention to the subject in his *Elective Affinities (Die Wahlverwandtschaften)* in 1809. The novel had a long popularity, due in part to its use of Goethe's experience of love outside marriage. A Boston publisher issued a new edition of the novel with an introduction by Woodhull. But this prestigious antecedent for her position failed to sway Beecher.

Paxton Hibben was right: Despite their differences, Woodhull and Beecher shared common ground. Both could magnetize their listeners, sweeping them along with their joy and zest for living. Both made love whenever they chose. And both had secrets in their pasts. Woodhull defied conventions, while Beecher usually managed to accommodate them, yet the personality parallels were striking. Woodhull had not given up on Beecher. Their encounter would lead both of them to the edge of ruin.

Annie Hummel Claflin
Holland-Martin Family Archives

Reuben Buckman Claflin
John Miles Thompson, Jr., Papers

Family Portrait ca. 1864-1865: Victoria
Woodhull, Dr. Canning Woodhull, Byron
Woodhull, and Zula Maud Woodhull
Holland-Martin Family Archives

Tennessee Celeste Claflin ca. 1870
Holland-Martin Family Archives

Colonel James Harvey Blood
Holland-Martin Family Archives

Cornelius Vanderbilt
New York Historical Society

Tennessee Claflin (left) Victoria Woodhull (right)
in the offices of Woodhull, Claflin & Company.
From *The Day's Doings,* February 26, 1870.
Holland-Martin Family Archives

Victoria Woodhull addressing the Judiciary Committee of the United States House of
Representatives in Washington, D.C. From *Frank Leslie's Illustrated Weekly,*
February 4, 1871

Victoria Woodhull attempting to vote in New York City, November 7, 1871, sketch by H. Balling, *Harper's Weekly*, November 25, 1871

Victoria Woodhull being nominated for the presidency by the equal rights party in New York City, May 10, 1872, *From One Moral Standard for All, M.F. Darwin, John Miles Thompson, Jr., Papers*

Reverend Henry Ward Beecher
New York Historical Society

Victoria Woodhull as "Mrs. Satan" Thomas
Nast From *Harper's Weekly*, February 17,
1872

Mr. and Mrs. John Biddulph Martin in the garden of 17 Hyde Park Gate, London
Holland-Martin Family Archives

Sir Francis and Lady Cook on the terrace at Monserrate, Cintra, Portugal
Jane Brabyn Collection

Zula Maude Woodhull ca. 1878
Holland-Martin Family Archives

The partners of Martin's Bank, Richard Martin (seated center) John
Martin (standing center)
Holland-Martin Family Archives

Victoria Woodhull Martin and Zula Maud Woodhull at Norton Park
Holland-Martin Family Archives

Victoria Woodhull Martin at Norton Park with Byron Woodhull and Zula Maud
Woodhull
Holland-Martin Family Archives

18
The Victoria League

During that summer of 1871, Woodhull threw herself into a new round of "at homes." She was returning to politics, believing that she had successfully defused Annie's day in court by her stand on free love. Her evening gatherings attracted a wide circle of potential supporters—bankers, editors, lawyers, clergymen, members of Congress, and even members of President Grant's family. The press attended and publicized Woodhull's connections with these notables.

Describing the evening of June 23, 1871, in the drawing room of East 38th Street, a reporter from the *New York Sun* said that the reflections of the many towering mirrors made him feel as though he were in a "magic chamber." The reporter had met the president's brother in Woodhull's drawing room the previous week. He had also seen his father, Jesse Grant.

On this particular evening he was told that "Congress" was in session in the next room. After a short wait, Woodhull and Tennie appeared. The reporter, who had a keen eye for women's clothing, gave a detailed account of what the sisters were wearing for this fashionable evening. Woodhull was in an elegant pink silk dress with an elaborate train and overskirt trimmed with broad black lace. An oversize white shawl was thrown across her shoulders. Tennie wore black silk *en train,* with a plain jacket of heavier material, trimmed with enormous jet buttons.

When the *Sun* reporter asked about the politicians in the next room, Woodhull said that the group included some of the most influential men in the country. Trade unions, women's suffrage organizations, and other reform movements were all represented, she added, taking advantage of the opportunity to publicize her new humanitarian goals. She brought up the theme that she had first discussed in her May speech to the labor reformers: that the established political parties were corrupt and controlled by special interests. The Republican Party was too corrupt to ever elect another president, she said. She was in touch with the "best men of the party," and they did not expect to succeed the next year.

The popularity of these evenings could not be explained by the power of the sisters' brokerage business or the power of their newspaper, the *Sun* reporter wrote. "If it be true that all the politicians and public men who flutter about . . . are drawn either by fear or by devotion to the cause, woman suffrage and the collateral reforms promised in the numerous pronunciamentos of Mrs. Woodhull and Miss Claflin may as well be accepted at once." Rather, he concluded, the charming company of the two "pretty brokers" attracted influential people. Woodhull was trying to turn the popularity of her evenings into something of political substance for herself.

What she had in mind was the new political party she had promoted at the May convention in her "Great Secession Speech." A letter in the *Weekly*, dated July 4, took her idea public. It was addressed to Woodhull herself:

> A number of your fellow-citizens, both men and women, have formed themselves into a working committee, borrowing its title from your name, and calling itself the Victoria League. Our object is to form a new national political organization, composed of the progressive elements in the existent Republican and Democratic parties, together with the Women of the Republic . . . to be called the Equal Rights Party.

With the Victoria League, with a new name—The Equal Rights Party—with Theodore Tilton's influence and support, and with her evening parties, Woodhull relaunched her political campaign. She intended to organize a national convention to meet in May of 1872 to ratify her candidacy by nominating her for president. The themes she introduced in the Victoria League letter would occupy her attention for the next year. Side-stepping free love for the time being, she stressed instead the less controversial humanitarian goals that could unite suffragists and labor reformers. These efforts would culminate in a major new speech on August 3 in New York.

The Victoria League announcement was a carefully planned, political device. The July 4 letter sent to Woodhull by "unnamed supporters" was actually her own creation. It laid out her goals and requested her leadership, giving her the opportunity to expand on them in her reply. It stated that the new party would ask Congress to pass a declaratory act at its next session and would urge women to vote in the off-year elections in the fall:

> We ask you to become the standard-bearer of this idea before the people, and for this purpose nominate you as our candidate for president of the United States, to be voted for in 1872 by the combined suffrages of both sexes . . . Offering . . . the assurance of our great esteem, and harboring in our minds the cheerful prescience of victory which your name inspires, we remain, Cordially yours, The Victoria League.

Woodhull created an aura of mystery around the league. The letter carried no signatures. Soon after it appeared, Woodhull implied that Vanderbilt was the power behind it. She used Tilton as her vehicle for this ruse. Tilton dropped the first hint in an interview he gave to the *Weekly*, saying he knew next to nothing about the Victoria League. He asked the *Weekly* interviewer if Vanderbilt was the group's president. In the biography of Woodhull that Tilton published that summer, he described the league as "an organization which, being somewhat Jacobinical in its secrecy, is popularly supposed, though not definitely known, to be presided over by Commodore Vanderbilt."

Tilton's speculation gave the Vanderbilt connection with the Victoria League public credibility, but Woodhull most likely created and financed the organization herself. She had, in fact, started criticizing Vanderbilt's capitalistic practices in the pages of the *Weekly*, further stretching the Commodore's patience. But Woodhull knew that speculation about the league's being secretly backed by Vanderbilt would make it more interesting to the public.

On July 20, Woodhull wrote a response to the Victoria League. After, she said, a period of "reflection," she had returned to her humanitarian objectives of uniting suffrage efforts with those of labor reform—her platform of "human rights."

She acknowledged that her announcement for president a year earlier had been for the "mere purpose of lifting a banner, of provoking agitation . . . a rallying point" for suffrage. Now she argued the case was quite different: "Little as the public think it, a woman who is now nominated may be elected next year." Whether or not Woodhull believed that a woman might be elected president, she believed absolutely that she could be nominated by the right kind of new splinter party. She expressed this confidence in terms of election success:

> The right woman to touch the right chord of the public sympathy and confidence . . . would arouse such a tempest of popularity as the country has never seen and as a consequence should ride triumphantly on the tide of a joyous popular tumult to the supreme political position . . . It is possible, therefore, that if I am your candidate I may be elected.

She touched briefly on suffrage, announcing that she planned to go to Washington to "claim" a "declaratory act," and saying, "I expect to succeed." Then she made her approach to the labor reformers.

> The freedom of women and the freedom of the laborer are conjointly the cause of humanity. Industry, finance and the home must all be rightly adjusted as transitional to the higher order . . . the fusion of the women and the workingmen and the Internationalists will render [the Democrats and Republicans] as parties unnecessary. The National Labor Union, just now convening in St. Louis has, for the first time, invited women upon equal terms to that convention. It is, of course, noticed that neither Republicans or Democrats have, with some exceptions in Massachusetts, invited us yet into their political assemblages.

She closed with a lyrical paragraph celebrating her name as an augury for her success, a self-serving piece of theater:

> Perhaps I ought not to pass unnoticed your courteous and graceful allusion to what you deem the favoring omen of my name. It is true that a Victoria rules the great rival nation opposite to us on the other shore of the Atlantic, and it might grace the amity . . . between the two nations . . . if a twin sisterhood of Victorias were to preside over the two nations. It is true also that in its mere etymology the name signifies Victory! and the victory for the right is what we are bent on securing . . . I have sometimes thought myself that there is perhaps something providential and prophetic in

the fact that my parents were prompted to confer on
me a name which forbids the very thought of failure.

The Equal Rights Party was a name with a history. In December
1865, Tilton had proposed the formation of an organization called
the National Equal Rights Society, to bring together the abolitionists
and suffragists. In May 1866, at simultaneous meetings of both
groups in New York, the suffragists had adopted the name American
Equal Rights Association, but the abolitionists had failed to join
them. The organization met in May of the three following years under another name—the Equal Rights Association—but the divisions
aired at the January 1869 suffrage meeting in Washington had produced not unity, but instead the divided New York and Boston wings
of the movement. The name Equal Rights Association fell into disuse.
Woodhull resurrected it again as the Equal Rights Party, preferring it
to Cosmopolitical, the name she had previously suggested in the
Weekly at Andrews's urging. The suffragists deplored Andrews's influence on Woodhull, and the name change moved her further away
from him and closer to them. The words Equal Rights were associated with unity and Theodore Tilton; they also had a clear meaning
which Cosmopolitical lacked. The change was a wise strategic move
on Woodhull's part.

As the summer went on, Woodhull's confidence grew. She expressed her excitement in a letter to Paulina Wright Davis on July 27,
reluctantly cancelling a visit to this highly regarded friend in Providence, "Such a rush of matters that my brain really whirls." She
hinted at new proposals and suggested Davis watch for the next
week's paper. Political matters were developing fast, she said. "I endeavor to make the most of everything, and expect something from
the Labor Convention which meets in St. Louis August 7."

On Thursday, August 3, Woodhull gave a major speech on "The
Principles of Finance" at Cooper Institute in New York City. This
was a forum for addressing, once again, the labor reformers. To establish her credentials on subjects of importance to them, and to ally
herself with their interests, she selected for her subject a proposal for
a new system of "national currency" based on the "entire wealth" of
the country. In this she was appealing to those who were supporters
of the newly emerging Greenback Movement, which opposed post-
war deflation and the government's return to the gold standard, favoring instead the expansion of greenbacks in circulation.

Woodhull's speech offered an astonishingly erudite economics lesson on wealth and money systems, as she proposed putting greenbacks into circulation and nationalizing banks. Her words showed the heavy touch of Stephen Pearl Andrews's theories and writing style, but exhibited her own flourishes. No woman had made this kind of speech in New York before. The *New York Times* of August 4 covered it sympathetically and in some detail, reporting that 1,000 people had attended and that Woodhull had been introduced by Theodore Tilton.

The speech, however, put Woodhull in a contradictory position. The first female broker and Wall Street banker, a woman who was personally speculating in gold almost recklessly, was now publicly opposing the gold standard and talking about abolishing private banks. She made no attempt to reconcile this inconsistency at this time, and no one, not even the *Times,* challenged her on it. Perhaps her subject was too abstruse for the reporters in the hall. As a subject to launch her candidacy with labor reformers, money was a wise choice, and there was little doubt in the minds of most that money was a subject Woodhull knew something about. To that extent, her speech was credible to the casual listener or reader. It succeeded in reactivating her campaign to bring suffragists and labor reformers together in support of common humanitarian goals.

19
The Spiritualists

Woodhull now began arduously to cultivate an esoteric base of supporters—the spiritualists. Vineland, New Jersey was the capital of spiritualist country, and Woodhull went there on Sunday, September 9, 1871. She had built bridges during the summer by reporting spiritualistic news in the *Weekly* and running announcements for their meetings. The Vineland spiritualists had organized a September weekend of activities, and Woodhull arranged to be on their schedule.

In embracing the spiritualists, Woodhull was taking the biggest gamble of her nascent political career. The spiritualists had never been politically active, but they were potentially a larger constituency than either the suffragists or the labor reformers. Woodhull meant to convince them that the millenium they believed in was the United States of America in 1872. If she could politicize them, she would create a powerful new voting bloc. It was an innovative and daring concept.

To succeed, Woodhull had to convince the spiritualists that she was one of them. She had never before been active in any of their meetings or organizations, but Vineland would change that. At her Sunday meeting, she and the assembled spiritualists listened to readings from Tilton's biography of her; the work had been intended by Woodhull as a campaign biography for spiritualist sensibilities. The reader began:

> I must now let out a secret. She [Woodhull] lived her life by the help (as she believes) of heavenly spirits . . . She has entertained angels, and not unawares. These gracious guests have been her constant companions . . . They dictate her life with daily revelation . . . Her writings and speeches are the products . . . of their indwelling in her soul.

The reading went on to Woodhull's childhood visions, and then to a somber picture of her home life, the abuse she suffered as a child, her unhappy marriage to Canning Woodhull, the birth of her mentally handicapped son—events intended to gain sympathy and understanding for Woodhull's unconventional home life.

The biography returned to a basic premise of Woodhull's: "She believes that intellectual power has its fountains in spiritual inspiration." As the work ventured into the details of Woodhull's "inspirations," Tilton's storytelling took over: "In pleasant weather she has a habit of sitting on the roof of her stately mansion on Murray Hill, and there communing hour by hour with the spirits." This kind of "divine inspiration" was an accepted convention among the spiritualists. Woodhull had calculated that they would respond to her ideas more favorably if she attributed them to otherworldly powers, and Tilton was placing Woodhull in this tradition.

Tilton described Blood as a "reverent husband to his spiritual bride, the sympathetic companion of her entranced modes, and their faithful historian to the world." He called Blood a "fine-grained transcendentalist." This picture of Blood and Woodhull working together duplicates the relationship between Andrew Jackson Davis, one of the most highly regarded spiritualist leaders, who was a trance recipient, and his wife, Mary, who recorded his words. It was a pattern familiar to spiritualists and a model for spiritualist marriage relationships. Tilton, with his subject's careful prompting, had succeeded in portraying Woodhull and Blood as a similarly ideal spiritual couple.

Tilton turned to the spiritual underpinnings of Woodhull's life as a public speaker. This episode also reflected a storyteller's guile. Woodhull had known her audience when she told her story to Tilton, knew that the spiritualists would respond to her invention: "The chief among her spiritual visitants . . . a matured man of stately figure, clad in a Greek tunic . . . prophesied to her that she would rise to great distinction; that she would emerge from her poverty . . . [to] become the ruler of her people." Woodhull identified her spirit guardian as Demosthenes, the great leader and orator of Athenian democracy. Her showmanship took over in the fabrication of an historical adult guardian angel, but she was capable of convincing herself that the Demosthenes vision contained an underlying truth. Demosthenes became her favorite invention.

The reading concluded with an account of Woodhull's religion.

"When under a strong spiritual influence, a strange and mystical light irradiates from her face," Tilton said, calling her a "spiritualist of the most mystical and ethereal type . . . led to speculate profoundly on the transformation from our mortal to our immortal state, deducing the idea that the time will come when the living human body instead of ending in death . . . will be gradually refined away until it is entirely sloughed off, and the soul only . . . remains."

With these words Woodhull identified herself with the most treasured belief among the spiritualists, that of a continuous life of the spirit. Serious spiritualism constituted an underground movement within established religion. It served as a way station for those abandoning the harsh Calvinism of an earlier generation but not yet ready to relinquish their belief in an afterlife. It expected, in the spirit of scientific inquiry, to establish a material basis for the soul. Rather than anticipating life in a distant heaven after death, it conceived of the spirit as experiencing a continuous and uninterrupted life. The concept appealed to Woodhull, and she would often speculate about it in the future.

Woodhull had judged the spiritualists astutely, and her biography was well received in Vineland. Following the reading, Colonel Blood proposed two resolutions, the first thanking the reader, the second stating that the meeting "deeply appreciated . . . Victoria Woodhull" and her Equal Rights Party.

By publicly identifying herself with spiritualism, Woodhull certainly risked losing credibility among those who considered it misguided. The Tilton biography provided ample material for censure and satire, but the response of the press was surprisingly muted. A "votive biography" was the consensus, reported by the *Brooklyn Eagle*. *Harper's Weekly* said more skeptically, "If apples are wormy this year and grapes mildewed, and ducks' eggs addle, and bladed corn be lodged, it may be ascribed to the unhallowed influence of Mr. Tilton's Life of V. W."

The suffragists reacted according to their tolerances for spiritualism. Olympia Brown, a Universalist minister from Bridgeport, Connecticut, who maintained good relations with both the Boston and New York suffragists, understood Woodhull's motives exactly. She wrote Hooker saying that she admired Woodhull's independence and energy and liked Woodhull's free-love theory and all her other theories and would "not hear her abused." But the Demosthenes story made Brown doubt Woodhull's sincerity. Demosthenes and the spirits are "humbug," she wrote, "calculated to be with the superstitious, and the crowd likes her."

Ellen Wright Garrison, niece of Lucretia Mott, expressed the conservative view, in a letter to her mother, asking, "How do you like Theodore Tilton's biography of Mrs. Woodhull? Can anything but infatuation or aberration explain its absurdities! Too ridiculous almost, even to ridicule!"

Elizabeth Cady Stanton, pragmatic as usual, called Woodhull a grand woman and accepted the theatrical invention of Demosthenes as a bit of poetic license. Later in the year she wrote Woodhull playfully, "Will you ask Demosthenes if there is any new argument not yet made on the 14th and 15th Amendments that he will bring out," assuming rightly, as had Olympia Brown, that Woodhull had enlarged on her spirit guide to pander to the credulous.

Woodhull's spiritualism was now public information, both the genuine and the embellishments, both her convictions and her showmanship. Those who assumed her new allegiance was opportunistically motivated did so with good reason.

However, Woodhull's spiritualism also formed the core of her personal beliefs. She extracted what she considered to be the spiritual from an increasingly material organized religion and made it the essence of her beliefs, looking for religious experience, not dogma. Quakers, Universalists, and Unitarians, and Woodhull's Methodists, the denominations that had always emphasized a subjective religious experience, were attracted to spiritualism. They were the emotional children of the transcendentalists, seeking for God and the God-like in themselves, for Emerson's "whisper of the voice within."

Despite their apolitical stance, spiritualists were drawn to reform movements. They saw reform as a way of realizing higher human development and promoting personal growth. Suffragists, labor reformers, free lovers, free thinkers, single taxers, anarchists, populists, vegetarians, communists, and socialists were welcomed by spiritualists as fellow searchers for new social truths. Woodhull hoped to bring this private moral fervor into the public sphere of politics. "Humanitarian government" was her name for this concept.

The spiritualistic trances Tilton had written about were theater on Woodhull's part, but she had also lived through the genuine article. As a young woman she had, from time to time, experienced altered states of consciousness that she considered trances. When she said "the sensation on returning to my body was that of having suddenly fallen from a height, but without harm . . . I began to feel as if I had something to do which was worth doing," she was describing feelings typical of a trance. It is a vivid sensory experience that leaves in its wake a profound sense of its importance. At the onset of a trance, the recipient often feels anxiety, which gives way to euphoria, ineffability, a joy too great to be described, an ecstasy akin to orgasm. Woodhull felt—as her mother had with her glossolalia—"a condition of exaltation which lifted her." Woodhull's trance experiences appear to have helped her through difficult events in her life and given her a sense of purpose.

Woodhull's evaluation of her trances was instructive. "Had we not been poor, uneducated, obscure people without position or prospects in the world, we should probably not have been so ready and willing to yield [to trances]." She rejected the word "hallucination." She insisted that she had experienced "something very different from ordinary imagination . . . a distinct class of mental phenomena having a quality and value of their own." Woodhull had discussed her altered states with ministers and doctors but found them "ignorant" or "pretentious"; they hadn't helped her understand herself any better. As Woodhull grew older and more sophisticated, she lost the ability to enter these altered states and regretted the loss.

Psychologists began to study the unconscious as the nineteenth century drew to a close, and trances were examined as a form of hysterical behavior, as possible manifestations of split or multiple personalities. However, Woodhull's trances were not a form of mental illness; rather they endowed her with a unique means of voicing authority, a means that was otherwise disallowed women by the conventions of the time. Difficult as it may be for those of us from another generation to believe, Woodhull's ingenuity and individualism, her admirable independence of thought, seem to have grown out of what we, like Olympia Brown, think of as superstition. That aspect of Woodhull's spiritualism was entirely genuine; she believed she had been "born and reared and educated under the influences from the unseen world for a special mission to the world."

Woodhull took a forceful stand against what she considered to be the charlatans among the spiritualists, the rappers and the table lifters. Not long after her biography came out, she wrote that spiritualism was "too materialistic," too dependent on "physical manifestations." When mediums have been exposed, the spiritualists "have shown too much readiness to defend them in spite of the evidence against them. This course has not only seriously weakened the public faith in the honesty of their convictions . . . but also in the general doctrines upon which spiritualism, as a whole, rests."

Woodhull's success in Vineland encouraged her to attend the American Association of Spiritualists' national convention in Troy, New York, a few days later. She prepared the way by making spiritualism the lead editorial in the *Weekly* on the week of the convention, saying spiritualism would "elevate the aspirations of humanity."

September 12 found Woodhull speaking in Troy. She had come prepared with a new subject, "The Training of Children—Good Advice to Mothers." It was a politic choice; the spiritualists' interest in education and their own Children's Lyceum had been on the agenda in Vineland. It was a subject of personal interest to Woodhull as she arranged for the education of her daughter, Zula Maud, now ten years old. She spoke for the first time on a subject that would become a recurring theme for her, the importance of providing children with sex education.

"I scarcely know how it has come about that I am on this rostrum in the midst of a spiritualistic convention," Woodhull began disingenuously. "I have been a spiritualist and a recipient of heavenly favors ever since I can remember . . . I have not been known to spiritualists, nor they to me. In my humble way I have been an earnest advocate of the principles of the spiritual philosophy . . . I thank the convention for its hand of fellowship." It was flawless spiritualistic language, and it came to her as easily as a drink of water.

In a wave of acclamation, the spiritualists nominated and elected Woodhull president of their organization. This response went beyond even Woodhull's expectations. If she had privately lobbied members of the convention for this position, no record of her efforts have survived. It seems to have been just as it appeared, a spontaneous outburst of enthusiasm. Woodhull was overwhelmed and later wrote in the *Weekly* that "her surprise at her reception, and her nomination to the presidency of the Society was equaled only by the gratitude she felt." She interpreted her election to this office as a confirmation of her political calling by higher powers, describing it as the "chief honor" of her life.

She turned this honor into a call to political action. In a "President's Message" to the association, a lengthy five-column editorial in the *Weekly* that ran in early November, she wrote, "I can only regard the fact of your election of me, personally a stranger among you, and by spontaneous action, as your president . . . as an intimation that the great and influential body of spiritualists has arrived at a state of readiness to intervene actively in the political affairs of the country." She talked about her suffrage work. She brought up her other constituency, labor reformers, and the strength they could wield together. She discussed the possibility of expanding the spiritualists' lyceums into a national education system. How appropriate, she said, for the spiritualists to establish a government of "the Good, the True and the Beautiful" to replace the present system ruled by corruption and influence peddling.

"I tell you frankly that I feel myself called upon by the higher powers to enact a great role in connection with this great change. It is not ambition in any common or low sense of the term . . . It is a swelling and overmastering desire for an immense usefulness to my suffering fellow-beings . . . it is inspiration . . . which I trace and ascribe to spiritual sources . . . and which has in it . . . the promise of undoubted and unbounded success."

20

A Famous Test Question

On Tuesday November 7, 1871, election day in New York City, twelve women met at 2:30 P.M. in the drawing room at East 38th Street. Their plan was to march as a group to the polls and become the first women voters in the city of New York. The *Herald,* on hand to report the historical moment, said Tennie Claflin read the Fourteenth and Fifteenth Amendments aloud from a "ponderous" volume, her "lily-white hands" turning the pages impatiently. The reporter couldn't hold back one aren't-they-cute jibe. "Unterrified, indomitable . . . each determined female unsheathed her parasol and swore to vote in spite of Democratic denunciations and Republican sneers."

The women marched to 682 6th Avenue, the polling place of the twenty-third District of the twenty-first ward, where Woodhull announced that she had come to "exercise her privilege as a citizen of the United States to vote."

The three polling inspectors stroked their beards and set their coat collars in order. When Woodhull handed them the ballots for the group of women, the Republican inspector reached out to accept them. His Democratic counterpart interrupted him, saying that Tammany Hall had given orders not to accept votes from women. The city elections of that year put the power of Tammany Hall to a serious test. The Committee of Seventy, led by Samuel J. Tilden, had obtained indictments against "Boss" Tweed, Mayor A. Oakley Hall, and other lesser Tammany officials shortly before election day. Would the voters now oust the Tammany ticket? Turnout all day had been large; the air was charged with high expectations.

Confronting the Tammany hack, Woodhull demanded to know if it was "a crime to be a woman." She had "registered," she said, and therefore claimed the right to deposit her vote. The inspectors were unmoved. A crowd collected, soon becoming several hundred people. Woodhull, seeing that she had an audience, pulled out a pocket-size copy of the Constitution, and pointing to the Fourteenth and Fifteenth Amendments, gave her suffrage speech on the spot.

As Woodhull distracted the polling inspectors with her speech, a reporter from *Harper's Weekly* noticed that one of the women accompanying her, a Mrs. Miller, had managed to slip her ballot into the voting box.

Claflin was not so successful. Directing her charms toward the Republican inspector, she said that the Tammany Democrats would soon be out of office. She was with the Republicans, she told him. They were the "guiding star of progress" and willing to allow "the fair sex all the privileges accorded to a man." Her words and wiles made no impact on the stony-faced inspector; he refused to accept her ballot.

The frustrated women returned to East 38th Street. But the Democratic inspector who had opposed them was in for a stunning surprise. The voters turned out Tammany Hall. Throughout the city, they rejected virtually all of Tweed's candidates. The would-be first women voters heard the news as they laid plans to bring a suit against the polling inspectors for illegally preventing legitimate voters from exercising the right of suffrage. The rights granted in the Wyoming Territory should come to New York, they said. J. D. Reymart, the lawyer who had first encouraged Woodhull to pursue her voting Memorial, offered to help them make their case a "famous test question." Woodhull put the speech she had given at the polls into a letter to the *New York Times*. "Much has been said in the daily Press about my claim being 'a farce,' " she wrote. "I trust that you may do your women readers the justice to publish [our argument] that women are legal voters under both the State and Federal Constitutions. One-sided and dogmatic journalism is too common, and I shall hail the day when a free press may be inaugurated."

Later in the month, *Harper's Weekly* reported the voting attempt, illustrated with a sketch by H. Balling. The magazine called the incident a "serio-humorous rencontre," but Woodhull was, in fact, depicted forcefully and impressively in the *Harper's* sketch. Her arm was upraised imperiously toward a shrugging poll official as she demanded her vote, and she stood her ground with determination among a group of sneering men. The sketch, rather than being humorous, accurately reflected the courage that had animated her attempt to cast her ballot.

21

"Yes, I Am a Free Lover"

The new Woodhull was in greater demand on the lecture circuit than the old. She had toured Cleveland, Chicago and Baltimore in September and October. Almost immediately after voting, she was off to Philadelphia to speak at Horticultural Hall on November 9, 1871, and then to Hartford, Connecticut, on November 14.

Woodhull's busy schedule had private motive: she needed the money that lecturing brought in. Her income had not kept pace with her lavish lifestyle, her extravagant parties, her expensive house on Murray Hill. Day by day her fortune seemed to be slipping away. She undoubtedly continued to speculate in the hope of recouping all, though no brokerage firm records from this period document her transactions. Woodhull maintained the posture that all was well, but Tennie, who was always more frank about their personal lives, acknowledged that their finances had become precarious.

Free love was the subject that drew the biggest crowds, and Woodhull now promoted her suffrage speech with the line, "She Will Also Discuss the Free Love System." Before Woodhull arrived in Hartford, a "citizen of Hartford," understood to be Catharine Beecher, requested that the governor of Connecticut ban Woodhull's speech on November 14. The governor refused, and Woodhull turned Catharine Beecher's opposition to her own advantage saying, "Miss Beecher told me . . . she would strike me . . . I will present her with my other cheek . . . She may profess Christ, but I hope I may exceed her in living his precepts."

Tilton's biography of Woodhull had included a succinct summary of Woodhull's free love philosophy:

> On social questions her theories are similar to those taught by John Stuart Mill and Elizabeth Cady Stanton, and which are styled by some as free love doc-

trines, while others reject this appellation on account
of its popular association with the idea of a promis-
cuous intimacy between the sexes—the essence of her
system being that marriage is of the heart and not of
the law, that when love ends marriage should end
with it, being dissolved by nature, and that no civil
statute should outwardly bind two hearts which have
been inwardly sundered.

The remarks Woodhull improvised during her suffrage speeches
usually began, "Agitation of thought is the beginning of wisdom.
Hence I like it," and continued, "I have never known any other love
than free . . . I protest . . . against all laws that would compel
[women] to maintain relations with men for whom they have no regard. I honor that purity of life which comes from the heart . . . If to
hold and practice such doctrines as these is to be a free lover, then I
am a free lover."

"Nastiness," spluttered the *Troy (New York) Times* after her
speech at the spiritualist convention in that city. Other newpapers
echoed this response. Yet people packed lecture halls to hear her.
Woodhull began preparing a major new speech on the subject, setting
aside her suffrage and labor reform efforts temporarily. She rented
Steinway Hall, the largest in New York City, for a lecture called "The
Principles of Social Freedom." The heavy-handed title was a device
to make the subject sound genteel and respectable, even erudite. And
she paid another call on Henry Ward Beecher.

As Woodhull remembered these events a year later, she had prepared the speech "in the hope of being able to persuade Mr. Beecher
to preside for me, and thus make a way for himself into a consistent
life on the radical platform. I made my speech as soft as I conscientiously could. I toned it down in order that it might not frighten him.
When it was in type I went to his study and gave him a copy, and
asked him to read it carefully and give me his candid opinion . . .

"Meantime, I had told Mr. Tilton and Mr. Moulton that I was going to ask Mr. Beecher to preside, and they agreed to press the matter with him. I explained to them that the only safety he had was in
coming out as soon as possible [as] an advocate of social freedom,
and thus palliate, if he could not completely justify, his practices, by
founding them at least on principle. I told them that this introduction

of me would bridge the way. Both the gentlemen agreed with me in the view, and I was for a time almost sure that my desire would be accomplished.

"A few days before the lecture I sent a note to Mr. Beecher asking him to preside for me. This alarmed him. He went with it to Messrs. Tilton and Moulton asking advice. They gave it in the affirmative, telling him they considered it eminently fitting that he should pursue the course indicated by me . . . Matters remained undecided until the day of the lecture."

Tilton was on a speaking tour of his own at the time, unavailable as an intermediary, and time was running out, so Woodhull sent off a fast but pointed note directly to Beecher:

> Dear Sir: For reasons in which you are deeply interested as well as myself and the cause of truth, I desire to have an interview with you, without fail at some hour tomorrow. Two of your sisters have gone out of their way to assail my character and purposes . . . You doubtless know that it is in my power to strike back . . . but I do not desire to do this. I simply desire justice . . . I speak guardedly, but I think you will understand me. I repeat that I must have an interview tomorrow, since I am to speak tomorrow evening at Steinway Hall . . . Please return answer by bearer.

Woodhull's later reconstruction of these events continued, "I went over again to press Mr. Beecher to a decision. I had then a long private interview with him, using all the arguments I could to induce him to consent. He said he agreed perfectly with what I was to say, but that he could not stand on the platform at Steinway Hall and introduce me."

"I should sink through the floor," Woodhull remembered Beecher saying. "I am a moral coward on this subject, and I know it, and I am not fit to stand by you, who go there to speak what you know to be the truth; I should stand there a living lie."

"He got upon the sofa on his knees beside me," Woodhull recalled, "and taking my face between his hands, while the tears streamed down his cheeks, begged me to let him off.

"Becoming thoroughly disgusted with what seemed to me pusillanimity, I left the room under the control of a feeling of contempt for the man, and reported to my friends what he had said."

Among those friends was Tilton, who had just returned from Boston. He persuaded Woodhull to talk to Beecher one more time, and accompanied her. Tilton said to Beecher, as Woodhull recounted it:

"Mr. Beecher, some day you have got to fall; go and introduce this woman and win the radicals of the country, and it will break your fall."

"Do you think," said Beecher, "that this thing will come out to the world?"

"Nothing is more certain in earth or in heaven, Mr. Beecher; and this may be your last chance to save yourself from complete ruin," Tilton responded.

"I can never endure such a terror." Beecher said, "Oh! if it must come, let me know of it twenty-four hours in advance, that I may take my own life. I cannot, cannot face this thing."

Woodhull remembered being thoroughly out of patience. She turned to leave, actually walked through the door, then returned for a last biting word. "Mr. Beecher, if I am compelled to go on that plat-form alone, I shall begin by telling the audience why I am alone, and why you are not with me." With that she left both Beecher and Tilton in Beecher's study. Tilton later told her that Beecher had agreed to preside if he could "bring his courage up to the terrible ordeal."

More than 3,000 people, undeterred by a drenching rain, went to Steinway Hall that Monday evening. A reporter from the *Herald* ar-rived an hour ahead of time. The entrance and vestibule were already crowded with people, though the doors would not open for 30 min-utes. Bold yellow placards sprawled Woodhull's name across the bul-letin boards on the walls. He saw "several young ladies of very bold behavior . . . evidently professional and unfortunate in character," a stream of respectable-looking people, both men and women, then a red-headed girl who bounced in, threw off her shawl, and said, "I hope, by gosh, I haven't come here for nothing in all this rain."

Entering through a side door, the reporter found Woodhull in a lit-tle room off a narrow passage, a roll of manuscript in her hands, talking with Claflin. "The Woodhull had an inspired look," he noted; her eyes were "burning with suppressed fire." She was dressed in black with a watch-chain pendant hanging from her neck. A fresh tea rose fastened near her neck "enhanced the fairness of her skin."

"I am glad to see the *Herald* reporter," she told him, "That paper has never misrepresented me, and I know it won't now." She handed him a fresh tea rose. He found himself eclipsed in Woodhull's attentions by the entrance of Tilton, whom the reporter recognized immediately as the "blond poet."

Woodhull remembered later that it was "four minutes of the time for me to go forward to the platform at Steinway Hall when Mr. Tilton and Mr. Moulton came into the anteroom asking for Mr. Beecher. When I told them that he had not come, they expressed astonishment. I told them I should faithfully keep my word, let the consequences be what they might. . . Mr. Tilton then insisted on going onto the platform with me and presiding." Woodhull told Tilton she would not mention Beecher's name, and turned away to go over her manuscript one more time.

Then, Tilton led Woodhull onto the stage, followed by Claflin and a body of reporters. At Woodhull's appearance, a shout went up from the audience. Every seat on the ground floor and in the two galleries was occupied, and people were standing in the aisles. The boxes on either side of the stage were occupied by Woodhull's friends and family. As Tilton stepped forward, Moulton whispered to him, "Are you going to introduce Mrs. Woodhull to the audience, Tilton?"

"Yes, by heaven," Tilton replied, "since no one else has the pluck to do it."

He led Woodhull to the front of the platform and introduced her. "I came to this meeting actuated by curiosity to know what my friend would have to say . . . I was told that she was coming upon this stand unattended and alone. . . It may be that she is a fanatic; it may be that I am a fool; but, before high heaven I would rather be both fanatic and fool in one than to be such a coward as would deny to a woman the sacred right of free speech." Applause interrupted Tilton. "With as much pride as ever prompted me to the performance of any act in fifteen or twenty years," he continued, "I have the honor of introducing to you Victoria C. Woodhull, who will address you upon the subject of social freedom."

Woodhull started hesitantly, "I come before the public at this time, upon this particular subject . . ." Scattered applause seemed to strengthen her, and she continued in a confident voice. She reviewed what she called the principles of freedom, the rights of individuals, drawn from social theories of "individual sovereignty." Woodhull had adopted Stephen Paul Andrews's term "self-ownership": An individual is "self owned . . . because he has the inherent right to self, which right cannot be delegated to any second person," she said, "a right—as the American Declaration of Independence has it—which is 'inalienable.'"

Women had the same rights to self-ownership as men, Woodhull declared, and should not be "owned and possessed by some second person . . . The sexual relation must be rescued from this insidious form of slavery. Women must rise from their positions as ministers to the passions of men to be their equals . . . They must be . . . independent individualities, [not] mere appendages or adjuncts . . ." Women have a "duty of selfhood."

Relations between the sexes are matters of emotions that the government has no right to control, she continued. "Law cannot compel two to love . . . Where two meet and realize the love elements of their natures are harmonious . . . a natural law . . . high above human law" operates. "They are sexually united . . . married by nature . . . and to be thus married is to be united by God."

Woodhull proposed that loveless marriages should be ended, that when the "unity" between the partners departed, the marriage ceased. "The government has no legitimate right to interfere."

As for monogamous relationships, she said, "I am fully persuaded that the very highest sexual unions are those that are monogamic, and that these are perfect in proportion as they are lasting."

But Woodhull's philosophy also supported the individual right to other kinds of relationships, to serial monogamy or "exclusionist" free love, and to sexual experimentation, or "varietist" free love. So long as the motives were "pure," by which Woodhull meant that partners felt genuine affection for each other, untainted by exploitation, sexual experimentation was a matter of individual choice. Her speech went on to her best lines of the evening:

> It can now be asked: What is the legitimate sequence of Social Freedom? To which I unhesitatingly reply: Free love, or freedom of the affections. "And are you a free lover?" is the almost incredulous query.
>
> I repeat a frequent reply: "I am; and I can honestly, in the fullness of my soul, raise my voice to my Maker, and thank Him that I am . . ."
>
> And to those who denounce me for this I reply: "Yes, I am a free lover. I have an inalienable, constitutional and natural right to love whom I may, to love

as long or as short a period as I can; to change that love every day if I please, and with that right neither you nor any law you can frame have any right to interfere."

Woodhull closed on a conciliatory note, saying, "I prize dearly the good opinion of my fellow-beings. I would, so gladly, have you think well of me, and not ill. It is because I love you all, and love your well-being still more than I love you, that I tell you my vision of the future . . . I believe, with the profoundest conviction, that what I have urged in this discourse is conducive to that end."

Applause ushered Woodhull off the stage. If she had spoken on free love to enhance her value on the lecture circuit, she had also convinced the thousands at Steinway Hall that she believed in it.

Woodhull's personal sexual history would follow the arc of her speech. Trapped in a loveless marriage, she had sought freedom. She admired long-lasting, monogamous relationships, but they were a model she could not live up to. She claimed the right to follow her own desires as a self-owned woman, calling this her personal "truth" and "purity." She had a strong hedonistic element in her makeup, and the philosophy of free love gave her a rationalization for acting it out. She lived through a period of sexual experimentation. One of her future lecture themes would be the right of every woman to sexual self-fulfillment. But Woodhull's sexual experimentation led to chaos in her personal and public life, and she eventually rejected sexual experimentation in favor of monogamy.

The following day, the *Times, Sun, World,* and *Herald* all gave the speech calm treatment, the *World* commenting with surprise that some of the audience had been disappointed by the "high moral ground" Woodhull had taken, and by "the limited license her definition of free love would allow." Even the *Tribune,* so critical since spring, acknowledged that "The Social Problem never had a bolder advocate than Mrs. Victoria C. Woodhull proved herself last night at Steinway Hall."

Woodhull scarcely had time to read her press notices. She was whistle-stopping again, speaking at Corinthian Hall in Rochester on Wednesday November 22, 1871, at the Opera House in Dunkirk, New York, on Thursday, at Case Hall in Cleveland on Friday, at the Young Men's Hall in Detroit on Saturday, at White's Hall in Toledo on Sunday, at St. James Hall in Buffalo on Monday, at Farrar Hall in

Erie, Pennsylvania, on Tuesday the 28th, in Wheeling, West Virginia, on the following Thursday, at the Mercantile Library Hall in Pittsburgh on Friday, and in Harrisburg, Pennsylvania, on Saturday December 2—11 cities in 13 days.

During this tour, her press notices were surprisingly muted, considering the controversial nature of her subject. The *Rochester Express* found her to be the ablest advocate of women's suffrage, "a woman of remarkable originality and power." The *Pittsburgh Dispatch* called her "the most prominent woman of our time."

While Woodhull was away, Claflin's name began appearing in the *Weekly*. In unpolished prose, she defended her sister when a writer at the *Sun* called Woodhull a woman devoid of all feminine delicacy. She also published a letter to Woodhull in the *Weekly*: "Honored Lady," the letter's author, Mary Bowles, wrote. "The brave words which you uttered at Steinway Hall the other night have touched the hearts of thousands of degraded women with a thrill of joy and hope." Through a series of unfortunate circumstances, Mary Bowles said, she had found herself, at age 20, "the inmate of a house of ill repute in this city." She had subsequently discovered in herself "a shrewd business capacity" and in time became "a successful mistress" of her own such house. But, she wrote, she had

> conceived an intense indignation, amounting almost to hatred, for society which had condemned and excluded me, and for men especially in their mean and hateful treatment of women of our class—intimate with and caressing us in private, and cooly passing us by without recognition before the world . . .
>
> My business has been successful, but I am tired of it. I am arranging to break it up . . . What occurred to me was this. If you, in the prosecution of your blessed mission as a social reformer, have any need to see more behind the scenes and to understand the real state of New York society better, I will give you access to my two big books . . . You will find in them the names of all classes—from doctors of divinity to counter jumpers and runners for mercantile houses. Make what use of them as you please. I do not know that they will ever be of any use to me . . .

In conclusion let me say that your lecture has awakened a soul in me which I thought was dead. If your views could prevail, virtue and happiness could be again mine. God bless you for your honest effort for women even though it should fail. Til now I had no hope but in the grave; now I have some.

With love and admiration, Mary Bowles.

Tennie explained to Mary Bowles that Woodhull was away, so it had fallen to her to answer the letter. She published her reply in the following edition of the *Weekly*.

Perhaps I, even more than my sister Victoria, am interested, as a specialty, in the social question . . . I shall be happy to receive you at my home at any time, alone, [or] with others of your class, and shall be as ready and willing to accompany you on the street, or to dine with you at [a] restaurant as if you were, in all respects, the first ladies in the land. It is enough for me that you are human beings, and such as Christ loved and associated with . . . I do not claim to be any better than you, but let us mutually help each other . . .

In respect to the books you speak of, I do not know what use can be made of them, for my sister and myself have scrupulously adopted the policy of avoiding personalities when possible. But the time may come when that policy will have to be abandoned, for our enemies do not scruple to resort to them in the most scandalous manner . . .

Very truly your friend, Tennie C. Claflin.

Both letters were generally, if nervously, attributed to Claflin. The consensus was that they had been published as a circulation builder for the *Weekly*. But a shiver ran down the collective spine of New Yorkers from Broadway to Broad Street. Woodhull's speech, with its attacks on hypocrisy, her veiled threats over the past months to expose Henry Ward Beecher, took on a new and more ominous color. It was one thing to threaten the exposure of a hypocritical preacher, another to scare all men in New York who had visited prostitutes during the past ten years. Those who had chuckled over their cigars and brandy about Beecher's predicament suddenly found the sisters less amusing.

Tennie had street smarts. There were more than two ledger books' worth of information packed away in her brain. Her humor concealed a bitterness toward men, apparent in the description of them "caressing us in private and coolly passing us by without recognition before the world." The plight of prostitutes had become a concern of the *Weekly*'s to the distaste of some suffragists, and Tennie would continue to sympathize with their lot and decry the double standard that held such women in contempt while winking at their male partners. In her own impetuous way, she sharpened the edge of the free love controversy. Criticism of the sisters quieted considerably after the Mary Bowles letters appeared.

22

A Suffragist Nomination for President

On January 10, 1872, another suffrage convention was meeting in Washington, and Woodhull intended to use it to politicize the spiritualists. She planned to pack the convention with them and then embrace them openly from the platform.

The first challenge to her objectives came when Susan B. Anthony and Isabella Beecher Hooker said that they wanted to limit the convention to women. Woodhull insisted that men should be invited. She needed them because of their importance among the spiritualists. "I think it an error to exclude men from the hall," she wrote Hooker. "In doing that you pattern after the old custom. It should be in reality a call for Equal Rights." Woodhull prevailed: men would attend the convention and speak.

She prevailed partly because she paid for the printed announcements of the meeting. The funds she had at her disposal, or the perception that she had funds available, gave weight to her preferences. The suffrage movement, always short of cash, couldn't afford to ignore the wishes of someone who could do their printing for them. Actually, Woodhull couldn't afford this donation to the suffrage movement, but she still behaved as though her funds were inexhaustible. The suffragists had no idea her finances were strained.

Woodhull's successful free love lectures had helped to balance her budget. She now received more requests for lectures than she could satisfy. She recommended substitute speakers and became a source of patronage for other women lecturers. These speakers included many spiritualist leaders whom Woodhull hoped to enlist politically. They were strategically placed to influence audiences all over the country, and Woodhull could count on their support at the January convention.

When the suffrage leaders took the stage of Lincoln Hall on January 10, Woodhull was one of them. Elizabeth Cady Stanton, president of the convention, led the way, an imposing figure in heavy black silk. Susan B. Anthony came next, her wiry build clothed in wine-colored silk with a white collar and a blue tie. Woodhull followed in a plain suit of blue broadcloth and a double-breasted chinchilla coat. Hooker, in black silk, followed Woodhull.

Woodhull's demeanor at this suffrage convention was markedly different from the preceding May. Now that she had been accepted among the leaders, she went out of her way to show deference. With political wisdom, she held herself back until they called on her.

Stanton opened the meeting with a proposal that women go to the courts to obtain voting rights if a declaratory act were not passed by Congress during its current session. Anthony spoke next, saying that since she had been in Washington a year ago she had traveled 15,000 miles and had spoken on 108 nights. "President Grant, in his message, has remembered all classes and conditions of men to Congress, but never said woman once, and we have made up our minds that he is not the woman's candidate for the White House." These words produced applause.

Woodhull then spoke. She became, on the spot, energetic and enthusiastic. She talked directly to the many spiritualists in the hall, asking all "evangelical"—that is, spiritualistic—bodies to organize for political purposes.

> Let spiritualists and all reformers tear from their political banners the names of Democrat and Republican, which have become a stench in the nostrils of all thoughtful people, and throw to the breeze that more comprehensive name "Equal Rights" . . . and let them battle for it stoutly and devotedly, never faltering until it shall be planted on the dome of the Capitol at Washington in the hands of the Goddess of Liberty, in whose keeping it may be entrusted for all future ages . . . This is the destiny of spiritualism.

Hooker later told the meeting, "If spiritualists have brains enough to comprehend and soul enough to come up to the position to which Victoria Woodhull invites them, spiritualists will rule the world."

Woodhull, the evening's featured speaker, presented a fresh, well-written reprise of her declaratory act argument. She was still the quiet, composed Woodhull, but she concluded in a more confrontational style, "[Women] citizens are entitled to a Constitution to represent them, and they have got the power to inaugurate it. I do not propose they shall wait sixty years for justice. I want it here and now." It was a measure of Woodhull's influence over the convention that she was able to have the first evening devoted entirely to her interests. By the close of the first day, Woodhull had accomplished her goals; she had reached out to the spiritualists and called them to political action. Her proposed Equal Rights Party aroused wide discussion.

At the next morning's meeting, Anthony stepped forward unannounced. In an unexpected and surprising display of personal temperament, she steered the meeting back to the subject of suffrage. Attempting to derail the talk of a new Equal Rights Party—and changing her position since her criticisms of Grant the previous day—she said she would support the Democrats or the Republicans, whichever would put "a woman's suffrage plank in its platform . . . That party is my party, and that party I will support." Applause interrupted her. "I shall take the stump for that party at the next presidential campaign. Women have a name and principle of their own—we have a kite to fly ourselves. Any party that is a woman's suffrage party I am in for, and I will help to fly its kite; but I am not willing to be the last little paper knot in the tail of any political kite." Laughter and more applause followed her words.

As Anthony continued, it became clear that she had ambivalent feelings about Woodhull and her performance the previous day. On the one hand, she wanted to give Woodhull credit for what she had accomplished. "When I heard of a woman on Wall Street, I went to see how a woman looked among the bulls and the bears," she said, referring to her interview with Tennie two years earlier. "Women have the same rights there as men.

"Who brought Victoria C. Woodhull to the front? I have been asked by many. Why did you drag her to the front?

"Now bless your souls she was not dragged to the front. She came to Washington from Wall Street with a powerful argument and with lots of cash behind her, and I bet you cash is a big thing with Congress." Loud applause interrupted her.

"She presented her memorial to Congress, and it was a power . . . [If we need] youth, beauty and money to capture Congress, Victoria is the woman we are after." More laughter and applause.

After these left-handed compliments, Anthony went on to publicly raise the questions that had circulated about Woodhull's past, though her words were phrased in the guise of defending Woodhull.

"Women have too much false modesty. I was asked by the editors of New York papers if I knew of Mrs. Woodhull's antecedents. I said I didn't, and I did not care any more about them than those of Congress. Her antecedents will compare favorably with any member of Congress." she said.

"I have been asked all along the line of the Pacific Coast, What about Woodhull? You make her your leader. Now, we don't make leaders, they make themselves. If any can accomplish a more brilliant effort than Victoria C. Woodhull, let him or her go ahead, and they shall be the leaders." Once again applause forced Anthony to pause.

She reached, then, the crux of the matter that agitated her. "The fountain head of this movement is in dispute. Spiritualists say they began it. I am a Quaker, and the Quakers say they sounded the tocsin. Then the Abolitionists claimed it. Next I presume the Presbyterians will claim it. Mrs. Hooker will perhaps say it was the Beecher family who originated it."

Hooker shook her head, muttering, "No, you must take that back." Anthony sailed on. "Now, all I want is that all shall come together on the platform of equal rights to all and work for woman suffrage. We don't endorse any sect, breed or political power. We don't endorse temperance, labor reform, or spiritualism, but we do emphatically endorse woman suffrage. Now do you understand our platform?"

A voice from the audience called out, "Yes. Long live Miss Anthony."

Anthony had been doing some thinking since the previous day and was positioning herself publicly against Woodhull, against her overtures to the spiritualists, and against the political program she was attempting to put together. Anthony had sounded an alarm for what would become a sharp disagreement with Woodhull and a divisive new issue among the suffragists.

Anthony continued to work against Woodhull. She read a letter from Henry Ward Beecher to the convention, in which Beecher said he was not sure suffrage was imminent, but that it would come ultimately. He closed with the words, "In every wise and Christian movement for the education and enfranchisement of woman I hope always to be in sympathy." The delegates understood that the phrase "wise and Christian movement" was intended to disassociate Beecher from a suffrage movement that endorsed Woodhull and free love. Laura Cuppy Smith, a suffragist who was also a spiritualist lecturer, objected immediately, saying, "Henry Ward Beecher's power and influence are limited by the extent of his courage . . . Victoria C. Woodhull's popularity is founded upon her high-souled vindication of the truth as she apprehends it . . . truth alone today will command the masses . . . I have alluded to Victoria C. Woodhull. I am not a hero worshiper, but my whole soul does homage to the principles of which I deem this grand woman to be the inspired representative."

The next morning Woodhull was one of six women representing the suffragists in the Senate Judiciary Committee room, where Stanton had been invited to speak. Hooker and Anthony made preliminary remarks, Stanton the main presentation. She referred to the action taken by Butler in the House. "The Woodhull Memorial and the able arguments . . . sustaining it have been before the nation for one year and as yet remain unanswered . . . the opinions of many of our most learned judges and lawyers, multiplying on all sides, sustain the position taken by the Woodhull Memorial." Stanton then restated the case.

Belva Lockwood, a suffragist who was a teacher in Washington, D.C. and who was also studying law, presented the Judiciary Committee with a heavy volume containing 20,000 signatures favoring a declaratory act.

The Judiciary Committee members tried to look impassive, one suffragist wrote afterward, but they unbent after a bit, and by the close of the meeting had become very cordial. They told the suffragists they would make a decision as soon as possible and then went into a closed door session. Meanwhile, the women were invited to lunch at the Senate restaurant. On learning that their bill had been paid, Lucretia Mott observed wryly that the senators "offered compliments in lieu of rights."

After lunch, Stanton reported back to the convention. The inconclusive morning meeting had made her more receptive to the formation of a new political party, despite Anthony's opposition. "The signs of the time indicate the formation of a third party, in the presence of which both the old parties may well tremble . . . We shall assemble in convention all over the country. Women would do well to . . . take up the studies pertaining to the science of government," she said.

The convention closed with another success for Woodhull, a resolution that said, "We rejoice in the rapidly organizing millions of spiritualists, labor reformers, temperance and educational forces now simultaneously waking to their need of woman's help in the cause of reform."

Stephen Pearl Andrews had led a body of labor reformers to Washington as Woodhull supporters at the convention, and Stanton had welcomed them, over Anthony's objections. As the meeting closed Andrews took the floor and promoted Woodhull's new political party, saying, "Perhaps the nucleus of that party, the Equal Rights Party, or the like, is now in this hall."

Then the audience called for Woodhull. She thanked the delegates for their "approbation." Ada Ballou, a suffragist who was also a spiritualist speaker known for her eloquence, rose from the audience and, carried away by the emotion of the moment, placed Woodhull's name in nomination for president of the United States. It is possible that Woodhull had planned this action with Ballou, but no evidence of their collusion has survived. The two women did not know each other well. It seems likely that Ballou's action was, as it appeared, an expression of the sentiment at the meeting.

Anthony immediately and strenuously objected. She said that she "thought it a little premature" and that "Mrs. Stanton, Mrs. Hooker, Mrs. Gage and [I, myself] all had claim to be considered, but not because [we] wanted office." Despite Anthony's objections, the nomination was put before the convention and passed.

With that endorsement Woodhull had gained everything she wanted from the convention. Her next task was to gain a similar pledge of support from labor reformers.

23
Jesus Christ and Karl Marx

On Tuesday, February 20, 1872, a crowd gathered at the Academy of Music, on 14th Street at Irving Place in New York, to hear Woodhull's speech, "The Impending Revolution." It was a cold night. The sky was filled with stars, the streets were clear—no snow had fallen since the beginning of the month—and the temperature was well above freezing. Woodhull had delivered this address in Boston and Washington, and word had gotten around that she had shocking things to say. The lecture in New York was sold out. Speculators began scalping the 50-cent tickets for $10. People milled around for almost an hour.

At eight o'clock, after the seats had been filled and the standing places taken, Woodhull came out onto the stage alone. She wore a black dress with a cutaway jacket and a large blue necktie. Her hair was cut short and hung loosely around her ears. The confidence gained from scores of evenings at the podium and a successful Washington convention cancelled any need for an introduction by an opinion-maker lending support.

Woodhull intended on that night to win the support of the labor reformers for her presidential campaign. She began speaking in a quiet, conversational tone: "Standing on the apex of the nineteenth century . . ." Her voice rose to a confrontational level as she attacked the leading money men of the country by name. She started with Vanderbilt, the power behind her own capitalistic venture, Woodhull, Claflin & Company. She had decided to cast her old patron aside in favor of a new idealistic doctrine that might enhance her presidential candidacy.

> A Vanderbilt may sit in his office and manipulate stocks, or make dividends, by which, in a few years, he amasses $50 million from the industries of the

country, and he is one of the remarkable men of the age. But if a poor, half-starved child were to take a loaf of bread from his cupboard, to prevent starvation, she would be sent first to the Tombs and thence to Blackwell's Island.

An Astor may sit in his sumptuous apartments and watch the property bequeathed him by his father rise in value from $1 million to $50 million, and everybody bows before his immense power and worships his business capacity. But if a tenant of his whose employer had discharged him because he did not vote the Republican ticket, and thereby fails to pay his month's rent to Mr. Astor, the law sets him and his family into the street in midwinter . . .

Mr. Stewart, [the leading New York retailer] by business tact and various practices known to trade, succeeds in twenty years in obtaining from customers . . . $50 million, and with his gains he builds costly public beneficiaries, and straightway the world makes him a philanthropist. But a poor devil who should come along with a bolt of cloth, which he had succeeded in smuggling into the country, and which consequently he could sell at a lower price than Mr. Stewart who paid the tariff, and is thereby authorized by law to add that sum to the piece, would be cast into prison . . .

Is there any common justice in such a state of things? Is it right that the millions should toil all their lives long, scarcely having comfortable food and clothes, while the few manage to control all the benefits? People may pretend that it is justice, and good Christians may excuse it upon that ground, but Christ would never have called it by that name. He would have . . . given him that labored but an hour as much as he that labored all the day, but to him that labored not at all he would take away even that which he hath . . .

A system of society which permits such arbitrary distributions of wealth is a disgrace to Christian civilization.

The inequitable distribution of wealth was Woodhull's underlying theme. The *Weekly*'s muckraking had opened her eyes to the fault lines in capitalism. She used the term "labor reform" as an umbrella to encompass this issue. The labor reformers included three distinct and differing groups who had, in fact, little in common except that they were outside the system. The National Labor Union, formed in 1866, was made up of skilled laborers whose goal was to obtain an eight-hour day. Elizabeth Cady Stanton and Susan B. Anthony had already discovered that these trade unionists had little common ground with women suffragists.

Financial reformers made up the second group. They were organized under such names as the Reform Labor League, the Anti-Usury Society, the New England Labor Reform League, the American Labor Reform League. These groups were looking to ensure fair play in the economic sphere; they anticipated a day when the excesses of the nineteenth-century robber barons would be controlled by government regulation.

The third group was Karl Marx's International Workingmen's Association, founded in 1864. Its goal was a socialist state in which workers owned the means of production, and it accepted violent revolution as a means of accomplishing this end. Stephen Pearl Andrews had been associated with the First Communist International for several years. In 1869, as a member of New Democracy, a group that aimed to harmonize all reform movements, he had contacted the General Council of the International in London to make an affiliation. Its sections in the United States were, for the most part, made up of foreign-born workers, the majority of them German.

Andrews's New Democracy disbanded and was replaced by two American sections of the International. One of these, Section 12, with the help of Andrews and Marie Stevens Howland, one of his disciples, became a women's section promoting political and social rights for women within the International Workingmen's Association. Howland had been a "workingman" once herself. She and her two younger sisters had worked in the infamous textile mills of Lowell, Massachusetts.

Through the efforts of Andrews and Howland, Woodhull and Claflin were named to head Section 12. Articles about the Internationals' meetings appeared regularly in the *Weekly*, usually written by an organizer named William West. From the little we know about them, most of the members of Section 12 were spiritualists as well as Internationals, and were unique among the spiritualists in their willingness to take political action. The section endorsed not only Marx, but also woman suffrage and free love. Section 12 was an anomaly within the International Workingmen's Association. Marxists accused the section members of being "pseudo-communists," "sensation-loving spirits" who merely played at the labor movement. With some justification, the leaders of the International repudiated the two lady bankers and brokers as "bourgeois intellectuals" and "parlor radicals" who were becoming a divisive force in the organization. The issue would soon be referred to the General Council in London.

Despite the opposition of the parent organization, Woodhull looked on the American Internationals as a potential constituency. She had marched down the streets of New York in a December 17, 1871, procession honoring Louis Nathaniel Rossel and his companions of the Paris Commune. Their insurrectionist group, in the wake of France's defeat in the Franco-Prussian War, had governed France earlier in the year, from March 18 to May 28, 1871. After their defeat and the subsequent execution of their leaders, Karl Marx invested the Commune's brief rule with a mythical stature as the first uprising of the proletariat against capitalism.

Marx's *Communist Manifesto,* written with Freidrich Engels, had appeared in the *Weekly,* timed to coincide with the 1871 memorial march. It had been the work's first appearance in the United States in English.

Weekly articles continued to expound Section 12's views on communism. On January 6, 1872, the paper editorialized that the beliefs of Marx were "Christlike" and stated, "We have no doubt that if Jesus Christ were among us today he would be found associating with [the Internationals], as all his doctrines were communistic in their tendencies." A profile of Marx appeared in the same issue, reprinted from Frank Leslie's *Illustrated Weekly.*

But Woodhull's efforts with the Internationals were doomed by a basic difference in values. She believed in individual freedom and wanted to make freedom available to excluded groups. The Internationals' collectivist outlook rejected individualism and private ownership of property and accepted the Marxist doctrine of unavoidable class conflict. Woodhull had absorbed more of Thomas Jefferson and Walt Whitman than Karl Marx; she and Section 12 were American in outlook as well as birth.

These basic incompatibilities would become apparent as time went on. For the moment, Woodhull naively took up communism as an idealized political expression of spiritualism, what the *Weekly* referred to as "Christian communism," a vaguely defined communal society that was also a worker's paradise.

In her speech at the Academy of Music, Woodhull talked of Christ and his disciples, "who had all things in common. Let professing Christians who . . . make long prayers think of that," she said, "and then denounce communism, if they can; and denounce me as a revolutionist for advocating it, if they dare.

"How is this to be remedied? I answer very easily . . . When a person worth millions dies, instead of leaving it to his children, who have no more title to it than anybody else's children have, it must revert to the people."

Woodhull's words indicate that she believed she was embracing a system that would promote a more equitable distribution of wealth, the goal of the financial reformers, not a state-controlled communist society. But her rhetoric did not make this distinction clear: "Now Christ was a communist of the strictest sort, and so am I, and of the most extreme kind. I believe that God is the Father of all humanity and that we are brothers and sisters, and that it is . . . a stern reality, to be reduced to a practical recognition." She made no attempt to rationalize her capitalistic brokerage business with the new doctrines she was expounding so enthusiastically.

Woodhull addressed the members of her audience as if they were a group of spiritualists, urging them as Christians to become politically active:

> Christianity of today is a failure . . . True religion will not shut itself up in any church away from humanity; it will not stand idly by and see the people suffer from any misery whatsoever . . . it is foolish for a Christian to say, 'I have nothing to do with politics' . . . It is the bounden duty of every Christian to support that political party which bases itself upon Human Rights, and if there is no such party existing, then to go about to construct one.

This time, Woodhull shocked the newspapers into silence. People who had been unable to get into the hall looked through the morning papers in vain. No word of Woodhull's speech appeared in the *Tribune,* the *Times* or the *Standard.* The *Herald,* usually so generous in its reporting of Woodhull's words, described the milling crowd at Irving Place, but omitted the main event, in the *Weekly*'s judgment making "a tremendous effort to say nothing and succeeding admirably." The *Sun* similarly described the size of the crowd but limited its report on the speech, saying vaguely, "Several passages of the speech were enthusiastically applauded, as much of what she said appealed directly to the prejudices of the audience."

Only the *World,* among the major New York dailies, reported the contents of the speech. A dozen lines referred elliptically to the slavery of the laboring classes, the evils of railroad and money monopolies, and the relation of Christianity to politics.

The mighty New York press, which had spared no ink covering Woodhull's defense of free love, controversial as it was, closed its columns to condemnation of the capitalist system. Not a single word of Woodhull's criticisms of Vanderbilt, Astor, and Stewart, mild and impersonal as those criticisms were, appeared in print. Nor did the unspeakable word, "communism."

Woodhull took the papers to task in the *Weekly.* "Ordinarily such a remarkable outpouring of the people would have received respectful attention from the press . . . the monopolies of all sorts do not desire that the people shall inquire [into themselves]: hence the press is muzzled; the people must not know too much . . . These men forget that the people will find out that newspapers and politicians are equally guilty of the wrongs which make reforms and revolutions necessary . . . the people will lose confidence in editors just as they have in political hucksters and tricksters."

Two days after the speech the *Times* published a column-long editorial attempting to trivialize Woodhull and so diminish her standing. She has been "married rather more extensively than most American matrons, and hence it might be deemed inappropriate to style her a foolish virgin," the *Times* began. Woodhull had recently proved her "folly," it said, and exhibited her "fondness for scolding men of respectability." Ignorant people might "receive her folly as though it were words of wisdom."

Then, the *Times* got to its real concern: "She is therefore capable of mischief in inflaming the unthinking hostility of the poor to the rich, and in fostering in the minds of the workingmen who applauded her during her recent lecture, the conviction that capitalists have no rights which workingmen are bound to respect." The *Times* defended Astor and Stewart by name and asked why Vanderbilt had been exempt from her criticisms. The *Times* was in error here, however, since Vanderbilt's name had been the first she'd mentioned.

The editorial went on to charge her with not practicing what she preached. This accusation had merit, for Woodhull had yet to explain how her own brokerage business fit her new communist ideology.

> Why should not Mrs. Woodhull prove her faith in the theory that property is crime . . . let her kindle a bonfire in Union Square and head a procession of women like-minded with herself, who will cast their wicked wealth into the flame. When her best black silk and her jaunty sealskin jacket, her diamond rings and her golden necklaces, her dainty high heeled boots and her most cherished chignons have crackled and burned and melted in the fire, the intelligent workingmen of the city will, at least, credit her with a desire not to enjoy luxuries which she has not earned by manual labor.

Woodhull immediately sent a reply, which the *Times* returned unpublished, saying "we cannot possibly afford the space for your letter." She printed it all in the *Weekly*. She rightly called the paper's characterization "burlesque if not blackguard." "I might," she said, "read the *Times* a homily on wife beating . . . but I shall treat the matter as if it were intended in good faith." Then she got to the point she had never addressed before, her own practice of capitalism. In reading her discussion of the subject, it becomes clear that her real concern, like that of the financial reformers, was in the equitable distribution of wealth and fair play.

> I never objected to the accumulation of wealth. I want everybody to have all the wealth of which he can make good use, and if equal conditions are secured everybody may have that amount. But I did, and always shall until it is remedied, object to a certain few

holding all the wealth . . . One class of people have no right first to monopolize the wealth, and afterward to put labor in bondage by its power.

Mrs. Woodhull does not monopolize either dresses, jewels or chignons; since of the first she only possesses sufficient to render her comfortable, while with the last two she has nothing to do . . . She believes humanity is capable of rising into a higher, nobler and more perfect life than that which makes money its God. She believes money should be simply the means to better ends, and not the end in itself; and she does not believe that anybody would suffer either hardship or injustice by the institution of such life among humanity . . .

Working people have rights which capital never has respected, and which the *Times,* and other papers conducted in the interests of bond-holders, money-lenders and Republican officials, are determined never shall be recognized. And this is the issue which . . . will be fully joined . . . before the next election.

It was a sharp defense, and probably helped Woodhull clarify her own thinking. But the *Times* did not change its position. The paper's coverage of her free love speech was the last considered, thoughtful copy Woodhull would receive. For the remainder of her public career, the influential *New York Times* would maintain the abusive tone she so aptly characterized as "wife beating."

It was not by chance that the most intensely negative response to Woodhull's free love views appeared after her communist speech. The famous Thomas Nast cartoon caricaturing her as Mrs. Satan, which did her public image so much damage, appeared in *Harper's* not after her free love speech, but on February 17, after her first speech on communism. Woodhull commented in the *Weekly,* "Harper—pious, godly, Methodistic Harper—indulges, feasts his Methodistic, pious, godly patrons with a feeble attempt at burlesquing the institution of divine marriage," using "divine marriage" as her euphemism for free love. But Woodhull's defense did little to deflect the cartoon's negative impact. *Harper's* led the diversion, and the daily press, uneasy about Woodhull's communism, followed.

They attacked not her political views, but an easier target, her free love views, intending to invalidate Woodhull's political voice.

Woodhull's association with International Section 12 would be brief. However, her own vision of Christian communism, her view of an ideal society in which financial fair play reigned, stayed with her, and for the rest of her life she would believe that the equitable distribution of wealth was society's "unsolved riddle."

24

A Collection of American Originals

On March 2, 1872, Woodhull announced in the *Weekly* "a grand consolidated convention" to be held in May. She hadn't expected the strong opposition that her overtures to labor reformers and her "Impending Revolution" speech had received. Her finances were still shaky. But she remained determined, despite all obstacles, to wage a real presidential campaign. Nomination by a political party in convention would put her name in contention.

She reached out to those she felt were still with her, saying, "the labor unionists are a power if they resolve to work for political purposes. So also are the temperance reformers, while the women suffragists are by no means to be ignored." Woodhull, along with many suffragists, expected to vote in November. If no declaratory act materialized, they would vote without it, casting their ballots to challenge the state laws that they believed were invalid. Woodhull continued, "The Spiritualists alone, acting in unison, can defeat any party . . . which does not [promise] Equal Humanitarian Rights."

A "rush of letters from every direction" arrived in response to her invitation, and on April 6 a "call" for a political convention to meet Friday May 10, 1872, at Apollo Hall in New York City appeared in the *Weekly*. It was supported by the names of 25 reformers. Fifty-nine additional names appeared the next week, part of an ever-lengthening list reported by the *Weekly* up until the start of the convention.

Conspicuously missing from the call were names of some of the groups she had hoped to carry with her. The National Labor Union had nominated Judge David Davis at their own convention in Columbus. The suffragists were planning to hold their convention on May 9 in New York, and their "call" also appeared in the *Weekly*. The dual calls represented a defeat for Woodhull; she had hoped to have the suffrage leaders sponsor *her* convention. The best she had been able to accomplish was an arrangement in which she could draw the suffragists from their meeting on Thursday into hers on Friday. The old-line Boston reformer William Lloyd Garrison sniffed to a friend, "You will see by her hodgepodge weekly that Mrs. Woodhull and her followers are preparing for a great political splurge."

In the midst of these political preoccupations, Canning Woodhull died on April 7, at the age of 48. Addicted to morphine as well as alcohol, he had told Woodhull that he knew he had destroyed his own health, and that he did not expect to reach the age of 50. Caring for him had been one of Woodhull's finest acts of compassion. She paused to run a long obituary in the *Weekly*, made burial arrangements, and then went back to her presidential campaign.

Woodhull promoted her convention with a hectic schedule of meetings and speeches up until the eve of the meeting. She talked to the financial reformers of the American Labor Reform League on Sunday May 5, saying, "I hope that this League will . . . take active part in both the organization and in the campaign." The next day she addressed the American Anti-Usury Society in Room 24 at Cooper Institute. She spoke to the spiritualists again on Wednesday May 8, ferrying across the Hudson River to open the second quarterly convention of the Spiritualist Society of New Jersey at Union Hall in Jersey City.

Immediately, she returned to New York to concentrate her full attention on the suffragist meeting, which started Thursday morning. Despite her failure to form a united convention, she still hoped to obtain a presidential nomination from their meeting, repeating the endorsement she had won in Washington four months earlier. It would strengthen her position in Apollo Hall on Friday.

On Thursday morning, the suffrage meeting was highly charged. Woodhull did not know that Anthony and Stanton had argued about supporting Woodhull until late into the night on Wednesday, and they had been unable to resolve their differences. Stanton, annoyed by what seemed to be pettiness on Anthony's part, refused to preside at the Thursday meeting. Anthony immediately took advantage of Stanton's refusal and had herself elected president of the meeting, and of the organization for the coming year.

But Stanton gave the keynote address as planned. In it, she supported Woodhull indirectly, urging the women present to vote in the November election, to exercise their rights under the Fourteenth Amendment and identify themselves as members of a new political party. Anthony urged the women to do nothing until after the major party conventions; if those conventions didn't properly recognize women, then the suffragists should hold their own convention to select a presidential ticket. The subject was debated throughout the day.

Woodhull was finally able to take the floor over Anthony's vigorous objections. She said, "The eyes of the world are upon this convention. Its enemies have sneered and laughed at the idea of combining reformers for any organized action. They say that women don't know enough to organize, and therefore are not to be feared as political opponents." Woodhull suggested that those opposed to her within the suffrage movement were elitists. "I have even heard some confessed reformers say they don't want anything to do with those who don't belong to 'our clique' . . . but I trust this policy may not succeed . . . I hope all friends of humanitarian reform will clasp hands with each other."

Woodhull moved that the meeting adjourn to Apollo Hall to nominate candidates. The motion was seconded amid wild confusion, but Anthony refused to call the question. Someone asked that the chair be overruled. Woodhull stood and demanded an immediate vote. Her motion passed.

"Out of order," Anthony declared.

Woodhull seized the podium and began talking.

Anthony tracked down the janitor and ordered him to turn off the lights, forcing the suffragists to end the meeting and leave the building.

Many delegates favored Woodhull and planned to attend the convention in Apollo Hall the next day, among them Belva Lockwood, Laura Cuppy Smith, and Ada Ballou, who had supported Woodhull in January. But Stanton and Hooker, who had defended Woodhull at the suffragists' meeting, remained loyal to Anthony and returned to Steinway Hall for another day of meetings on Friday.

Apollo Hall was busy Friday morning. As the delegates made their way inside, they were greeted by long banners on the walls. Reformers of all persuasions could find their own comfortable homilies.

INTEREST ON MONEY IS A DIRECT TAX ON LABOR, TO SUPPORT
WEALTHY PAUPERS.
NATURALIZATION OF LAND, LABOR, EDUCATION AND INSURANCE.

EQUAL RIGHTS, PEACE AND CO-OPERATION.
THE WORLD IS OUR COUNTRY, TO DO GOOD OUR RELIGION.
THE UNEMPLOYED DEMAND WORK OF THE GOVERNMENT.

A holiday mood engulfed the convention delegates, a sense that their day had come at last. Many women among them came from backgrounds similar to Woodhull's. A disadvantaged early life had forced them to rely on their native talents, attractiveness, and courage. Spiritualism, of whatever individualistic interpretation, had given them a way out. They now looked indistinguishable from the suffragists, the middle-class elitists they had emulated. However, the spiritualists and Woodhull did differ from most suffragists in significant ways. Unconventional, less educated, but upwardly mobile and immensely gifted, they had turned their talents into professional success before the concept of a professional woman had been born. They were young and idealistic. Woodhull's achievements were their own. She, as a representative woman, was about to fulfill the ultimate ambition—to run for president. The spiritualists were at Apollo Hall to be a part of it.

The women attending, and the men, were a collection of American originals. Ada Ballou and Laura Cuppy Smith were there, of course, and Marie Stevens Howland, who had helped form Section 12 of the International. So were J. D. Reymart, Woodhull's friend and legal adviser, and Stephen Pearl Andrews, her political mentor.

Moses Hull of Vineland, New Jersey, would become a leader of the convention. A one-time abolitionist, he now wrote on free thought and free love in his journal *Hull's Crucible*. He had found marriage restrictive, and, with his wife's agreement, had moved on to what he described as "diviner impulses." Thereafter he and his diviner impulse, Mattie Sawyer, had lived and lectured together.

Caroline Hinckley Spear had started life as a trance speaker and had become a spiritualist lecturer. She graduated from Penn Medical University, a nontraditional medical school founded by the Longshores, a Philadelphia Quaker family of spiritualist views, and served for a time on the school's faculty. Her husband John Murray Spear, a Universalist minister, founded a utopian community, Kiantone, in upstate New York and divorced his first wife to marry Caroline Hinckley. In 1870 the couple moved to California and joined in organizing the state's first woman suffrage organization.

Belva Lockwood, the educator and suffragist from Washington,

D.C., was unusual among the women present in that she did not have a background as a spiritualist or a medium. An unhappy early life had led her into teaching, and she had founded her own school in Washington. She had just been admitted to law school at Columbian College (later George Washington University), and she would become the first woman admitted to practice before the Supreme Court of the United States. She would later run for president herself, nominated by another splinter party that owed something of its invention to her experience at this convention.

Angela Tilton and her husband, Ezra H. Heywood, a Presbyterian minister, represented the financial reformers. J. S. Sands considered himself a Christian capitalist. Theodore Banks was a rising star among the Internationals. J. K. Ingalls of New York was an agrarian reformer. Horace Dresser of New York was a spiritualist leader and lecturer who had graduated from Penn Medical University. William West, a member of Plymouth Church, was a Christian communist and an International. Robert Dale Owen, a reformer and freethinker, was a son of the Scottish industrialist Robert Owen, who had founded a utopian community in New Harmony, Indiana.

Another delegate, Dr. E. B. Foote of New York City, had been elevated to sainthood in the minds of many of the convention delegates. A fair-minded progressive and a highly regarded professional, Foote became radicalized when his works on sex education made him the target of obscenity charges. *Medical Common Sense,* his first book, had sold a quarter of a million copies in its first ten years, and in 1870 he had updated it in *Plain Home Talk.* Foote invented the first cervical cap used in the United States and sold birth control devices by mail. His son E. B. Foote, Jr., would coin the term "contraception."

Almost all of the delegates had lived lives of individual battle. It illuminates the strength of Woodhull's character that she could have attracted these iconoclasts to herself and united them sufficiently to bring the convention into being. At Apollo Hall in May 1872, they found common cause and would, for the first time, perhaps play a role in the political process. It was a euphoric moment of communion and high hopes.

At noon the choir sang "Hail, Columbia" to open the proceedings. The delegates were in such good humor that they didn't quiet down until the last words of the song had been sung. George Maddox of Maine, the temporary chairman, welcomed the members and got to the first order of business, the name for the new party. An Oregon delegate suggested Human Rights Party, but after a short discussion they chose Equal Rights Party, the name Woodhull favored.

Then the convention organized itself, forming committees, passing resolutions, and naming J. D. Reymart president. The Committee on Resolutions and Platform would direct the convention's activities. Through that committee, Colonel Blood managed the convention on Woodhull's behalf. Blood had taken a complete platform document, already printed, into the committee's meeting room. After vigorous discussion, the committee adopted the platform without changes.

Twenty-three planks covered education, suffrage, and a series of social and industrial reforms. Several planks would eventually become part of American life: graduated direct taxation, regulation of monopolies, laws to protect laborers, and a civil service based on merit. Other planks set forth radical economic positions redistributing wealth by nationalizing railroads and other industries; giving ownership of land, mineral, and water resources to the people; abolishing interest payments; and guaranteeing employment to all. A visionary plank called for the establishment of a universal government with international arbitration for wars.

The platform was read aloud to enthusiastic applause. Temperance reformers urged the committee to add a plank calling for total abstinence, but the delegates couldn't agree on the wording, so they passed a resolution discouraging the use of intoxicating liquors. A more fully organized temperance movement would get under way in the next year, 1873, with the formation of the Woman's Christian Temperance Union.

When the meeting reconvened at 8 P.M., the committee on credentials reported that 668 people, representing 22 states and 4 territories, were present. The delegates congratulated each other on the broad representation and unity of the convention. Nobody was thinking beyond the excitement of the moment, the sense of heightened anticipation that filled the air. A resolution was introduced and unanimously adopted inviting Victoria Woodhull to address the convention. Following her rousing speech, she was nominated by the new party for president of the United States.

25
Crisis

*A*fter Woodhull's nomination, fund-raising became her first priority. She had thrown no lavish convention parties—just one small, if exuberant, victory reception in Apollo Hall. Champagne no longer flowed at the house on East 38th Street. Back in April when the lease for the house had come due, she could not afford to renew it. So she had taken modest quarters near Apollo Hall as a temporary expedient, confident that her financial problems would solve themselves once she had obtained the presidential nomination. Her speech income had been exhausted by convention expenses, the rental of the hall, printing costs, the *Weekly,* constant travel. Still ahead of her was the process of getting her name on the ballot, a meticulous procedure that would entail petitions, legal expenses, and filing costs state by state.

Isabella Beecher Hooker told her friends that Woodhull had "sunk $100,000 in women suffrage" (almost $1 million in today's dollars), a figure that likely originated with Woodhull herself. Woodhull had undoubtedly exaggerated this figure to dramatize her contributions to suffrage, and to silence the women who felt aggrieved that her promised $10,000 donation had never been put directly into their hands. The exact mix of political activities, speculation, and high living that had depleted Woodhull's Black Friday winnings remains unclear, but she was now holding off creditors. However, she kept these worries to herself and her inner circle.

Saturday morning, the convention turned its attention to a novel financing program. After forming committees to continue the work of the new party—and after selecting a party banner featuring the Goddess of Liberty on a field of white, with the words "Equal Rights" underneath—the executive committee, led by Colonel Blood, proposed issuing non-interest-bearing bonds that would be redeemable when the Equal Rights Party was in power. The bonds would be "only for the necessary expenses of this campaign." They would be printed on the best-quality bank note paper with the name of the candidate and the party banner. Delegates immediately purchased bonds worth $1,600 and pledged another $4,700. Woodhull, expressing more wishful thinking than common sense, said that capitalists with vision, with "humanitarian instincts," would see the merits of a more equitable distribution of wealth and come to support the Equal Rights Party. She reported that the first bond had been purchased by a capitalist, J. Q. Sands, "wise enough to see the injustice of present conditions."

Reymart, president of the convention, ended the meeting with similarily idealistic optimism. "Victoria C. Woodhull . . . is full of humanity and full of inspiration, spirit and love . . . truth and justice can crush ignorance and prejudice . . . It devolves upon us to render this work effective . . . we call on earth and heaven to inspire us."

Within 24 hours, Woodhull began putting all her private affairs under the newly endowed umbrella of the Equal Rights Party. Sunday evening the executive committee of the party met to plan the campaign ahead. Her long-time advisers, Blood, Andrews, and Reymart, were present, as well as Theodore Banks, Anna Middlebrook, John and Carrie Spear, and Mary H. Leland.

Woodhull made a new residence her first order of business. It would be used as the headquarters for the party and a location for committee meetings, and part of it would be occupied by the "prospective Presidentress." Woodhull and a committee of three were appointed to secure a house in some "prominent locality" at a rental not to exceed $1,000 per month. This was a queenly sum, indicating Woodhull saw the Equal Rights Party as a new and lucrative source of income. The *Times*, getting word of this scheme, wrote sarcastically, "If Mrs. Woodhull's nomination for the presidency be the means, as it promises to be, of furnishing that excellent woman with a comfortable house, at a rent not less than twelve thousand dollars [per year], we have no personal reason to complain."

Undeterred, Woodhull, with the support of her executive committee, continued to merge her interests under the party banner. They determined that the *Weekly* would be issued as the official organ of the Equal Righters, and that the business of the brokerage firm would be transferred to the proposed new residence. By making the paper and the brokerage firm tools of the new party, they would become part of the "necessary expenses of the campaign." The bonds sold at the convention provided seed money for these new arrangements. Additional bond sales were expected to cover operating expenses.

Woodhull's fund-raising device was in keeping with her image as a Wall Streeter. Her bonds looked impressive and official. At the same time, they protected her from any liability for repaying them. No one seems to have considered the dubious ethics of mixing personal and party finances.

Assuming that she had found a way out of her money problems, Woodhull told the press with confidence that "money to support the party is being sent in rapidly," and she expected to have "$100,000 in the treasury within a few days." Campaign clubs called Victoria Leagues were forming and, she predicted, soon would number 50,000, with memberships in the millions. Speakers would be sent all over the country to advocate the cause, and she and Claflin would "stump the country from Maine to California." "A grand ratification meeting" at the Grand Opera House would begin the campaign.

The meeting would also provide an occasion for publicly identifying Woodhull with the running mate the party had selected, the Negro leader Frederick Douglass. His choice had been a spontaneous act on the part of the delegates under the determined leadership of abolitionist Moses Hull. "Woodhull represented the oppressed sex," Hull said, "and the ticket needed the oppressed race as well." After energetic discussions in which many names were offered, the delegates agreed that Douglass could add stature to the ticket and bring the new black voters with him. Woodhull had acceded to this desire of the convention with pleasure, for she had admired Douglass since the January 1869 suffrage convention in Washington, D.C.

He was, however, a problematic choice. None of Woodhull's reform efforts had been directed to the new black voters. Douglass had not been present in Apollo Hall, and no evidence indicates that any other black men or women were there. At Hull's urging the party slogan had been worded the Women's, Negroes' and Workingman's Ticket, in honor of Douglass. Hull had apparently convinced Woodhull that Douglass would accept the position on the ticket, for she announced to the press that "Mr. Douglass's acceptance will be read [at the ratification meeting], as it is well known he will not decline." But Douglass was occupied organizing a national convention of black citizens in New Orleans. It is unlikely he would have supported the Equal Rights Party had he been in New York, for he was committed to Grant and the Republicans, the party of the great emancipator, Abraham Lincoln. Nor would he appear at the ratification meeting. Woodhull, politically inexperienced, had set herself up for public humiliation when she casually accepted Douglass as her running mate.

A second public humiliation followed: the Grand Opera House cancelled the ratification meeting, objecting to "the class of people" expected to attend, declaring, "No, not for $10,000 could a ratification meeting of the Equal Rights Party be held there." Woodhull lashed out in the *Weekly* against this "despicable despotism," but she was forced to reschedule the meeting for Cooper Institute on Thursday June 6, 1872. This incident was a foretaste of the future, the start of a series of public harassments, frustrations and embarrassments.

Despite the setbacks, Woodhull took the podium before a full house. Every seat was filled, and every standing place occupied. Her speech was short and designed to appeal to workingmen who lived and voted in New York City. In a more realistic appraisal of her situation than she had previously made, Woodhull recognized that her last hope for any real presidential campaign lay with these men. She knew that they were legally accepted as voters, unlike the suffragists, and that they would go to the polls, unlike the spiritualists whose commitment to politics was still to be tested. All her magnetism went out to them. In her most ebullient and exhortative style, she urged them to

> waste no opportunity to help in the glorious work . . .
> I would have every workingman or working woman
> feel that he or she is equal in all respects to any
> wealthy person. I would have every laborer in the
> country demand that eight hours should constitute a
> day's work, and stick to the demand . . . Stand firm,
> then, in your demands. Yield not a single inch . . . In
> this city there are 125,000 workingmen's votes; but is
> there a workingman sent to Albany or to Washington
> . . . I advise you upon the next election day [to be
> heard] by your votes . . .
> When this movement overturns the old systems, the
> millions now paid into the pockets of Wealth will re-
> main in the pockets of industrial people, and instead
> of there being the very rich few, and the very poor

many, all will be rich enough to have all the comforts
that wealth and enjoyment demand.

To the tune of "Comin' through the Rye," Cooper Institute re-
sounded with

> *Yes! Victoria we've selected*
> *For our chosen head:*
> *With Fred Douglass on the ticket*
> *We will raise the dead.*
>
> *Then around them let us rally*
> *Without fear or dread,*
> *And next March we'll put the Grundys*
> *In their little bed.*

Woodhull's performance was convincing, and the meeting appeared to be a noisy success.

But she and those closest to her had begun to realize that her presidential campaign was coming apart. She did not tell the ratification
meeting that Douglass had not accepted a place on the ticket, or that
her only formal connection with workingmen was about to be sev-
ered. The International Workingmen's Association was in the process
of expelling Section 12, the branch of the organization she headed,
on the grounds that she was a "pseudo-communist" and that her section was not composed of wage laborers. Woodhull would appeal
this "summary ejectment," but the decision would stand.

The reform groups that had become her supporters at the Equal
Rights Party convention returned to their 22 states. Loosely struc-
tured, without money, and with widely disparate interests, they were
more accustomed to cutting each other apart than working in harmony. Woodhull had outlined a party structure to keep them together, but she needed money and manpower to continue it.

Her Equal Rights Party bonds were not selling. Capitalists were
not buying, and she now acknowledged that she could not expect any
aid from "wealth." She had tried to sell the bonds to the workingmen, those with a "direct interest" in the Equal Rights Party, at the
ratification meeting, but had been equally unsuccessful. She had not
a penny to finance an Equal Rights Party structure. In fact, bill collectors were already threatening her with lawsuits. She couldn't or-

ganize the petitions or pay the legal expenses and filing fees required to get her name on state ballots.

She could not understand how the tide of public opinion had turned away from her so abruptly. She did not realize that her embrace of communism, even the innocent and idealistic version she described as Christian communism, had aroused deep feelings against her. The Wall Street establishment was genuinely shocked that the woman they had taken up had turned on them. The *New York Times* had expressed an anger and disavowal that was widely felt.

"We were at a loss ourselves to account for the intense bitterness that existed at that time," Woodhull later wrote. "Our eyes have since been widely opened to the causes." As offensive as her revolutionary talk was her willingness to form a radical political party. She was experiencing the odium attached to any new splinter party. This response would be reenacted a few years later. Those who formed the Greenback-Labor Party, an organization made up of many of the same strands Woodhull was trying to weave together, would make an impressive showing at the polls in 1878, but one participant wrote, "To admit sympathy with the detestable Greenbackers was to be ostracized socially, commercially and culturally. Respectable men refused to speak on the street to Greenbacker acquaintances, brothers and sisters withdrew the hand of fellowship at the prayer meeting and it was seriously debated whether a Greenbacker ought not to be expelled from the church."

As the spring of 1872 became summer, Woodhull came to understand these realities for herself. She explained, "We have learned that so long as we merely talked and wrote, the people did not mind it; but the moment a practical movement was contemplated, the alarm . . . began to spread . . . immediately following the May convention every opposer to our program rose up in arms . . . and they left no means untried."

"Those with whom we had transacted business were sought out, their minds poisoned against us," Woodhull said later. "To our astonishment one by one they fell away until we stood alone . . . on every hand we were undermined, and, in a word, in two short months, completely ruined financially."

Business friends falling away included, of course, Vanderbilt. She had publicly attacked him in her "Impending Revolution" speech, and however idealistic her motives may have been, she had made the person most responsible for her first successes look foolish in having encouraged her. She paid for her lack of loyalty. Woodhull, Claflin & Company was no longer seen as a front for Vanderbilt's intentions in the market, and its special position in the financial community evaporated. Gone were the periodic rushes of transactions placed through the firm—and the commissions they generated.

Woodhull rightly realized that her political activities had killed the brokerage business and she said later, "Our presence among the Internationalists . . . was the beginning of our financial ruin, as those who were supporting us could not understand why we should connect ourselves with the parties of whom that movement was made up."

Other factors worked against her as well. What nobody yet realized was that the country was entering the worst recession of the nineteenth century. Railroad construction had been growing at the rate of 12 percent, 6,000 new miles of track each year. Railroad finance had dominated Wall Street. Now overoptimism and overbuilding had reached a critical point. Some 4,000 businesses failed in 1872. The crash of banking houses, for which few were prepared, began in September of 1873. The Stock Exchange closed for ten days. The majority of American railroads, which had been heavily overinvested, went into bankruptcy. Unemployment became endemic. A severe recession would be followed by five long years of depression. Even in 1876 and 1877, 18,000 businesses would fail; not until 1879 would commerce and industry revive. The decade would be known as the black seventies and Woodhull, Claflin & Company was an early casualty. Overextended and operating on margin, it would be one of the first companies to go under.

"A series of pecuniary disasters stripped us . . . and forced us into a desperate struggle for mere existence," Woodhull wrote later. Those who had found her a refreshing novelty when she was rich fell away when she became poor. She was forced to face the unpleasant reality that the secret ingredient of her success had been money. Without it, her voice fell on deaf ears. "Persons whom we accounted friends . . . we found vomiting forth the bitterest gall against us; many whom we thought personal friends used every possible occasion to stab us in the back. These things, which we did not expect, added to all that we did expect, produced the desired effect—we were paralyzed in health, strength and purse, and reduced to a condition in which we were obliged to stop all business."

The suffragists backed away from Woodhull. Susan B. Anthony

was forcing those in the New York wing of the movement to choose sides. Isabella Beecher Hooker remained loyal; she had written a letter for Woodhull to publish in the *Weekly,* giving her public support to Douglass as Woodhull's running mate. She promptly received a reproving note from Anthony that diminished Woodhull in every way. "How can you urge Douglass to accept the post of lieutenant to Woodhull—which neither you nor Stanton would even think of. I cannot understand. The probability is that Douglass has not thought his Apollo Hall nomination of sufficient importance to even notice it. I marvel that you should ask a monied favor of Victoria again—do you not see that you at once compromise yourself by so doing."

Hooker was her own woman, however, and despite these rebukes, she maintained her friendship with Woodhull. She chided her for her "communist cry," and criticized Woodhull's free love views as opening the door to a "weak or vicious soul who now moves carelessly from flower to flower sucking poisonous sweets," but in July 1872, Hooker replied sympathetically to what she called a "sad letter" from Woodhull, saying, "Whenever I can help you to make men and women better and happier command me."

Woodhull's immediate problem after the ratification meeting was finding a permanent place to live. For six weeks she looked for a house. Not a house agent in the city would rent to her. The story she heard was always the same, "We personally don't object to you, but you know there is such a prejudice against you, that really we can't do it." Woodhull finally found a place in a public hotel, the Gilsey, but when the proprietor learned the identity of his guest, he asked her to get out, saying that if she remained in the hotel all his family boarders would leave. When Woodhull pressed him on his reasons, he replied that she "published a paper and made speeches in which free love was advocated, and the people would not tolerate any such thing." Woodhull refused to leave and, standing on her "rights as a citizen," said that unless some misdemeanor could be proved against her, she would not leave until she had found other suitable accommodations.

Then, late one evening after a long day at the office, Woodhull found all her possessions piled outside her door. A guard had been hired to keep her out. She spent hours looking for some place to spend the night. Finally, at one o'clock in the morning, Woodhull gave up the search and took her tired and frightened children to her office on Broad Street. There they slept "as best we could," she remembered later, "upon the floor." It was a humiliating experience for a proud woman. She and Zula Maud both became ill from the stress.

Life at the office was equally trying. Immediately after the convention, her landlord had increased her rent by $1,000 a year and had asked for the full amount in advance. In mid-June she found a better place at a lower rent, at 48 rather than 44 Broad Street, and she was able to shelter her family there when they were without a place to spend the night.

For weeks she continued to sleep in the office. Growing desperate, Woodhull finally wrote a public letter to Beecher. If he represented the forces of the establishment arrayed against her, a public expression of sympathy from him would soften the opposition. She said bluntly, "I want your assistance. I have been shut out of hotel after hotel . . . and am hunted down . . . I have submitted to this persecution just so long as I can endure. My business, my projects, in fact everything for which I live, suffers from it, and it must cease. Will you lend me your aid in this?"

Beecher called it a "whining letter."

In August Woodhull was brought to court and sued for nonpayment of her debts. She testified that she did not own even the clothes she wore. She had borrowed the furniture for her office and owned no property. Her sister Maggie Miles had found a house, and Woodhull was living with her. Woodhull's day in court was another moment of public humiliation.

While she looked on in helpless frustration, her old supporters began to campaign for other presidential candidates. In April, Grant's opponents had organized a Liberal Republican party. Desiring a government not of the rich but of what has been described as the intellectually well endowed, the Liberal Republicans abhorred political patronage and a host of vulgarities that they associated with Grant. Favoring civil service reform, free trade, hard currency and gentility in general, they wanted a government that was liberal but limited. They nominated Horace Greeley as their candidate, and they won the support of the Democrats. In June Grant had been renominated by the Republicans. His posters featured "The Tanner," referring to his own family's background in the tannery business, and "The Cobbler," vice-presidential candidate Henry Wilson of Massachusetts, who had once operated a shoe factory.

Woodhull had to watch from the sidelines as Theodore Tilton campaigned for Greeley. Belva Lockwood also went to work for Greeley after Woodhull's campaign began to collapse. Susan B. Anthony had hoped to see a woman suffrage plank in the regular Republican platform. When a token statement on behalf of women was included, she campaigned for Grant. Frederick Douglass campaigned extensively for Grant.

"The press, suddenly divided between the other two great parties, refused all notice of the new reformatory movement," Woodhull wrote. "The inauguration of the new party, and my nomination, seemed to fall dead upon the country."

She struggled with her own despairs during the summer and fall of 1872. The June 15 issue of the *Weekly* had reported that subscribers were not receiving copies of the paper: "Newsmen were being bribed to exclude it from their stands. Postmen have not been delivering it. Since the inauguration of the Equal Rights Party these problems have become . . . so frequent." The paper cost Woodhull and Claflin $300 each week over the income it generated. The two-year plan underwritten by Vanderbilt had run out at the end of April. Apart from other considerations, the Commodore had made a business investment in the paper, and it had not been profitable. On June 22 Woodhull was "compelled to suspend the paper . . . completely worn out both in body and mind, and rendered incapable of ministering to the needs of the *Weekly*." Of all the terrible choices she faced that summer, suspending the *Weekly* seems to have been the hardest. The paper had become part of her own persona, and she was psychically mute without it.

"I had not even the means of communicating my condition to my own circle of friends," she admitted later. In fact, she had kept her declining fortunes a secret for as long as she was able. Only after the *Weekly* had failed to appear for several issues did the public, and even many of Woodhull's close friends, suspect the financial problems.

"Circumstances being in this state," she recalled, "the year rolled round, and the next annual convention of the American Association of Spiritualists occurred in September 1872, in Boston. I went there—dragged by the sense of duty—tired, sick and discouraged." The presidency had eluded Woodhull, and she felt rudderless and uncertain. She carried a speech to Boston about the social good that spiritualists could accomplish through political action. It was heavy with Andrews's prose; she had spent little time on it herself. Months had passed since she had last spoken in public.

"I listened to the speeches of others and tried to gather the sentiment of the great meeting," she later recounted. "I rose finally to my feet to render my account of my stewardship, to surrender the charge and retire. Standing there before that audience I was seized by one of those overwhelming gusts of inspiration which sometimes come upon me, from I know not where, taken out of myself . . . and made by some power stronger than I, to pour out into the ears of that assembly . . . the whole history of the Beecher-Tilton scandal in Plymouth Church."

26
Beecher Exposed

Woodhull had found her voice again after an enforced silence of four months. The enthusiastic spiritualists reelected her as their president. Energized by their acclaim, she set off on a long lecture tour, her notoriety working in her favor. She also decided to revive the *Weekly*.

The paper emerged in a reckless spirit of revenge. The Beecher article that Woodhull had considered printing earlier in the year, before Tilton had persuaded her otherwise, now went into type. She telegraphed her nightly lecture receipts back to New York to pay the printer. She remembered many years later the circumstances that had brought about her final decision: one evening, after a speaking engagement, she had experienced "a flood of inspiration" under which her "soul became illuminated." She wrote down the thoughts that rose into her consciousness: "Paradise lost in Genesis through woman and regained in Revelation through woman. Through woman and not through man will the world be saved." She had interpreted this insight to mean that she should expose Beecher to save the world from the hell of a sexual double standard and sexual hypocrisy. "Paradise found" she called it. With this rationalization in place, she took action against those who had humiliated and vilified her. The new *Weekly* served as her scourge.

That Beecher was guilty of the infidelities Woodhull charged him with, there is little doubt. Her own sources, which included Tilton, his wife Elizabeth, Beecher's sister Isabella Beecher Hooker, and her own personal sexual adventure with Beecher, had given Woodhull ample confirmation that Beecher was an adulterer. She had further verifications from two reliable suffragists, Elizabeth Cady Stanton and Paulina Wright Davis. And subsequent events would lead all thoughtful observers to conclude that Beecher was "guilty of the charge brought against him," as the *New York Times* phrased it.

Woodhull had exposed business fraud for over two years and now she turned to social fraud. But her decision to go ahead was not dispassionate; it was visceral, calculated to do harm. The exposé was timed to coincide with Beecher's "silver anniversary," the twenty-fifth anniversary of his coming to Plymouth Church in Brooklyn, at the peak of the church's festivities.

The *Weekly*'s bland front page, now covered with Wall Street advertisements, gave no hint of the ticking bomb inside. The editorial page apologized to readers for the paper's disappearance, saying, "It has never entered our thoughts that the *Weekly* was dead." A pious speech on spiritualism took up five pages at the front of the paper.

But back on page nine under an inconspicuous one-column headline, " The Beecher-Tilton Scandal Case, the Detailed Statement of the Whole Matter," the bomb exploded. The article began with Woodhull's justification for publishing it.

> I propose . . . aggressive moral warfare on the social question, to begin in this article with ventilating one of the most stupendous scandals which has ever occurred in any community. I refer to . . . the conduct of the Rev. Henry Ward Beecher in his relations with the family of Theodore Tilton. I intend that this article shall burst like a bomb-shell into the ranks of the moralistic social camp.
>
> I am engaged in officering, and in some sense conducting, a social revolution on the marriage question. I have strong convictions to the effect that this institution, as a bond or promise to love one another to the end of life, and forgo all other loves or other passional gratifications, has outlived its day of usefulness; that the most intelligent and virtuous of our citizens . . . have outgrown it . . . and only submit . . . to it from the dread of a sham public opinion.

Woodhull was correct that loveless marriage deserved a better remedy than adultery and hypocrisy. She recklessly overstated her argument, however, when she predicted the end of the marriage institution.

Woodhull cast her article in the popular form of an on-scene interview. An unnamed reporter asked her all the appropriate questions. "Mrs. Woodhull, I have called to ask if you are prepared and willing to furnish a full statement of the Beecher-Tilton scandal for publication in the city papers?"

"I do not know that I ought to object to repeating whatever I know in relation to it. You understand, of course, that I take a different view of such matters from those usually avowed by other people. Still I have good reason to think that far more people entertain views corresponding to mine than dare to assert them openly or live up to them."

"Mrs. Woodhull, would you state in the most condensed way, your opinions on this subject, as they differ from those avowed and ostensibly lived by the public at large?"

Woodhull responded by faulting Beecher not for his infidelity but for his hypocrisy. "I believe that the marriage institution, like slavery and monarchy and many other things which have been good or necessary in their day, is now effete, and in a general sense injurious, instead of being beneficial to the community."

The reporter responded, "I confess, then, I cannot understand why you of all persons should have any fault to find with Mr. Beecher, even assuming everything to be true of him which I have hitherto heard only vaguely hinted at."

"I have no fault to find with him in any such sense . . . I have no doubt that he has done the very best which he could do under all the circumstances—with his demanding physical nature, and with the terrible restrictions upon clergymen's lives . . . The fault I find with Mr. Beecher is of a wholly different character, as I have told him repeatedly and frankly, and as he knows very well. It is indeed the exact opposite to that for which the world will condemn him. I condemn him because I know . . . that he entertains . . . substantially the same views which I entertain on the social question; that . . . he has lived for many years, perhaps for his whole adult life, in a manner which the religious and moralistic public . . . condemn; that he has permitted himself, nevertheless, to be overawed by public opinion, to profess to believe otherwise . . . and that he has, in a word, consented, and still consents to be a hypocrite. . . Speaking from my feelings, I am prone to denounce him as a poltroon, a coward and a sneak . . . for failing . . . to stand shoulder to shoulder with me and others who are endeavoring to hasten a social regeneration."

With this rationale in place, Woodhull was ready for the next question: "You speak very confidently, Mrs. Woodhull, of Mr. Beecher's opinions and life. Will you now please to resume that subject and tell me exactly what you know of both?"

Woodhull recounted the tale as she knew it, starting with the rumors she had heard in Washington in the winter of 1871. She described Tilton's distracted mental state when he had raved to her, seemingly on the verge of insanity, "Oh! that that damned lecherous scoundrel should have defiled my bed for ten years, and at the same time have professed to be my best friend! Had he come like a man to me and confessed his guilt, I could perhaps have endured it, but to have him creep like a snake into my house leaving his pollution behind him, and I so blind as not to see, and esteeming him all the while as a saint—oh! it is too much."

"Is it possible that Mr. Tilton confided this story to you?" the reporter asked. "It seems too monstrous to be believed."

"He certainly did, and what is more I am persuaded that in his inmost mind he will not be otherwise than glad when the skeleton in his closet is revealed to the world . . . Mr. Tilton looks deeper into the soul of things than most men, and is braver than most." Woodhull was being disingenuous here, for she well knew Tilton wished to keep this skeleton in his closet.

"Do you not fear that by taking the responsibility of this exposé you may involve yourself in trouble? Even if all you relate should be true, may not those involved deny it in toto, even the fact of their having made the statements?"

"I do not fear anything of the sort. I know this thing must come out, and the statement of the plain ungarnished truth will outweigh all the perjuries that can be invented, if it come to that pass. I have been charged with attempts at blackmailing, but I tell you sir there is not money enough in these two cities to purchase my silence in this matter. I believe it is my duty and mission to carry the torch to light up and destroy the heap of rottenness which, in the name of religion, marital sanctity, and social purity, now passes as the social system."

Having unburdened herself of this impetuous tirade, Woodhull accepted the reporter's interjection, "You speak like some weird prophetess, madam."

"I am a Prophetess—I am an evangel—I am a Savior, if you would but see it; but I, too, come not to bring peace, but a sword," she responded. Carried away with herself, Woodhull let an unattractive edge of hubris emerge.

Continuing, she related what Tilton had told her about his suspicions of Beecher after returning from his lecture tour, questioning his daughter and confronting his wife, his anger that the child she carried was not his and how he had stripped the wedding ring from her finger, his wife's miscarriage, and the shattered homelife he had lived ever since.

"I ridiculed the maudlin sentiment and mock heroics and 'dreadful suzz' he was exhibiting," Woodhull said, "over an event the most natural in the world, and the most intrinsically innocent . . . I assumed at once and got a sufficient admission that his real life was something very different from the awful 'virtue' he was preaching . . . as if women could 'sin' in this matter without men, and men without women . . . that the dreadful suzz was mearly a bogus sentimentality, pumped in his imagination, because our sickly religious literature, and Sunday School morality, and pulpit phariseeism had humbugged him all his life into the belief that he ought to feel and act in this harlequin and absurd way on such an occasion—that in a word neither Mr. Beecher nor Mrs. Tilton had done anything wrong . . . I tried to show him that a true manliness would protect . . . the absolute freedom of the woman who was loved, whether called wife, mistress or by any other name, and that the true sense of honor in the future will be not to know, even, what relations our lovers have with any and all other persons than ourselves—as true courtesy never seeks to spy over or to pry into other people's private affairs."

Here, Woodhull was justifying sexual experimentation as an individual right, as she had at Steinway Hall a year earlier. "Love" could and should be shared with anyone with whom an "affinity"—that favorite nineteenth century code word for sexual attraction—existed.

"The wrong point," she continued, "and the radically wrong thing, if not, indeed, quite the only wrong thing in the matter, was the idea of ownership of human beings, which was essentially the same in the two institutions of slavery and marriage . . . Every human being belongs to himself or herself by a higher title than any which, by surrenders or arrangements or promises, he or she can confer upon any other human being. Self ownership is inalienable."

Woodhull concluded by saying, "It is nobody's business but their own what Mr. Beecher and Mrs. Tilton have done . . . I am the champion of that very right of privacy and of individual sovereignty . . . It is not . . . Mr. Beecher as the individual that I pursue, but Mr. Beecher as the representative man . . . The evil and the whole evil lies . . . in the compulsory hypocrisy and systematic falsehood which is thus enforced and inwrought into the very structure of society . . . Mr. Beecher is today . . . as good, as pure and as noble a man as he ever was in the past, or as the world has held him to be . . . Mrs. Tilton is still the pure, charming, cultured woman. It is, then, the public opinion that is wrong."

Woodhull then frankly stated her intention to turn New York's secrets into a source of power for herself. "Whenever a person whom we know to be a hypocrite stands up and denounces us because of our doctrines . . . we shall unmask him . . . we will propose to put our lives and characters in comparison with any or all of the various persons who have daubed our reputations with slurs of sexual debauchery generated in their own imaginations. That is plain, terse and impossible of misconception . . . We are prepared to take all the responsibility for libel suits and imprisonment," she added.

A further justification for publishing the exposure followed the article, in a letter from Laura Cuppy Smith, in which she pointed to Harriet Beecher Stowe's account of the Byron affair as a precedent for Woodhull's exposure of Beecher. Stowe's publication would be cited frequently as an exemplar for the public airing of her brother's indiscretions.

Woodhull enjoyed the ambrosia of revenge. She had started at the top, with Henry Ward Beecher, and she announced that she did not plan to stop there. She had, the editorial page of the *Weekly* stated, "five hundred biographies of various persons, in all walks of life . . . people must be compelled to live [as they] want the public to think they live."

Was this blackmail? Not for money. No evidence exists that Woodhull ever attempted to blackmail anyone for money. As she had said, there was not enough money in New York or Brooklyn to buy her silence. Woodhull had stated specifically in the first issue that she would not deal in personalities, that she would not write a damaging profile simply to invite a buy-off. And she never did. But a factual, though damaging profile, to gain the respect she felt was her due, *that* was another matter. *That* was street justice. Thousands of such articles appeared every year. She would play by the same free-for-all rules men accorded themselves.

Woodhull made it clear that she was not bluffing when she exposed Luther C. Challis, a minor Wall Street figure, in the same issue as Beecher. The paper explained that it was the first of a series entitled, "The Philosophy and Illustration of Modern Hypocrisy." Challis's misdeeds were selected for inclusion at Tennie Claflin's insistence, and Tennie wrote the article. She clearly had some old scores to settle with Challis.

Tennie began the article with the French Ball, which had recently been celebrated at the Academy of Music. She and Woodhull had covered the event for the *Weekly*, and had met Challis and a friend with two young girls, 15 or 16 years old, fresh from school in Baltimore. The sisters watched as the young girls were plied with wine. Tennie added, "You may be sure I followed the girls up and got the history of their connection with the men. They were seduced by them." With some anger, Tennie added that the men continued to be considered models of Wall Street integrity, while the two young girls' reputations were soiled forever. "And, this scoundrel Challis," wrote Tennie, "to prove that he had seduced a maiden, carried for days on his finger, exhibiting in triumph, the red trophy of her virginity." These colorful words would later provide the basis for obscenity and libel charges against Tennie, Woodhull, and Blood.

Woodhull and Claflin would not, however, expose women in the *Weekly*. And despite being sorely provoked by some of the suffragists, they did not. Anti-Woodhull suffragists had spread gossip about her at the time of the May, 1872, convention; among them was Laura Curtis Bullard. Bullard had taken over Stanton and Anthony's failing newspaper, *The Revolution;* her name had been romantically linked with Tilton's in the summer of 1870. Woodhull threatened to retaliate against the gossip in an article called "Tit for Tat," in which she said she would make their own "hypocrisies" public. Word of these charges and countercharges reached Anthony. She was irreproachably honest but not unbiased in her interpretation of these events, as she was looking for ways to lessen Woodhull's influence among the suffragists. Anthony told Ezra H. Heywood, a Woodhull supporter, that Woodhull had "resorted to blackmailing intentionally." Anthony's name and reputation gave the "blackmail" rumors credence. Paulina Wright Davis had convinced Woodhull not to act against the women, writing her, "Dear child, I wish you had let [the women] pass and taken hold of these men whose souls are black with crimes and who set up to be the censors of morality . . . Give women a fair field of equality."

Hearing these whispers of blackmail, Woodhull explicitly denied all charges that had been made against her, saying, "Members of the press, both in this city and various other places, have made the charge of blackmailing against us . . . to these journals we say plainly, you have charged a crime which we have never either committed nor attempted to commit . . . retract the ungallant, ungraceful and untruthful statements which have placed us so disparagingly before the public . . . it is a right to which we are entitled."

The *Weekly* was back in business with renewed vigor. It survived for almost four more years, published week after week during the worst depression of the century—a remarkable accomplishment for a small weekly reform paper.

Woodhull later regretted what the Beecher exposure cost her personally, saying with mixed feelings in her autobiographical notes, "My being instrumental in exposing the Beecher scandal has been the shadow which has obscured everything that I did or said . . . I had no idea in the beginning of the battle I was waging . . . Probably if I had, I should have fainted by the wayside; but there was always some power impelling me onward." An astute self-assessment, but only half realized. Although she was unable to acknowledge that revenge impelled her onward, this powerful motive led Woodhull to air the hypocrisies and double standards that masqueraded as nineteenth-century morality.

27
Ludlow Street Jail

*T*he first edition of the new *Woodhull and Claflin's Weekly*, detailing the Beecher-Tilton scandal, dated November 2, 1872, reached the New York City newsstands on Monday October 28. "Strictest secrecy" had made the delivery possible, Woodhull said. The entire mail edition had been shipped out over the weekend—including copies to newspapers throughout the country—before a single paper was released in New York. Woodhull had taken these precautions to prevent the paper from being stopped in the New York post office.

The first run of 100,000 copies sold out. "The presses, though kept running constantly, could not supply the demand," Woodhull said. Then the distributor, American News Company, refused to replace the paper on its stands; an army of newsboys and newsdealers descended on Broad Street to obtain copies directly from Woodhull and Claflin. The curious, unwilling to wait for additional press runs, upped the cover price of 10 cents to 50 cents, then to $2.50. One of the daily newspapers later reported that a single copy had sold for $40 and that those fortunate to have copies in hand were leasing them out for $1 a day. "Sales reached 150,000 and promised to go as high as two million," said another paper.

A reporter pushed his way into the *Weekly* office and found Woodhull and Claflin "jubilant—the exposé had gone off like buttered hot cakes." Once again, every newspaper in New York wanted to interview Woodhull.

Beecher and his friends, caught unaware by Woodhull's new *Weekly*, went from newsstand to newsstand in Brooklyn, buying up and destroying copies of the paper. But it was useless. During the course of that week, Woodhull remembered later, "the city was in an uproar . . . We were constantly on the lookout for some defensive movement, but Tuesday, Wednesday, Thursday, Friday passed and none was made. We began to think that the whole movement would be allowed to go by default."

Beecher refused to comment on the *Weekly* story, saying only, "In passing along the way any one is liable to have a bucket of slop thrown upon him. It is disagreeable, but does not particularly harm." His nonchalant pose belied the fury of activity going on around him. Beecher stood at the center of a large circle of financial interests, interlocking associations of church, book, and newspaper publishing relationships. His friends were not prepared to be so casual. But they appeared to be incapable of deciding on any course of action.

While they floundered, Anthony Comstock, a self-appointed guardian of public morals, offered himself as their savior. Comstock was a self-rightous prig who had made a name for himself condemning pornographic literature and dime novels, which he called "traps for the young." He went around the city noting evils in a small diary bound in purple leather. The Young Men's Christian Association had rewarded him by appointing him head of their Committee for the Suppression of Vice. He had managed to lobby a law through Congress, passed earlier that year, on June 8, 1872, that made it illegal to send obscene publications through the mail. He was widely disliked; "cheap and dirty," one contemporary magazine called him. But he was obsessed, unstoppable, and he usually left a nasty cloud of fear in his wake.

The *Weekly* exposé outraged him and he determined to bring Woodhull and Claflin to heel. He sent several copies of the paper to Henry Bowen's *Independent,* specifically arranging that they be sent through the United States mail.

As soon as the *Weekly* arrived, Comstock obtained a Federal warrant for the arrest of Woodhull and her colleagues on the charge of sending obscene literature through the mail. The warrant also authorized the seizing of all copies of the issue. Comstock intended to take the paper out of circulation.

Two deputy United States marshals found the sisters at 12:15 P.M. on Saturday November 2, 1872, in a carriage on Broad Street. They had 3,000 copies of the *Weekly* with them. The marshals confiscated the papers and took the sisters to the Federal Building for arraignment. A large crowd followed behind.

"They were dressed in plain dark suits of alpaca, and wore hats of the most jaunty style," the *New York Dispatch* reported. "Tennie was flushed like a rose, and her blue eyes sparkled nervously. As she glanced around the room, a smile of contempt seemed to gather about her ruby lips. She has splendid teeth and takes care to show them. In fact Tennie is a pretty looking woman, round faced with well-cut features, and a bright animated expression."

The sisters were rushed not into open court, but into a "star chamber," a private examination room. Woodhull and Claflin sent for J. D. Reymart, their lawyer, and insisted on being examined in open court. They succeeded in moving the proceedings to a public room.

Noah Davis, the United States Attorney for the Southern District of New York, a member of Plymouth Church and a distant relative of Beecher's, began the examination. He said, "Not only have the defendants, by circulating an obscene publication through the mails, committed an offense against the law, but they have been guilty of a most abominable and unjust charge against one of the purest and best citizens of this State, or in the United States, and they have, as far as possible, aggravated the offense by atrocious, malicious, gross and untrue libel upon the character of the gentleman whom the whole country reveres, and whose character it is well worth the while of the government of the United States to vindicate." The gentleman's name was not mentioned.

Davis had tipped the hand of the prosecution. It was evident that a U.S. court was being used to prosecute two women on the pretext of obscenity, when their only conceivable offense was libel— *if* Henry Ward Beecher had elected to bring libel charges. Beecher chose not to charge libel, so his associates found an alternative legal action.

Reymart pointed out that his clients were charged with sending obscene literature through the mails, not with libel. His words were ignored. The presiding officer of the Federal court set bail at $8,000 each, only slightly below the $10,000 requested by the U.S. attorney, saying, "An example is needed and we propose to make one of these women." The bail was a foretaste of things to come. Charge after charge would be leveled against the sisters, trumped-up misdemeanors would be used as pretexts for jailing them and setting exhorbitant bail demands. It was blatant harassment, an obvious bending of the judicial system.

The temperance advocate George Francis Train, a prominent and rich eccentric, offered to put up the $16,000 bail, but Woodhull and Claflin declined. Reymart had advised them that if they were freed they would be promptly arrested again on other charges. Luther C. Challis, the subject of Tennie's *Weekly* article, had secured warrants for the arrests of Woodhull and her associates on charges of libel in the Second District Police Court. Five members of the paper's staff, including Colonel Blood and Stephen Pearl Andrews, had already been jailed and were in Jefferson Market Prison, one of the worst in the country. Reymart advised Woodhull and Tennie that Ludlow Street Jail, to which the Federal court would consign them, was far more tolerable. So instead of posting bail, Woodhull and Tennie decided to spend Saturday night and Sunday in Ludlow Street Jail, remaining there until their appearance in Federal court on Monday, November 4, 1872.

At 3:30 Saturday afternoon, they left the Federal Building for jail. Deputy Warden William H. Gardner escorted them to cell 11 and allowed them to receive visitors. A crowd of reporters shouted questions through the bars. Woodhull refused to say anything except that their quarters were not "wholly unpleasant." Tennie responded more cordially, offering a lecture on their martyrdom.

The office on Broad Street, emptied of all *Weekly* personnel, was raided by the police. They confiscated all copies of the *Weekly,* scattered the type, tore through trunks and private letter files, broke furniture, and seized the company books. If there were 500 biographies stored in that office, as the *Weekly* had suggested, the authorities were intent on finding them. Sunday morning, after the raid, the staff members being held in Jefferson Market Prison were released for lack of evidence. Colonel Blood was not allowed to leave with them, however; he, like the sisters, had months of legal harassments ahead of him.

After the sisters' arrests, their press coverage turned negative again. The *Times* said sourly, "The female name never has been more disgraced and degraded than by these women." Even their long time friend the *Herald* said, "These women cannot even be classed with unfortunates. It is a greater depth of infamy to which they glory to belong."

On Monday Woodhull and Tennie returned to the Federal Building. They had obtained additional legal counsel—William F. Howe, a well-known criminal lawyer. Howe, in plaid pantaloons and a purple vest, proclaimed that "this case is instigated by the malice and revenge of certain persons in high station, who dare not come forward and face public opposition." The case was a flagrant example of malicious persecution, Howe said, and he challenged the newspapers to come to the aid of the defendants and preserve freedom of the press.

The sisters were discharged by the Federal court and then immediately rearrested on Federal grand-jury indictments and returned to Ludlow Street Jail. Their bail remained set at $8,000 each.

The next day, Tuesday November 5, was election day. Woodhull learned of President Ulysses S. Grant's reelection while she was in cell 11. She had ample time for private contemplation of what might have been, but she has left no record of her reflections. Her public views, however, were before the electorate in the November 2 *Weekly*. Believing now that the push for a declaratory act was dead, she proposed an innovative new idea: the winning candidate should be brought to trial for performing the functions of president illegally by not allowing the one-half of citizens, who were women, to vote. Let the courts decide the issue of suffrage for women, the *Weekly* challenged.

Before Woodhull left her cell, Grant's opponent, Horace Greeley, died, collapsing under the twin disappointments of his election loss and his wife's unexpected death.

Susan B. Anthony found election day to her liking. Single-minded as always, she went to the poll in her hometown, Rochester, New York, and succeeded in voting. She wrote gleefully to Stanton, "Well I have been and gone and done it! Positively voted the Republican ticket—straight—this AM at 7 o'clock . . . so we are in for a fine agitation in Rochester on the question."

While the sisters waited in jail for the Federal grand jury to take action on the obscenity charge against them, Luther B. Challis took *his* libel case to the press. He told reporters that he hardly knew Tennie—that she was blackmailing him. Six months earlier she had demanded $200, he said, and when he had refused she had shown him the proof of the article that had since been published in the *Weekly*.

The reporters went to cell 11 to get Tennie's side of the story, and Tennie obliged them. Challis, she told them, had been on "intimate terms" with her, and they could consider this expression to mean whatever they pleased. Tennie had made several speeches supporting Woodhull's campaign. She told the reporters that she had asked Challis to contribute to the expenses of one of her lectures. Jim Fisk, Henry Clews, and other brokers had made donations from time to time. She also revealed she had some affectionate letters from Challis that might make interesting reading.

On Friday November 8, a packed courtroom in Jefferson Market Court attended a preliminary hearing on the charge of libel that Challis had manufactured. Challis testified that he scarcely knew Tennie, that he and a friend had met her and Woodhull at a party. He acknowledged that they had met two fairly young girls at the ball, but insisted that they had drunk only one small bottle of wine with them. Challis and his friend had tired of the scene and gone home early, he said. He denied under cross-examination that he had courted Tennie, or become her sweetheart, or given her silken under-things, as she had claimed. A "sensational comedy of free love," declared the *Herald*.

Decision in the case was reserved, and Woodhull and Tennie returned to federal custody and Ludlow Street Jail. Day followed day in cell 11, and Woodhull's spirits flagged. She wrote a letter to the *Herald* asking for "fair play" and "justice." Her letter was reprinted in papers throughout the country.

On December 5, 1872, the sisters were freed when two men who sympathized with their situation, Dr. Augustus D. Ruggles and James Kiernan, paid the $8,000 bail for each of them. Both sisters were immediately arrested again on new charges of libel and sending obscene matter through the mails. A deputy from the sheriff's office was waiting to serve the papers. But with the help of new friends outraged by the unfair treatment the sisters were receiving, all the various bonds were finally paid.

Eight charges were eventually brought against Woodhull and Claflin, but one charge never appeared: Beecher never sued for libel. Nor did he or anyone in his circle deny the *Weekly*'s accusations.

Woodhull was convinced that the *Weekly* was the real object of their opponents, saying later that had she promised "the *Weekly* would never again be issued, from such time the persecution would have ceased."

Finally free, Woodhull went on the offensive once more. Another issue of the *Weekly* appeared in a fortnight. As it went to press, Woodhull learned that her first postprison speech, "Moral Cowardice and Modern Hypocrisy, or Four Weeks in Ludlow Street Jail," had been banned in Boston.

The ban was apparently the work of Harriet Beecher Stowe. Stowe had gone to her friend Mary Claflin, the wife of the governor of Massachusetts (and no relation to Woodhull's family). Stowe had found Mary Claflin "all on fire with indignation" at the prospect of Woodhull's lecture, and, likely at Stowe's urging, the governor and Mrs. Claflin arranged with the mayor of Boston to stop the lecture. Stowe wrote her daughters, "Those vile women jailbirds had the impudence to undertake . . . a lecture in the Music hall . . . It appears that lectures cannot be given without a license from the city government which is not to be forthcoming."

Woodhull next engaged Cooper Institute in New York for January 9, 1873, to give a speech titled: "The Naked Truth." But when Anthony Comstock learned of Woodhull's plans, he manufactured new charges against her. He went to Greenwich, Connecticut, and, adopting the alias J. Beardsley, ordered copies of the paper to be mailed to him there. On January 9, he swore out new obscenity warrants against Woodhull, Claflin, and Blood. He took the warrants directly to Broad Street, where he found Blood and had him arrested. Unable to pay the $5,000 bail, Blood was imprisoned again. That evening Comstock wrote in his purple book, "In my heart I feel God approves, and what care I more. If Jesus be pleased, I care for nothing else."

Warned by Blood's arrest, Woodhull was certain that Comstock intended to prevent her speech at the Cooper Institute that evening. She stayed in Taylor's Hotel in Jersey City until after dark and then returned to New York with a plan. "I resolved to assume a disguise," she reported later in the *Weekly*. "Some willing friends assisted, and I soon presented the appearance of an old and decrepit Quaker lady. In this costume I confidently entered the hall, passing half a dozen or more United States marshals, who stood guarding the entrances and warning the people that there was to be no lecture that night . . . But I passed them all safely, one of them even essaying to assist me through the crowd. On the pretense of deafness, I gradually worked my way down to the stage and finally upon it, and just as Laura Cuppy Smith was announcing that she still believed that I would appear, I suddenly advanced to the center of the stage and exclaimed, 'Yes, I am here,' and began speaking before having entirely cast aside my Quaker garb so that the marshals who were on the platform would have to interrupt my speech if they attempted to arrest me then." This victory over Anthony Comstock became one of Woodhull's favorite stories.

A member of the audience gave his version of what happened next. "With the celerity of a flash of lightning the old Quaker lady dashed from behind the pillar. Old age, coal-scuttle bonnet and grey dress disappeared like magic. Had a thunderbolt fallen upon the audience, they could not have been any more surprised and astonished. There stood Victoria C. Woodhull, an overwhelming inspirational fire scintillating from her eyes and beaming from her face . . . with her breast heaving in long suppressed nervous emotion, her arms raised aloft in nervous excitement, her hair in wild and graceful confusion, and her head thrown back defiantly . . . she looked the personification of Liberty in Arms. Her voice rose in clear and piercing tones, like a song of love, blended with the war cry of battle, and the pent-up forces of her soul rushed forth in an impetuous and irresistible torrent of burning, glowing words."

About 1,000 people listened to her comeback, according to the *Times.* She spoke about her jailing, about Comstock's role, and about the weaknesses in his case, about her belief that he was Beecher's agent. The object of the persecution, Woodhull continued, was to harass her and keep the *Weekly* from being published.

Woodhull drew a parallel between her case and that of Walt Whitman, when he had been removed from his position in the Office of the Interior in Washington on the grounds that some of his poems were obscene. Such a storm of indignation arose at Whitman's treatment, she reminded them, that he had been offered a higher office in another department.

She expressed a new sense of mission: "I speak of myself as conducting a warfare on the present impacted mass of love and hate, of confidence and jealousy, of prudery and flippancy, of deceit and hypocrisy, marital infidelity, sexual debauchery, seduction, abortion, and consequent general moral degradation, all mingled in frightful confusion and labeled the social system. When I think of this as being the foundation of morality . . . to the label ought to be added 'to be shaken well before taken.' "

At the end of her speech, Woodhull bowed low to the three U.S. marshals standing in the wings and extended her wrists dramatically as if to receive handcuffs. They took her from the hall amid jeers from the audience, and conducted her once again to Ludlow Street Jail.

This time, the case was heard promptly. Anthony Comstock was the chief Federal witness, and he was aggressively cross-examined.

Was a passage from the book of Deuteronomy obscene? Howe asked. Did Comstock favor censoring Lord Byron, Shakespeare, and Fielding? Comstock refused to answer. Realizing that his testimony did not support an obscenity case against the Beecher article, Comstock shifted his ground to say that Claflin's Challis article was obscene.

Comstock contradicted himself and made a thoroughly bad impression, according to the *Sun*. It was the consensus of the press that he had made a fool of himself. The prosecution now had no case against the sisters for obscenity in the Beecher article. Decision was reserved and the defendants were released on bail.

The grounds for protecting Beecher, that gentleman whose character "it is well worth the while of the government of the United States to vindicate," as U.S. Attorney Noah Davis had put it more than two months before, had slipped away. The prosecution now shifted its ground to follow Comstock's testimony and developed a new obscenity case based on the Challis article. The sisters protested that the prosecution had changed its position, but to no avail.

As the weaknesses in the new case against the sisters became apparent, public opinion began to turn in their favor. Woodhull planned a speaking tour to tell her side of the story.

But before her lecture series could get under way, she was arrested again. Howe pleaded for a reasonable bail, saying that for simple misdemeanors his clients were under $60,000 bail in various suits, while Boss Tweed, who was accused of looting the city treasury of millions, was under only $51,000 bail. Howe was successful and the sisters obtained bail backing.

Killing the *Weekly* was the real object of these persecutions, Woodhull said again, but she would "flaunt" the paper and "defy our persectuors." Supporters helped with contributions. The December 28, 1872, issue had sold well, and a new issue dated January 25, 1873, was having an "immense sale in the streets of the city by newsboys, a thing unknown of any other weekly paper." The *Weekly* would be published regularly "whether in jail or out," Woodhull declared.

General Benjamin Butler came to the sisters' aid in an open letter in the February 3 issue of the *Sun*, saying the obscenity law was not intended to cover newspapers:

> The action of the United States Prosecuting Attorney was based wholly upon a misconstruction and mis-

conception of that statute . . . The statute was meant to cover . . . lithographs, prints, engravings, licentious books and other matters which are published by bad men for the purpose of corruption of youth . . . If I were your counsel I should advise you to make no further defense but mere matter of law . . . I do not believe that a legal wrong can be done you in this behalf before any learned and intelligent judge . . . Benjamin F. Butler.

The court issued a decision in accordance with Butler's interpretation, but refrained from releasing the accused from their bonds, saying that was due to "the importance as well as the subtlety of the questions involved" and "the anxiety of the prisoners, as well as the community, for a definite settlement of the whole matter." Woodhull and Claflin had to wait for a grand jury decision.

Woodhull began her lecture tour, and became once again "the Woodhull." The press reported her refinement and her earnestness, and, as in days past, many who expected to condemn her were won over after seeing her in person.

The *Weekly* came out regularly. Beecher, Tilton, and Bowen were a continuing story. On May 17 the original November 2, 1872, exposure of Beecher was reprinted. No arrests followed, no suits, no word from Henry Ward Beecher or Anthony Comstock.

In Troy, New York, Edward H. G. Clark of the *Troy Whig and Daily Press* wrote: "Through Victoria Woodhull and Tennie Claflin, American law has been outraged, the rights of the press assailed, freedom of speech endangered and the functions of republican government usurped to cloak the reputation of one or two prominent individuals." Clark had done his own research, and he called the charges brought againt Woodhull "a fraud born of a plot." Yet, Clark hated free love and all radicalism. Of Woodhull, he said:

She struck me as a rapt idealist—"out of her head" in the sense of "enthusiasm;" a nature so intense that she might see visions of angels or devils, and as many as St. John or Luther . . . At one time she sinks every vestige of egotism in the absorbed expression of ideas; and at another time she would steal the genius of a friend to aid her in "putting on airs." It seems as if she loves notoriety more than any other being on earth, yet she loves her notions of duty even more than notoriety. She is ignorant: and her strong signature in letters and on the backs of photographs, is commonly the handiwork of Colonel Blood. It is probable that she never wrote, unaided and alone, any of her "great speeches" or her stirring editorials—the Beecher-Tilton scandal being no exception. Yet she is the inspiration, the vitality and the mouthpiece of her clan and her "cause." Her organ, *Woodhull and Claflin's Weekly* has voices from the "seventh heaven," and the gabblings of a frog pond . . . yet the amazing journal is crowded with thought and with needed information that can be got nowhere else. And today it stands as the test of a free press, and the possibility of a better breed of men.

It was a perceptive assessment, but it came as a blow to Woodhull. Clark's newspaper had been the first to come to her defense, and she had expected kinder words. The momentum she had regained began to flag. On June 2, 1873, the obscenity case was finally called. Various legal wranglings resulted in yet another postponement, this time for two more weeks. One more legal delay seemed more than Woodhull could tolerate. She had exhausted her reserves of energy.

28
Reported Dead

On a hot muggy June Friday, following the postponement of the latest trial, Woodhull felt ill. She had a cup of tea and then, when climbing the stairs to her bedroom, she fell suddenly and heavily. Everyone in the house rushed to her side. Tennie and Annie found Colonel Blood leaning over her. Woodhull's face had turned gray, and all three feared that she was dead. Frantically they searched for signs of life. They could find no pulse. They held a mirror to her lips, a feather. Nothing stirred.

Dr. Comins, her physician, arrived. Tennie told him that Woodhull had complained of pains in her chest on the way home from the office. She had a history of chest pain, which she and Tennie both attributed to a weak heart. Dr. Comins examined Woodhull. Detecting a faint heartbeat, he attempted to revive her. As blood oozed from her mouth Comins and two other doctors he had called in talked in hushed whispers. Finally Dr. Comins announced that Woodhull had probably "ruptured a blood vessel of her lungs." The three doctors and Woodhull's frightened family saw her lips move. Dr. Comins said softly into her ear, "You must not speak; do not move. Your life depends on your remaining quiet."

Woodhull's hands and feet were put into hot water; mustard plasters were applied to her body. She remained unconscious, a trickle of blood still issuing from her mouth. Everyone was banished from her room except Claflin and the Colonel.

Tennie was convinced that Woodhull would not make it through the night. She telegraphed a newspaper friend, Johnnie Green of the *Sun,* that her sister was dying. Saturday morning headlines announced Woodhull's imminent death. Bouquets and baskets of flowers arrived all through the day.

At one o'clock Sunday morning, Woodhull briefly regained consciousness. She seemed to be recovering; then on Monday afternoon she developed a fever, lost consciousness again, and passed a restless night. Tuesday afternoon her fever broke and she slept quietly.

On Wednesday morning at six o'clock she awoke feeling fully alert for the first time since her fall. She was able to sit up in bed. From that point on she began to improve steadily, and it was clear that she would recover.

Woodhull, too, was afraid she was dying. Blood later reported in the *Weekly* that her only thoughts were that her work and the paper might survive her. Given the circumstances, we can assume he was inventing what he thought the *Weekly* readers wanted to hear, or, with his commitment to the paper, what he wanted them to hear.

Some newspapers interpreted her illness as an invention to enable her to postpone her trial, but Woodhull wanted to get the trial over with as quickly as possible. "Only yesterday morning," Blood wrote in the *Weekly* the day after she became ill, "she said that she feared she was not to be treated with fairness by the courts, and that in the case of her conviction she could not survive . . . she was anxious to be tried, she said, and be done with it. The anxiety was killing her."

The stress she was under had undoubtedly contributed to her collapse. Not only the trial worried her. Money problems were critical again, too. "She and her sister had worked hard for the past few months to make up for their losses sustained during their imprisonment, but made scarcely more than enough to pay the current expenses of their office and home," Blood wrote. "Some of her bondsmen showed a disposition to desert her, and this, too, added to her misery."

"When persons asserted that she and her sister wore an air of indifference and were brazen, they little knew how much they really suffered and with what difficulty they could refrain from giving way," Blood said loyally. "The treatment she had received from her own sex troubled her most. Although she had spent a fortune in the advocacy of women's rights, the leaders of that movement now had seemingly forgotten her labors and were said to be anxious to have her sent to state prison."

One of Woodhull's first acts after her release had been a letter to Susan B. Anthony. Legal action had been taken against the suffrage leader because she had voted. Woodhull wrote her on January 2, 1873:

There is no time now to indulge in personal enmity. I have none toward anybody, and I ask everybody to put aside whatever there may be against me and permit as great a unity as possible . . . I fear [the administration] intend to crush out, in your person, the constitutional question of women's right to suffrage . . . I may be able to help you if any is required. You know that I have considered the legal aspect of the question, perhaps more thoroughly than any other person, and there is no phase of it I do not thoroughly understand. Your case is my own and that of every other woman's who thinks much . . . For myself I have a pretty large fight of my own on hand, but I can find time to do my share to assist you . . . Hoping to hear from you by return mail permit me to subscribe myself, your friend for the cause, Victoria Woodhull.

Anthony never replied. Undeterred, Woodhull continued to persevere with the suffragists. She reran earlier letters of support from their leaders, including Anthony. She publicized the coming May 6, 1873, suffrage convention and printed the names of the speakers, even though hers was not among them.

A major new obstacle had come Woodhull's way in the form of a public letter written by Catharine Beecher and published in the *Tribune* on March 28. It was the latest weapon in a covert campaign being waged against her by her implacable enemies, Henry Ward Beecher's older sisters Catharine Beecher and Harriet Beecher Stowe. They could not bring themselves to believe what had become widely accepted, that Woodhull's charges against their brother were true. Ironically it was Stowe, the crusader who had exposed another famous sex scandal in her defense of Lady Byron, who chose to be the most vindictive, calling Woodhull a "vile jailbird," an "impudent witch."

In her March letter to the *Tribune,* Catharine Beecher made fresh accusations of blackmailing against Woodhull. She called Woodhull "insane," adopting a frequently used masculine ploy to undermine the credibility of unconventional women. Catharine Beecher broke the pact of silence the two women had adopted after their Central

Park carriage ride almost two years earlier and revealed in her letter the details of the conversation she had had with Woodhull at that time. She said that Woodhull had "calmly informed me that several distinguished editors, clergymen, and lady authors of this city, some of them my personal friends . . . not only held her opinions on free love, but practiced accordingly, and that it was only a lack of moral courage that prevented their open avowal of such opinions." But Catharine Beecher's clumsy maneuver simply increased public awareness of Woodhull's charges.

In her explicit charges of blackmail, Catharine Beecher wrote that "this woman or her associates have been carrying out a plan for making money by maligning or threatening conspicuous persons of such purity and sensibility that it would be expected they or their friends would pay large sums rather than come in collision with such antagonists and their filthy weapons." The implication of this was that her brother Henry had been blackmailed, and, refusing to pay, had been falsely exposed in the *Weekly*. Catharine Beecher had no basis in fact for these charges, but she was desperate to defend her brother, who still remained silent on the subject and refused to defend himself. Since the prosecution had redefined its obscenity charges against Woodhull to cover only the Challis article, she was now proposing that the state take some new action to clear her brother's name. "Imprisonment for life, without the power for pardon in any human hands," would be appropriate punishment, she said, and called on the women and the clergymen of New York to work toward this end.

Woodhull responded with an April 2 letter to Whitelaw Reid at the *Tribune*, and Charles A. Dana at the *Sun*, which had also printed Catharine Beecher's letter. She said that Catharine Beecher's statement was a "lie." She had never extorted money, and no one had ever proved a "single instance" against her.

The *Tribune* and the *Sun* refused to print Woodhull's letter. Their only explanation was the thin excuse that there was too great a sentiment against her and in favor of Henry Ward Beecher to allow her reply to appear in print. The Catharine Beecher letter was reprinted by newspapers all over the country.

On May 17 Woodhull devoted the entire *Weekly*, on the stands at the time of the suffrage convention, to an extended defense of herself and her reputation. She made a frank reply to Catharine Beecher's letter. She acknowledged that the earlier silence between the two women, after their drive in Central Park, had been purchased with threats, not understanding. Woodhull had told Catharine Beecher about her brother's philandering. She remembered that Catharine Beecher had refused to believe her and had attacked her, saying, "I will strike you in every way I can and will kill you if possible."

She also took Tilton to task on May 17 for not standing on principle and supporting free love. Tilton had written a poem titled "Sir Marmaduke's Musings"—

> *I won a noble fame;*
> *But with a sudden frown,*
> *The people snatched my crown,*
> *And in the mire trod down*
> *My lofty name . . .*
>
> *I clasped a woman's breast.*
> *As if her heart I knew*
> *Or fancied, would be true,*
> *Who proved—alas she too—*
> *False, like the rest . . .*

—suggesting that Woodhull was the false woman Tilton was describing. In fact, Tilton was pointing a finger at his wife, not at Woodhull, and she explained: "The poem was written by Mr. Tilton, so he informed me, in Young's hotel in Boston . . . a revolver lying beside him . . . as an explanation of his suicide. Returning, however, to his better sense, he . . . returned home, called at my residence . . . , read me the poem in manuscript, and gave me this history of it. It was immediately published in the *Golden Age* . . ." Woodhull had published it in the *Weekly* as well. The story exposed Tilton's adolescent posturing as no accusation could.

Woodhull had written to Tilton on her release from prison, hoping that he might now be persuaded to form an alliance with her. She had appealed to his manliness, saying, "You have the most glorious opportunity to strike toward the future and become a hero." She had received no reply, so she published the letter, with this afterthought: "Since then I am grieved to confess I have believed him lost, lost to the cause, lost to himself."

Despite Woodhull's vigorous defense of herself in the May 17 *Weekly*, she was not invited to attend the suffrage convention. It was a crushing public humiliation. Even the gentle and tolerant stateswoman of suffrage, Lucretia Mott, avoided appearing in print on Woodhull's behalf and wrote to her sister that "E. C. Stanton is disposed to be very cautious how she identifies herself in any way with [Woodhull] now."

But Woodhull's loyal friend Isabella Beecher Hooker would not allow the convention to ignore Woodhull. Though illness prevented her from attending the meeting, she sent a letter that was read aloud to the body. In describing the suffrage accomplishments of the past 25 years, she paid tribute to "the work of a woman, young and inexperienced, a tender mother . . . but with a heart bolder than a lion and a will firmer for the right than the granite rock. From a reluctant congressional committee she wrung the first recognition that women citizens of the United States" had a right to the ballot. "The Memorial of Victoria C. Woodhull, together with her own argument thereon" has laid the foundations for an "absolute equality of rights," she wrote. With that tribute Woodhull had to be content.

Almost lost in the May 17 *Weekly* was a brief notice on the editorial page, stating that Tennessee Claflin was leaving the *Weekly.* "Valedictory," read the headline, and below the announcement appeared this "notice":

> The firm of Woodhull and Claflin, proprietors and publishers of *Woodhull and Claflin's Weekly* is hereby dissolved by the retirement of Tennie C. Claflin, who had transferred all her right, title and interest in the *Weekly* to Victoria C. Woodhull. The paper will still continue to be published under its original title of *Woodhull and Claflin's Weekly.* Victoria C. Woodhull. Tennie C. Claflin.

Poor health was the pretext for this action, though there were no indications that Tennie was ill. She may have wanted to sign over her *Weekly* contract to Woodhull so she would not be liable for the losses the *Weekly* incurred. She did not have income from lecturing, as Woodhull did, to cover those losses.

During her gradual recovery from her illness in June, Woodhull found scant reason for optimism. Into her sickroom floated the first word from Henry Ward Beecher on the *Weekly*'s exposure. One of his parishioners had mentioned the "Woodhull outrage" to him, adding that the world knew "the whole thing was a fraud from beginning to end." "Entirely," Beecher had responded. His supporters, hungry for a denial from their beloved preacher, fanned the word "entirely" all over New York and Brooklyn.

It would have given Woodhull some comfort if she had known that Susan B. Anthony, on hearing this, had been unable to resist writing Isabella Beecher Hooker to say that if God had ever struck anyone dead for telling a lie, He should have done so then.

Hooker wrote to her brother begging him to tell the truth. Henry counseled her to remain silent. Their brother Thomas wrote Hooker, "In my judgment Henry is following his slippery doctrines of expediency, and in the cry of progress and nobleness of spirit, has sacrificed clear, exact integrity. Of the two, Woodhull is my hero, and Henry my coward . . . You cannot help Henry. You must be true to Woodhull." Eventually all these letters found their way into print, but Woodhull had no access to them at the time they could have given her the most encouragement.

On Thursday June 26, 1873, the obscenity trial finally began. Woodhull looked ill, and she wilted further in the muggy heat. She fanned herself with her hat, but "still showed that the hot air in the room was affecting her very disagreeably," the *Sun* reported. She sat in the courtroom beside her new trial attorney, Charles Brooke. A jury was chosen with some difficulty; and one juror had to be excused on the grounds that he was a member of the YMCA.

The next morning at 11 the prosecution's witness, Anthony Comstock, was called to the stand. He testified about the *Weekly*s he had mailed to himself in Greenwich, Connecticut, under the name J. Beardsley.

Eventually Brooke was able to present his case for the defendants. He argued that the statutes of 1865 and 1872 under which the defendants had been charged did not apply to newspapers. And since a new statute specifically including newspapers had been passed only in 1873, the defendants could not be tried under a law that had come into existence after the prosecution of their case had begun. Brooke cited General Butler's opinions to the judge.

After a close review of the details, the judge stated that "the prosecution could not be maintained." The assistant U.S. attorney agreed and issued a formal notice that the criminal case be ended. But Brooke objected, saying the defendants were entitled to a verdict. The judge ruled in his favor and instructed the jury that since no case had been presented by the prosecution, they were to find the defendants not guilty.

The jury complied, and the case against Woodhull, Claflin, and Blood ended. The question of what words had constituted obscenity never came up. Nor did the names of Henry Beecher or Luther Challis. After eight months of legal harassment, Woodhull had won an undisputed victory.

No carefree celebrations followed, for the Challis libel case was still ahead. Though drained, Woodhull went on the offensive. "This persecution . . . was purely . . . to vindicate the reputation of a revered citizen," she said in the *Weekly*. She sent a petition for damages resulting from the *Weekly*'s suppression, to the Senate Committtee on Claims.

Now that Woodhull had succeeded in clearing her name of these baseless charges, the press and the public were having new thoughts about the whole matter. The *Sun* chronicled the change of heart, writing on June 30:

> Mrs. Woodhull and Miss Claflin were arrested some time ago, charged with offence against the United States, jailed for a considerable number of days, and finally released on giving heavy bail.
>
> Their business is broken up, and they were put to much inconvenience and subjected to many indignities.
>
> The prosecution opens—it proceeds—it closes; then what?
>
> Why then the learned Judge of the United States District Court, who presides at the trials, informs the accused that there is no occasion for them to introduce any evidence in their defence; that no case has been proved against them; and he instructs the jury to render a verdict of not guilty, which they immediately do without leaving their seats.
>
> For the wrong which has been done to these women, they have no redress. The injury is irremediable.

The suffrage leaders, too, were having second thoughts. Elizabeth Cady Stanton defended Woodhull privately. She wrote Anthony that if her testimony would rescue Woodhull and at the same time dethrone Beecher, she would willingly give it. In Anthony's response, she set aside her differences with Woodhull and quoted from an earlier letter she had written supporting her: "We have had women enough sacrificed . . . let us end this ignoble record and henceforth stand by womanhood."

As if sniffing out this change in sentiment, Henry Ward Beecher was finally heard from. On June 30, 1873, the same day the *Sun* defended Woodhull so vigorously, he wrote to the *Brooklyn Eagle:*

> I have returned to the city to learn that application has been made to Mrs. Victoria Woodhull for letters of mine supposed to contain information respecting certain infamous stories against me. I have no objection to have the *Eagle* state in any way it deems fit, that Mrs. Woodhull, or any person or persons who may have letters of mine in their possession, have my cordial consent to publish them. In this connection, and at this time, I will only add that the stories and rumors which have for some time past been circulated about me are grossly untrue, and I stamp them in general and particular as utterly false.

Later that year Stanton wrote to Hooker stating in no uncertain terms that Woodhull's story was essentially accurate so far as she knew the situation, and expressing her anger at the power bloc that had persecuted Woodhull and defended Beecher.

> Susan [B. Anthony] heard the story from the lips of Mrs. Tilton—I from him at a different time and place—neither knowing what the other has heard . . . Victoria's story is exaggerated—rather higher colored than I heard it—but the main facts correspond with what Susan and I had heard.
>
> I have not a shadow of doubt of the truth . . . There is too much money locked up in Beecher's success for him to be sacrificed. The public, especially those who have a financial interest in this matter, would rather see every woman in the nation sacrificed than one of their idols of gold. They think if they can separate us one from another, prevent us writing or meeting, sowing seeds of discord all around they can manage the public. The outrageous persecution of Mrs. Woodhull in our courts shows money and power behind, and

she may thank Plymouth Church, Ford & Co. etc. for all she has suffered . . . I have been crucified in this matter as much as you—have lost friends in the family and out and am beset every day with some phase of "the Woodhull" coming up by word and letter until at times I feel like shirking everything disagreeable. But through it all I see one thing, we must stand by each other. Women must be as true to women as men are to men. This is the first thing I have committed to paper on this T[ilton] and B[eecher] matter, so use it judiciously for your defense.

It would not be long before Stanton's point of view would be published in the *Chicago Tribune* and reach thousands of readers. Though Stanton continued to avoid associating with Woodhull publicly, she made her attitude toward Beecher widely known.

You ask if it is possible for Mr. Beecher to maintain his position in the face of the facts. His position will be maintained for him, as he is the soul and center of three powerful religious rings: (1) Plymouth Church; (2) the *Christian Union;* (3) *The Life of Christ.* The church property is not taxed, its bonds in the hands of wealthy men of that organization are valuable, and the bondholders, alive to their financial interests, stand around Mr. Beecher, a faithful, protecting band, not loving truth and justice less, but their own pockets more. Next the *Christian Union*—a dull paper that represents no new thought in morals, religion or politics . . . If then his good name is shadowed, another circle of suffering stockholders would be brought to grief. As to *The Life of Christ,* in the words of one of the fold, that would indeed be blown "higher than a kite" were the author proved an unworthy shepherd. I have heard that he was paid $20,000 for that work before he put pen to paper.

Supporting words from Paulina Wright Davis, as well, reached Woodhull, with the request that Woodhull not make them public until after Davis's death. She was too ill to withstand controversy, she told Woodhull. "Sweet, loving, beautiful as your two letters have been to me, I can only just say a word in reply . . . I have been with you in prison, in bondage, and in sickness . . . Believe in me, believe that I never betrayed a trust, never was false to a friend, and that at all times truth is dearer to me than ought else in this life; but there are times when silence is all there is for me."

Both women Woodhull had quoted as her sources in the Beecher exposure had now supported Woodhull's story in all it essentials. But neither wanted to be publicly identified with her because she was still notorious for her positions on free love and Christian communism. Woodhull had hoped and expected that they, and the entire New York wing of the suffrage movement, would come to her defense when she was jailed—that whatever past differences had divided them, the women would make a show of solidarity on her behalf. She couldn't erase the disappointment she felt when once again she was abandoned. But her image as a martyr to freedom of the press and radical reform had turned up a new circle of friends, most of them from the ranks of spiritualists, and she enjoyed their attention and support.

While still fragile, Woodhull had to confront a new emotional crisis in her family circle—the death of her sister Utica on July 9. Only 31 years old, Utica, like Canning Woodhull a year earlier, succumbed to the effects of addiction to alcohol and narcotics. Woodhull had been aware of her sister's problems, "driven to intemperance by sheer desperation . . . habitual use of narcotics . . . stimulants to drown her griefs and disappointments," but she was shocked that death had come so quickly. Still face to face with her own mortality, feeling the sense of vulnerability that serious illness leaves behind, the death of her younger sister produced an unexpected aftershock.

A private funeral service was followed by burial in Green Wood Cemetery in Brooklyn, the fashionable resting place of the time. Woodhull and Claflin told the funeral director that there was to be no display, and he complied with a plain casket strewn with a few white flowers. The immediate family formed a cortege to Brooklyn, accompanied by an unidentified "intimate friend of the family." Oddly enough, Colonel Blood was not among the mourners.

"What she needed most of all things was a master mate—some one before whom even her regal nature could bow and seek wisdom," Woodhull wrote in her sister's obituary. "Hers was a nature too large and demanding, too conscious of its own capacity to be counter-parted and commanded by any other than a superior." One senses that Woodhull was talking more about herself than her sister at this time of crisis, introspection, and vulnerability, fantasizing about a "superior," a "mastermate" who would help guide her through the maze of her present difficulties.

After her illness, Woodhull was never quite the same. Some part of her unquenchable spirit disappeared, her spontaneous zest replaced by a sense of desperation. Still ambition and ego drove her onward.

29

"Perfected Sexuality"

Woodhull surged back to life and health with a powerful series of bold speeches on the sexual emancipation of women. While paying lip service to political action, she preached sexual enlightenment as a means of self-realization. Making the rounds of spiritualist summer camp meetings, she told her audiences that the "free consent of women is a necessary precedent to sexuality . . . Women of America! Will you, can you, dare you begin this glorious work?

"Nine of every ten wives, at some time in their marriage, are compelled . . . to submit themselves to their husbands when every sentiment of their souls revolts at the act," Woodhull said. "The poor young woman who is a Christian believes she can escape hell only by obeying St. Paul's injunction that wives should submit to their husbands. I say damn such Christianity as that." Woodhull's words projected an anger that her listeners found exciting. During that summer of 1873 she was as popular as she had ever been.

"The sexual emancipation of woman" was the "sublime mission of spiritualism," Woodhull declared, using her speeches as a platform for reelection as president of the spiritualists. The *Weekly* moved in tandem with her, exposing fraudulent mediums and promoting spiritualist meetings and speakers. Political copy still appeared in the paper; during the course of the summer the platform of the Equal Rights Party was reprinted and the American Labor Reform League received coverage, but the paper's most frequent subject was spiritualism.

In a marked change, the *Weekly* now offered negative comments on Stephen Pearl Andrews, his meandering talk and "peculiar views on everything under the sun." Andrews no longer sought Woodhull's company. In fact, he had seldom been heard from since his brief arrest with Blood and the other *Weekly* staff members, and he never returned to the paper. A new inner circle, composed of family and special friends among the spiritualists, now supported Woodhull's interests. Suffragists, Wall Street friends, labor radicals—all had gone.

The experiences of the past few months had drawn Woodhull, Claflin, and Colonel Blood closer together. "Ours is a trinity . . . to which we are all equally devoted . . . 'we three are one' in spirit and purpose, and [therein] lies all the strength we have," Woodhull wrote in the *Weekly*.

Blood and Claflin usually accompanied Woodhull on her lecture tours. Their presence and emotional support were essential to her sense of well-being. Woodhull supported the paper and her extended family with the $280 she earned from each lecture. When she was unable to speak, it threw "us all on our oars," Blood said in one of his rare comments on their working relationship. "We can work up the audience, get the people together, but it needs her to finish the work. I am afraid it would be an up-hill business to attempt to run the machine without her." When Woodhull became ill, for she had recurring bouts of ill health after her June collapse, Blood did not step in as a substitute, explaining, "I am not in any sense a public speaker. I am a worker, and I hope I am doing my work well." Tennie would occasionally speak in Woodhull's place.

Blood and Claflin could travel with Woodhull because George Blood, the Colonel's younger brother, now managed the *Weekly* on a day-to-day basis. George did not resemble his handsome and stylish older brother; he was short, frail, and blond, and an untrimmed beard cascaded over his vest. He was devoted to his brother, and also cheerfully saw to Woodhull's son Byron's care in addition to his other responsibilities. The Colonel would send him somewhat casual reminders about details at the paper, confident of his brother's ability to carry on without him. Another full-time employee was Robert E. Hume, stout, mild in manner, a Scot and a land reformer of the Henry George school. A "true believer" who delivered lectures on "radical spiritualism," he wrote copy on economic subjects as well as spiritualism. The Colonel commented in a letter to his brother, "by the way, what a splendid assistant he makes," and apologized that he and Woodhull could provide no editorials that week—Hume would have to do it.

That summer Woodhull wrote a brief autobiography that was attuned, as Theodore Tilton's biography of her had been two years earlier, to spiritualist sensibilities. She was positioning herself for the

September spiritualists' convention. She called it *A Glance Behind the Scenes in Her Own and Sister's Lives,* and in it she reviewed her public career step by step, attributing each move to spirit guidance. Although she deplored frauds in spiritualism and dependence on physical manifestations, she declared that her life was "a series of constant spiritual experiences . . . the minutest details of every day existence as well as . . . the efforts of a whole career."

On September 16, 1873, she was in Chicago for the annual spiritualists' convention, presenting herself with uncharacteristic modesty as a "weak, unlettered woman." Unlettered, yes. Weak? Not likely. But her words were in keeping with the spiritualist belief that the most important knowledge came from the humble and unlearned, not the mighty.

The convention presented a contest between the "conservative respectables" and the more radical "New York ring." The conservatives, opposed to free love and its association with spiritualism, were attempting to undermine Woodhull and her leadership. Woodhull was pressed by a man named Cotton about her free love views. He asked her persistent questions about her personal life. Cotton led a group of spiritualists who had a prying and prurient interest in Woodhull's sex life. They felt that her exposure of Beecher obligated her to answer any questions they might put to her.

Woodhull went on the offensive, asking, "Has Mr. Cotton ever had sexual intercourse with Mrs. Woodhull?"

"No," he replied.

"Do you know of any man who has?" she pursued.

"No."

"Then what in the name of heaven can you prove? . . . I never had sexual intercourse with any man of whom I am ashamed to stand side by side before the world . . . I am not ashamed of any act of my life. At the time it was the best I knew. Nor am I ashamed of any desire that has been gratified or of any passion alluded to. Every one of them are a part of my own soul's life, for which, thank God, I am not accountable to you."

Woodhull continued, "I had to live, or I should assuredly be sent to Sing Sing. Hence I went to the world's people. I went to your bankers, presidents of railroads, gamblers, prostitutes, and got the money that has sent you the paper you have been reading, and I do not think that any of you are the worse for handling it." Cheers greeted her words. "I used whatever influence I had to get that money, and that's my own business and none of yours; and if I devoted my body to my work, and my soul to God, that is my business and not yours. I have gone before the world devoting my heart and soul to this cause . . . [The spirits] have entrusted me with a mission . . .

"Let me assure the highly respectable gentleman from Vineland [Cotton] that I have done whatever was necessary to perform what I conceived to be my duty . . . [even] a thing so utterly abhorrent to me as to submit sexually for money to a man I do not love. If Mr. Cotton or any of you are so terribly alarmed lest I may have been obliged to do this let him and you manifest your alarm by rallying to my support so as to insure that no such exigency shall shall ever again arise. I hope Mr. Cotton that you are answered . . .

"And this sexual intercourse business may just as well be discussed now, and discussed until you become so familiar with your sexual organs until a reference to them will no longer make the blush mount to your face any more than a reference to any other part of your body. Have I not done my work? Have I not done everything that was demanded of me? . . . I do not propose to have any blush on my face for any act of my life. My life has been my own. I have nothing to apologize for."

Prolonged applause followed Woodhull's words, and the convention reelected her president of the association for another year. The delegates collected a generous subscription for her and formed a committee to reorganize themselves in accordance with her wishes. She had, at least for the moment, faced down the conservatives.

Woodhull closed the convention with her most radical speech. After spending the summer talking about a woman's right to say no, she turned now to a woman's right to say yes, about a woman's right to sexual pleasure and fulfillment in orgasm. She would tell them, she said, "the plain unvarnished truth about the most important question that has ever interested and distracted the human mind." Throw away the "sickly sentimentalism about sexual love," she said. "This problem of sexual love is the most important one that has ever engaged the human mind.

"Sexual intercourse that is in accordance with nature, and is therefore proper, is that which is based upon mutual love and desire, and that culminates in reciprocal benefit . . . First love; Second desire based on love; and Third mutual happiness the result." Woodhull used the words "reciprocal benefit" to mean orgasm. "Fully half of women seldom or never experience any pleasure whatever in the sexual act . . . Almost every woman, at some time in her life, has suffered from false sexual relations" (Woodhull's term for orgasmic failure), which left a "void in the inner soul."

Woodhull concluded with a lyrical paean to orgasmic fulfillment, saying, "What a revelation. Words are insignificant to express it . . . The heart beats faster; the eye sparkles . . . the whole being thrills with ecstasy as it recognizes and embraces the companion." Woodhull left the convention having convinced the spiritualsts that she preached and practiced a new enlightened sexuality.

Woodhull's frankness about sex excited a young man named Benjamin Tucker. "She stood fixed on her pedestal, I, at her feet, a clod of common clay," he said later. Tucker was a student at the Massachusetts Institute of Technology; he was a nineteenth-century "reform groupie" who circled briefly in her orbit. Woodhull's sexual experimentation was extended to him, and many years later, he gave an account of their "experiment in friendship"; it offers a revealing picture of Woodhull as a sexual person.

Tucker had first met his idol when she had spoken in Boston. In her rush to catch the night train back to New York, Woodhull had left her wrap behind, and Tucker ran after her, arriving as the train was about to pull out. He had leaped aboard and found Woodhull, he said, who "accepted the wrap with thanks . . . Then, suddenly and to my intense astonishment, she put her face up to mine and kissed me squarely on the mouth. The train was already moving. I ran to the door and leaped off, a much excited and wondering youth."

The next time Woodhull spoke in Boston, Tucker sought her out at her hotel. He met Colonel Blood, who asked the eager young man if he would like to help with some of Woodhull's speaking arrangements. Tucker completed his assignment and returned to report back to Blood. As he entered their room, Woodhull "came forward, her face wreathed with cordial smiles, and her two hands, both outstretched, clasped mine and shook them warmly." Tucker's joy knew no bounds. Two other women and Blood were with Woodhull, and the party chatted until about ten, when Woodhull asked Blood if he would escort the ladies to their homes.

"Before we were 20 feet from the door, Mrs. Woodhull turned the key and hung a wrap upon the knob to cover the keyhole," Tucker remembered. "Then, always in a quiet, earnest, charming manner, she marched straight to the chair in which I was seated, leaned over and kissed me, remarking then: 'I've been wanting to do that so long!' Then with a grace all her own she gently swung herself around and placed herself upon my knee, I behaving always like a puzzled brute . . . A few moments later she took another chair and sat in it by my side." The conversation continued. When Colonel Blood returned he asked Woodhull if she did not feel the need of another meal after her day's journey.

"Oh no," she answered with a meaning smile, "we have just had refreshment that you know not of."

Tucker said goodnight and promised to return the next day, a Sunday. When he arrived the next morning, Colonel Blood was not present. Tucker and Woodhull chatted amiably, and then Woodhull said, "Do you know, I should dearly love to sleep with you."

As Tucker recalled his response years later, he said, "Any man a thousandth part less stupid than myself would have thrown his arms about her neck and smothered her with kisses. But I simply remarked that were her desire to be gratified, it would be my first experience in that line."

Woodhull looked at him with amazement. "How can that be?" she asked.

Colonel Blood returned, and Tucker left for lunch. He returned at three and found Blood writing at a table in one corner of the room. Woodhull was stretched out on a lounge. She complained of a headache and asked Tucker to place his hand on her forehead. As Tucker obliged, Blood rose, gathered his papers and said, "I must go down to the reading room to finish my work. There's altogether too much magnetism about here for me."

Tucker's account continued: "After that, affairs moved rather more rapidly. Mrs. Woodhull was still obliged to make all the advances; I, as before, was slow and hesitating, because of my lack of savoir faire. But, despite all obstacles, within an hour my 'ruin' was complete, and I, nevertheless, a proud and happy youth."

"What will Colonel Blood think of this?" Tucker finally had the courage to ask.

"Oh, that will be all right," Woodhull replied, "and besides, he cannot deny that it's largely his own fault. Why, only the other day he wrote to me of you in glowing terms, declaring, 'I know very well what I would do were he a girl.' "

As Tucker rose to go Woodhull said, "Be sure to come back this evening; and, as you pass out, please step into the reading-room and speak to Colonel Blood in order that he may know you are no longer with me."

"I did as told and was received by the Colonel in a most natural and hospitable manner, after which I departed, walking on air," Tucker recalled.

He returned in the evening. He remembered that, "Toward ten o'clock Colonel Blood, without saying a word, pulled the lounge into [an adjoining] room, shut himself up there, and went to bed, leaving the sleeping-room to Mrs. Woodhull and myself. At one o'clock in the morning I left the hotel, in order that Colonel Blood might not be obliged to pass the entire night so uncomfortably."

Benjamin Tucker was no longer a virgin. He remembered later that Woodhull "was not vulgar in her love making, simply enraptured and happy. She was not indifferent, not insatiable. She did not make love in order to be accommodating . . . She was never very gay but almost always cheerful and charming." He observed that she "had the stuff in her to be a 'true pagan,' but in reality was rather a 'perverted puritan.'"

Blood's role in all of this is problematic. The relationship between Blood and Woodhull had never been closer, they were "one" in "spirit and purpose," as Woodhull had said not long before. Tucker described Blood with affection and respect, calling him an "honest" and "generous" gentleman. He "was cognizant of the intimacy," Tucker said. He was convinced that Woodhull loved Blood during this time and was "entirely frank with him."

Fifty years later, Tucker gave an account of his infatuation with Woodhull to Emanie Sachs, Woodhull's first full-length biographer. He needed money and talked Sachs into paying him $3,500 for his story. Neither party revealed this transaction at the time Sachs's book was published. When Sachs asked whether Blood "always quietly got out of the way," Tucker speculated that "opportunities were abundant when Blood was working at the paper." Tucker believed that both Blood and Woodhull were fond of him, and that the situation was entirely to Blood's liking. Blood did not bring it about for the sake of variety, Tucker told Sachs; Blood felt secure in his relationship with Woodhull, but feeling secure, it was an additional satisfaction to have Tucker on the scene. "That may seem strange," Tucker told Sachs, "and it is certainly unusual, but I feel sure that I am right about it." He assured her that he never saw the least evidence of ill feelings in the relations between Woodhull and Blood. Blood clearly accepted Woodhull's sexual experimentation in practice as well as in theory.

When Sachs printed Tucker's account, verbatim, from Tucker's letters to her, Tucker was outraged, saying it portrayed Blood as a procurer and himself as the one procured. He wrote Sachs that he didn't like what she had done with his material, and he was in the "depths of despair." "Great damage" had been done, he said. Yet Sachs had simply printed Tucker's words.

There is no reason to doubt that Tucker's story is essentially accurate. Though Tucker was the only man to talk about his intimacy with Woodhull, such "experiments in friendship" were part of Woodhull's emancipation. Tucker was not, however, typical of Woodhull's liaisons, not a "mastermate."

Power, money, success, men more in the mold of Charles Brooke and George H. Ellery interested Woodhull. Ellery was a successful business man of some wealth, originally from Indiana. He had come to her aid during her days of imprisonment, and she had turned to him for advice when Henry Bowen of Plymouth Church had approached her for several letters Beecher had written to her. Woodhull had given Ellery the letters for safekeeping. She considered him "the peer of any man" and went on to have a lifelong friendship with his children, and to remember his son Ellery years later in her will, leaving him a legacy with the words "to the son of an old and valued friend." Charles Brooke, the lawyer who had defended her so competently in her obscenity case, was fortyish and dashing, with heavy hair that swept over his forehead. He had made a reputation for himself in Philadelphia and then transferred his practice to New York. Woodhull appreciated his "wise conduct," "his coolness," his "dignity and moral force." Both Ellery and Brooke were men Woodhull responded to, though there is no evidence to confirm that Woodhull had affairs with either of them.

Woodhull put her reawakened sensuality to an eminently practical purpose; she imbued her speeches of this time with an emotional conviction that contributed to their immense success.

On Friday, September 18, 1873, the financial markets crashed in New York. Woodhull prepared a timely response to the new realities in a speech titled, "Reformation or Revolution, Which?" She delivered it on October 17 to a large audience at Cooper Institute. It contained the germ of a big idea, wrested from her own experience. The church, she said, had allied itself with money and power, when it should be speaking for the powerless. The church had joined capitalism to rule the country. "The government, all the wealth of the country, backed up by the church [are] the strongest power in the world . . . the people of this country are today powerless against such a combination." She warned that the "Christian Bigots" might well be "installed as God's vice-regents on Earth." During her recent imprisonment, Woodhull had seen this misuse of public office enacted against herself. But Woodhull's new concept was not presented effectively. The speech didn't work and she cancelled her planned tour.

Her energies went immediately into another lecture on sexuality. It would be the most successful of her career, a distillation of all her speeches on sexual topics, frank, personal, and wise. She called it "Tried as by Fire, or the True and the False, Socially." The spiritualist language she had been using was stripped away, for she intended this production for wider audiences. Without Stephen Pearl Andrews's influence, her speeches were now freer and more compelling. Her mode had become even more like that of the exhorting Methodist preacher. It was a style her audiences were familiar with and responded to.

She gave them candid talk about forbidden subjects, and permission to think about them in a new way. She said that sexuality was good, the "physiological basis of character . . . to kill out the sexual instinct by . . . repression is to emasculate character." But sexual gifts must be used wisely to enable one to breed and bear healthy children, she cautioned. She continued to discuss female orgasm, but she put it in the context of sex education for men and women, part of the knowledge essential for a sound sexual relationship, a proto-family planning program. She called this her religion. Woodhull spent the remainder of the year, and most of 1874, on the road with "Tried as by Fire," speaking on 150 nights to what she estimated was a quarter of a million people. The success of this lecture temporarily eased her financial strains.

Woodhull made her son, Byron, an important part of this speech, using him as an example of how not to bear children. It was the first time she had discussed him publicly. She considered his impairments the result of a pregnancy forced on her when she was an uneducated, unprepared mother:

> Go home with me and see desolation and devastation
> . . . My boy, now 19 years of age, who should have
> been my pride and joy, has never been blessed by the
> dawning of reasoning. I was married at 14, ignorant
> of everything that related to my maternal functions.
> For this ignorance, and because I knew no better than
> to surrender my maternal functions to a drunken
> man, I am cursed with this living death . . . Do you
> think I can ever hesitate to warn the young maidens
> against my fate, or advise them never to surrender the
> control of their maternal functions to any man!

Woodhull apparently believed that impregnation "under perfect conditions of love" and with "mutual consummation" would alter the laws of heredity so that negative traits, such as her son's mental defects, would not be passed on. We now know her thinking about heredity was flawed. But her belief in the concept motivated her strongest and most intelligent words on sex education. Woodhull opened the minds of her generation to the value of sexual knowledge for young women—and men—as a preparation for marriage, making a valuable and courageous contribution to her time.

She was "the Woodhull" again, but the pleasure she once took in her prominence was evaporating. She dragged herself behind the never-ending echo of a train whistle—to Detroit, Bay City, St. Johns, Lowell, Lansing, Jackson, and Port Huron in Michigan; then on to Lincoln, Omaha, and Nebraska City in Nebraska; Lawrence, Emporia, Topeka, and Leavenworth in Kansas; St. Joseph in Missouri; Dubuque, Council Bluffs, Des Moines, Keokuk, and Burlington in Iowa; Freeport, Peoria, Quincy, Galesburg, Jacksonville, and Springfield in Illinois; Janesville, Madison, and La Crosse in Wisconsin; Winona, St. Paul, and Red Wing in Minnesota. The local papers referred to her unconventional subject matter as the "social question."

Woodhull was forced to return from Milwaukee to New York for the Challis libel trial in March, 1874. It was a tense affair that went on for ten days. Charles Brooke's strategy for the defense was to put Woodhull on the stand, not Tennie, who had actually written the article about Challis. It was a wise move, considering Tennie's tendency to blurt. In fact Tennie's formal separation from the paper may have been motivated by legal strategy—it was now advantageous in court for Woodhull to be the sole proprietor of the paper.

The prosecutor attempted to influence the jury by bringing Woodhull's exposure of Beecher, and her unconventional private life, into the case. The presiding judge was openly biased against the defendants. Woodhull was effective on the stand, and as the case continued, the judge's obvious prejudice turned the jurors against him and predisposed them toward Woodhull. Brooke used these advantages capably. Further, Challis did not make a good impression, and he did not convince the jury that the story printed in the *Weekly* was false.

Still, the outcome was in doubt. A decision from the jury was expected on March 13. At 11 o'clock that morning, the judge took his seat on the bench, the jury filed into court, and quiet came over the room.

"How say you? Do you find the [defendants] guilty or not guilty?" asked the clerk of the court.

The foreman of the jury responded "Not guilty!" in a clear loud voice.

The room burst into applause, and Woodhull and Claflin burst into tears. Colonel Blood sat immobile. Annie Claflin, who had attended every day of the trial, called down blessings on the jury amid her tears. George Ellery, who had also been in court every day, gave a shout of joy and threw his hat in the air.

The judge grumped, "It is the most outrageous verdict ever recorded; it is shameful and infamous, and I am ashamed of the jury who rendered such a verdict." He quickly adjourned the court.

Woodhull attributed the outcome to Brooke's able defense, saying, "It is with pride and gratitude that we speak of Charles W. Brooke, Esq., [our] able, eloquent and eminent counsel." Brooke's was "the ablest defense on record," Woodhull believed, and she printed his summation in the *Weekly* word for word from the court stenographer's records.

Woodhull scarcely paused to enjoy the public support building around her. She returned doggedly to the lecture circuit. "I do not believe it is possible for a woman to produce her best child, except by the man whom she loves best, and for whom she has the keenest sexual desire," she told the thousands who came to listen. She introduced the term "sociology" to her audiences as "that science which deals with every range of human affairs." She talked sometimes to women only, and she discussed birth control. Returning often to her favorite catchphrase, "perfected sexuality," she steadfastly insisted that the sexual emancipation of women was as important as their political equality.

30
"Deluges of Filth"

Dr. Joseph Treat was aroused by Woodhull's sexual frankness. A medical doctor and a spiritualist who was also a radical pamphleteer, Treat had helped found Berlin Heights, an experimental community in Ohio. He believed in free love of the "continence" school, which favored a variety of partners but opposed sexual "ultimation." Treat advocated "sexual fasting," abstinence except for procreation. He was obsessed with prostitutes, female anatomy, female diseases. Unluckily for Woodhull, he also became obsessed with her.

Woodhull had responded to Treat's overtures of friendship while she was in prison, thinking him another large-hearted medical man, in the tradition of Dr. E. B. Foote, the author of books on sex education, who had supported her May convention. Treat's ambition in life was to cure disease and "checkmate death," a subject for which Woodhull had considerable enthusiasm.

During the spring of 1873, Treat made flattering speeches about Woodhull and criticized Beecher and Comstock. He became a welcomed contributor to the *Weekly*. He wrote "The Martyr Woman of the Nineteenth Century" in March. In April he wrote, "Victoria the Brave; She Is Intellect, But She Is More—She Is Intuition, Inspiration, Genius. Her Law, Her Propulsion Is in Herself. She Is Not Vanity, but She Is Necessity." Soon after, he ran a notice in the *Weekly* announcing that he and his wife, Mary, a well known naturalist, were separating.

Treat wrote about his infatuation with Woodhull later that year: "I idealized you as the embodiment . . . of the principle of Social Freedom . . . you stood to me as one sacred and holy and the very room in which I sat and wrote was transfigured every time you entered it, and the very sound of your voice heard through open doors thrilled every fiber of my being."

He couldn't have believed that Woodhull shared his view of free love—her words on the subject were too frank for misinterpretation—but perhaps he hoped to convert her to his "continence" school. More likely, his obsession had blinded him to all rational thought.

After six months of unrequited adulation, Treat turned on Woodhull. He had joined the faction that asked her to reveal her sexual life at the September 1873 spiritualists' convention. After the convention, Treat began a poisonous anti-Woodhull letter-writing campaign.

Treat's venom began to undermine Woodhull's standing among the spiritualists. He capitalized on a "doctrine of disclosure," a tenet among some spiritualists that secrecy poisoned social life, giving power to men and depriving women of it, while openness encouraged egalitarian relationships among the sexes and removed social evils. He used this concept to promote the idea that Woodhull should publicly disclose her personal sexual history. Woodhull had acted on this philosophy herself when she had disclosed Beecher's hypocrisy. Now Treat was asking her to expose herself as she had exposed Beecher, ignoring the pertinent detail that Woodhull had not been a hypocrite, but had openly espoused what she practiced. Woodhull assumed correctly that Treat's spitefulness was that of a rejected suitor. Later she said that she had "from time to time been surrounded by [those] who think that a person who claims to be a free lover thereby invites the advances of any and every person."

The *Weekly* began to run articles against Treat's sexual continence school of thought. Woodhull's comments in the paper goaded Treat into making more scurrilous charges against her and her family. He prepared a pamphlet intended to expose her as "the greatest fraud in the world." "Prostitutes," "Magdalens," "harlots," "whores"—the words rolled lubriciously off of his tongue and onto the page. He accused Woodhull, all of her sisters, her daughter, Zula, her nieces and nephews, even her aged mother, of sexual misconduct.

Woodhull decided to maintain a dignified silence, hoping that Treat would fade away. She went on a long and successful speaking tour in the West with her "Tried as by Fire" speech. She scheduled a long stay in California, and Tennie, Blood, and Zula accompanied her. But the Treat furor did not die down. Rumors circulated that Woodhull was leaving New York, closing down the *Weekly* and moving to California. In July 1874, she finally addressed these rumors in the *Weekly*, writing that the paper would continue "so long as we have life and strength to carry it along. We love the *Weekly* as if it were our natural child."

Woodhull returned to New York on August 1, 1874, after her last speaking engagement in San Francisco. Treat pressed her to publish his pamphlet in the *Weekly*. She evaded him and decided to take a European vacation, telling her readers that she looked on "an ocean voyage as a necessary step to entering on our fall lecture campaign." Woodhull departed on August 8 with her extended family.

In Paris, Woodhull was unsettled by reports that New York authorities had warned the Paris police about her, and that her entire party would be kept under observation. Her fears may have been more for her psychological than her physical safety. On the eve of her departure for Europe, Treat had succeeded in publishing his treatise as a pamphlet, and his spite would cause her public career great damage. From among Woodhull's own spiritualist friends had come the very kind of ammunition Beecher—and anyone else who wanted to discredit her—had hoped for. Many deplored Treat's pamphlet, but the mainstream press found a story there and attacked Woodhull once again. "Infamous woman," said the *New York Tribune;* "black as ravens," said the *New York Herald;* "advocates harlotry," said the *Chicago Times.*

Word of Treat's pamphlet reached Woodhull, and she decided to skip the 1874 spiritualists' convention being held in Boston. Still president of the organization, she apologized for her absence in the *Weekly,* saying she had calculated on returning in time for the meeting, but that mechanical difficulties and bad weather had slowed her crossing. Despite this explanation, it is certain that if she had intended to be at the convention, she could have returned to New York in time. In giving up the spiritualists, Woodhull relinquished her emotional home.

Her problems hadn't blown over while she was away. Treat had invented new charges: Woodhull had taken "hush-money" from Beecher. Rumors circulated that Woodhull had run away to Europe with Beecher money and that the *Weekly* would be discontinued.

Woodhull responded immediately. Twice in October she made a public and categorical denial of Treat's allegations. "We have never received a dollar or any other consideration from Mr. Beecher, or from anyone for Mr. Beecher, or from any other party connected with this scandal, or from anyone for any party connected with it, either to offer, or to withhold, any testimony," she wrote. "We trust this may be received as final." As her best evidence for the truth that no one had hushed her, she printed and reprinted details of the unfolding Beecher-Tilton story.

Hoping that the uproar would finally subside, Woodhull began another ambitious lecture tour. But hundreds of Treat's pamphlets, a gift to Beecher's supporters, started turning up outside the halls. Blood blamed the "slimy crawlings of the secret snake" when illness began to plague Woodhull again. The enemy this time was pleurisy, and the Philadelphia doctor who treated her recommended several weeks of bed rest.

Eventually Colonel Blood brought libel charges against Treat on Woodhull's behalf. On August 7, 1876, Treat was arrested. He pleaded not guilty on September 21, 1876, and posted $1,500 bail, but Treat died on February 4, 1879, at the age of 52, before the case was finally brought to trial.

Nothing Woodhull said or did could remove the accusation of harlotry. Treat's pamphlet was picked up by the press and quoted without attribution wherever she lectured. In December 1874 she had spoken again in the *Weekly*. "In regard to advocating harlotry I am entitled to be judged by my speeches and writings," she said. She reviewed all of them going back to her "Social Freedom" speech of November 1871, quoting herself as consistently advocating "monogamic unions" as the highest and best sexual relationships, and promiscuity as a lower stage of development practiced by those not able to achieve the higher plane. That was accurate so far as it went; her writings did applaud monogamy. But she conveniently left out her impassioned words defending the right of the individual to depart from monogamy, should "amativeness" strike. Woodhull had been a sexual experimenter, but she had never been a harlot, available to any buyer. The epithet unfairly distorted her legitimate aim to bring women's position in marriage out of the Dark Ages and her desire to, as she put it, "bless her sex by what she has learned regarding the science of life." After months of silence, her pent-up frustration found a voice. And once started, she held nothing back:

> The press will denounce me [having no] conception of what I am laboring to effect or of what I teach . . . they follow me up and down the earth as if I were a pestilence that it is their duty to combat, wilfully and maliciously misrepresenting all my acts and views. I

have endured this . . . until I am worn out. Constant drippings wear the hardest stones. I am made of no such flinty stuff as to be impervious to the constant deluges of filth that are poured upon me . . . I say shame upon the press for thus pursuing me . . . shame upon shame upon them for refusing . . . to undo their wrongs by publishing the right and the truth.

Treat, a man from among her own spiritualists, had succeeded in doing what Beecher and his minions of the law had been unable to accomplish. He had soiled Woodhull. She couldn't escape him. She began to alter her life to recover her pride.

31

"The End of the World Is at Hand"

W oodhull's sexual frankness ended; she disengaged from contro- versy and sought refuge in respectability. Religious ferment was in the air, and Woodhull now rummaged among her various as- sets, past and present, and proceeded to invent her own religion. Tap- ping into the more esoteric fervors of the era, she took up the Bible as an occult text and looked for secrets she believed she could decipher through her spiritualistic inspirations.

News of materializations reached Woodhull from Vermont. Two brothers, William and Horatio Eddy, had opened a spiritualist board- inghouse in the town of Crittenden, conducting nightly seances dur- ing which spectral figures allegedly appeared in their "spirit room." A New York attorney named Colonel Henry S. Olcott had visited and found a house full of "long-haired men and short-haired women," and wrote extensive reports for the *New York Sun* and the *Daily Graphic.* Crittenden, Vermont, became a mecca for spiritual- ists, and materializations became a vogue.

In the *Weekly,* Woodhull devoted gallons of ink to debating the meaning of these manifestations, and to exposing fraudulent materi- alizations. But the frauds that Woodhull uncovered didn't persuade her to relinquish her own secret conviction that somewhere genuine materializations could occur. Among the spiritualists, she said, "manifestations are accepted as evidence that there is life beyond the grave."

Two women far more substantial than any apparition emerged from all this turmoil. A star from the international circle of the oc- cult, Helena Petrovna Blavatsky, joined Olcott in Crittenden. To- gether they turned his newspaper accounts into a book. During 1875, he helped her found a new religion called Theosophy, a mix of faiths and philosophies with an Eastern coloring. Two years later she pub- lished *Isis Unveiled,* the textbook of Theosophy. Her emphasis on mystical experience, the supernatural, and higher spiritual powers appealed to the spiritualists, and many became her disciples. At the same time, Mary Baker Eddy was inventing Christian Science, a belief system that accepted the spiritualistic outlook but rejected materializations. It differed from spiritualism in that it had a single founder with an authoritative text that became the basis of the faith.

Woodhull clearly shared some of the impulses driving Eddy and Blavatsky. On April 17, 1875, she plunged into the quickening religious environment with a "new departure" in the *Weekly*. "There is a hidden thing permeating the whole Bible," she wrote. "The book itself purports to be a mystery [clothed] in parables and in allegorical pictures . . . shrouded in imagery and spoken of in language which none but the initiated ever for a moment suspect has the remotest reference to the thing really involved." Woodhull's new view of the Bible as an occult text owed a debt to the Theosophical ideas circulating, and in her autobiographical notes she later said of Blavatsky and Olcott that they had discovered "wonderful truths."

The spiritualistic concept of continuous life was at the core of Woodhull's new religious inquiries. She quoted St. Paul, in Corinthians I, Chapter 15:20, the "last enemy that shall be destroyed is death." Ever since her own brush with death in 1873, she had been preoccupied with this concept, the belief that a life rightly lived could lead to eternal life—not life in heaven after death, but an "immortal state without passing through death." She felt convinced that continuous life related in some way to the sexual emancipation of women. These metaphysical contemplations became the themes of her speeches and her private ruminations.

Woodhull's philosophical inquiries were periodically interrupted by the various aftershocks from her Beecher exposé. Theodore Tilton had instituted a suit in city court against Beecher for willful alienation of his wife's affections. It came to trial on January 11, 1875, and lasted almost six months, stringing out a million words of testimony.

Tilton's legal action had been precipitated by a series of provocations on the part of Beecher loyalists. Plymouth Church had expelled Tilton for slandering Beecher. Tilton sympathizers had called an advisory council of sister churches, but its action had been indecisive. The *Herald* commented on the mild rebuke meted out to Beecher: "Not guilty. But don't do it again." Beecher had then put together a team of legal advisers that included an established politician, General William Tracy. Tracy threatened Tilton, and Frank Moulton as well, calling them blackmailers, and offered to send Tilton and his family abroad indefinitely. Tilton angrily rejected the proposal, recognizing this strategy was to smear him, just as the Beecher forces had previously smeared Woodhull.

At a church hearing, Beecher's friends persuaded Tilton's wife, Elizabeth, that she had an obligation to help Beecher. She testified that Beecher's behavior toward her had always been proper, and that her husband was insanely jealous of Beecher, that he was a free lover, and that he was godless. Tilton rose up in wrath and gave full details of the long affair.

Beecher promptly repaid Elizabeth Tilton's loyalty by claiming she had "thrust her affections on me unsought," and, for good measure, he accused Tilton of hatred and greed. He added that Woodhull, his original accuser, was a woman with an appetite for all that was vile. The six presiding churchmen reached the conclusion that Tilton was malicious and revengeful, that Elizabeth Tilton was guilty of "inordinate affection," and that Beecher himself was innocent of all charges; his only fault was that he had been too trusting. Tilton, angry, bitter, desperate to clear his own name, had then instituted his legal action against Beecher.

When the case began in January, Woodhull was in Washington presenting her petition for damages. She appeared before the Senate Committee on Claims on January 12, and the House Committee on January 13. Public courts had been used for private purposes, she said, in a clear miscarriage of justice. Her petition had merit, and the *Washington Chronicle* reported that she was listened to patiently and respectfully. But she was awarded no compensation.

The Beecher-Tilton trial dragged on until June. Woodhull was subpoenaed by the defense, not to testify but to deliver some letters from Tilton she had in her possession. The letters had been written to arrange several meetings between Woodhull and Tilton, showing a closer intimacy between them than Tilton had testified to but nothing more. After her court appearance, Woodhull left the publicity cauldron of the Beecher trial, satisfied to "keep out of the imbroglio." Tilton's case against Beecher eventually ended in a divided jury (nine to three against Tilton), and Beecher was acquitted.

From January 13, when she spoke in Washington, through that year, Woodhull maintained a grueling cross-country schedule, appearing in small-town music halls and big-city opera houses nationwide. Train whistles held her captive, releasing her to unpredictable food and strange beds. She remembered these days later as her "weary years of public life in America." Her tours were interrupted by bouts of illness. Benign uterine tumors that caused excessive menstrual bleeding and anemia, problems she referred to as the "monthly waste," further wore her down.

Yet Woodhull could still sell out the houses, and she slowly restored her bank account. At the end of 1875, she reworked her sex education speech, giving it a religious coloring and title: "The Human Body, the Temple of God." She launched it at Cooper Institute in New York and began another bone-wearying tour.

In June 1876, she printed the last issue of the *Weekly*. The paper no longer provided Woodhull with a power base. Her religious message was building no following, and other papers had taken the *Weekly*'s place among the spiritualists. Even her husband, Colonel Blood, disagreed with her new direction.

The decision to close the paper reflected the deterioration of their relationship. She had said in one of her speeches that "it is the common experience among the married who have lived together . . . from five to ten years, that they are sexually estranged . . . Think of it!" In July she and Blood would celebrate the tenth anniversary of their ceremony in Dayton.

Woodhull and Blood's partnership had been based on mutual ambitions and goals, an empathy that went beyond sexual exclusivity. They had seen the top and the bottom of celebrity together. Now Blood no longer accompanied Woodhull on her lecture tours, they no longer had their work or their reform ideas in common, and the *Weekly*, the offspring of their union, withered and died. "True love gone out of fashion," ran a *Weekly* article before it closed. Divorce, a subject never previously broached in the paper, had become a regular editorial topic.

Woodhull applied for a divorce from Blood on September 18, 1876, on the grounds of adultery. The divorce was granted October 6. Since adultery was the only grounds for divorce in New York at this time, the charge was probably arranged to meet legal requirements. Woodhull had decried this practice in the *Weekly* but appears to have followed it anyway.

The most likely reason for the final estrangement of Woodhull and Blood was Treat and his pamphlet. Blood may have brought Treat into their circle. In any case, Woodhull always blamed Blood, fairly or not, for the appearance of the pamphlet. She felt he should have been able to prevent it or, if not prevent it, bury it. Even after the Beecher-Tilton trial was over, the pamphlets kept turning up at her speaking engagements.

In New York, an era was ending. The raw, naive, vigorous search for money, power and ideas that had followed the Civil War wound down during the recession of the 1870s. As if to confirm its demise, Vanderbilt died on January 4, 1877. A sedate and respectable New York was emerging, the world of Edith Wharton's proper brownstones and rigid proprieties. It had no room for Victoria Woodhull or Theodore Tilton, and not much space for Henry Ward Beecher, either.

After the unsuccessful outcome of his case against Beecher, Tilton left New York for Paris. He gave the impression that he was broken and impoverished, but in fact he, like Woodhull, had made enough money from his lectures to live comfortably for the remainder of his life. He joined the expatriate chess players of the Café de la Régence, who included Judah P. Benjamin, the secretary of state for the Confederacy. Tilton died in obscurity in 1907. Elizabeth Tilton reversed herself once again in 1878, writing to the *Times* that her husband's charge of adultery between herself and Beecher had indeed been true. She died in 1897.

As for Beecher, the *Times* had expressed the general consensus of thoughtful people after the trial, that he was guilty. He remained "the impure and perjured man which any rational construction of his own letters proved him to be," said the paper. Beecher was even more successful than Woodhull and Tilton in capitalizing on his notoriety, and he lectured successfully and gainfully to almost half a million people. His standing as a serious leader of the community may have been compromised, but he remained popular with the crowd until he also died in 1897.

Colonel Blood floundered aimlessly after he and Woodhull divorced. Woodhull and Claflin had accused him of taking funds from the *Weekly* at the time the decision was made to close it down. The accusation seems to have been more of a family quarrel over the allocation of funds than a matter of embezzlement. He drifted into Auburn, Maine, where he wrote on radical reform for the *Greenback Labor Chronicle*. Blood cultivated an aura of romantic sadness, seeming to be a "man with a bleeding heart," and he became a minor celebrity in Maine because of his former association with Woodhull. The only words he spoke about her recalled by those who knew him were simply that "the grandest woman in the world went back on me."

Blood's new life ended when the *Chronicle* failed. He married the mother of his former employers, and with her financial help set off for the Gold Coast of Africa, where he died on December 29, 1885.

Stephen Pearl Andrews lived with his son Charles on East 34th Street in New York City, still writing impenetrable prose and reading it regularly at meetings of the Manhattan Liberal Club. He died peacefully in his bed on May 21, 1886.

When Commodore Vanderbilt died in 1877, the newspapers reported that he had left $100 million. William, the son Vanderbilt had found to be so like himself, received 97 percent of the fortune. The will was contested by William's siblings and by Tennessee Claflin. Woodhull had arranged a lecture tour in England and rumors circulated that the sisters were paid to go to London while the will was contested in court. Woodhull denied the rumors, saying that "William H. Vanderbilt had no more to do with [my] departure for England than a child unborn."

Woodhull had been rudderless for some time. When Beecher's success in court seemed to prove that false respectability could defeat truth, it had seemed to be a victory for Treat and his pamphlet. She had lost her psychological center. "The end of the world . . . is at hand," she said in June of 1876. She made a startling turnaround on free love shortly before she left for England. In her last speeches, she described free love as the "love of God . . . free to all." She had first heard the phrase from a Methodist minister, she said, when she attended one of those protracted meetings in which the minister told everybody to come forward to receive "God's free love." Woodhull had faded into middle-age conventionality.

Prepared to go to any lengths to erase Treat's ugly picture of her and her family, she left New York for England in August of 1877 with the prim explanation that "I have a fair daughter just budding into womanhood, to whom I wish to leave an untarnished name. [I leave] for her sake, much more than for my own."

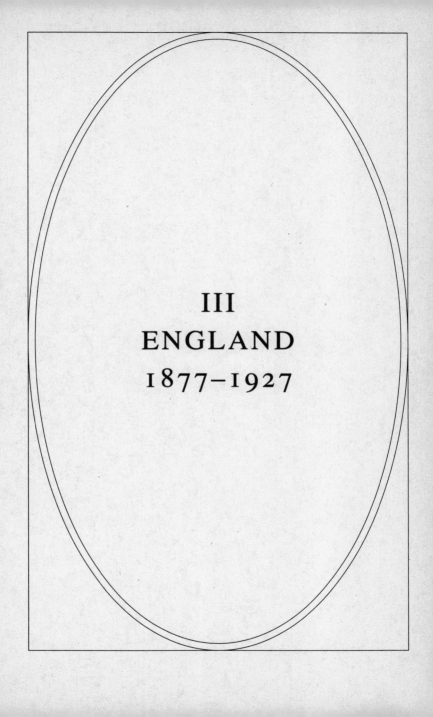

III

ENGLAND

1877–1927

32

Inventing "Mrs. Woodhall"

*I*n London, Woodhull dealt herself a new hand. A respectable widow of impeccable antecedents, possessing some means and many accomplishments, emerged. She adopted the name Woodhall to disassociate herself from the woman Joseph Treat had reviled. She portrayed her past as having been "quiet and aristocratic." Old families were part of her New York neighborhood, and the church was one door away, she said.

Warwick Road in South Kensington became her London address. She had sailed with her children, Byron and Zula, her mother, Annie, and Tennie. In June of 1878, her sister, Maggie Miles, and Buck Claflin, her father, reborn as a retired lawyer of "clear and learned views," joined them, as well as Maggie's two daughters, Ella Celeste, 20, and Carrie Zula, 16 . The cousins Carrie Zula and Zula Maud, born only a year apart and sharing the same unusual name, had always been close. Ella Celeste had been named for Tennie Celeste and was a particular favorite of her Aunt Tennie's. Woodhull presented her close-knit clan as a model of Victorian rectitude. Theirs was a family "of union and happiness and of perfect accord," she said, and she explained that she and Tennie had been always devoted to the "teaching and elevation of their sex."

Like many parents who have lived free lives themselves, Woodhull was overprotective of her daughter and nieces. The three young women lived exemplary and genteel lives in London. "Such a lady, but with charm too," was the way one of Woodhull's biographers later described Carrie after meeting her. The same could be said of any one of the three. Woodhull had protected them so well they had no knowledge of the scandals that had surrounded their "aunties" in New York.

On Warwick Road, Woodhull and Tennie recreated something of their early, happy days in New York. First on Woodhull's agenda was the speaking tour she had arranged before sailing for England. September found her in Nottingham speaking about sex education. The *Nottingham Guardian* reported enthusiastically that Woodhull spoke in "impassioned and fearless language," saying that "The child too often gathers from ignorant and vicious companions knowledge which ought to be imparted by a loving and intelligent mother." She is "unquestionably a great orator," the paper declared.

In December, when Woodhull faced more critical London audiences at St. James Hall, her press notices were mixed. The London reporters looked into their transatlantic files and wrote about her notoriety. Her lectures—she gave a series of ten that concluded in February of 1878—got better comments than her life. One reporter declared that "no man would dare discuss such subjects." Apparently charmed despite this disclaimer, however, he went on, "Her half-nervous style of utterance, her little womanly ways, so out of keeping with the matter of her lecture, pleased the audience."

Woodhull tried to make contact with the London suffragists but was rebuffed. The formidable British suffrage leader Millicent Garrett Fawcett had written to Susan B. Anthony about Woodhull. Anthony's reply had been sharp and harsh: "Let her severely alone. Both sisters are regarded as lewd and indecent. I would advise against any contact." Fawcett followed Anthony's advice. The rejection reinforced Woodhull's conclusion that respectability was her only course.

Tennie had her own agenda in London. She soon found a London Vanderbilt and lost interest in contesting the Commodore's will. Francis Cook was an immensely wealthy man in his sixties, married, with three grown children, and a well-known taste for philandering. He was tall with gray eyes that projected a sharp intelligence. He headed Cook, Son & Company of St. Paul's Churchyard, London, Great Britain's largest manufacturer and distributor of fabrics. He owned a marble palace called Monserrate, at Cintra near Lisbon, and held the title of Viscount of Monserrate, an honor bestowed by Dom Luiz, King of Portugal, for his beneficences to the country. The viscount also had a palatial London residence, Doughty House, overlooking the Thames on Richmond Hill. It housed a famous collection of paintings by Van Eyck, Rubens, and Rembrandt.

Tennie captivated Cook, and he became the sisters' sponsor and protector, an amiable relationship that pleased them all. The arrangement was different from New York days in one respect: Tennie and Cook did not appear in public together. They saw each other discreetly and quietly, screened by the propriety that prevailed on Warwick Road.

At about this time, an Englishman became interested in Woodhull. John Biddulph Martin had attended one of Woodhull's London lectures, drawn because of his late sister Penelope's interest in women's rights. Not yet 40, Martin was a main managing partner in Martin's Bank, the fifth generation of Martins in the family business at the Sign of the Grasshopper in Lombard Street. A tall, handsome man with dark eyes and a full dark beard, he had power, money, and social standing, and served on the boards of various businesses, hospitals, and charitable organizations. He had taken classical honors at Oxford, but had been better known there as a runner, graduating with a shelf full of silver trophies and, college archives record, "an athletic record unequalled by any other member." He was still an avid sportsman.

Though Martin appeared to have everything, he was a melancholy man. At the end of 1876, when he was 35, he had written in his diary, a pocket-size volume bound in green silk, "a very disappointing year . . . Is it possible to become more amiable and happy as one grows older?"

One cause of his unhappiness was Penelope's death in 1873. She had died unexpectedly after giving birth to her second child. John and Penelope were only a year apart in age. Martin's feelings toward his older siblings, Richard and Julia, had never been strongly affectionate, and when Penelope died John lost his best friend.

Penelope had been a free spirit. She had written a series of essays on women's rights—always anonymously, as was fitting for a woman of her social position in the England of her time. Martin honored his sister in the way he felt would mean the most to her. He encouraged the family to print her essays privately in a slim, leather-bound, gold-edged volume.

Martin had attended Victoria Woodhull's lecture hoping to find something of the spirit of the sister he had lost. He had followed Woodhull's career, "in the press, long before I ever saw her," he said later. He found enough in the lecture hall to pique his interest. On a fine fresh day in September of 1878, he paid a call on Warwick Road. "A very remarkable interview," he reported in his diary. He called again on November 24 and had a long talk with Zula but did not see Woodhull.

Almost a year passed before Martin called again. He had been preoccupied with another romantic interest, but that relationship had floundered. A sexual dysfunction, the exact nature of which he never confided to his journal, had held him back. It was not the first time. "Had not the old obstacle intervened I should certainly have asked EH to be my wife, and the news of her engagement affected me very much," he wrote in his diary.

In August of 1879, Martin again sought out Woodhull, and then in November, noting in his book "a singular interview with a stranger." But he had doubts as well. "Can I believe that this is anything but a sham?" he asked himself. Then, overcoming his reservations, Martin began paying regular visits to Warwick Road. "Stranger interview than ever," he noted at the beginning of 1880, "tête-à-tête, dinner and singularly sentimental evening."

Martin filled all of Woodhull's requirements for a mastermate. Her lifetime experience came to bear on him: he was wounded sexually, and she was in a position to help. Martin stayed later into the evening, "an emotional interview, almost ending in a climax," he confided to his diary. More late evenings followed.

On Valentine's Day, 1880, he went down in the afternoon to see Woodhull in her new quarters at 47 Warwick Road. Martin's comments about this new house are cryptic, but he had apparently arranged to rent a "home" for just the two of them adjacent to her family residence. He stayed to dinner. "Afterwards taken up to sanctum: a critical passage," he noted. He added a few words in classical Greek, expressing his most private thoughts. Translated, they read, "This is worthy of the world." In a letter he wrote to a friend later in his life, he gives an idea of what had drawn him to Woodhull almost against his will: "There were only two sorts of women, the ones in whom you lost yourself and the ones in whom you found yourself. She was more alive than anyone I have ever met. Ordinary words don't describe her. When you were with her everything became so thrilling, so worthwhile. You looked at the world through her eyes and you saw miracles all around you. The commonplace, the dull, the everyday had disappeared. She believed that people were interesting and wonderful and they became it. She wanted people to be happy and she made them happy."

Starting with this date in February 1880, Martin coded his journal with a red asterisk every time he spent the night with Woodhull. Once or twice a week the red asterisk decorated its pages. "Strange that under my acquaintance with Victoria my old enemy should have disappeared," he confided to his diary. "Her forbearance in this respect created a debt of gratitude from me that I could never forget, and forms perhaps the strongest link between us." Woodhull had helped Martin heal his sexual incapacity.

In the middle of March, Woodhull and Martin spent an entire weekend together. On Sunday they drove around Richmond Park and Kew Gardens, enjoying the first flowers of spring. Woodhull selected this time to let Martin know she expected a proposal of marriage from him. As Martin put it in his diary, "The great question came up and continued in a very maudlin, question of honor [way,] a wretched change . . .very much upset all day." The relationship continued with the question of marriage constantly between them. A period of anguished partings and impassioned reunions followed. Through the spring and summer of 1880, Martin attempted to cool his infatuation by going to Spain for six weeks. It didn't work and he went to see Woodhull immediately on his return. Then, once again, Martin attempted to break off the relationship. "A very sad parting with V." The next day "felt very seedy all day."

On August 26, 1880, he found Victoria alone and stayed with her. "Much said about establishment; wanted me to take her down to Overbury, very pointedly." Overbury Court was the Martin family's country estate, and Woodhull was pressing Martin to be properly introduced to his family. Three months later, Martin was ready to make the relationship permanent, willing to defy convention and take a leap into the unknown. He told his mother and his sister Julia about Woodhull. That evening Woodhull and Martin attended a pops concert, their first public appearance together. Woodhull pushed things along. On November 26, 1880, Martin "discovered" that Woodhull had bought a ring. Woodhull convinced him to make her put it on her finger.

On December 1, 1880, Martin wrote his mother to arrange for Woodhull to spend the weekend with her in the country. Preparing the way for this momentous event, he told his mother that his brother, Richard, after having had a long talk with Woodhull, had said simply, "I like her very much." Woodhull had said, he reported to his mother, that she was afraid "you would not like her except for my sake, and that she would not come between me and my own people; but I hope we shall get over that. I hope I shall find you all friends on Friday."

On December 2, Martin's sister, Julia, took Victoria to Overbury

Court to meet her parents. Even Woodhull's queenly ambitions were intimidated by the grandeur. The house was built in 1738 and had been modified over the years to satisfy the Martins' taste for refined country life. The building was in the Georgian style with two nineteenth-century wings. The surrounding gardens included the latest in landscaping art—waterfalls, an ornamental lake, a large rockery and a lily pond—all laid out with aesthetic skill and care. A large conservatory occupied part of one wing of the house.

Martin's parents were, if anything, more imposing than their surroundings. His father was the fourth generation in the family bank. His mother, Mary Ann Biddulph Martin, was the daughter of another banking family, that of Cocks, Biddulph and Company. Woodhull was keyed up to the breaking point. On Friday, when John arrived at Overbury Court, he found "all well, but V. very excited and nervous with strain." But he felt they were "all getting on well together."

Despite her nervousness, Woodhull was a success with Martin's family, and during the course of the weekend at Overbury she and Martin made marriage plans, deciding "to try to arrange a wedding before Christmas."

Then Woodhull's past caught up with her—both the false and the true—in the hands of Richard Martin. In early December, he did some checking on Woodhull's life in America, and had asked his brother-in-law, Douglas Henty, to make additional inquiries. When Martin arrived at Lombard Street after the weekend at Overbury Court, he found his brother Richard "with an appalling story of V's antecedents." Once again Treat's pamphlet had surfaced. Richard assured his brother that his beloved was "well known as a gay lady on the other side." "A wretched day," Martin confided to his diary, "very miserable."

Woodhull asked Francis Cook to talk to Martin on her behalf, and Martin agreed to see him, but their meeting was inconclusive. Martin wrote to his mother that he would do as she wished and break off with Woodhull. A series of sad evenings together followed. "A most tearful parting. She was quite beside herself. Left the house in a frantic state," he noted December 23. "The year closes in chaos."

Woodhull did not creep away quietly. Her pen became the instrument of her defense. Still affecting the altered spelling of her name, she issued *Woodhall and Claflin's Journal*, "a Journal Devoted to the Advocacy of Great Social Questions and for the Higher Instruction and Improvement of Women." Under "Notices to Correspondents," buried on page four, she explained that "Mrs. Woodhall, for special reasons, has altered the last vowel in her name, so as to render it uniform with that adopted by the old Woodhall family in the West of England."

From the tone of this sheet, we can get the flavor of her defense to Martin and his family. The clumsiness of her effort is still obvious. Torn between present desires and past life, she dissembled. Having lived quietly for almost five years, she had, perhaps, convinced herself that she was respectable. In any case, she wanted John Martin and all he represented so much that she was willing to toss aside her life's work. Presenting herself as having been a public figure who had lectured on women's rights, and who had been deceived by the men publishing her paper while she was away—men who promoted free love and other radical social ideas—she said, "I could not always read and select the contributions . . . My lecturing engagements in distant parts of the States, sometimes extending over 100 nights, prevented such rigid supervision."

She disavowed free love and named her enemy: "Stephen Pearl Andrews—the originator of the most immeasurable infamy . . . I impeach thee before the judgment bar." She added, "Thank Heaven his teachings had no effect on our mind. The pure stream of our life was never sullied by it." She named Colonel Blood her second enemy and blamed him for allowing the publication of the Treat pamphlet. She accused Blood of adultery and printed a copy of her divorce decree.

She declared that she had never believed in free love: "I now openly avow, with all the earnestness of righteous indignation, that during no part of my life did I favor free love even tacitly." Significantly, she chose to reprint one small portion of the Beecher article, the part that described his amative nature as a fine thing, "one of God's best gifts to the world," the description that had fit her as neatly as it had fit Beecher. Now she called it "filthy," "prurient," "obscene," and denied having written any part of it. The minority of free lovers who still held to their radical views maintained them with religious intensity, and to them, Woodhull's change of heart was a shocking apostasy. She was behaving just as Henry Ward Beecher had behaved, and her dissembling was just as obvious.

To force Martin's hand, Woodhull talked about returning to America, and she asked him for money to carry on her work. In February 1881, he gave her £5,000. In March Martin told Woodhull he was going abroad again, so she adopted desperate measures. She asked Francis Cook to act on her behalf again. Cook met with Douglas Henty, Martin's brother-in-law, and told him that unless Martin agreed to "fix a day" to marry Woodhull, she might "claim damages." Woodhull had, Cook said, "confidence in [Martin's] pledge and word to her as a gentleman that he will carry out his engagement."

To Henty's feelers about some kind of financial settlement, Cook responded that Woodhull "does not want J. Martin's money . . . [she] wants him as a husband." Cook said he considered it "one of the noblest acts of his life" to uphold Woodhull, a phrase that sounds as though it came directly from Woodhull's lips. Cook confessed to Henty, however, that his own wife did not know Woodhull, "but will be introduced as soon as she becomes Mrs. John Martin." No one in the Martin family was aware of Cook's relationship with Tennie.

Henty wanted to go to court to accuse Cook and Woodhull of a conspiracy to attempt to obtain money under false pretenses. But, he concluded, "we have a poor case and JBM will only appear as the dupe of a clever harlot." The language of the Treat pamphlet still dogged Woodhull.

After Martin returned from his trip abroad, he continued to see Woodhull. He often commented on her fondness and affection. Despite her opportunistic pursuit of him, Woodhull's relationship with Martin had developed into love.

The year 1882 and early 1883 produced no resolution of the marriage question. Woodhull returned to the original spelling of her name, but her new persona was complete. She had recreated herself as the dutiful "wife" who wrote her "husband," as she liked to call Martin, "God bless my precious husband for sustaining me and aiding me with his wise counsel that I may not stumble."

By the fall of 1883 Martin, growing "more and more attached to Victoria," was unwilling "to conceal any longer." He resolved to "make her happy."

33
17 Hyde Park Gate

On October 31, 1883, a dull, foggy day, Victoria Woodhull married John Martin at 9:30 A.M. in a Presbyterian chapel. Annie, Tennie, Zula, and her cousin Carrie attended the ceremony. After the ceremony, Woodhull walked home with Zula and Carrie while Martin went off to his usual day in Lombard Street. Preoccupied and concerned, he wrote to reassure Woodhull that the ceremony hadn't been needed to legitimize his love for her. "My darling wife. You are not a bit nearer to my heart than you were yesterday. Today is nothing to us. Let us forget it and the past. Be happy in the future. Keep yourself quiet in our sacred love until I come this evening."

It was the first of many such notes that would pass between them, written in the oversweet tone of the time, but expressing real and deep affection. A period of quiet happiness and domestic contentment followed, interrupted only by small household crises. John Martin's complaint to his diary was that he didn't get enough time alone with Victoria.

No one from Martin's family had attended the wedding. He had written to his mother with some qualms, asking her blessing. "I have a letter from you written long ago in which you felt that you should not be happy until you had seen all your children happy. You know how much unhappiness I have had . . . my life at times [has been] almost unbearable. I was looking forward to some happiness in this fashion . . . will you help me attain it?" While Martin waited anxiously for a response, he told his brother, Richard, of his marriage. Richard told Martin flatly that he would refuse to receive Woodhull. Martin began giving serious consideration to leaving the bank at the end of the year. He also drew up a new will, which, with some changes over the years, left his entire estate unconditionally to Woodhull.

When he told his sister, Julia, she responded that she would receive Woodhull privately but "could not insult my friends by introducing her." She wrote spitefully: [John] "is so weak and she is so clever I always feared she would eventually get hold of him." Henty, her husband, wrote to Richard that they would treat Martin and Woodhull like a man and his mistress, "cut her when I like and be civil when I like . . . she was a harlot, cunning and deceitful." The family still saw Woodhull as the woman the Treat pamphlet had portrayed and gave no consideration to John's happiness.

Except for Martin's mother, to her credit. Mary Ann Martin had presided over her family with confidence; she had brought money and the strength of her personality into her marriage. Her son, deeply attached to her, had hesitated to legitimize his relationship with Victoria primarily out of respect for her wishes. But a week after the marriage, a particularly "kind letter" from Mary Ann Martin arrived followed by one from John's father. They would receive Woodhull as their daughter-in-law. Martin's mother instructed her children to do likewise, and in November John Martin and Woodhull visited Overbury. "V. seemed quite at ease and happy," Martin observed. And the next day, "V. happy and in good spirits."

In February 1884, Woodhull and Martin found a house at 17 Hyde Park Gate that dated back to the time when the suburb had been a village neighboring Kensington Palace. Built of red bricks, behind high brick walls that were covered with ivy, climbing roses, and Virginia creeper, it had half a dozen gables which rose against the sky. Inside, large rooms were joined together by winding stairs and odd nooks and corners. Rejecting the dark, heavy decor of the period, the Martins made everything light, bright, and graceful. Woodhull designed the entrance hall with a domed ceiling in sky blue. In the morning room, a bay window looked out on green lawns and Woodhull's rose garden. They both took pleasure in furnishing what they called their "dear nest."

It was a good summer. "My heart becomes lighter and happier when I turn towards you and home," Martin wrote Woodhull. His diary recorded their days. "Took Victoria to concert, some good singing." "Fidelio, very good." "Public concert with Victoria, very good." "Pop concerts." "Walked in zoo gardens and saw the white elephant." "Went with V. to Electric and Invention Exhibit to look at electric lights and telephone." "Took V. to Savoy theater." "To Haymarket to see 'Peril.'"

At the end of the year Martin reported "the happiest year of very many that had passed . . . my love and esteem for Victoria grew every day." Their happiness was, ironically, a triumph for Victoria's doctrine of free love, for it was her unconventional past that brought them together, and the theraputic powers of sex she'd advocated that had helped heal her husband. Woodhull finally had a "monogamic" union, the kind of relationship she had admired from the speaker's rostrum as the "very highest sexual union" but had been unable to achieve. She couldn't transform the United States of America, but she did succeed in transforming herself and her husband. She had found her "mastermate," and together they lived out the love she had always wanted.

Shortly after their marriage, Martin came home one Friday evening to find Francis Cook visiting. Woodhull was trying to arrange a rapproachment between her husband and the man who had acted as her go-between with Martin's family. The Sunday after Cook's call, the Martins visited Doughty House, to Woodhull's great satisfaction, and Cook showed them his pictures. "A very fine collection," acknowledged Martin, who regularly visited the London picture galleries and considered himself something of a connoisseur.

Mrs. Cook died August 12, 1884. On September 7, Cook told Martin that he and Tennie were planning to be married, and there followed a flurry of getting papers in order. Tennie's early marriage to John Bortel had to be dealt with. She insisted that she had obtained a divorce through a lawyer in Chicago, and that she had "never seen or heard from Bortel since." To be sure there would be no legal problems, Cook married his "sass wife" twice, once as a spinster and again some time later as a divorced woman.

About the same time, Cook became engaged in the philanthropic work he would be most remembered for, the building of a student hostel, Alexandra House in South Kensington, as a tribute to the Princess of Wales. A concert hall in the building was under construction and students would soon be in residence. The building was constructed on a grand scale at a cost of £80,000 ($5 million in today's dollars). Cook's philanthropy was recognized when he was made a baronet on March 10, 1886. Tennie thereafter enjoyed the pleasure of being known as Lady Cook.

Still, petty aggravations marred these happy days. Woodhull's Claflin siblings showed up in London hoping to cash in on their sisters' financial comfort. A parade of letters from people of former days—some total strangers, many asking for money—arrived with each morning's mail. Blackmail and extortion threats appeared. A policeman named Byrnes, a woman named Schoenberg, a lawyer named MacKinley were particularly irksome.

Fictitious stories of famous snubs made the rounds of American papers. The wife of a General Taylor had objected to Woodhull by leading the boycott of a banquet at the London Athletic Club, wrote the *Chicago Times.* "The whole story was a fabrication," Martin told his lawyer. "There was no General Taylor [nor] any banquet." As president of the club, Martin awarded the athletic prizes each year, and Woodhull had also done the honors. Martin dug to the bottom of each threat against Woodhull. His anger "grew strong," and he appointed Channing Ellery, the son of Woodhull's New York friend, George Ellery, to act as his agent against those who had done her wrong.

The American novelist Henry James, now living in England, created consternation at 17 Hyde Park Gate when his novel, *The Siege of London* appeared. It was the story of Nancy Headway, a divorced American who wanted to marry into London society. James's slight novel treated the American adventuress gently and censured London society as "bad manners organized." But more than one source pointed out the character's resemblance to Woodhull, among them the *New York World.* On November 17 Martin and Woodhull called on James and obtained a letter from the author that stated he had had no intention of "representing or suggesting Mrs. Victoria Woodhull" in his novel. Despite this denial, a reader will find Nancy Headway to be a deft composite of Woodhull and Tennie, and her intended, Sir Arthur Demesne, to bear more than a passing likeness to Martin and Cook.

James was in the process of completing a much more substantial novel with another character that would remind many people of Woodhull. *The Bostonians* was a serious study of the "situation of women," as James put it. It dealt with suffragists, free lovers, and journalists, and featured Verena Tarrant as a lecturer whose "charm" enabled her to say almost anything and enchant her audience. She extemporized so successfully that those who had come to jeer went away converted. To many who read James's book, Victoria Woodhull was a flesh and blood Verena Tarrant. Woodhull made no comment on *The Bostonians,* but in her autobiographical notes she described James as "one of your greatest intellectual snobs."

On November 18, 1885, Buck Claflin, the sisters' father, died quietly at 17 Hyde Park Gate. Putting aside her early distrust of him,

Woodhull said, "God has taken from our home circle the most noble of fathers, the wisest of counsellors, the holiest of men . . . my dear father has become a thousand times dearer to us all." The flamboyant Buck Claflin wouldn't have recognized himself in these words, but Woodhull undoubtedly found some comfort in remembering him as she wished he had been. Annie Claflin died at Doughty House on June 11, 1889, and was buried beside her husband at Highgate Cemetery. Whatever mixed emotions Woodhull and Claflin had felt for their parents, they had cared for them compassionately to the end.

The maturing relationship between Woodhull and Martin was affectionate and tolerant. Woodhull frequently found herself "too ill" to go with Martin to Overbury. Martin wrote, sometimes with gentle barbs, "Father and mother are really sorry that you are not here with us. They know I only half enjoy being here without you." She responded, "I would be so nervous that I would annoy my darling if I went down to Overbury." Martin controlled and Woodhull manipulated, and they maintained a balance which satisfied them both. "Johnny," signed his letters "your boy" or "your loving boy." Woodhull closed hers with "mizpah," considered in nineteenth-century England to be a pledge between lovers, meaning "May the Lord watch between me and thee."

The physical component of their marriage remained strong. Woodhull wrote once when they were separated, "I need your precious arms around me this moment," and again, "feel dear wife's arms and kisses over you." They shared a bedroom throughout their marriage, and Woodhull complained during another absence, "I caught a severe cold sleeping alone."

Evenings and weekends meant lawn tennis, visits to Kew, exhibits of Turner watercolors, Oxford and Cambridge boat races, London Athletic Club events, dinner parties at home—for which Martin carefully decided the seating arrangements in little diagrams he recorded in his diary. On quiet evenings he would talk about the banking business and try out his speeches on Woodhull. They experimented with a new typewriter.

Each year included trips abroad—the United States, Switzerland, Gilbraltar, Malta, Italy, Greece, and Canada. They collected treasures for their "nest," shipping home marble busts, watercolors, and furniture. In March of 1889, the house was wired for electricity, and the following summer the garden was illuminated. Woodhull and Martin began a series of annual Fourth of July "Interdependence Day" parties, to which swarms of guests were invited. At the first of these events, Martin draped the flags of England and the United States together as the centerpiece of their decorations, and this placement of flags became an important tradition.

In April 1887, Martin and Woodhull helped celebrate his parents' golden wedding anniversary at Overbury Court. The entire family was photographed under a triumphal arch, and there was a reception in the front hall. Woodhull had gained her mother-in-law's affections to the extent that when the older woman died, she received part of her collection of family jewels.

Faces from the past emerged. In 1887, around Easter, Woodhull met Frederick Douglass, her erstwhile running mate, in Rome. Douglass recorded in his journal that at his hotel one day "a great surprise came to me . . . a lady of very fine appearance who introduced herself as Mrs. John Biddulph Martin of 17 Hyde Park Gate S. W. She frankly—and I thought somewhat proudly—told me she was formerly Mrs. Victoria Woodhull. I am not sure that I quite concealed my surprise." Douglass remembered Woodhull and the controversy that had surrounded her name, but had forgotten that he had been selected to be her Equal Rights Party running mate 15 years earlier. Woodhull won Douglass over, and he recorded his second thoughts: "I do not know that she is not in her life as pure as she seems to be. I treated her politely and respectfully—and she departed apparently not displeased with her call."

On January 5, 1888, Martin found Woodhull "much excited by a visit from Mrs. [Elizabeth Cady] Stanton." Stanton had replied to overtures from Woodhull in late 1886, thanking Woodhull for some papers she had sent along with a copy of a speech on statistics by John Martin. She had written that she was "pleased to hear from your sister that your domestic trials have ended so happily and that you are now in a safe harbor at last. Accept my congratulations with sincere wishes for your happiness. As ever your friend." When Stanton later spent a few days at the Hotel Metropole in London, she arranged to see Woodhull—a visit that gave Woodhull considerable satisfaction.

In 1888 Isabella Beecher Hooker wrote Woodhull that she was coming to England and would like to "renew an old friendship." Hooker, alone among the suffragists, had continued to see Woodhull in New York, though she had done so privately because of the objections of her Beecher siblings and her husband. Henry Ward Beecher had died the previous year, releasing Hooker from the old family pressures.

Hooker settled in at 17 Hyde Park Gate, dining and sleeping there, writing to her husband that this would be her address in London. She visited Doughty House and took "deep delight" in the picture gallery. She saw Alexandra House and read about Monserrate, the Cook estate in Portugal. Hooker, Woodhull, and Martin discussed Henry Ward Beecher during Hooker's visit. Martin found these conversations reassuring. Hooker confirmed to him that Woodhull's exposure of Beecher had been justified, contrary to the views expressed in current idolatrous biographies of Beecher.

Despite the victories Woodhull felt in the visits of the suffragists, and the happiness and security she enjoyed with Martin, she was becoming nervous and anxious again. In 1888 she was 50 years old, and experiencing a difficult menopause. Her benign uterine tumors were finally diagnosed, and surgery was considered. Woodhull was able to avoid the surgery, but she returned to normal health with a certain restlessness. A doctor she consulted told Martin that Woodhull should be kept "employed and occupied." With the support of such an authority figure to help her persuade Martin, she began making arrangements to resume her "calling." Woodhull wrote, "God helping me, I will not rest until I am known for what I am, not what others have made me out to be."

34

The Grasshopper and the Humanitarian

In 1890 John Martin was working on a history of the bank; it was published two years later as *The Grasshopper in Lombard Street,* and it became a reference work on financial history. Woodhull also began work on a book in 1890, and later that year she published *The Human Body, The Temple of God.* A vanity publication, its primary value today is the self-portrait of a misunderstood reformer that Woodhull offered for posterity. It is also a useful repository of some of her earlier works on suffrage and of her press clippings from the United States. Tennie is listed as coauthor, and pictures of both women in their middle years, still as attractive as ever, open the volume.

A new note appeared in the subtitle: *The Philosophy of Sociology.* Woodhull had presented her last speeches on sex education from a new perspective, that of a would-be sociologist looking for the "proper understanding of the growth and development of man" in relation to social, religious, and political institutions.

In July 1892, *The Humanitarian, a Monthly Magazine of Sociology,* followed. The science of sociology was in its infancy, and the journal was a companion innovation to her book. However much Woodhull had disparaged Stephen Pearl Andrews, she now put his tutelage to good use. Her new "calling" was to disseminate information on "applied scientific knowledge . . . exalting and purifying the entire human race." In the scientifically planned world Woodhull envisioned, governments would provide tribunals of health, and bureaus of anthropology would serve every police station. Laboratories would analyze impure foods and liquors; physicians would examine children in schools; the poor would be provided with improved dwellings. The "aristocracy of blood," her euphemism for family planning and birth control, would prevail. In her idea that social science could solve social problems, Woodhull anticipated the liberal agenda of the twentieth century.

With this platform, Woodhull now decided to run for president of the United States again. Her reawakened ambitions had been stimulated by a visit with Belva Lockwood in 1890. Her old friend had become a lawyer, and then a candidate for president in 1884, nominated by the National Equal Rights Party. She had received votes in six states and had run again in 1888. Susan B. Anthony had opposed Lockwood, but the public had found her candidacy interesting.

To inaugurate her own campaign, Woodhull launched the *Humanitarian* in the United States. She and Martin spent April through June, 1892 in New York City, where she sent out a call to the old Victoria Leagues, to Lockwood's supporters, and to all "friends of Equal Rights." Then, on September 22, she met with 28 delegates of the National Equal Rights Committee in a parlor of the Willard Hotel in Washington, D.C. Once more, Woodhull was nominated for president of the United States. J. Lindon Knight of Kansas put her name before the committee with the words, "In Victoria Woodhull Martin we recognize our standardbearer for the campaign of 1892 . . . [She] has done more than any other individual for the cause of women." Mary L. Stowe of California was nominated for vice president. The delegates also issued a resolution, that "by the united efforts of the women voters of this nation we will drive anarchy, crime, insanity and drunkenness from our midst."

Woodhull met the press in New York, in the house that the Martins had taken at 142 West 70th Street. She called her campaign "educational" and predicted that "before many years there will be a woman president."

Susan B. Anthony and the suffragists spurned Woodhull again. But Frances Willard, the temperance leader, expressed a more tolerant view, saying to the *New York World* that she had "nothing to say against Victoria Woodhull. If she wants to be president of the United States that is her business, but it is a mistake to say that she is a candidate of that numerous body of women saints like Susan B. Anthony, who devoted their lives to woman suffrage. Victoria Woodhull has stood more pelting than she deserved. I was right glad when she married an English gentleman and had someone to defend and care for her."

On election day, when Grover Cleveland was returned to office, Woodhull invited the press to tea in her library. She told a reporter: "To be perfectly frank, I hardly expected to be elected. The truth is I am too many years ahead of this age, and the exalted views and objects of humanitarianism can scarcely be grasped as yet by the unenlightened mind of the average man."

Woodhull began making plans to lecture in England. A woman who had declared herself a candidate for president of the United States, no matter how feeble her campaign, could command attention and lecture fees. She announced a tour of England, Scotland, and Wales on the topic of "Humanitarian Government." She spoke first at St. James Hall in London on March 24, 1893, but the response wasn't strong enough to encourage Woodhull to continue; she cancelled her tour.

The couple returned to the United States in 1893, where Martin served as one of the British commissioners to the Chicago World's Fair. In the autumn of 1894, Woodhull lectured one last time at Carnegie Hall. She wore a violet dress, with violets at her throat (the flowers that John Martin frequently gave her, enclosing them with his letters from Overbury, had replaced the rose as her sentimental favorite). She wore spectacles to read her manuscript. In her speech, Woodhull proposed to "waken mothers to the crime of propagating children to live upon their betters and become a curse to the race." The speech was not a success, however, and Woodhull recognized that she had lost her platform touch. She cancelled an American lecture tour, "in compliance with the wishes of my husband."

Back in London again, Woodhull put her last efforts for public recognition into the *Humanitarian,* its credibility having been enhanced, she hoped, by her presidential candidacy and her lectures. She created her own small zone of power in the journal. Her list of authors was soon decorated with sirs, honorables, archdeacons, and an occasional lord or lady. The young Arnold Bennett appeared. She reprinted an address by her neighbor Sir Leslie Stephen.

The journal's New York office was managed by Zula Maud, who also wrote articles from time to time. Contributions on health and medicine came from Dr. Charles Stuart Welles, a medical doctor married to Woodhull's niece Ellie Celeste. But Woodhull retained control of the publication in London, where she recreated something of her early, happy days with the *Weekly.* Martin participated reluctantly at first, but he eventually developed a commitment equal to Woodhull's, marking his "corrections in ink . . . comments in pencil" and warning her while she was in America, "Don't give up your grip on the *Humanitarian*. If it ceased . . . to be . . . in our control there would be an end of it." He cautioned her to be wary of contributors who "only came to see you for what advantage they think they will get . . . for themselves."

Woodhull wrote more than 100 articles over the years. The journal was her university. She had a writer's instinct for educating herself on a subject by writing an article, researching it, and consulting experts. Her writing style improved with practice. "Air and Exercise," "Profit vs. Equity," "Remedies for Drunkenness," marriage, athletics, horticulture, psychology, farming, and poetry were early subjects. Spiritualism and the occult received little space. She turned later to Anglo-American relations and the equitable distribution of wealth.

She began to study eugenics and the processes of heredity. She amended her earlier misconceptions, but she continued to believe that children who were wanted, planned for, and loved would be healthier children. Taking up new, provocative stances, she promoted birth control and wrote "The Rapid Multiplication of the Unfit." After the Nazis and the Holocaust, no one can read such titles today without flinching, but this was 40 years before the Third Reich, when eugenics was still considered a respectable scientific field.

For all its substance, the journal, like Woodhull's book, was intended primarily to project the image of Mrs. John Biddulph Martin as a leader among nineteenth-century women. Flattering biographical sketches appeared. Copies were mailed to libraries all over the world. Woodhull had each year's issues carefully bound in leather to be preserved for the future.

Tennie was developing her own humanitarian side, as well, presiding over Cook's painting collection and personally escorting visitors through the gallery. The world-famous critic Bernard Berenson was one of her guests. But Tennie's marriage was not serene. "Great row" at Doughty House, Martin noted in his diary in 1893. "Ladies excited and wanting to take rash action."

The "row" had stemmed from a suit brought against Cook by a former housekeeper, on charges of seduction and breach of promise. Mrs. Maidy Holland testified in court that she had lived at Doughty House and that Sir Francis had promised to marry her after the first

Mrs. Cook died. A sister of Lady Cook, Mrs. Victoria Woodhull Martin, had talked her out of her letters from Sir Francis for the sum of 30 pounds. Cook took the stand and confessed to the liaison but said he had never promised to marry the lady. The jury found in favor of Mrs. Holland, and Cook was required to pay nominal damages. It was understood that Cook made an additional private settlement with Mrs. Holland as well.

The relationship between Doughty House and 17 Hyde Park Gate cooled. Martin had no tolerance for "libertine" behavior. Woodhull wrote to Tennie that Sir Francis had "openly" insulted Tennie and she had "bow[ed] her head and murmur[ed] not." A rift developed between the sisters that continued, to some extent, for the rest of their lives.

In the same year, 1893, Woodhull's niece Carrie married in New York City. Woodhull disapproved of the marriage and became concerned that Zula Maud, who had been enjoying her freedom in New York, might follow Carrie's example. Unable to persuade Zula to return to London, she asked her niece and nephew, Ellie Celeste and Charles Stuart Welles, to keep an eye on her daughter. In January of 1895, they wrote Woodhull saying that Zula, now 33 years old, wanted to marry a man named McCormick, and suggested that McCormick was after her money. Zula retaliated, evicting the Welleses from the house for which she held the lease, and firing Welles from the *Humanitarian*. The Welleses went to court. Woodhull left immediately for New York, cancelled the lease on the house, and returned home, forfeiting bail to avoid appearing in the Welles case. Zula accompanied her mother back to London, without McCormick. Woodhull extracted a promise from her daughter that she would never marry.

It was a harsh demand, and Woodhull's motives were mixed. Her mentally impaired son Byron was a consideration. Since the deaths of Woodhull's parents, Zula had helped to care for Byron. He had spent some time in New York with her under Dr. Welles's supervision. Further, Woodhull genuinely feared that if Zula were to marry, she might bear a child with Byron's deficiencies. Woodhull had written in the *Humanitarian* that the mentally unfit should remain childless. Now she became neurotically possessive of her daughter. Her letters to Zula were emotional and manipulative. "As long as I live, my child, I shall grieve every moment that I am not near the best, the noblest and purist child God ever blest a mother with . . . Mamma['s] heart is weeping for the sound of your sweet voice . . . Oh, may God watch over you."

In the middle of this family strife, Woodhull faced new legal problems of her own. A researcher at the British Museum library discovered a pamphlet hostile to Woodhull, and she suspected that the pamphlet was Treat's. The Martins instituted legal action against the museum. The institution withdrew the pamphlet from circulation. Then another damaging pamphlet turned up, and the Martins proceeded with a libel suit for damages. It subsequently developed that neither pamphlet was Treat's; both were compilations of news articles—including some of Treat's material—that had been published about the Beecher-Tilton trial. Still, the case created a stir. No one had ever sued the British Museum for libel.

Sir Richard Webster, the Martins's counsel, told the court that Woodhull felt compelled to clear her spotless reputation. The two works that the Museum had in circulation had accused her of immorality, a charge that had grown out of the "strong view" she had taken of the "Beecher-Tilton imbroglio."

Sir Charles Russell, the counsel for the museum, had a reputation as the most adept cross-examiner in England. He called Woodhull to the stand. "Had she ever been guilty of immorality?" he asked.

"Gracious, no!" she replied. She had been constantly before the American public from 1870 to 1877, and "during all that time not one single charge had been made against her character."

"Demosthenes interests me," Sir Charles said, and asked if it were true that he was Woodhull's spiritual adviser.

"There is an apparition appearing before me now," she retorted, and the courtroom burst into laughter.

Sir Charles bowed low to acknowledge her point, but pursued his question. Had Demosthenes dictated her speeches or merely suggested the general context?

"I do not feel disposed to tell you," she responded tartly.

What about Woodhull's two divorces and her intimacies with Theodore Tilton?

Woodhull said she had barely known Tilton, if that were his name. Free love? "I never knew that love was anything but free."

Why had she written the article, a copy of which the defense wished to enter in evidence, that had brought on the Beecher-Tilton scandal?

Woodhull said she had not written it, that when it appeared she was thousands of miles away lecturing. "Why am I so persecuted?" she asked. The trial transcript reveals that Woodhull soared and swooped, flew off on tangents, and when all else failed, simply lied. She fashioned her own case, presenting herself as a defenseless woman hounded by male justice.

Her closing statment had the ring of the old Woodhull: "I am quite willing to state what I do believe quietly. Women are struggling for their freedom from sexual slavery. It may [seem] ridiculous, but all the same, the time will come when a woman will stand before the judge . . . cross questioning a man perhaps, and she will have just as good a right to do it . . . as the men now take it upon themselves to judge of women."

The judge, caught uncomfortably between two British institutions, Martin's Bank and the British Museum, instructed the jury in a way meant to satisfy both. The jury, following his lead, found that the museum trustees were guilty of allowing slanderous publications to be placed on their shelves, and that they could have taken more care, but also found that the trustees were "not guilty of negligence" in the legal sense of the word. Damages of 20 shillings were awarded to the Martins. They accepted the decision, feeling they had been vindicated, "that there was absolutely no foundation for the libels."

Woodhull returned, with relief, to the comfortable life of publishing the *Humanitarian,* entertaining at salons and dinner parties, and attending cultural events, museums, concerts, and the opera.

In the summer of 1895 the Martins took up bicycling. Woodhull introduced her husband to this new London rage. "V interested in learning to ride a bicycle," he noted in August. But he soon took it up with a passion. "Practicing on bicycle with V in the street." "Bicycle practice spoilt by storm." "Took V to Battersea Park and rode with her." "Rode all around park and back without a stop." By the following summer Martin was doing bicycle tours of 40 miles and more. Bicycling articles turned up in the *Humanitarian.*

In 1896, the Martins's most celebrated "Interdependence Day" party took place. "Strong breeze, fine night," Martin noted. "Hard at work for party . . . busy all afternoon with preparations, but got all ready in time. A large gathering of all sorts. Garden very effective. Everyone seemed [happy] and [party] went off well. Difficult to clear the house at the end, not over til 1:30. V very unwell all day with a bad cold."

Woodhull wore a pink and dove-gray silk dress trimmed with lace and wrapped herself warmly in a crimson and white shawl. Her garden was lighted by hundreds of electric lights. An orchestra played dance music, and Woodhull and Martin led their guests in a waltz. Woodhull felt better the next day, "pleased at success of our party," Martin noted. Nothing more serious than a head cold seemed to threaten their charmed life.

35

The Courage to Stand
in the Path of Man

During the fall of 1896, John Martin fell ill. For the first time, he was confined to his bed. He stayed there for three weeks. Chronic upper respiratory infections developed into pleurisy and pneumonia, and his usual cure for all ailments, bracing exercise, was out of the question. His doctor recommended that he get away from the London winter. In January 1897, somewhat improved, Martin booked passage to the Canary Islands on the *Lusitania*. Woodhull didn't feel up to making the trip with him. Worried about her, he confided his feelings to his diary: "Both of us unhappy at my going away alone." But on January 13, he reluctantly left London without her.

"Well darling, I am sitting in the dear old library at the desk where your presence lingers," Woodhull wrote him. "I am longing for your sweet kiss and loving embrace . . . If you wish me to come and return with you when this reaches you, wire me." Her letter crossed his, which said that he was sailing for the most remote islands and would be cut off from the world for ten days, but that he would be home before the end of the month. It was no longer worth her making the trip out to join him. "God bless my little wife . . . and keep her heart as full of love for her boy as his is for her."

Within a week, shocking news reached London: Martin was desperately ill. He had gone riding in the mountains, at an elevation of 8,600 feet, and had taken a fall into a watercourse. He had insisted on continuing on in wet clothing. Martin's nephew, Robert Holland, left for the Canaries to bring him home, but he arrived too late. John Martin had died of pneumonia, on Saturday, March 20, 1897.

His body was returned to England and cremated, in accordance with his wishes, after which his ashes were scattered at sea. Woodhull paid tribute to her husband with a long biographical memoir in the May, 1897 *Humanitarian*. She saluted his "unruffled and courteous" manner, his "innate nobility of character," his "intensely sensitive nature which shrank from publicity . . . to the end he remained chivalrous, long suffering and generous, a gentleman in the truest sense of the word."

At first Woodhull's life changed little, at least outwardly. She inherited £171,778 ($14 million in today's dollars). The *Humanitarian* continued with Zula Maud as associate editor. Gradually, Woodhull began a round of social activities and travel. The *London Court Journal* for July 4, 1898, reported that Woodhull and "her beautiful and distinguished daughter" had not given their usual Fourth of July reception because of her "fairly recent bereavement," but they had been seen "at many of the great social functions, including the Duchess of Westminster's reception to meet Lord Salisbury and the members of the United Club, and the garden party at Stafford House in connection with the Scottish Home Industries." She and Zula had been in the ladies' gallery of the House of Lords, and, the *Journal* reported, "She has been entertaining in a quiet way at her beautiful house in Hyde Park Gate, and many eminent professors and men of science from English and foreign universities have been among her guests and are contributing to her magazine, the *Humanitarian*."

Woodhull got in touch with Elizabeth Cady Stanton again, sending her copies of the *Humanitarian*. Yes, Stanton was interested in doing some writing for the magazine. Stanton liked Woodhull's articles on marriage and divorce, saying she was the only woman to discuss the subject intelligently in the past 30 years.

Woodhull bought an automobile, an electric Victoria, and was the first to drive a motorcar into Hyde Park. When neighbor Sir Leslie Stephen told her it was "unladylike to go out in an electric Victoria," she assured him, "It *will* be."

In 1901, four years after Martin's death, Woodhull decided to close down the *Humanitarian*. She had published it for nine years, three years longer than *Woodhull and Claflin's Weekly*, and she planned to retire to the "tranquil" environment of the country and write her autobiography.

As Woodhull was preparing for her move, Tennie's husband, Sir Francis Cook, died. Over the years Woodhull had made overtures to her sister, but had never succeeded in restoring their old intimacy. Now the men who had divided them, Cook and Martin, were both gone. Woodhull wrote, "My darling blessed sister, I so long to come and see you. How is it that our lives cannot be brought together now in our few remaining years of life?" Woodhull was 63, Tennie 58. De-

spite Woodhull's efforts, the sisters never regained their old cama-
raderie.

Tennie remained loyal to her niece and nephew, the Welleses, who
had named their daughter Utica Celestia after the long-dead Utica
and the very much alive Tennessee Celeste. The little girl grew up to
be a dark-haired, blue-eyed beauty. Dr. Welles obtained a job as first
secretary at the United States embassy in London, and the Welles
family moved to England. Tennie "adopted" her grandniece. She
arranged for Utica to be presented to Queen Victoria.

On July 27, 1903, Utica Celestia married 24-year-old Thomas
Beecham, the future conductor Sir Thomas Beecham, heir to the
Beecham pharmaceutical fortune. Three obscure American Claflins
had now married three of the richest men in England. The marriage
produced two sons, much strife, and ended in divorce. Utica said, "I
am the unhappiest woman in England. And the happiest. That is
what it means to have been married to Thomas Beecham."

Tennie traveled constantly, living in hotels and visiting relatives.
She was generous and jolly, fond of "just a little light wine." She and
Woodhull enjoyed occasional brief visits. Tennie died on January 18,
1923, without a will. Cook had left her well provided for, and her
fractious relatives fought over her fortune in court.

Woodhull settled into her new country "seat," Norton Park in
Worcestershire. She announced her arrival with seven pages and 11
photographs in the June 14, 1902, issue of *Country Life,* and a full-
page photograph of Zula Maud appeared on the cover. The house
was "true old English, with high pitched gables, mullioned windows,
quaint doorways, and panelled walls of dark old oak." Photographs
showed comfortable chairs with casually draped throws, tall potted
palms, and flowers everywhere. Woodhull chose to show her study
and the library, both with walls of bookshelves, reminding readers
that she and her daughter had entered into English "intellectual society," as she expressed it. They liked to call their new home "Brain-
rest," she confided. Outside the house were terraced gardens, grass
lawns, monumental trees, and hawthorns twisted with age. Paths
named for Tennyson, Longfellow, and Swinburne led to orchards of
apple, cherry, and pear.

Norton Park, or Bredon's Norton as it was often called, was located 109 miles from London on the lower part of Bredon Hill, looking westward over the Avon and Severn Rivers toward the Malvern

Hills. The 1,100 acres of land had been in John Martin's family for several generations. Pastoral tranquility prevailed. Various houses, cottages, and outbuildings made up the estate: An ancient manor house dating back to the sixteenth century, a Norman church recently restored, a tithe barn—named for the ancient custom of giving one tenth of the produce from the farmland to the church, with narrow slits for windows that indicated it had been defended by bow and arrow. Woodhull renamed two of the cottages, one Homer, the other Ohio. She painted the word "Kismet" on her front door in gold letters.

The history and romance of Bredon Hill attracted Woodhull; legend held that Queen Boudicca, the ruler and priestess who led an uprising against Roman rule in the year 60 A.D., had come to Bredon Hill to consult soothsayers and gather troops. In a moment of spiritualistic introspection, Woodhull confided in her autobiographical notes that "Queen Boudicca once had her camp on Bredon Hill. Now the queen of the soul's laboratory reigns at its base." Woodhull and Zula often bicycled on the hill.

Woodhull's social cachet in the countryside was enhanced after the prince of Wales, about to become Edward VII, visited Norton in January 1891. He was shooting in the area and, something of an automobile buff, paid a call to talk motor cars with Woodhull. The talk turned into an outing in Woodhull's automobile, and she afterward enjoyed telling friends that she had given King Edward VII his first motor car ride. Lunch followed the drive. Woodhull had draped Old Glory and the Union Jack in her dining room, and the prince complimented her on this "happy" symbol of Anglo-American friendship. The next day he sent a thank-you gift of grouse.

Bruised by a world that considered impeccable ancestors important, she took up the social game and played it with determination, creating her own set of forebears, whom she posted on an easel in the great hall. She claimed descent from the kings of Scotland and England on her father's side, through Thomas Hamilton, her great-grandfather, back to Alexander Hamilton, and further back to the dukes of Hamilton. In her research, Woodhull connected John Martin to George Washington through the Biddulph side of his family. She had found a great-grandmother of John Martin's named Penelope Dandridge and through her claimed kinship to Martha Dandridge, the wife of the first president. "Thus," she said, "after the lapse of a century the families of Washington and of his dearest friend, Alexander Hamilton, are again united!"

She had turned her finances over to Zula when they left London. On November 20, 1901, Woodhull conveyed the Norton estate to her daughter, a golden string that kept Zula at her side. Woodhull tried to make Zula's life happy without marriage, and wrote in her old age, "My daughter has stood by my side for years never thinking of self, watching over me with a devotion that knew not self." Zula left no record that she resented the control her mother maintained over her life.

Comfortably settled at Norton with Zula and Byron, Woodhull's mind once more sought stimulation. Her ego still demanded an audience. She turned the manor house into a salon and packed it with guests. Recreating the *Humanitarian* on a modest scale, she issued a newsletter called the *Manor House Causeries*.

In the past, Woodhull had made gifts as a way of gaining public attention. At Norton, she gave privately and freely, remembering the less fortunate when she had the means. Putting theories she had expounded in the *Humanitarian* into practice, she started a Women's Agricultural College that offered instruction in gardening, poultry keeping, and dairying. She started an annual agricultural show. She gave an organ to the Bredon's Norton Church. She converted her tithe barn into a village hall, with seats for lectures, plays, and concerts, and eventually a screen for magic lantern slides. Each year "Father Christmas" served Christmas dinner and gave out presents to 150 villagers. Local children received new boots. Zula Maud sponsored a kindergarten for the village children. She also provided funds for the villagers' medical and dental care.

The manor house became the headquarters for the Ladies' Automobile Club, the International Peace Society, and, in 1912, the Women's Aerial League of Great Britain. Woodhull had not lost her pioneering spirit; she announced she would give "5,000 dollars to the first man or woman to fly across the Atlantic."

Woodhull's best-known benefaction during these years was Sulgrave Manor in Northamptonshire. She gave £1,000 to help preserve the ancestral home of the family of George Washington. The project became a popular cause, and in 1919 the property was purchased and saved. Woodhull's association with Sulgrave Manor brought celebrity visitors to Norton, among them Prime Minister Arthur Balfour and Nicholas Murray Butler, the president of Columbia University.

When World War I came, Woodhull supported allied intervention and urged the U.S. Congress to act. She worked for the Allies by organizing Red Cross sewing sessions in the tithe barn and arranging for lectures, pageants, and milking contests. She donated hats for the Village Land Army. During the war, she flew the American flag over Norton Park, and her name became associated with Anglo-American friendship.

Over the years Woodhull maintained correct, if unenthusiastic, relations with Overbury Court, the Martin country seat nearby. But she had always been genuinely fond of Robert Holland, the son of Martin's sister Penelope. He had spent many weekends at 17 Hyde Park Gate during his Eton and Oxford days. A generous and engaging person, Robert had not censured his uncle's marriage to Woodhull. It was he who had brought John Martin's body back to England in 1897. He had taken his place at the bank that same year. In time, he and his wife, Eleanor Mary, and their six sons became the occupants of Overbury Court. Robert was the sole male descendant of his generation and in response to a request in his Uncle Richard's will, he adopted the name, Holland-Martin. As Robert became a leader in the City of London and the world of business, he still found time to bring his sons to Norton to call on "Aunt Victoria" and Zula. Robert later remembered Woodhull with a commemorative plaque in Tewkesbury Abbey.

As the years went by, Woodhull's autobiography remained unwritten. She scratched and blotted and wrote copious notes, but nothing pleased her. She had made one false start: "Sitting here today in this north room of 17 Hyde Park Gate—dreary, smoky, foggy . . ." and then dropped it.

As she reached back into her memories, the early experiences she had shared with her mother—dreams, trances, magical events—preoccupied her. She had yet to find the great revelation that would satisfy her quest, her search for "the truth of nature." Once again, she dropped her autobiography. She called on the talents of a parade of biographers, none of whom satisfied her. She finally assigned the task to Zula.

In old age, Woodhull enjoyed small eccentricities. She refused to shake hands. She said that "how are you," "good-bye" or "good morning" were meaningless expressions and a waste of time. She came down early one day while a young gardener named Jack Opperman was weeding the stone terrace. "Murderer! murderer!" she shouted, breaking the quiet of the morning, "Those weeds have the courage to grow in the path of man. Don't murder them."

Standing in the path of man had been Victoria Woodhull's lifework. She died in her ninetieth year on June 10, 1927. She had issued a last, enigmatic command: "There must be no screws used when I embark. My ashes by loving hands I wish thrown into the sea." As she requested, her ashes were scattered over the Atlantic Ocean, to rest eternally as "a link between my two countries."

EPILOGUE

"Women Must Own Themselves"

*I*n 1905, Victoria Woodhull had received a letter from Marilla M. Ricker, an attorney in Dover, New Hampshire. Ricker reminisced about the time she had traveled with Woodhull from Boston to Portsmouth for a lecture, and about the reception they had attended together afterwards. She made a simple, direct evaluation of Woodhull's impact, writing, "You gave women the idea that they must own themselves."

It had taken a Walt Whitman to understand Woodhull. She came out of the landscape he had peopled in *Leaves of Grass;* she had the same protean energies—a child of "nature" in the "swarming vortex of life"—that had been 1870s New York. She had given his "object lesson to the whole world," his "prophecy of the future."

The Nineteenth Amendment to the Constitution finally gave American women the vote in 1920. When Woodhull died in 1927, the nineteenth-century suffrage movement had been set aside as dusty history. Her obituaries recognized her as a promoter of Anglo-American friendship who had been, early in life, some kind of pioneer suffragist and social reformer. Her historical role, when it was considered, was drawn from the many bland and self-laudatory pamphlets she had published.

Woodhull had been written out of the suffrage movement during her lifetime. Elizabeth Cady Stanton, Susan B. Anthony, and Matilda Joslyn Gage published a three-volume work that became the historical record of the movement and volume two, which covered the 1870s, appeared in 1882. It was elitist history. The authors were intent on disassociating themselves from Woodhull's various scandals; they conveniently dismissed the role she had played during those years. Even though Woodhull had dominated four national conventions—January 1871, May 1871, January 1872 and May 1872—the suffrage historians reported her activities at those meetings only obliquely and in footnotes. The volume did print her Memorial, and accorded her passing credit for her work toward a declaratory act. But a reader would have no idea that Woodhull had been the first woman to address a congressional committee, in January 1871, that she had made a "Great Secession" speech in "the Woodhull" convention of May 1871, or that she had been nominated for president at the Washington suffrage convention of January 1872, prior to her Equal Rights Party convention in May 1872.

The 1920s brought jazz to biography, and the lives of many nineteenth-century figures received discordant reappraisals, among them Henry Ward Beecher, Anthony Comstock, and Cornelius Vanderbilt. When a novelist named Emanie Sachs had lunch with her friend, Katharine Angell, an editor at a new magazine called the *New Yorker,* Angell told Sachs about the Claflins. Sachs thought a biography would be a refreshing change of pace, and in researching Tennessee Claflin she came upon her sister Victoria. In 1928, *The Terrible Siren* appeared.

Sachs's work took its cue from suffrage history. It was another elitist putdown that failed to report Woodhull's role in the suffrage movement. Sachs presented Woodhull's ambition as a fatal character flaw, her sexuality as déclassé. She rightfully skewered Woodhull's image building and falsifications, providing a healthy counterpoint to Woodhull's own white washing of herself. Then, because of these flaws, Sachs discarded Woodhull's life as worthless.

The Terrible Siren intruded into Zula's mourning for her mother. Now 66, Zula wrote a friend that she felt unable to carry out the biographical task her mother had left. But she spent her remaining 13 years preoccupied with it, while caring for her brother, Byron, her "constant companion" until his death at 77 on January 17, 1932.

Unable to write her mother's life story, but wanting to carry out her wishes, Zula set aside £5,000 in her will for an authorized biography. When she died, aged 80, in September 1940, she left an estate of £337,976. ($16 million in today's dollars). Generous bequests also went to members of her mother's family, and the Norton land was returned to the Martin family. She gave the residuary to the Royal Institution of Great Britain to set up a Victoria Woodhull endowment for the study of eugenics, a subject that had shaped the course of her life.

C. K. Ogden of the Orthological Institute, a research institution in London, was invited by Zula's trustees to investigate a life of Woodhull. In 1951, he summarized his conclusions:

The general picture presented by Mrs. Emanie Sachs in *The Terrible Siren* is now accepted by historians . . . If no further account of Mrs. Woodhull-Martin's pioneer activities is made available *The Terrible Siren* will hold the field . . . In my opinion the emphasis could now be shifted to aspects of Mrs. Woodhull-Martin's record as a pioneer reformer which will otherwise be neglected. Her associates were remarkable people, about whom little is known in America and nothing in England. The orthodox feminist historians failed to do her justice in their anxiety not to be associated with campaigns against abuses which are now freely admitted.

The trustees decided against a biography, apparently believing a subsidized work would simply revive interest in Sachs's interpretation of Woodhull's life.

As the twenty-first century approaches, the elitist deprecations of Woodhull appear petty and puny. How did she dare, we want to know. What did she accomplish?

Woodhull's true family tree was rooted in primitive America, a land of mad visions, sharp trading, and titanic energies. Hers was a robber baron's spirit. She saw no reason why she should not play by the same free-for-all rules as men. Her strengths lay in her will power, her sheer energy, her quick reflexes. She looked with a sharp eye for male weaknesses and used men rather than being used by them. Cowardice and hypocrisy disgusted her. So did cant in talking about sex. She had a primal desire to be first and a storyteller's capacity for guile.

She cared about the lot of women. In her self-appointed role as a "representative woman," she reenergized a flagging suffrage movement. Certainly, she uttered empty rhetoric and played to the crowd, but she also gave impassioned speeches on important social issues. She went after what she wanted with single-mindedness of purpose and defied anything that got in her way. For better and for worse, Woodhull owned herself. She *was* a prophecy of the future, her life a song of herself.

Bibliography

PRIVATE PAPERS

Holland-Martin Family Archives, London. Victoria Woodhull's autobiographical notes and Zula's records for her proposed biography of her mother (handwritten notes, typeset pages, letters, family and business records, photographs, a painting, cartoons, *Humanitarian* correspondence and articles) were scattered after the trustees' decision not to publish an authorized biography. The bulk remained with the Holland-Martin family. The members of the family have generously made their archives available for this work, and their collection is a major source. Some of this autobiographical collection has found its way to Southern Illinois University at Carbondale, and some to the Boston Public Library (consisting primarily of the correspondence between Woodhull and John Biddulph Martin after their marriage). In the notes, I have designated these sources as A Papers-HM, A Papers-SIU, and A Papers-BPL.

John Miles Thompson, Jr., Papers, Plymouth, Minn. Mr. Thomspon, the grandson of Woodhull's niece Carrie Zula Miles Thompson, has kindly made his family recollections and papers available for this work.

Anthony Comstock Papers, YMCA Archives, New York.

James Lowe and Sal Alberti, autograph collection, New York.

Howard S. Mott, Inc., Rare Books and Autographs, Sheffield, Mass.

Library Collections

Colonel James H. Blood Correspondence, New-York Historical Society, New York.

Cook Collection, Richmond Local History Collection, London.

Paulina Wright Davis Papers, Alma Lutz Collection, Vassar College Library, Poughkeepsie, N.Y.

William Lloyd Garrison Correspondence, Boston Public Library Manuscript Collection, Boston.

Rutherford B. Hayes Presidential Center, Fremont, Ohio.

Isabella Beecher Hooker Collection, Stowe-Day Library, Hartford.

Isabella Beecher Hooker Correspondence, Ashton Willard Papers, Vermont Historical Society, Montpelier, Vt.

The Huntington Library, San Marino, Calif.

National American Woman Suffrage Association Collection, Library of Congress, Washington, D.C.

Whitelaw Reid Collection, Library of Congress, Washington, D.C.

Schlesinger Library, Radcliffe College, Cambridge, Mass.

Sophia Smith Collection, Women's History Archive, Smith College, Northampton, Mass.

Elizabeth Cady Stanton and Susan B. Anthony Papers, University of Massachusetts, Amherst, Mass.

Elizabeth Cady Stanton Correspondence, New York Public Library Manuscript Collection, New York.

Theodore Tilton Correspondence, New York Public Library Manuscript Collection, New York.

Tucker-Sachs Correspondence, New York Public Library Manuscript Collection, New York.

Victoria Claflin Woodhull Correspondence, Butler Library, Columbia University, New York.

Victoria Claflin Woodhull Correspondence, Manuscript Collection, Historical Society of Pennsylvania, Philadelphia.

Victoria Claflin Woodhull Correspondence, Alma Lutz Collection, Vassar College Library, Poughkeepsie, N.Y.

Victoria Claflin (Martin) Woodhull Correspondence, New-York Historical Society, New York.

Victoria Claflin (Martin) Woodhull Papers, Boston Public Library Manuscript Collection, Boston.

Victoria Claflin (Martin) Woodhull Papers, Southern Illinois University Special Collections, Morris Library, Carbondale, Ill.

Victoria Claflin (Martin) Woodhull Papers, Hamilton College Special Collections, Clinton, N.Y.

Additional regional collections are identified in the notes.

PAMPHLETS, ARTICLES, NEWSPAPERS

Andrews, Stephen Pearl, Henry James, and Horace Greeley. *Love, Marriage and Divorce: A Discussion.* New York: Stringer and Townsend, 1853.

Beecher-Tilton Trial. Scrapbook of newspaper clippings, New York Public Library, New York.

The Beecher Trial: A Review of the Evidence. Reprinted from the *New York Times,* July 3, 1875, with some revisions and additions. New York: n.p.,1875.

Chrisman, Michael Leroy. *The Past and Present of Homer.* Granville, Ohio: Homer Historical Society, 1979.

Clark, Edward H. G. *The Thunderbolt.* New York, Albany, and Troy: n.p., May, 1873.

Darewin, G. S. *Synopsis of the Lives of Victoria C. Woohull, Now Mrs. John Biddulph Martin, and Tennessee Claflin, Now Lady Cook: The First Two Lady Bankers and Reformers of America.* London: n.p., 1891.

Darwin, M. F. *One Moral Standard for All: Extracts from the Lives of Victoria Claflin Woodhull, Now Mrs. John Biddulph Martin, and Tennessee Claflin, Now Lady Cook.* New York: Caulon Press, n.d.

Davis, Julia. "Victoria Woodhull: Victorians Thought Her a Downright Scandal — As She Was." *Smithsonian Magazine,* October 1977.

Davis, Paulina Wright. *A History of the National Woman's Rights Movement for Twenty Years, with the Proceedings of the Decade Meeting held at Apollo Hall, October 20, 1870, from 1850 to 1870, with an Appendix Containing the History of the Movement during the winter of 1871, in the National Capitol.* New York: Journeymen Printers' Co-operative Association, 1871. Reprint, New York: Kraus Reprint, 1971.

D'Onston, Rosyln. *Brief Sketches of the Life of Victoria Woodhull (Now Mrs. John Biddulph Martin.)* London: n.p., 1893.

Fisher, Dr. Charles A. *Snyder County Pioneers.* Selinsgrove, Pa.: Snyder County Historical Society, 1938. (See also his unpublished notes, Snyder County Historical Society.)

The Great Scandal Case. New York: American News Company, 1874.

The Humanitarian: A Monthly Review of Sociological Science, New York and London, vols. 1–19, 1892–1901.

Johnson, Gerald W. "Dynamic Victoria." *American Heritage,* June 1956.

Legge, Madeleine. *Two Noble Women, Nobly Planned.* London: Phelps Brothers, 1893.

Lorey, Frederick N. History of Knox County, Ohio. Mount Vernon, Ohio: Knox County Historical Society, 1976.

Martin, John Biddulph. *Future of the United States.* London: Blades, East & Blades, 1884.

Margolis, Anne Throne, ed. *The Isabella Beecher Hooker Project.* Hartford: The Stowe-Day Foundation, 1979.

Meiser, Joseph A., Jr. *A Genealogy of Selected Northumberland County, Pennsylvania, Pioneer Families,* part 11, *The Johan Jacob Hummel Family.* Elysburg, Pa.: n. p., 1983.

"Mrs. Satan." *Harper's Weekly,* February 17, 1872.

Nelson, James M. "America's Victoria." Paper presented to the Literary Club, Cincinnati, February 10, 1958. Cincinnati: Historical and Philosophical Society of Ohio, 1958.

Stanton, Elizabeth Cady, and Susan B. Anthony. "Wall Street Aroused." *The Revolution,* February 24, 1870.

———— "The Working Woman." *The Revolution,* March 10, 1870.

————"Carrying the War into Africa." *The Revolution,* March 24, 1870.

Stern, Madeleine B. "Notable Women of 19th-Century America." *Manuscripts,* vol. 34, no. 1 (winter 1982):19. (Autograph of Woodhull).

Story of Henry Ward Beecher and Theodore and Mrs. Tilton with Portraits. London: Anglo-American Times, 1874.

Tilton, Theodore. "Victoria C. Woodhull, A Biographical Sketch: Mr. Tilton's Account of Mrs. Woodhull." *The Golden Age,* tract 3, New York: 1871.

Treat, Joseph, M.D. *Beecher, Tilton, Woodhull, the Creation of Society: All Four of Them Exposed, and If Possible Reformed and Forgiven, in Dr. Treat's Celebrated Letter to Victoria C. Woodhull.* Published by the author. New York, 1874.

The Vanderbilt Will Case. Scrapbook of newspaper clippings, New York Public Library, New York.

"Women at the Polls," *Harper's Weekly,* November 25, 1871.

Woodhull, Victoria Claflin. "Tendencies of Government." *New York Herald.* April 16, 25; May 2, 9, 16, 27; June 4, 19; July 4, 11, 1870. (Probably ghostwritten by Stephen Pearl Andrews.)

Woodhull, Victoria Claflin (Mrs. John Biddulph Martin). *Manor House Causeries.* Bredon's Norton near Tewkesbury, n.d.

Woodhull, Zula Maud. *Affinities: A Play.* London: n.d. 1896.

————. *The Proposal: A Dialogue.* London: Norgate & Co., c. 1899. Reprint, Cheltenham, England: Norman, Sawyer & Co., 1907.

Woodhull and Claflin's Weekly, New York. May 14, 1870–June 10, 1876; publication suspended for part of 1872. (Victoria Woodhull's speeches were printed in the *Weekly* and were also sold as pamphlets.)

See also newspaper sources identified in the text and the notes.

BOOKS

Abbot, Austin, ed. *The Official Report of the Trial of Henry Ward Beecher,* 2 vols. New York: G. W. Smith & Co., 1875.

Adlard, Eleanor, ed. *Robert Holland Martin: A Symposium*. London: Frederick Muller Ltd., 1947.

Ahlstrom, Sydney E. *A Religious History of the American People*. New Haven: Yale University Press, 1972.

Andrews, Stephen Pearl. *The Basic Outline of Universology*. New York: Dion Thomas, 1872.

———. *The Primary Synopsis of Universology and Alwato, the New Scientific Universal Language*. New York: Dion Thomas, 1871. Reprint, Weston, Mass.: M & S Press, 1971.

Andrews, Wayne. *The Vanderbilt Legend*. New York: Harcourt, Brace and Co., 1941.

Auchincloss, Louis, *The Vanderbilt Era: Profiles of a Gilded Age*. New York: Charles Scribner's Sons, 1989.

Barry, Kathleen. *Susan B. Anthony: A Biography of a Singular Feminist*. New York: New York University Press, 1988.

Biographical Directory of the American Congress, 1774–1971. Washington, D.C.: United States Government Printing Office, 1971.

Boydston, Jeanne, Mary Kelley, and Anne Margolis. *The Limits of Sisterhood: The Beecher Sisters on Women's Rights and Women's Sphere*. Chapel Hill: University of North Carolina Press, 1988.

Braude, Ann. *Radical Spirits: Spiritualism and Women's Rights in Nineteenth-Century America*. Boston: Beacon Press, 1989.

Brendon, Piers. *The Life and Death of the Press Barons*. New York: Atheneum, 1983.

Brister, E. M. P. *1909 Centennial History of the City of Newark and Licking County, Ohio*, volume 1. Chicago: S. J. Clarke Publishing, 1909. Reprint, 1982.

Broun, Heywood, and Margaret Leech. *Anthony Comstock: Roundsman of the Lord*. New York: Albert and Charles Boni, 1927.

Butler, Benjamin F. *Autobiography and Personal Reminiscences of Major-General Benj. F. Butler; Butler's Book*. Boston: n.d., 1892.

Butler, Jon. *Awash in a Sea of Faith: Christianizing the American People*. Cambridge, Mass.: Harvard University Press, 1990.

Cate, Curtis. *George Sand: A Biography*. Boston: Houghton Mifflin, 1975.

Clews, Henry. *Fifty Years in Wall Street*. New York: Irving Publishing, 1908.

Claflin, Tennessee, Lady Cook. *Essays on Social Topics*. London: The Roxburghe Press, c. 1895.

Croffut, A. *The Vanderbilts and the Story of Their Fortune*. New York: Belford, Clarke & Co., 1886.

Derks, Scott, ed. *The Value of a Dollar: Prices and Incomes in the United States, 1860-1989*. Washington, D.C.: Gale Research, 1994.

Dickenson, Donna. *George Sand: A Brave Man—The Most Womanly Woman*. New York: Berg, 1988; distributed by St. Martin's Press.

DuBois, Carol Ellen, ed. *Elizabeth Cady Stanton / Susan B. Anthony: Correspondence, Writings, Speeches*. New York: Schocken Books, 1981.

————. *Feminism and Suffrage: The Emergence of an Independent Women's Movement in America 1848–1869*. Ithaca, N.Y.: Cornell University Press, 1978.

Dunkelberger, George F. *The Story of Snyder County*. Selinsgrove, Pa.: Snyder County Historical Society, 1948.

Dyer, Frederick H. *A Compendium of the War of the Rebellion,* volume 3. New York: T. Yoseloff, 1959.

Edel, Leon. *Henry James: The Conquest of London,* vol. 2. Philadelphia: J. B. Lippincott, 1962; New York: Avon Books, 1978.

Foner, Eric, and John A. Garraty, eds. *The Reader's Companion to American History*. Boston: Houghton Mifflin, 1991.

Foster, William Zebulon. *History of the Three Internationals*. New York: International Publishers, 1955.

Fraser, Antonia. *The Warrior Queens*. New York: Alfred A. Knopf, 1989.

Freud, Sigmund, and Josef Breuer. *Studies on Hysteria*. Trans. and ed. James Strachey, in collaboration with Anna Freud. New York: Basic Books, 1957.

Goethe, Johann Wolfgang von. *Elective Affinities,* trans. and with an introduction by Victoria Woodhull. Boston: D. W. Niles, 1872. See also the edition trans. and with an introduction by R. J. Hollingdale. New York: Penguin, 1983. Originally published in 1809 as *Die Wahlverwandtschaften*.

Gompers, Samuel. *Seventy Years of Life and Labor,* vol. 1. New York: Dutton, 1925.

Gordon, John Steele. *The Scarlet Woman of Wall Street: Jay Gould, Jim Fisk, Cornelius Vanderbilt, the Erie Railway Wars, and the Birth of Wall Street*. New York: Weidenfeld & Nicolson, 1988.

Griffith, Elisabeth. *In Her Own Right: The Life of Elizabeth Cady Stanton*. New York: Oxford University Press, 1984.

Hedrick, Joan. *Harriet Beecher Stowe: A Life*. New York: Oxford University Press, 1994.

Hibben, Paxton. *Henry Ward Beecher: An American Portrait*. New York: George H. Doran, 1927.

Hudson, Frederick. *Journalism in America*. New York: Harper & Brothers, 1873.

Holzman, Robert S. *Stormy Ben Butler*. New York: Macmillan, 1954.

James, Edward T., Janet Wilson James, and Paul S. Boyer, eds. *Notable American Women, 1607–1950: A Biographical Dictionary*. Cambridge, Mass.: Harvard University Press, Belknap Press, 1971.

James, Henry. *The Bostonians.* New York: Macmillan, 1886; New York: Penguin, 1983.

———. *The Great Short Novels of Henry James: The Siege of London.* New York: Dial Press, 1944; New York: Penguin, 1983. (*The Siege of London* first appeared in *Cornhill Magazine,* January–February 1883.)

James, William. *The Varieties of Religious Experience: A Study in Human Nature, Being the Gifford Lectures on Natural Religion Delivered at Edinburgh in 1901–1902.* New York: Random House, Modern Library, n.d.

Johnson, Gerald W. *The Lunatic Fringe.* Philadelphia: J. B. Lippincott, 1957.

Johnston, Johanna. *Mrs. Satan: The Incredible Saga of Victoria Woodhull.* New York: G. P. Putnam's Sons, 1967; London: Macmillan, 1967.

Kindleberger, Charles Poor. *Manias, Panics and Crashes.* New York: Basic Books, 1978.

Klaw, Spencer. *Without Sin: The Life and Death of the Oneida Community.* New York: Penguin, Allen Lane, 1993.

Lutz, Alma. *Created Equal: A Biography of Elizabeth Cady Stanton, 1815–1902.* New York: John Day, 1940.

———. *Susan B. Anthony: Rebel, Crusader, Humanitarian.* Boston: Beacon Press, 1959.

Lane, Wheaton J. *Commodore Vanderbilt: An Epic of the Steam Age.* New York: Alfred A. Knopf, 1942.

Leach, William. *True Love and Perfect Union: The Feminist Reform of Sex and Society.* New York: Basic Books, 1980.

Martin, John Biddulph. *The Grasshopper in Lombard Street.* London: Simpkin Marshall Hamilton Kent & Co.; New York: Scribner & Welford, 1892.

Moore, R. Laurence. *Religious Outsiders and the Making of Americans.* New York: Oxford University Press, 1986.

———. *In Search of White Crows: Spiritualism, Parapsychology, and American Culture.* New York: Oxford University Press, 1977.

Marberry, M. M. *Vicky: A Biography of Victoria C. Woodhull.* New York: Funk & Wagnalls, 1967.

McCabe, James D., Jr. *Lights and Shadows of New York Life; or the Sights and Sensations of the Great City.* Philadelphia: National Publishing, 1872.

McFeely, William S. *Frederick Douglass.* New York: W. W. Norton & Co., 1991.

———. *Grant: A Biography.* New York: W. W. Norton & Co., 1982.

Meade, Marion. *Free Woman: The Life and Times of Victoria Woodhull.* New York: Alfred A. Knopf, a Borzoi Book, 1976. (For young readers.)

————. *Madame Blavatsky: The Woman behind the Myth.* New York: G. P. Putnam's Sons, 1980.

Nevins, Allan. *Hamilton Fish: The Inner History of the Grant Administration.* New York: Dodd, Mead & Co., 1936.

Newman, Peter, Murray Milgate, and John Eatwell. *The New Palgrave Dictionary of Money and Finance.* New York: Macmillan, 1992.

Papachristou, Judith. *Women Together: A History in Documents of the Women's Movement in the United States.* New York: Alfred A. Knopf, a Borzoi Book, 1976.

Reid, Charles. *Thomas Beecham: An Independent Biography.* New York: E. P. Dutton & Co., 1962.

Rugoff, Milton. *America's Gilded Age: Intimate Portraits from an Era of Extravagance and Change, 1850–1890.* New York: Henry Holt and Co., 1989.

————. *The Beechers: An American Family in the Nineteenth Century.* New York: Harper & Row, 1981.

Sachs, Emanie. *The Terrible Siren: Victoria Woodhull.* New York: Harper & Brothers, 1928. Reprint, New York: Arno Press, 1978.

Sears, Hal D. *The Sex Radicals: Free Love in High Victorian America.* Lawrence, Kans.: Regents Press of Kansas, 1977.

Seitz, Don C. *The Dreadful Decade: Detailing Some Phases in the History of the United States from Reconstruction to Resumption, 1869–1879.* Indianapolis: Bobbs-Merrill, 1966.

Shaplen, Robert. *Free Love and Heavenly Sinners: The Story of the Great Henry Ward Beecher Scandal.* New York: Alfred A. Knopf, a Borzoi Book, 1954. Originally published in *The New Yorker,* June 5 and 12, 1954, under the title, "That Was New York."

Smith, Arthur D. *Commodore Vanderbilt: An Epic of American Achievement.* New York: Robert M. McBride & Co., 1927.

Smith, Matthew Hale. *Sunshine and Shadow in New York.* Hartford: J. B. Burr and Co., 1868.

————. *Twenty Years among the Bulls and Bears of Wall Street.* Hartford: J. B. Burr and Co., 1870.

Smith, Page. *The Rise of Industrial America: A People's History of the Post-Reconstruction Era.* New York: McGraw-Hill, 1984.

Snyder, Charles M. *Union County, Pennsylvania: A Bicentennial History.* Lewisburg, Pa.: Colonial Printing House, 1976.

Stanton, Elizabeth Cady, Susan B. Anthony, and Matilda Joslyn Gage, eds. *History of Woman Suffrage, in Three Volumes,* vol. 2. New York: Fowler & Wells, 1882.

Starr, Paul. *Social Transformation of American Medicine.* New York: Basic Books, 1982.

Stasz, Clarice. *The Vanderbilt Women: Dynasty of Wealth, Glamour, and Tragedy.* New York: St. Martin's Press, 1991.

Steinem, Gloria, *Moving Beyond Words.* New York: Simon & Schuster, 1994.

Stern, Madeleine B. *The Pantarch: A Biography of Stephen Pearl Andrews.* Austin: University of Texas Press, 1968.

———, ed. *The Victoria Woodhull Reader.* Weston, Mass.: M&S Press, 1974. (This work is a helpful reprinting of Woodhull's speeches and articles; it lacks consecutive page numbers.)

———. *We the Women: Career Firsts of Nineteenth-Century America.* New York: Schulte Publishing, 1963.

Stoehr, Taylor. *Free Love in America: A Documentary History.* New York: AMS Press, 1979.

Stowe, Harriet Beecher. *Lady Byron Vindicated.* Boston: Fields Osgood & Co., 1870.

———. *My Wife and I.* Serialized in the *Christian Union,* 1871. New York: J. B. Ford & Co., 1871. Reprint, Boston: Houghton Mifflin, 1896.

Teltscher, Herry O. *Handwriting, A Revelation of Self: A Source Book of Psychographology.* Alexandria, Va.: Red Dragon Press, Hawthorn Books, 1971.

———. *Handwriting Analysis for Business and Personal Success.* New York: Shapolsky Publishing, 1994.

Terry, Edwin W. "Theodore Tilton as Social Reformer, Radical Republican, Newspaper Editor, 1863–1872." Ph.D. diss., St. John's University, 1971; University Microfilms International Dissertation Information Service, Ann Arbor, Mich.

Tilton, Theodore. *Tempest Tossed.* New York: Sheldon, 1874.

Tilton vs. Beecher: Action for Criminal Conversation. Verbatim report by the Official Stenographer, 3 vols. New York: McDivitt, Campbell & Co., 1875.

Trollope, Frances. *Domestic Manners of the Americans.* London: Whittaker, 1832. Reprint, New York: Vintage Books, 1960.

Vanderbilt, Arthur T., II. *Fortune's Children: The Fall of the House of Vanderbilt.* New York: William Morrow, 1989.

Waller, Altina L. *The Reverend Beecher and Mrs. Tilton: Sex and Class in Victorian America.* Amherst: University of Massachusetts Press, 1982.

West, Richard S., Jr. *Lincoln's Scapegoat General.* Boston: Houghton Mifflin, 1965.

Wight, Charles Henry. *Genealogy of the Claflin Family.* New York: William Green, 1903.

Wilder, Louise Beebe. *Color in My Garden.* Garden City: Doubleday, 1918. Reprint, New York: Atlantic Monthly Press, 1990.

Woodhull, Mary Gould and Francis Bowes Stevens. *Woodhull Genealogy.* Philadelphia: n.p., 1904.

Woodhull, Victoria Claflin (Mrs. John Biddulph Martin). *A Fragmentary Record of Public Work Done in America, 1871–1877.* London: G. Norman & Son, 1887.

Woodhull, Victoria Claflin. *The Origin, Tendencies and Principles of Government: A Review of the Rise and Fall of Nations from Early Historic Time to the Present; with Special Consideration Regarding the Future of the United States as the Representative Government of the World.* New York: Woodhull, Claflin & Co., 1871. (Probably ghostwritten by Stephen Pearl Andrews.)

Woodhull, Victoria Claflin (Mrs. John Biddulph Martin), and Tennessee C. Claflin (Lady Cook). *The Human Body, the Temple of God; or The Philosophy of Sociology.* Published by the authors. London, 1890. (Includes Woodhull's announcement for president, her memorial to Congress, the majority and minority committee reports, her major suffrage speeches, and reprints of many newspaper clippings useful to the researcher.)

Wrobel, Arthur, ed. *Pseudo-Science and Society in Nineteenth Century America.* Lexington: University Press of Kentucky, 1987.

Notes

For full citations of works listed in shortened form in the notes, see the bibliography. The following abbreviations are used:

A Papers-BPL   Woodhull's autobiographical papers in the Boston Public Library, Boston, Mass.

A Papers-HM   Woodhull's autobiographical papers in the Holland-Martin Family Archives, London, England

A Papers-SIU   Woodhull's autobiographical papers at Southern Illinois University, Carbondale, Ill.

HB   Victoria Woodhull, *The Human Body, the Temple of God*

HC   Isabella Beecher Hooker Collection, Stowe-Day Library, Hartford, Conn.

HWS   Elizabeth Cady Stanton, Susan B. Anthony, and Matilda Joslyn Gage, *History of Woman Suffrage*

NAW   Edward T. James, editor, *Notable American Women*

VWR   Madeleine B. Stern, editor, *The Victoria Woodhull Reader*

WCW   *Woodhull and Claflin's Weekly*

INTRODUCTION

xi   "A pedestal . . .": This quote has been attributed to Steinem, but she first heard it while organizing in the South in the early 1970s and was told it had been said by a black woman of the abolitionist and suffragist era to her white Southern sisters. If any reader knows its source, she would love to have it.

xii   "I have an inalienable . . .": Marberry, p. 70.

xii   "An Astor may sit . . .": Marberry, p. 83.

Steinem also consulted *VWR* and Sachs on Woodhull's life.

PROLOGUE

3   Convention events: *WCW*, May 18, 25, 1871, and June 1, 1871, including reprints of reports from the *Cincinnati Commercial*.

3   "Yes, I am a free lover": *VWR*, "Principles of Social Freedom" speech.

3   Nast cartoon: *Harper's Weekly* published Thomas Nast's "Mrs. Satan" on February 17, 1872.

6   *New York Herald* letter and "we want no expediency...", *WCW,:* May 4, 1872.

7   "Wild men and women...": *New York Herald,* May 12, 1872.

7   "The career of V...": *New York Times,* reprinted in *WCW,* June 1, 1872.

1   "A FAVORING OMEN"

12   Woodhull talked about the "favoring omen" of her name in a July 20, 1871, letter to the Victoria League, *VWR.*

12   Life in Homer: Tilton, pp. 5–11; Licking County Land Record Index and deeds; 1850 Census of the United States; Homer Historical Society; Licking County Historical Society; National Archives Record of Appointments of Postmasters; Lorey, p. 211; Licking County Genealogical Society and its 1982 *History of Licking County;* Chrisman; and Homer Library. The "windows were for light" quotation comes from a Homer resident Harriet Smythe, interviewed on June 14, 1988. On September 23, 1988, Homer erected an Ohio State historical marker to mark the 150th anniversary of Woodhull's birth, ending years of silence about its famous resident.

12   Hummel family history: Meiser, Jr., and others; Fisher and Fisher's unpublished notes at the Snyder County Historical Society. A rich source of information on Pennsylvania German customs and superstitions is Dunkelberger.

12   Claflin family history: Wight, pp. 124–125; local history collection of Sandisfield, Mass., Free Public Library; A Papers-HM.

13   Buck's career as a river trader: A Papers-SIU; Snyder.

15   The Methodists and their camp meetings: Ahlstrom, pp. 436–440; Trollope, pp. 167–175.

16   Dyslexia: Woodhull's description of Utica's learning problem fits the classic description of learning disability. Though Utica had "intellect," Woodhull said, "she had no application, no concentration, no continuity. As a child at school, study, even, was impossible, and this characteristic grew in strength ... [She] lacked the capacity to conquer it," *WCW,* July 26, 1873.

17   Woodhull on her parents' financial failure: Tilton, pp. 5, 6.

18   Woodhull's trance stories: Tilton, pp. 3–35; A Papers-HM.

19–20   "Whose watchful eyes..." and "O merciful father...": from one of Annie's typical prayers, quoted by Woodhull in A Papers-HM.

2   "SEND FOR THE SPIRITS"

22–39   Tilton, pp. 3–35, contains the most extensive material on this period of Woodhull's life and is the source of quotations in the text.

23   Fourth of July celebrations: Trollope, pp. 86, 87.

22   Miles family: Mt. Gilead Historical Society, Miles family genealogy.

24   Marriage: Records of the Cleveland probate court.

24 Canning Woodhull: Woodhull family genealogy: Gould, p. 211; practice of medicine: Starr, pp. 43–63.

25 "Ignorant . . .": *WCW,* October 25, 1873.

25 Byron's illness: A Papers-HM, SIU, Tilton, pp.19–21.

30 Zulu tulips: Wilder, p. 45.

30 Tennie's fortune telling: Sachs, pp. 32–38.

33 Mediumship as a career for enterprising young nineteenth-century women: Braude, pp. 84–116, a groundbreaking work on this neglected topic.

35 Jesse Grant: McFeely's *Grant,* p. 5. Grant's poem is in the local history collection of the Missouri Historical Library, St. Louis.

35 Blood: Dyer, vol. 3, p. 1325; Veterans Records of the National Archives, records of Missouri Adj. Gen. Office; local history collection of the Missouri Historical Library, St. Louis.

37 Family portrait: Holland-Martin Family Archives.

38 Dayton and Rev. Thomas E. Thomas: local history collection of the Montgomery County Historical Society; A Papers-HM; *HB.*

3   COMMODORE VANDERBILT

43–49 Commodore Vanderbilt: Vanderbilt's *Fortune's Children,* pp. 1–54 provides a fine, although brief, account of the Commodore's life. See also the books by Land, Croffut, Smith, Andrews, Auchincloss (pp. 13–24), and Stasz. I relied primarily on Croffut and Vanderbilt for the Commodore's words, quoted in the newspapers of his day. "Many young ladies . . .": *New York Tribune,* March 2, 1878; "it would go up 22 percent . . .": *New York Tribune,* October 16, 1878; make her a queen . . .: *New York Tribune,* March 2, 1878.

44 Meeting: "directed . . .": quotation from a letter to Vanderbilt published in *WCW,* April 8, 1875; A Papers-HM.

46 Tennie's reading newspapers to Vanderbilt: "The Vanderbilt Will Case," New York Public Library scrapbook of newspaper clippings.

49 John Bortel: Richmond Local History Collection, London, England, newspaper clippings. In 1899 Tennie Claflin, through her husband Sir Francis Cook, told the press she had once been married to, and divorced from, John Bortel. The name has been spelled Bartels by some sources. They probably relied on the 1928 biography of Victoria Woodhull by Emanie Sachs. In this work we have followed Tennie Claflin's 1899 spelling.

49 *Aurora* painting: Marberry, pp. 9, 191, 236.

51 Owed "all that they had done . . .": *WCW,* April 8, 1875.

4   "THE COMING WOMAN"

52 Woodhull memoir of suffrage meeting: A Papers-HM.

52 2. Reports of and quotations from suffrage convention: *HWS,* vol. 2, pp. 345–362.

53 Kansas campaign, racism and elitism of the suffragists: See DuBois's *Feminism* for a thoughtful account of these events, also Terry.

54 Douglass: McFeely's *Douglass*, pp. 268, 269.

56 "Alpha": *New York World,* January 28, 1869.

5 "GOLD, GOLD, GOLD WAS THE CRY"

57 Woodhull "operating heavily": A Papers-HM.

58 Newspaper reports of the Black Friday panic: McFeely's *Grant,* pp. 320–331; Gordon, pp. 271–278, 285; Rugoff's *Gilded Age,* pp. 58–61.

59 Vanderbilt purchase of securities to stabilize the market: Seitz, p. 74.

59 "I came . . .": A Papers-HM.

59 Today's dollars: Derks, p. 2.

59 "Bold operator . . .": A Papers-BPL.

60 Might have been Mrs. Vanderbilt: *New York Tribune,* March 2, 1878.

6 WOODHULL, CLAFLIN & COMPANY

61 European trip: A Papers-HM. Woodhull's account did not mention Vanderbilt's name, but the circumstances identify him.

62 Check for $7,000 from Vanderbilt deposited with Henry Clews: Clews, pp. 430–441.

62 "It was you . . .": *WCW,* April 8, 1875.

63 *New York Herald:* January 20, 22, 1870.

66 Walt Whitman: A Papers-BPL, SIU.

67 Quotations from *The Revolution,* March 10, 1870, p. 159; March 24, 1870, p. 188.

69 Randall Foote: A Papers-SIU.

69 Gould: *Wall Street Journal,* August 11, 1927.

69 "The secrets of money . . .": A Papers-HM.

7 THE ART OF THE SOIRÉE

70 Salons: Smith; Marberry, p. 176; Clews quoted in the *Wall Street Journal,* August 11, 1927; Tennie quotations from the *New York Courier,* Feburary, 14, 1870, *HB.*

71 Reid: Whitelaw Reid Collection, Library of Congress; *NAW.*

72 Blood relationship: Tilton, pp. 23–26.

72 Brokerage contract: A Papers-HM.

73 Woodhull's handwriting: The noted graphologist Herry O. Teltscher guided me through the mysteries of Woodhull's penmanship. The autograph dealers James Lowe and Sal Alberti were also helpful as were Sterns's article in *Manuscripts,* p. 19, and the curators of the collections of Woodhull's letters. The conclusions in the text are my own.

74 Check fraud: *New York World,* March 20, 1870, *HB.*

75 Delmonico story: A Papers-SIU, Darwin, p. 26.

75–76 Andrews: "the salon of Mme Roland ..." quotation is from Stern, p. 113; the "Queer Philosopher" quotation is from the *New York World,* October 2, 1870; Andrews's free love debate appeared in the pages of the *New York Tribune* in 1852.

8 "I ANNOUNCE MYSELF AS A CANDIDATE FOR THE PRESIDENCY"

77 Announcement of the candidacy and accompanying editorials: *New York Herald,* April 2, 1870.

79 Stanton for Congress: Lutz, pp. 140, 141.

79 Suffrage divisions: Terry.

81 "More sagacity ...": *Philadelphia Press,* April 7, 1870; HB.

81 Reid correspondence: Whitelaw Reid Collection, Library of Congress.

82 Greeley: Brendon, pp. 50–57.

82 Woodhull's articles in the *New York Herald:* April 16 and 25, May 2, 9, 16, and 27, June 4 and 19, July 4 and 11, 1870.

84 Cole letter to Woodhull: A Papers-SIU, May 3, 1910.

84 "Whence the truth ...": WCW, June 19, 1875.

84 Semiramis: Fraser, pp. 28, 29.

85 "Masculine grasp ...": *New York World,* January 28, 1869, HB.

85 "Spend a fortune ...": *New York Dispatch,* April 3, 1870, HB.

9 *WOODHULL AND CLAFLIN'S WEEKLY*

86 WCW: May 14, 1870, and subsequent issues.

88 Sand: Dickenson; Cate, pp. 709–719.

88 Stowe attacked Sand in the *Woman's Journal* and Stanton defended her in *The Revolution,* September 15, 1870, Papachristou, p. 69.

89 "We nursed it ...": WCW, July 11, 1874.

89 WCW business plan: WCW, May 14 and December 17, 1870; May 20 and July 1, 1871; April 27 and November 2, 1872; May 3 and August 9, 1873; July 25, 1874.

90 "Abundance of her assurance": Tucker-Sachs correspondence, New York Public Library Manuscript Collection.

91 "Handsome ...": *New York Standard,* May 18, 1870, HB; *Philadelphia Day,* June 7, 1870, HB.

91 "Hostile divisions": *New York Herald,* May 18, 1870, HB.

92 *The Independent:* Terry, pp. 246–262.

10 WHISPERING IN THE PRESIDENT'S EAR

94 The Willard Hotel and "universal habit ...": Rugoff's *Gilded Age,* p. 15.

94 "Third house ...": VWR, pp. 21–22.

95 Isabella Beecher Hooker: HC; Hooker often repeated herself to more than one correspondent. I have quoted her letters in "quarrel ...", "no time ...", "When I ...", "the victory and the credit ..." and "actually feared us ...".

95 Suffragists and the Fifteenth Amendment: Terry; Dubois's *Feminism;* "deliberate insult to American womanhood . . .": *HWS,* vol. 2, p. 354; "monster of selfishness": Dubois's *Feminism,* p. 72.

96 Butler: *Butler's Book* by Benjamin Butler; Holzman; West, Jr.; "the truth . . .": Holzman, p. 202; "half truths . . .": A Papers-BPL; "very lonely . . ." and "you have been away . . .": West, p. 319; "opportunity to feast . . .": Tucker-Sachs correspondence, New York Public Library Manuscript Collection; "went at night . . .": A Papers-BPL.

99 Memorial: *VWR* gives the full text.

99 "Men could never . . .": Johnston, p. 86.

99 Memorial presentation: *VWR* gives the full text; see also *HWS,* pp. 442–481, Davis, pp. 86–95, and *WCW,* January 28, 1871; "Her voice trembled . . .": HC; "in as good . . .": *New York Herald,* January 12, 1871; "all the past efforts . . .": *New York Tribune,* January 16, 1871.

104–105 Grant: "whispering in the president's ear": *New York Tribune,* January 16, 1871; "He stands . . .": *WCW,* January 21, 1871; "President's cigar" and "married woman two votes": Nevins, p. 135; "Some day you will occupy . . .": A Papers-SIU; "president is with us . . ." and "Weak men . . .": *New York Sun,* June 23, 1871; "Mrs. Grant has filed in . . .": Anthony to Woodhull, in *WCW,* February 4, 1871.

106 "Republican dodge": Stanton to Woodhull, in *WCW,* February 11, 1871.

106 Majority and Minority opinions: *VWR* gives the full text.

11 THE WOODHULL

108–110 New political direction in *WCW:* "Cosmo-political Party . . .": began appearing January 28, 1871; Claflin Memorial to New York State Legislature: *WCW,* January 28, 1871; "The male citizen . . ." and "The point shirked . . .": *WCW,* February 11, 1871; "I am satisfied . . .": *WCW,* February 18, 1871; request to speak to the House: *WCW,* February 11, 1871; 79 votes: *WCW,* August 5, 1871; "Resolved . . .": *WCW,* February 25, 1871.

110 Griffing: "Consciousness . . .": Davis, p. 83.

110–112 February 16, 1871 speech: This and Woodhull's "Great Secession" speech, delivered May 11, 1871, were variations of the same speech. Texts appear in Davis, pp. 112–119, *HB,* pp. 145–183, and *VWR.* The *VWR* version, though dated February 16, 1871, includes the rousing "Great Secession" ending. Ticket: A Papers-HM; "objective . . .": Davis, *WCW,* March 4, 1871; "perfect composure . . ." *Washington Chronicle,* February 17, 1871, *HB;* "Involuntarily . . ." and "a most enviable . . .": HC; "very effective speech . . .": *Herald,* February 17, 1871; "Applauded . . .": *Washington Sunday Gazette,* February 19, 1871 and "Brave . . .": *Washington Daily Republican,* January 20, 1871, *HB;* "graceful . . .": *New York Tribune,* January 16, 1971..

113 Butler: "You are . . .": A Papers-SIU.

113 Petitions: "Everyone should feel . . .": *WCW,* February 4, 1871.

113–115   Growing stature: "We have waited . . .": Stanton to Woodhull, in *WCW*, March 11, 1871; "loudly cheered . . .": *New York Times*, March 2, 1871; "head and front . . .": *New York Herald*, February 17, 1871, *HB*.
114    $10,000: Marberry, p. 28.

12   THE GREAT SECESSION SPEECH

116   May 8, 1871 speech:*VWR* gives the full text; *New York Times*, January 21, 1871.
117   Mott: "You won my heart . . .": Woodhull to Mott, February 27, 1873; "We were all charmed . . .": Wright to Garrison, March 15, 1871, both Sophia Smith Collection, Smith College, Northampton, Mass.
117   Davis: *NAW* article by Alice Felt Tyler; "A thousand thanks . . .": Woodhull to Davis, April 11, 1871, Alma Lutz Collection, Vassar College Library, Poughkeepsie, New York.
119   Stanton: Lutz; Griffith; "I have watched . . ." and "I read your journal . . .": Stanton to Woodhull, February 20, 1871 in *WCW*, March 18, 1871; "I have thought much . . .": HC.
120   Anthony: Lutz; Barry; "strong spirit . . .": Anthony to Woodhull, February 4, 1871, in *WCW*, February 25, 1871.
121–123   The Beechers: Rugoff's *Beechers* is a fine biography of this family. *The Limits of Sisterhood* by Jeanne Boydston, Mary Kelley, and Anne Margolis is a useful collection of the sisters' correspondence. Hooker: "I can't write . . .": Rugoff's *Beechers*, p. 421; "I dare not . . .": Boydston, p. 348; "whole nature is spiritual . . .", "such a powerful woman . . .", and "You were drawn . . .": HC. Catharine: "My soul . . .": Rugoff's *Beechers*, p. 314; "Is it not possible . . .": *WCW*, January 14, 1871; "Catharine wanted . . .": Johnston, p. 101, and Sachs, p. 86; "Griffin": Rugoff's *Beechers*, p. 397; "How unhappy . . .": *WCW*, May 17, 1873. Stowe: Hedrick; Stowe's *Lady Byron Vindicated* and *My Wife and I*.
124   Dickinson: "Does not hesitate . . .": Milo Townsend to Stanton, March 22, 1871, Stanton reply, April 5, 1871, Sophia Smith Collection, Smith College, Northampton, Mass.
125–127   "Great Secession" speech:*VWR* gives the full text; see Davis for an account of the meeting. Responses: "no one could . . .", "affectionately welcomed . . .", and "rebellion threat . . .": Wright-Garrison correspondence, May 14, 1871, Sophia Smith Collection, Smith College, Northampton, Mass.

13   MUCKRAKING DAYS

128   Woodhull, Claflin & Company operations: fragmentary records in A Papers-HM. Giles Holland-Martin, CA, and Chris Leonard, CPA, helped me interpret the records.
129–133   Exposures: The *Weekly* muckraked 36 years before Theodore Roosevelt coined the word that has become part of the language. *WCW*, September 1870 through June 1871 and resuming December 1871 through June

1872. When regular publication resumed in 1873, exposures moved from business subjects to social subjects.

132   "Financial schemes . . .": A Papers-HM.

14   ANNIE'S DAY IN COURT

134   Court report: *New York Herald,* May 16, 17, 1871.

140   Stowe letter: Stowe to Annie Adams Fields, December 25, 1872, The Huntington Library, San Marino, Calif.

141   Woodhull's reaction to Stowe's accusations: Woodhull to Bladen, June 22, 1871, Sophia Smith Collection, Smith College, Northampton, Mass.

141–142   "A gentleman . . ." and "I suppose . . .": HC.

142   "Perfect defense": *New York Sun,* June 23, 1871.

15   "I DO NOT INTEND TO BE THE SCAPEGOAT"

143   Woodhull's letters to the *New York Times: Times,* May 22 and 24, 1871.

144   Free love: Stoehr; Sears; Oneida Colony and Noyes's doctrine of stirpi-culture: *WCW,* October 15, 1871 and Klaw, p. 175.

145   Woodhull-Greeley exchange: *WCW,* June-August, 1871.

147   Suffragist reaction: "The grief I felt . . .": Stanton to Woodhull, June 21, 1871, in *WCW,* July 15, 1871; "the leader . . .": HC; "tender pity . . .": Stearns, HC.

148   "Already . . .": Woodhull to Bladen, June 22, 1871, Sophia Smith Collection, Smith College, Northampton, Mass.

16   "THE SWEETER IMPULSES OF NATURE"

149   Woodhull's account of Tilton: *WCW,* November 2, 1872, and May 17, 1873.

149   Tilton: Terry's is the only biography of Tilton and covers just the early years. Shaplen's is still the best account of the Beecher-Tilton scandal, and Waller discusses the impact of the scandal on social institutions. Rugoff's *Beechers* offers a perceptive view of Tilton's life.

150   "Very expressive [eyes] . . .": Terry, p. 3.

150   "He slept every night . . .": Treat, p. 15, attributed by Treat to the *Chicago Times.*

150   "Sweeter impulses . . .": Johnston, p. 113.

150   "My dear Victoria . . .": Marberry, p. 51–52.

151   Confirmation of Tilton-Woodhull affair: Tucker-Sachs Correspondence, New York Public Library Manuscript Collection.

151   "She never goes": Tilton, p. 33.

153   "What hours . . .": Rugoff's *Beechers,* p. 386.

154   "I thought of you . . .": Davis to Woodhull, *WCW,* November 2, 1872.

157   "Sparkled in every line . . .": Marberry, p. 43.

157   "Should she be elected . . .": Tilton, p. 28.

17 THE GRAND ENDOWMENTS OF HENRY WARD BEECHER

158   "I have arranged . . .": Sachs, p. 116. Woodhull's account of Beecher: *WCW*, November 2, 1872.

158–162   Beecher: Hibben is the best in a large field of biographies. Rugoff's *Beechers* is a masterly update of Hibben's book. The quotations on Beecher are from Rugoff, pp. 369–398.

159   Beecher-Woodhull affair: "had sexual relations . . .": Tucker-Sachs correspondence, New York Public Library Manuscript Collection; "I never loved . . .": *Chicago Times,* Marberry, pp. 109–111.

160–161   Moulton: *The Great Scandal,* distributed by the American News Co., 1874, included reports of the Plymouth Church trial on pp. 100, 101; "My wife is a broad-minded, self-preserving woman . . .": *WCW,* October 31, 1874.

161   Hibben on the Beecher-Woodhull affair: "Mr. Beecher's mistress, as I have strong evidence indicating that she was": Hibben to the lawyers Collyer-Bristow & Co., December 31, 1927, A Papers-HM; "understood . . .": Hibben, p. 324.

162   Goethe's *Elective Affinities*: *WCW*, December 2, 1871, advertisement.

18 THE VICTORIA LEAGUE

165   "An organization . . .": Tilton, p. 28.

167   Equal Rights: Terry, pp. 132–170.

167   "Such a rush . . .": Woodhull to Davis, July 27, 1871, Vassar College Library, Poughkeepsie, N.Y.

165–167   "Victoria League" letters and "Principles of Finance": *VWR* gives the texts: *New York Times* report on speech, August 4, 1871.

19 THE SPIRITUALISTS

169   Spiritualism: Moore's *Crows* and *Religious Outsiders;* Leach; Sears; Braude.

169–172   Vineland meeting: *WCW*, September 9, 30, 1871; Tilton, pp. 3–35; children's lyceums: Leach, p. 295; "deeply appreciated . . .": *WCW,* September 30, 1871; "votive . . .": *Brooklyn Eagle,* "if apples . . .": *Harper's Weekly,* Marberry, pp. 51–52; "not hear . . .": Brown to Hooker, October 26, 1871, HC; "How do you . . .": Garrison to Wright, September 27, 1871, Sophia Smith Collection, Smith College, Northampton, Mass.; "Will you ask . . .": Stanton to Woodhull, December 29, [1871], Stanton Correspondence, New York Public Library Manuscript Collection.

172–173   Trances: "sensation . . .": *WCW*, May 6, 1876; "had we not . . .": *WCW*, April 17, 1875; "something very different . . .": speech entitled "Reformation or Revolution, Which?" October 17, 1873, *VWR*. I found James's *Varieties of Religious Experience,* pp. 370–420, pertinent in considering Woodhull's trances. See also Breuer and Freud. I received help-

ful perspectives on Woodhull's psyche from the psychotherapists Ruth
Conkey, Ronee Herman, MD, Louise Kaplan, Sue Shapiro, and Eileen
Simpson. Marilyn Rossener, who calls herself a medium and clairvoyant,
shared her views with me.

174   Troy meeting: *WCW,* August 12, 1871; Woodhull's speech: *WCW,* October 7, 1871.

174   Woodhull's message to spiritualists: *WCW,* November 11, 1871.

20 A FAMOUS TEST QUESTION

176   "Lily white hands . . .": *New York Herald,* November 8, 1871.

176   Voting attempt: *Harper's Weekly,* November 25, 1871.

177   "Much has been said . . .": *New York Times,* November 8, 1871.

21. "YES, I AM A FREE LOVER"

178   Speaking tour: *WCW,* September 30, October 14, and November 25, 1871; "Miss Beecher . . .": Sachs, p. 125 and Marberry, p. 63; "Agitation of thought . . .": *WCW,* December 2, 1871.

178   Free love philosophy: Tilton, p. 32.

179–184   Woodhull on "Social Freedom" speech: *WCW,* November 2, 1872, full text in *VWR;* "several young . . .": *New York Herald,* November 21, 1871, Sachs, p. 129.

185   "A woman of . . .": *Rochester Express,* November 21, 1871, *HB.*

185   "Most prominent . . .": *Pittsburgh Dispatch,* December 2, 1871, *HB.*

185   Mary Bowles letter: *WCW,* December 16, 1871.

22 A SUFFRAGIST NOMINATION FOR PRESIDENT

188   "I think it . . .": Woodhull to Hooker, October 19, 1871, HC.

188–192   Convention: *WCW,* January 27, 1872; *New York Herald,* January 11, 12, 1872.

23 JESUS CHRIST AND KARL MARX

194   "Impending Revolution" speech: *VWR* gives the full text; See also *WCW,* March 2, 1872. Weather: Weather bureau of the New York Meterological Observatory.

197   Internationals: "Pseudo communists . . .": Stern's *Pantarch,* pp. 114–115; Gompers, vol. 1, pp. 55–57; Foster, p. 121; Foner, pp. 900–901.

197   Rossel march: *Frank Leslie's Illustrated Weekly,* January 6, 1872; *WCW,* December 23, 1871.

197   *Communist Manifesto*: *WCW,* December 30, 1871.

199–201   Woodhull's defense: "Ordinarily . . ." and "burlesquing . . .": *WCW,* March 2–16, 1872; "Harper . . .": *WCW,* February 24, 1872.

202   "unsolved riddle": *VWR.*

24   A COLLECTION OF AMERICAN ORIGINALS

204   "You will see . . .": Garrison to Johnson, April 23, 1871, Boston Public Library Manuscript Collection.

204   Canning Woodhull's death: *WCW,* April 27, 1872.

205   May 9, 1872 suffrage meeting: "The eyes of the world . . .": *WCW,* May 18, 25, 1872; Griffith, p. 152.

206–207   Delegate biographies: *WCW,* May 18, 1872; Smith; *NAW;* Braude; Leach; Moore; Stoehr; Sears. Lacking a roster of delegates, I have relied on the sponsor list published in the *Weekly.*

207–208   Equal Rights Convention: *WCW,* May 18, 25, 1872, and June 1, 1872.

25   CRISIS

210   Post-convention arrangments: *WCW,* May 25, 1872, June 1, 15, and 22, 1872; "If Mrs. Woodhull's nomination . . .": *New York Times* reprinted in *WCW,* June 1, 1872.

211   Ratification meeting: *WCW,* June 15, 22, 1872; *VWR* gives the full text of the speech.

211   Douglass's selection as vice presidential nominee: *WCW,* May 25, 1872; McFeely's *Douglass,* pp. 270–281.

213   Section 12 ejected: Sachs, p. 123.

214   "We were at a loss . . .": *WCW,* November 2, 1872.

214   "To admit . . .": Smith, p. 456.

214   "We have learned . . ." and "Our presence among the Internationalists . . .": A Papers-SIU.

215   Financial crash: Kindleberger, p. 213.

215   "Pecuniary disasters . . .": *WCW,* November 2, 1872, Sachs, pp. 167, 168, A Papers-SIU.

216   Hooker loyalty: *WCW,* June 1, 1872.

216   "How can you . . .": Anthony to Hooker, HC.

216   "weak or vicious . . ." and "sad letter," July 28, 1872, HC.

216   Sued for debt, owns nothing . . . : John Hooker to his wife, September 22, 1872, HC.

216–217   "We personally don't object . . ." and "upon the floor . . .": *WCW,* November 2, 1872.

217   "I want your assistance . . .": Woodhull to Beecher, June 3, 1872, in *WCW,* September 5, 1874.

217   "Whining letter . . .": Marberry, p. 97.

218   "The press . . .", "Newspapers were being bribed . . .", "compelled to suspend . . .", and "I had not even the means . . .": *WCW,* November 2, 1872.

26 BEECHER EXPOSED

220   Exposure: "a flood . . .": A Papers-HM; "guilty of . . .": *New York Times,* April 16, 1878; Exposure published in *WCW,* November 2, 1872.

226   Blackmail charges: "Resorted to blackmailing . . .": Anthony to Heywood, *WCW,* November 2, 1872; "Dear Child . . .": Davis to Woodhull, *WCW,* December 28, 1872; "Members of the press . . .": *WCW,* December 28, 1872.

227   "My being instrumental . . .": A Papers-HM.

27 LUDLOW STREET JAIL

228–229   *Weekly* published: "Strictest secrecy . . ." and "the city was . . .": A Papers-HM; "Like buttered hotcakes . . .": Marberry, p. 108; "In passing . . .": Marberry, p. 111.

229   Comstock: Broun and Leech.

230   Train: *WCW,* May 17, 1873, and in Marberry, p. 120.

230–233   For accounts of the complex legal proceedings and the quoted material in the text see *WCW,* December 28, 1872, January 25, 1873, February 8 and 22, 1873; Broun, pp. 90–127; Shaplen, pp. 162–170; Marberry, pp. 110–142; and Sachs, pp. 173–192. These accounts confuse the statements of Noah Davis, the U.S. Attorney for the Southern District of New York, and Henry E. Davies, his assistant. Since both men spoke on behalf of the U.S. Attorney's office, I have attributed all their statements to U.S. Attorney Davis.

232   "Well I . . .": Lutz, p. 232.

233   Stowe's opposition: Hedrick, p. 376.

234–235   "The Naked Truth" speech: the full text is in *VWR* and *WCW,* January 25, 1873; "I resolved . . .": *WCW,* February 8, 1873, A Papers-HM; "With the celerity . . .": A Papers-HM; Broun, p. 118.

236   "Immense sale . . .": *WCW,* February 8, 1873 and March 8, 1873.

236   Butler's advice: Butler to Woodhull, January 19, 1873, published in the *New York Sun,* February 3, 1873.

237   "She struck . . .": *Troy Whig,* November 25, 1871, *Thunderbolt,* May 1873; *WCW,* May 17, 24, 1873.

28 REPORTED DEAD

239–240   Woodhull's illness: According to Cynthia MacKay, M.D., Woodhull's symptoms suggest a pulmonary embolism in which a blood clot breaks and travels to the lungs. A person so afflicted spits blood, runs a fever, suffers chest pains, and has difficulty breathing. She also may have experienced a vaso vagal reaction in which the vagus nerve, which runs through the body and regulates unconscious functions, overfires from shock or pain. When the nerve overfires blood rushes to the extremities, the heart slows down, and the person loses consciousness. Woodhull may have hit her head in her sudden, unexpected fall and experienced the further complication of a concussion. Woodhull's physical condition was reported regularly in *WCW* in June and July of 1873.

240   Anthony: Woodhull to Anthony, January 2, 1873, The Huntington Library, San Marino, Calif.

244   Mott letter: "Cautious...": Mott to her sister, February 27, 1873, Sophia Smith Collection, Smith College, Northampton, Mass.

244   Hooker: tribute to Woodhull, *WCW*, May 24, 1873.

244–245   Beecher: "Entirely", "God had struck...", and "In my judgment...": Sachs, pp. 188–189.

245   Obscenity trial: *WCW*, July 12, 1873; Broun, p. 122; Marberry, p. 147; Sachs, pp. 196, 214–215.

247–248   Stanton: "heard the story...": letter to Hooker, November 3, 1873, HC; "You ask if...": August 24, 1874, letter in *Chicago Tribune*, also in *WCW*, October 17, 1874; see also Lutz's *Created Equal*, pp. 226–227.

248   Davis to Woodhull, n.d.: Letter is in the National American Woman Suffrage Association Collection, Library of Congress.

249   Utica's death: *WCW*, July 26, 1873.

29 "PERFECTED SEXUALITY"

251   Sexuality speeches: "free consent..." and "Scarecrows of Sexual Slavery": *WCW*, August 23, 1873; the full text is in *WCW*, September 27, 1873, and in a pamphlet in the Sophia Smith Collection, Smith College, Northampton, Mass.

252   Working relationships: "we three are one...": *WCW*, February 8, 1873; "on our oars...": *WCW*, November 28, 1874; "splendid assistant...": *WCW*, December 11, 1875; Travel together: *WCW*, December 5 and 19, 1874.

253   September 16, 1873, spiritualist convention: "Weak, unlettered...": *WCW*, October 4, 1873, also Sears, p. 20; full convention reports, including material quoted in the text, are in *WCW*, October 4 and 25, 1873.

255   Tucker: Tucker-Sachs correspondence, New York Public Library Manscript Collection, published in part by Sachs, pp. 236–266.

258–259   Ellery: A Papers-HM.

259   "Reformation or Revolution, Which?" and "Tried as by Fire..." speeches: for full texts see *VWR,WCW*, October 11, 25, 1873.

259   Woodhull's lecture income: *WCW*, October 18, 1873.

260   Woodhull's travel schedule: *WCW*, September 27, 1873, December 13, 1873, and January 24, 1874.

260   Challis trial: *WCW*, March 28, 1874, and April 4, 1874, for a full report and the quotations in text.

30 "DELUGES OF FILTH"

263   Treat: Stoehr, pp. 344–345, 421; "I idealized...": Treat, p. 3.

264–265   Woodhull against Treat: *WCW*, October 25, 1874; "from time to time . . .": *WCW,* July 4, 1874; "so long as . . .": *WCW,* July 14, 1874; "an ocean voyage . . .": *WCW,* October 3, 1874.

265–266   "We have never . . .": *WCW,* October 3, 1874; "Slimy crawlings . . .": *WCW,* November 21, 1874; "In regard to . . ." and "The press will . . .": *WCW,* December 12, 1874.

266   Charges against Treat, his illness and death: A Papers-HM.

31   "THE END OF THE WORLD IS AT HAND"

268   Religious ferment: Meade's *Blavatsky;* Butler; and especially Moore's *Religious Outsiders* and *Crows.*

269   "There is a hidden . . .":*WCW,* April 17, 1875.

269–270   Beecher-Tilton trial: Rugoff's *Beechers* provides a good, brief report, as does Shaplen. For a partial transcript, see Abbot; this transcript was published by Beecher supporters and ends on the thirty-fifth day of the trial, before Beecher's testimony began. McDivitt provides a complete transcript. Many pamphlets were published based on the voluminous newspaper accounts of the trial.

270   Petition to Congress: *Washington Chronicle,* January 13, 1876, reprinted in *WCW,* January 29, 1876.

271   "Weary years . . .": A Papers-HM.

271   "The Human Body, the Temple of God": this speech had many variations; see *WCW,* January 1, 1876, for one.

271–272   Grounds for divorce: Lawyer Stanford Lotwin; Blood's late life: Sachs, pp. 306–311.

272   "The impure . . .": *New York Times,* April 16, 1878.

273   "William Vanderbilt has no more . . .": Johnston, p. 255.

273   "End of the world . . .": *WCW,* April 15, 1876.

273   "Love of God . . .": Boston farewell lecture, "Review of a Century," October 2, 1876, *HB.*

273   "I have a fair . . .": *New York Sun,* April 17, 1876, *HB.*

32   INVENTING "MRS. WOODHALL"

277   Woodhull's new life: A Papers-HM; *HB.*

277   Reports of Woodhull's England lectures: Johnston, pp. 266–267.

278   "Let her . . .": Anthony to Fawcett, courtesy of Bayley Silleck.

278   Tennie and Vanderbilt: Tennie lent credence to rumors that she and Woodhull were paid to go to England during the Vanderbilt Will case by claiming that Vanderbilt had invested money for her which she had never received. But Tennie's statements may simply have been part of her plan to obtain money from the Vanderbilt estate. Her correspondence from Warwick Road in London to William Vanderbilt, and to her father still in New York, suggests that William Vanderbilt had paid her nothing. She wrote her father, A Papers - SIU c. 1877, "Now father I believe if you and Maggie would call on Vanderbilt and tell him I would rather take any principal and interest than have to return to New York . . . Father see if

you cannot persuade him to give me any principal and interest . . . Father try and get someone to help you and make the proposition. I will take any principal and interest . . . if Vanderbilt was concerned that I am in need of any money he would at least give me the principal." After learning that William Vanderbilt was coming to London, she wrote him directly, A Papers-SIU, c. 1877, ". . . if I could have the opportunity of stating my claim to you in person . . . it [would] not be necessary for me to return to New York as advised by Scott Lord [the lawyer for the siblings challenging the will]. I pray you grant me an interview and after hearing my statement of fact I will leave the settlement . . . to your honor." The accepted view is that Tennie received about $15,000 from William Vanderbilt, but no evidence supports that conclusion. The A Papers-HM, SIU include several references to a box of Vanderbilt papers and suggest that it was later destroyed by Zula or her cousin Carrie.

278   Cook: A Papers-HM, Richmond Local History Collection, London, England.
280–284 Martin: A Papers-HM; "There were only two . . .": fragment of a letter in Martin's handwriting, A Papers-SIU; John Martin's diary, Holland-Martin Family Archives, London, England; "God bless . . .": A Papers-BPL.

33   17 HYDE PARK GATE

285–290 Married life and correspondence: A Papers-BPL, HM, SIU.
288   Henry James: James was living in Cambridge, Mass. in the early 1870s when Woodhull spoke in Boston. He attended many lectures during the Boston winters, listening to "speeches by ardent young reformers," Edel, vol. 2, p. 26. It is quite likely that he heard Woodhull during that time.
290   "A great surprise . . .": McFeely's *Douglass,* pp. 332–333.

34   THE GRASSHOPPER AND THE HUMANITARIAN

292   *The Human Body, the Temple of God* expanded a *Fragmentary Record* of Woodhull's life work which she had printed in 1877.
293   Return to public life, family complications, British Museum Case, correspondence and quotes: A Papers-BPL, HM, SIU.
293   National Equal Rights Committee: Hamilton College Special Collection, Clinton, N.Y.
294   Leslie Stephen: Stephen lived at 22 Hyde Park Gate, a few doors from Woodhull. His daughter, Virginia Woolf, the voice for women of another generation, grew up near Woodhull's "dear nest." James's *Siege of London* was published in Stephen's *Cornhill Magazine,* and it is possible James learned of Woodhull's new life through Stephen.

35 THE COURAGE TO STAND IN THE PATH OF MAN

302–306   Life at Norton: A Papers-BPL, HM, SIU; Boudicca: See also Fraser, pp. 27–42.
302   Beecham: Reid; "I am the . . .": Reid, p. 30. In an interview on May 6, 1987, Beecham's grandson, Thomas Beecham, told me of Tennie's visits to her relatives. He was a teenager at the time. He said of Victoria that in old age she was still "impressive" and "wasn't afraid to express an opinion."
303   Prince of Wales's visit: Johnston, p. 296, A Papers-HM.
305   Holland-Martin: Adlard.
306   "Murderer . . .": interview with Opperman, April 28, 1987.
306   "No screws . . .": A Papers-SIU.

EPILOGUE

309   "You gave women . . .": Ricker to Woodhull, September 15, 1905, A Papers-SIU.
309   "Swarming vortex . . .": A Papers-BPL.
309   "Object lesson . . .": A Papers-SIU.
311   "The general picture . . .": A Papers-SIU.

Index

"Alpha," 56
abolition, 5, 53, 191; and suffragists, 79
Amendments: Fifteenth, 53, 81, 95, 176; Fourteenth, 53, 55, 98, 176, 204; Nineteenth, 309; Sixteenth, 94–95
American Anti-Usury Society, 204
American Association of Spiritualists, 174, 218
American Labor Reform League, 196, 251
American Woman Suffrage Association, 79, 95
Ames, Adelbert, 97, 112
Andrews, Stephen Pearl, 81, 83, 135, 147, 206, 210, 251, 259, 283, 293; communism and, 196; death of, 273; on free love, 144; in jail, 231; at suffragist convention, 193; *Weekly* essays of, 129; and Woodhull, 75–76; as Woodhull ghostwriter, 84, 88, 126, 168, 219
Angell, Katharine, 310
Anthony, Susan B., 3, 52, 53, 79, 95, 102, 104, 105, 125, 188, 196, 204, 218, 226, 245; interview of Tennessee Claflin by, 67–68; letters to, 240–241, 246; position against Woodhull by, 190–193, 215, 278, 293; suffrage and, 95, 101, 189, 309; voting by, 232; Woodhull supported by, 113, 120, 124, 147
Anti-Usury Society, 196
Apollo Hall convention, 3–4, 6–7, 154, 205–210
Atlantic Monthly, 122
Aurora (painting), 49

Bacon, Dr. Leonard 122
Balfour, Arthur, 304
Ballou, Ada, 193, 205, 206
Banks, Theodore, 207, 210
Beecham, Sir Thomas, 302
Beecham, Utica Celestia (Welles), 302
Beecher, Catharine, 121, 124, 178, 241–242
Beecher, Charles, 122
Beecher, Edward, 122
Beecher, Henry Ward, 5–6, 88, 124, 158–162, 241, 242, 246, 258, 263, 264, 272, 273, 283, 310; Susan B. Anthony and, 191–192; Beecher-Tilton trial and, 270, 297; Anthony Comstock and, 235; death of, 291; Equal Rights Association and, 79; siblings of, 121–122; Elizabeth Tilton and, 79; Theodore Tilton and, 152–155, 269; Joseph Treat's allegations and, 264–266; Woodhull and, 158–162, 179, 186; Woodhull's exposure of, 221–225,

FOR THE BEST IN PAPERBACKS, LOOK FOR THE

In every corner of the world, on every subject under the sun, Penguin represents quality and variety—the very best in publishing today.

For complete information about books available from Penguin—including Puffins, Penguin Classics, and Arkana—and how to order them, write to us at the appropriate address below. Please note that for copyright reasons the selection of books varies from country to country.

In the United Kingdom: Please write to *Dept. JC, Penguin Books Ltd, FREEPOST, West Drayton, Middlesex UB7 0BR.*

If you have any difficulty in obtaining a title, please send your order with the correct money, plus ten percent for postage and packaging, to *P.O. Box No. 11, West Drayton, Middlesex UB7 0BR*

In the United States: Please write to *Consumer Sales, Penguin USA, P.O. Box 999, Dept. 17109, Bergenfield, New Jersey 07621-0120.* VISA and MasterCard holders call 1-800-253-6476 to order all Penguin titles

In Canada: Please write to *Penguin Books Canada Ltd, 10 Alcorn Avenue, Suite 300, Toronto, Ontario M4V 3B2*

In Australia: Please write to *Penguin Books Australia Ltd, P.O. Box 257, Ringwood, Victoria 3134*

In New Zealand: Please write to *Penguin Books (NZ) Ltd, Private Bag 102902, North Shore Mail Centre, Auckland 10*

In India: Please write to *Penguin Books India Pvt Ltd, 706 Eros Apartments, 56 Nehru Place, New Delhi 110 019*

In the Netherlands: Please write to *Penguin Books Netherlands bv, Postbus 3507, NL-1001 AH Amsterdam*

In Germany: Please write to *Penguin Books Deutschland GmbH, Metzlerstrasse 26, 60594 Frankfurt am Main*

In Spain: Please write to *Penguin Books S. A., Bravo Murillo 19, 1° B, 28015 Madrid*

In Italy: Please write to *Penguin Italia s.r.l., Via Felice Casati 20, I-20124 Milano*

In France: Please write to *Penguin France S. A., 17 rue Lejeune, F−31000 Toulouse*

In Japan: Please write to *Penguin Books Japan, Ishikiribashi Building, 2−5−4, Suido, Bunkyo-ku, Tokyo 112*

In Greece: Please write to *Penguin Hellas Ltd, Dimocritou 3, GR−106 71 Athens*

In South Africa: Please write to *Longman Penguin Southern Africa (Pty) Ltd, Private Bag X08, Bertsham 2013*